SANTA ANNA'S ARMY IN THE TEXAS REVOLUTION, 1835

THE TEXAS EXPERIENCE
Books made possible by
Sarah '84 and Mark '77 Philpy

SANTA ANNA'S ARMY IN THE TEXAS REVOLUTION, 1835

GREGG J. DIMMICK

TRANSLATIONS BY

John R. Wheat

ILLUSTRATIONS BY

Manuel Hinojosa

TEXAS A&M UNIVERSITY PRESS
College Station

First edition

♾ This paper meets the requirements of ANSI/NISO Z39.48–1992 (Permanence of Paper).
Binding materials have been chosen for durability.
Manufactured in the United States of America

Library of Congress Cataloging-in-Publication Data

Names: Dimmick, Gregg J., author. | Wheat, John, translator. | Hinojosa, Manuel, illustrator.
Title: Santa Anna's Army in the Texas Revolution, 1835 / Gregg J. Dimmick ; translations by John R. Wheat ; illustrated by Manuel Hinojosa.
Other titles: Texas experience (Texas A & M University Press)
Description: First edition. | College Station : Texas A&M University Press, [2025] | Series: The Texas experience | Includes bibliographical references and index.
Identifiers: LCCN 2025030595 (print) | LCCN 2025030596 (ebook) | ISBN 9781648431418 (hardcover) | ISBN 9781648431425 (ebook)
Subjects: LCSH: Santa Anna, Antonio López de, 1794–1876—Military leadership. | Mexico. Ejército—History—19th century. | Texas—History—Revolution, 1835–1836—Personal narratives, Mexican—Translations into English. | San Antonio (Tex.)—History—Siege, 1835. | Mexico—History—1821–1861—Sources. | BISAC: HISTORY / Military / Revolutions & Wars of Independence (see also United States / Revolutionary Period (1775–1800)) | HISTORY / Latin America / Mexico
Classification: LCC F390 .D547 2025 (print) | LCC F390 (ebook)
LC record available at https://lccn.loc.gov/2025030595
LC ebook record available at https://lccn.loc.gov/2025030596

CONTENTS

PREFACE

In 2010, as part of the two hundredth anniversary of Father Hidalgo's "Grito de Delores" speech, which marks the beginning of the Mexican Revolution, the Mexican Military Archives (Archivo Historico Militar) were digitized and placed online.[1] They were sorted by folders or *expedientes* based on subject matter. Each folder had a varying number of pages or *fojas*. The earliest folders dated back to 1821, when Mexico became a nation, and they extended into the mid-1800s. Nearly all the documents were handwritten in Spanish, and some were in extremely poor condition. These documents, for the most part, were letters written to the secretary of war, or letters by him to other officials. Luckily, it was standard practice in the Mexican army to send a copy of dispatches sent between officers or officials to the secretary of war for his knowledge.

Soon after these fantastic digitized photos of documents were put online, I was sent a link to the site by Dr. Roger Moore, a well-known archeologist in Houston. Dr. Moore was aware of my interest in the Mexican army and knew of my archeological reports and book on the Mexican army's struggle through the Sea of Mud.

When I got the link, I immediately visited the website and was able to familiarize myself with its organization quickly. The amount of material was overwhelming. I had it in the back of my mind that the site might not be up forever and made a lucky decision not to try to worry about the details of the documents but just focus on downloading as many documents as possible that had to do with the Texas Revolution. Little did I know at the time that over the next several years I would end up downloading well over two thousand documents.

There were a few times over those years that the website would not function, and each time I would stress out, as I did not know if the site would come back up. Luckily it would eventually return to normal, and I would continue downloading documents. I was able to get most of the documents that had to do with Texas regarding the period from about 1832 to 1841. It was lucky that I took this path since, for the last several years, even though the site is still up, the search engine for the site does not work. Now, when you click on the link to a specific document, another random document comes up. Therefore, it will not be possible to easily find the documents that I footnote in this work online unless they get the search engine for the site working. I am beginning to think that may not happen.

Because the original documents are unavailable through the Mexican archive website, I plan to provide a complete list of the documents and their digital versions to the Cushing Library at Texas A&M University in College Station. My artifacts from the Sea of Mud are already in their collection, so it seems natural to keep them together. I am going to make sure to make all the images of the downloaded documents available, not just those that I use in the book, so that other researchers can find and use them. I will also include in the files a copy of the rough translations that I have done, as well as any that were professionally translated by John Wheat. There are close to two thousand documents available in the collection that are not used in the book. There will also be a master list of all the Mexican documents from all the sources that I have examined over the years, organized by the date they were written.

It was great to have all these documents, but the big question, once I got the images downloaded, was what to do with them. My Spanish has slowly improved over the years, owing to all the research and to talking with Spanish-speaking patients in my office, to the point that I was able to tell what the documents were about and whether they were worth downloading. There was a vast amount of material about the internal struggles in Mexico that had nothing to do with Texas, which I opted not to download. I eventually decided that I needed to write a book about the Mexican army in the Texas Revolution. I knew that the basis of the book would primarily be the contents of these documents, the majority of which have not been seen by Texas history researchers, and the vast majority of which have never been translated into English.

I decided that I would try to do a rough translation of the significant documents. I then contacted John Wheat at the Briscoe Center for American History in Austin, Texas, to do the final translation of the documents that I planned to transcribe into the book.

Another source that I have used that is essentially untapped is the Archivo General de la Nación (AGN) files at the Briscoe.[2] These documents were generated when Professor Eugene C. Barker from the University of Texas went to

Mexico City and had typewritten copies made of the documents in the AGN that related to Texas. There are a moderate number of documents that exist in both the AGN and the military archives, so when possible I have used the AGN copy as the source since it is available at the Briscoe and the items there are typewritten (caution is needed, though, as there are a moderate number of errors in the transcriptions).

Due to the vast number of documents and the fact that there is so much previously unexamined material, it will be necessary to make this a three-volume book. The first will deal with the year 1835, the second with 1836 through the assault on the Alamo, and the third with San Jacinto and the aftermath of the campaign. There are a far greater number of documents from 1835 than 1836. It is likely that much of the material from 1836 was lost during the war, and it could be argued that the Mexican officers were much more distracted in 1836.

Other sources will be used as well, but it should be noted that even though there are more documents from 1835, there are far fewer Mexican writers who documented these actions than those of 1836. Gen. Vicente Filisola and José Juan Sánchez Navarro are two sources for 1835 material, but it should be noted that Filisola's 1835 material is not firsthand and Sánchez Navarro's 1835 material only deals with the later stages of the siege of Béjar.[3] By contrast, there are many more books written by the participants of the 1836 campaign.

A few notes on the documents themselves should be added. When Professor Eugene Barker of the University of Texas wrote an article on the difficulties of the commander of the customhouse in Anáhuac in 1835, he added an interesting footnote.[4] It stated that Mexican official etiquette forbade the discussion of more than one subject in a single letter; thus, they would often write several letters to the same recipient on the same day. This seems often to be the case in the documents that were downloaded, but on occasion the letters address many different subjects.

The reader and future researchers should also be made aware of the fact that Mexican officers would often write two letters on the same day to the same person regarding the same subject. One was the official letter, and apparently this document is the one that would often be copied and sent on to the war department. The private letter would be less formal and might include more personal information. It appears this letter would usually be destroyed. This is consistent with the fact that several of the private letters from 1836 were probably captured by the Texans and are still in existence. It is uncommon to find these personal letters among the 1835 documents.

Another detail that needs to be highlighted is the fact that when the letters arrived at the war department and were examined by the secretary of war, José María Tornel y Mendívil, he would often write, or have his clerk write, margin notes that would summarize the document and often detail the response that he wanted to be given to the senders. One should also be aware that in the military archives there are often short notes with poor handwriting that are signed with only a rubric. These are usually giving orders or responses by Tornel. Sometimes the archives include a very similar letter, with good handwriting, which is the official letter written by his clerks. It is easy to recognize Tornel's rubric, but on occasion one must guess based on the information.

The letters were usually written by the clerks of the officers but signed by the officers themselves. For the most part the Mexican officers and officials would end the document with a very polite ending, especially if sent to a superior. They would close with the town from which the letter was written, the date, and a signature. Following the signature, they would often include the name of the person to whom they were sending the dispatch, along with the city where the recipient was located.

A short note on translations should be made as well. The language was not totally the same in the 1830s as it is now. Military terms were especially different at the time. Just a few examples to help any researchers that attack some of these untranslated documents in the future: at the time a *fusil* was a musket and a *rifle* was a rifle; an *obus* was a howitzer, not a mortar or cannon; in military terms *rancho* could also be the mess that an army would eat; *plaza* could mean an enlisted man as well as the town square. These are just a few of the terms, but hopefully this will give an idea of a few of the pitfalls of translating period material.

Terminology can also be an issue. The Mexicans referred to the United States as the United States of the North, as their own country was officially the United States of Mexico. Tejano was usually used for a person of Spanish or Mexican descent who lived in Texas. The immigrants that came to Texas from elsewhere, mostly the United States, were called Texans, Texians, Anglos, colonists, immigrants, etc. One needs to realize that these immigrants, until the later stages of colonization, were legalized Mexican citizens living in Mexico. Also, it is incorrect to refer to the Mexican army as an invading army as an army cannot invade its own country.

It should be noted that it was difficult to decide which and how many of the documents to use. It was not the plan to write a book that was just a list of documents. However, many of these documents have never been accessed, much less translated, and they contain a vast number of small details that are, in my mind, fascinating. Trying to summarize such documents tends to either leave out the small details or make the summary longer than the document. Therefore, many documents are transcribed in the entirety. Sadly, far more are not even mentioned. It is tempting to summarize many of the longer documents, but I have tried to avoid doing so. In my research I have found that many of the translations of the period works left out parts of the books or only gave summaries of documents. These omitted or summarized parts of the work often contained the very details that I needed for my research. This was especially true of trying to use the Mexican sources to document the location of the Sea of Mud. Thus, some of the documents summarized in the text are included in full in the appendices.

The issue of the spelling of many of the Mexican names also became an issue. I consulted noted author and researcher Dr. Jesús F. de la Teja, former state historian for Texas, on this issue. His recommendation was to use the *Diccionario Purrua de Historia, Biografia, y Geografia de Mexico,* and I have followed this resource in the majority of cases.

Lastly, it should be noted that the purpose of this work is to show what the Mexicans knew about and were thinking about, as well as the actions they were taking. As is the case with the Texans, the information they had at their disposal was occasionally wrong, but they did not know it at the time, and it still shaped their thoughts and actions. A handful of documents written from one Texan to another are included in the work, but only in the case that they were located in one of the Mexican archives. This means that it may have influenced the thinking of the Mexican officials at the time. In short, the Texans' side of the story has already been told. This work is to tell the other side of the story.

ACKNOWLEDGMENTS

There are many people I would like to thank for making it possible for me to write this work on the Mexican army. The first person I need to mention is a gentleman whom I consider my mentor in all my years of chasing down the Mexican army, both archeologically and historically. Dr. James Crisp was one of the first people I talked to after we started discovering Mexican army artifacts in the Sea of Mud. In a lengthy phone call, he gave me many recommendations concerning historical research. He let me know that if I was going to become a serious archival researcher on this subject, I was going to have to learn Spanish, and not just modern Spanish but 1830s Castilian Spanish. After I got off the phone with him there was no doubt that this would happen. I now speak reasonably good Spanish and have become a passable translator for Alamo-period, handwritten Mexican documents. After I wrote my first book on the history and archeology of the Sea of Mud, Jim was the first person whom I asked to read my manuscript. He not only did so but forwarded it to the Texas State Historical Association with a recommendation that they publish the work. For over twenty years now he has been a sounding board for me and given me great advice when needed.

Another contributor and friend, Manuel Hinojosa, an architect from the valley, is the only person I know who might possibly be more obsessed with the history of the Mexican army than I. He happens to be the illustrator for my books, and due to his knowledge of the Mexican army, I can trust him to be fully accurate in his artwork.

Dr. Roger Moore, a prominent archeologist from Houston, was also a major contributor to this work. I had the privilege being a volunteer at the San Jacinto Battleground for many excavations under his direction. Knowing my particular interest in the Mexican army, he forwarded a link to me many years ago. The link was to the website of the digitalized Archivo Historico Militar, the archives of the secretary of war of Mexico from 1821 to the early twentieth century. It was a treasure trove of documents and was the motivation for me to write this work.

Another particularly important person in my work over the years is John R. Wheat, archives translator for the Briscoe Center for American History. John and I collaborated on the publication of Filisola's 1838 book, *General Vicente Filisola's Analysis of José Urrea's Military Diary*. He agreed to check all my translation for this work so that the translations would be excellent as opposed to passable.

I would be amiss if I did not mention three gentlemen who paved the path and encouraged my interest in the Mexican army. I have found that there are far fewer "experts" on the 1836 Mexican army, even in Mexico, than on most other aspects of the Texas Revolution. Even though they are no longer with us, the works of these men live on and serve as great resources for this work. These men are Kevin Young, Jack Jackson, and Thomas Ricks Lindley. All three of these men succeeded in casting light not only on the Texans but also on the Mexican side of the Texas Revolution.

Another person who was critical in my development as an amateur historian and Texas Revolution enthusiast is Jan DeVault. Jan died a few years ago, but her love and devotion for all things Texas were contagious, and I was exposed and caught her obsession.

I had a discussion with my wife as to her part in my work, and we came to an agreement that she has tolerated my passion for the Mexican army. Despite having no real interest in the subject, she has attended many of my lectures, put up with my speaking Spanish to her for years, and most of all she put up with all my muddy clothes and dirty artifacts.

A special thanks goes out to Jim Woodrick, an exceptional researcher. Living in Austin, Jim has been glad to go to the Briscoe and find archival documents for me. He is exceptionally knowledgeable regarding the cannons of the Texas Revolution, both on the Texan and Mexican sides.

I would like to thank several other people for their involvement on this work: Marsha Dardenne and Rick Range for helping me proofread the book; Frank de la Teja, Jeff Dunn, and Stephen Hardin for giving me help with documents, details, and direction for the work; and Texas A&M University Press, whom I greatly appreciate for their trust in my work and their willingness to publish it.

Last but certainly not least I would like to thank all those folks who have helped with the archeology in the Sea of Mud over the years. If not for the hundreds of Mexican army artifacts (most of which are now housed at the Cushing Library at Texas A&M University), I seriously doubt that my interest in the Mexican army would have come about. The Houston Archeological Society was integral in the early excavations and published two archeological reports on the site. Individuals involved have included Joe Hudgins, Ed Person, Terry Kieler, John Wicke, and George Ressler.

SANTA ANNA'S ARMY IN THE TEXAS REVOLUTION, 1835

Introduction

The value of Texas and its resources were recognized early on by the Spanish as they migrated into northern Mexico. In July 1777, the commander of the internal presidios, Hugo O'Connor, wrote to the viceroy, Teodoro de Croix:

> That of Texas, which is also found more than a degree beyond our line, has been of the overseas possessions of Spain the most costly, although of very little utility; the largest, although unknown, and the one that has produced the most hostilities; but the one of greatest importance, on many counts, since none of the others can match it. It borders on the east that of Louisiana, or New Orleans; on the west, the Río Medina; on the north the Missouri; and on the south the sea or Gulf of Mexico. It has abundant rivers that water it; sierras that surround it and protect it; valleys and plains that rightly call for farmers; and it is peopled by numerous *gentiles* [peaceful people] who when attracted to recognition and vassalage of the monarchy would make it more fertile and richer than the other provinces because of its location, multitude of people, and fine climate.[1]

At that time, most people considered Texas as *tierra despoblada* (unpopulated land) but it is obvious that O'Connor recognized the potential of the area. Later, colonists from many parts of the world would covet this land, and the Mexicans would do everything in their power to retain it.

The history of the Mexican army's participation in the Texas Revolution is very well documented. No doubt, many of the most important documents (battalion logs, captured Alamo papers, Col. Juan Nepomuceno Almonte's original journal, etc.) have been lost or destroyed, but an amazing amount of period documentation has survived the years. The problem is that these documents are handwritten, in Spanish, and have been shelved in the back rooms of museums and libraries long enough to have been forgotten. These archives are scattered from Spain to California, from Mexico City to Yale University. A great number of them exist in Texas, but very few of the historical pieces have been translated into English and even fewer have been published.

Most of the published pieces on the Texas Revolution are published in English and, for the most part, only detail the events from the Texans' perspective. Unfortunately, many of these publications were written years after the fact and were taken from accounts of participants who were elderly and trying to recall events that took place many years prior.

The opposite is true of the Mexican documents. Much of the documentation was done at the very time of the events and was written for their superiors, giving details in the form of orders, accounts, and reports. They were not writing historical pieces and were generally not trying to put any spin on the events. Certainly, there are exceptions, such as the writings of the Mexican commander, Gen. Antonio López de Santa Anna. He would often skew the events to make himself look as if he always made the right decisions. If the results of his decisions were poor, he would attribute them to someone else's failures.

It is extremely hard to downplay the veracity of daily battalion logs, battle reports, and official documents that were contemporary and written by direct eyewitnesses. The purpose of this work is to publish many of the translated documents from the Mexican army and detail their motivations, actions, and thoughts on what was occurring in Texas in 1835–36. Almost all the documentation will be from the Mexican side, the rare exception being Texan or US documents that show up in the Mexican archives and would have influenced the thinking of the Mexican decision-makers.

For a better understanding of the condition of the Mexican nation at the outset of the Texas Revolution one must look at details from the early onset of its history. When one considers that Nueva España was established in 1521 and was occupied and pillaged by the Spanish for three hundred years, it is not difficult to understand why the Mexican nation struggled with becoming a self-reliant nation after winning their independence in 1821.

Mexico also took a different approach when it came to the handling of the indigenous peoples of their land. Rather than the policy of extinction practiced by the Spanish and their American neighbors, they tried to incorporate these people into their society. This was successful to a degree, but when they tried to settle the vast northern lands of their nation, they encountered Native Americans who were often more belligerent and not easily dealt with.

Gen. Vicente Filisola, the military commander of the Internal States of the East, had an interesting take on the treatment of Native Americans by the

United States: "With the population of the United States growing at an astonishing rate because of the emigration from Europe, they began to feel as an embarrassment the continuance in their territory of the Indian tribes who inhabited it, and whose existence there was consecrated by treaties and solemn agreements. In no part of the globe are so noticeable as in the United States the prejudices of the white race against people of colors, and this was sufficient to exclude the bronzed or red men from their lands and despoil them of it."[2]

After Mexico became a nation in 1821, there were several matters that had a huge impact on their ability to respond to the actions of the colonists in Texas. Two factors were especially important in disrupting the ability of the government and the army to function in an efficient manner. The first was the fact that the Mexican nation could not settle on a form of government.

There was a strong movement to form a democratic republic and pattern themselves after the United States.[3] Another faction seemed to favor some sort of a modified monarchy, using a relative of one of the European royals to take the throne. Agustín de Iturbide's ill-fated attempt to declare himself emperor lasted less than a year, and a representative government came into power. After Iturbide's exit the nation still could not settle on whether they wanted to have a more liberal government, with more states' rights and personal freedom, or a stricter conservative government that gave more power to the president and national congress in Mexico City.

The second factor was even more devastating than the first. Changes in leadership and types of government are acceptable and tolerable if they can be accomplished peacefully and within the limits of the nation's laws. Unfortunately, this was not to be the case in Mexico. In the early stages of the Mexican Republic, a young, brash officer started to become active in politics. Antonio López de Santa Anna, though he had no widespread support and little in the way of military backing, began to take advantage of his most unique talents. He seemed to have a true gift for reading the will of the people of Mexico, his fellow officers, and the politicians of the country. For the most part, Santa Anna was a step ahead of the rest of the power brokers and had the gall and unbridled confidence to attempt the seemingly impossible. He did not hesitate to use the troops under his command to decide which politicians were in power. On several occasions Santa Anna would take inferior forces, both in number and quality, and would win the day with his brash actions. He seemed to realize that if he had any early success in an uprising it would be easy to get other, more powerful, forces to join him and eventually defeat his opponent. Thus, military rebellions, or *pronunciamientos,* as they were called in Mexico at the time, against the government became an accepted form of political action. The resulting constant warfare was terrible for the economy, political stability, foreign trade, and manpower of the country.

The scope of this work is to focus on the story of the Mexican army's involvement in the Texas Revolution in 1835–36. The term "Texas Revolution" is used lightly, as this term gives the reader a very restricted concept regarding the true nature of this event. This uprising was not an isolated incident and did not occur in a vacuum. It was the result of an extremely complex chain of events that essentially led to an ongoing civil war in Mexico from its inception as a country in 1821. During the period of the Texas Revolution, the Mexican government and its military leaders were occupied in putting down revolts in several states, battling each other for political control, and dealing with Spanish attempts to reacquire Mexico. At the same time, they were trying to fend off foreign powers, especially the United States and Britain, who were constantly interfering with their internal affairs.

It is not difficult to understand why the Mexican nation was so suspicious of the motives of the United States. Mexico expected the Americans to support them as a fellow republic, but this happened in word only. A long succession of events did nothing but reinforce to the Mexican government that their suspicions were well founded. The Philip Nolan expedition in 1801, the Juan de la Casas coup in Béjar in 1811, the Gutiérrez-Magee expedition of 1811–13, the James Long expedition of 1819–21, and the Fredonian Revolution led by Hayden Edwards in 1826–27 were all events, among many others, that destroyed any hope of the Mexican nation's laws and territories being respected by the Americans. The fact-finding trips of General Manuel de Mier y Terán[4] and Juan Almonte[5] reinforced the feeling of mistrust when their reports were published. The American claim that the border between Mexico and the United States was not the Sabine but the Nueces, or even the Río Grande, did nothing to help matters. The above factors helped form the eventual abyss that separated Mexican Texas from the rest of Mexico by 1835.

Even though the movement to make Mexico a republic won out over those who favored a monarchy, the political scene did not stabilize. Over time two political parties developed in Mexico. For the most part, the further the Mexican people lived from Mexico City, the more likely they were to lean toward the Federalist, or liberal, political view. These people, living in relative isolation, had little to no financial or material support from their national government. The military presence on the frontiers was minimal at best. Due to these factors the people living on the fringes of the country were more likely to support the concept of local rule and individual freedoms.

The conservative, or Centralist, party was basically comprised of the wealthy, the Catholic Church, and the military. The conservatives favored the government being centralized in Mexico City, where they could make laws that would be advantageous for the church and the military. They favored colonization in the far reaches of the nation, to stabilize the frontiers, but seemed to have little desire to finance such ventures.

To better understand the feelings of the Mexican people toward the Texans at the outbreak of the Texas Revolution, one must understand how the Anglo migration to Texas came about. On January 3, 1823, the Mexican government passed a colonization law permitting colonists from other countries to settle in Mexico under certain conditions. Stephen F. Austin was the first to take advantage of this law and brought three hundred colonists to his land grant between the Brazos and the Colorado Rivers. These new arrivals were required to take an oath of loyalty to the Mexican Republic. They were also required to profess to be Christian. As the state religion of Mexico was Catholic, they were required to swear to be members of that denomination or be willing to convert to it. As there were very few Catholic priests in Texas at the time, the requirement to practice the faith was not strictly enforced.

Each head of a family (male or female) could claim a headright of 4,605 acres for approximately four cents an acre, payable over six years (the going rate in the United States at that time was about $1.25 per acre). Cheap land was by far the most common motivation that spurred the migration into Texas. This resulted in land companies, with no permission from the Mexican government, being organized in New York and New Orleans to sell Texas lands to immigrants.[6] This temptation to get a new start was especially true for American settlers who were deep in debt, as their indebtedness did not legally follow them across the Mexican border.

The new arrivals were also given relief from all tithing, taxes, and duties (on goods up to two thousand dollars) for their first six years in Mexico. They only had to pay half of what was due for the following six years. As these monies started to come due, there were major conflicts between the colonists and the Mexican authorities. This was especially true at the customhouses, where tariffs were collected. Contraband trade and smuggling became major points of contention between the colonists and the authorities.

In considering these factors, it is easy to see why the Mexican government and people would have expected the newly arriving colonists in Texas to be happy with the agreements. They anticipated that the colonists would be willing to abide by the stipulations set for them to become Mexican citizens and own land in their newly adopted country. There certainly were immigrants who obeyed the rules and became good Mexican citizens, but as the Mexican people and leaders were soon to find out, this was not the norm. The colonists that migrated to Texas tended to be rugged individualists and brought with them their American ideals of individual freedoms. They were often self-reliant and had a great deal of experience in the use of firearms. In contrast, this was not often the case with the Mexican settlers who migrated to Texas. Some were presidial soldiers, but many had been reliant on their landowners for protection and had little to no experience with firearms.

In 1824, with the liberal Federalist party in power, a new constitution was adopted. This constitution provided for more individual freedom and states' rights. For the most part the colonists in Texas felt that they could thrive under this document and supported it.

Another issue that raised its head was the matter of slavery. Slavery was officially outlawed in Mexico in 1829, but Texas was declared exempt. After Guerrero fell from power, the anti-slavery decree was annulled for the rest of Mexico by the congress.[7] During this time the Texans began a practice of requiring slaves to sign papers that bound them as indentured servants. Mexico already had a system that was remarkably like indentured servanthood, in that hacienda owners were free to forcefully keep their peons on site until they had paid all debts to the landowner.

The slavery issue did not seem to be a major factor in the Texas Revolution, however. In the myriad of Mexican documents that I examined for this book, I found only a few that dealt with this issue. There was an interesting document written by Secretary of War José María Tornel to the military commander of the Internal States of the East, General Cos, and other commanders regarding the penalties that could be imposed on obstinate rebel colonists who refused to obey the laws. Tornel noted that they could lose their lands and added: "It could serve as an action, in an extreme case, to declare the freedom of all the slaves that serve the settlers, according to the laws of the Republic."[8]

One possible reason for the Mexican government's lack of anti-slavery action is that the slaveholding departments of Texas exported far more goods than the non-slaveholding parts of the states. In 1834 the department of Béjar, mostly Tejano with few slaves, exported no goods, while the slaveholding department of the Brazos exported six hundred thousand pesos' worth of goods, including five thousand bales of cotton.

A vast amount of research and documentation has been done on the Anglo settlers in Texas during this time and their difficulties in dealing with the Mexican government. Many scholars of Texas history have tried to get at the root of the dissent among the colonists that settled one of Mexico's most remote states, Coahuila y Tejas. The consensus seems to be that the Mexican government did not provide the Texan colonists with protection, a judicial system, or an educational system. Furthermore, the settlers did not like the fact that they were not allowed to practice the religion of their choice; they were distressed when the Mexican government finally tried to clamp down on the active importation of slaves; and they were bitterly upset when customs officials came to Texas to start collecting import taxes, which had been forgiven for their first six years. There were also great delays, because of the vast distances involved, in getting any official word from the Mexican government on land matters, judicial decisions, etc.

Extraordinarily little research has been done on the opinions of the Mexican populace of 1835–36 toward the Texan colonists. Up to this point there has been little attempt to try to understand why the average Mexican was so anxious to do what was necessary to put down this uprising and save this valuable territory for their young country. Even though this question is not the focus of this book, it must be addressed if one is to fully comprehend the motivations and behaviors of the Mexican army in this campaign.

To better understand how the thoughts of the Mexican government and people about the Texans evolved, several events need to be considered. In 1828–29, the Mexican government sent General Mier y Terán at the head of a boundary commission to determine the border between the United States and Mexico. He was also charged with observing the situation with the indigenous tribes along the border, as well as determining the number and attitudes of the Americans living there.

The report of Mier y Terán is particularly useful in showing the awareness of what was taking place in the colonies in Texas. A portion of his report to the war department follows. It was amazingly insightful as to the behavior and motivations that the colonists had brought with them from the United States.

The department of Texas is contiguous to the most avid nation in the world. The North Americans have conquered whatever territory adjoins them. In less than half a century, they have become masters of extensive colonies that formerly belonged to Spain and France, and of even more spacious territories from which have disappeared the former owners, the Indian tribes. There is no power like that to the north, which by silent means has made conquests of momentous importance. Such dexterity, such constancy in their designs, such uniformity of means of execution that always are completely successful, arouses admiration.

Instead of armies, battles, or invasions—which make a great noise and for the most part are unsuccessful—these men lay hand on means that, if considered one by one, would be rejected as slow, ineffective, and at times palpably absurd. They begin by assuming rights, as in Texas, which are impossible to sustain in a serious discussion, making ridiculous pretensions based on historical incidents that no one admits—such as the voyage of La Salle, which was an absurd fiasco, but serves as a basis for their claim to Texas.

. . . At this stage it is alleged that there is a national demand for the step that the government mediates. In the meantime the territory against which these machinations are directed, and which has usually remained unsettled, begins to be visited by adventurers and empresarios; some of these take up their residence in the country, pretending that their location has no bearing upon the question of their government's claim or the boundary dispute; shortly some of these forerunners develop complaints, even threats, begin to be heard, working on the loyalty of the legitimate settlers, discrediting the efficiency of the existing authority and administration; and the matter having arrived at this stage—which is precisely that of Texas at this moment—diplomatic maneuvers begin. They incite uprisings in the territory in question and usually manifest a deep concern for the rights of the inhabitants. There follows a matter of notes in which are found equitable and moderate phrases, until with the aid of other incidents, which are never lacking in the course of diplomatic relations, finally comes to the desired conclusion of a transaction as onerous for one side as advantageous for the other. They used such a method to dispossess the powers of Europe of vast territories, which under the name of colonies they once possessed in America, but which were of secondary interest.

The question with respect to Mexico is quite different. It is a matter of attacking primary interests intimately tied up with the political existence of our country. Mexico, imitating the conduct of France and Spain, might alienate or cede unproductive lands in Africa or Asia. But how can it be

> expected to cut itself off from its own soul, give up to a rival power territory advantageously placed in the extremity of its states, which joins some of them and serves as a buffer to all? How can it be expected to alienate two hundred and fifty leagues of coast, leaving on them vast resources for the construction of boats, the shortest channels for commerce and navigation, the most fertile lands, and the most copious elements for providing means of attack and defense? If Mexico should consent to this base act, it would degenerate from the most elevated class of American powers to that of a contemptible mediocrity, reduced to the necessity of buying a precarious existence at the cost of many humiliations.
>
> In the act of ceding Texas, it would have to renounce all pretensions of having its own industries with which to maintain and enrich its eight million inhabitants, who within a few years could not avoid seeing the bread and sugar, and even the corn and beans consumed in the federal district, furnished by the foreign harvest of Texas. The sale of this department would reduce the territorial property, it would reduce the value of the land in all the rest of Mexico by one half of that which it now has. These assertions, which carry their own evidence, should be manifest to such an extent . . . that they will establish a conviction in every Mexican heart that he who consents to and does not oppose the loss of Texas is an execrable traitor who ought to be punished with every kind of death. . . . If war should break out [in Texas] it would be expedient to suppress it in a single campaign—a less expensive method than to be always on the defensive. But even this would be useless until a colony of one thousand Mexican families is planted there, an economical measure when it is remembered that the funds spent once in establishing a colony would be spent many times in maintaining garrisons.[9]

Terán's report added that if military garrisons were not established immediately, if Mexican colonists were not sent to Texas, and if the flood of illegal immigrants from the United States was not abated, Texas would be lost.

As a result of his report the Mexican government passed the law of April 6, 1830, which banned any further colonization of the border states of Mexico by immigrants from adjacent countries and prohibited the import of any new slaves. More military posts were established, and soldiers were sent to garrison them. The law also encouraged Mexican colonization of Texas with similar enticements to those given to the American colonists; put new land distribution under federal control instead of that of the states; and sent convicts to Texas to help with building projects. The tax delay previously granted to the

Texans was rescinded, and the tariffs were increased. These measures were well and good; however, most Mexican troops were occupied by dealing with various revolutions in Mexico, and there were no means to enforce the law that had been passed. The new law had no serious effect on the situation in Texas other than making the colonists of Texas upset with the government. Owing to political pressure, the main part of the 1830 law—outlawing immigration from the United States—was soon repealed, and little was done in Texas for several more years.

On May 2, 1830, the state legislature of Coahuila y Tejas passed a liberal colonization law, ignoring the federal law of April 6. The governor of Coahuila y Tejas, Don José María Letona, sent two land commissioners, Don Francisco Madero and Don José Carbajal, to survey the new lands. General Mier y Terán, now the military commander of the Internal States of the East, ordered Juan Davis Bradburn, commander of the post at Anáhuac, to arrest the two commissioners, but he was not able to locate them. Bradburn tried to strictly enforce the tariffs on incoming goods, but the Texans resisted.

At about that time, with emotions already high, a female colonist in Texas was outraged by some Mexican soldiers. As a result of this a Mexican soldier was tarred and feathered. Subsequently, there was a small skirmish in which several Texans were arrested, William B. Travis among them.

Mier y Terán, wanting to keep the peace because of the small numbers of Mexican soldiers at the post (approximately 150), got news of the rough tactics of Bradburn and ordered Col. José de las Piedras to proceed from Nacogdoches to Anáhuac to quiet the disturbance. In Anáhuac, the colonists captured some Mexican cavalrymen. After some minor fighting an agreement was reached. The Texans were to release their captives and retire from the town.

Soon afterward one of the Texan leaders, John Austin, gave command of the Texans to W. C. Hall and went to Brazoria for cannons, arms, and soldiers. Trying to justify their actions, the insurgents held a meeting and declared their loyalty to Santa Anna, the leader of the Federalists at the time. Austin got 112 soldiers and mounted a cannon on a schooner; Johnson attacked the fort at Velasco on June 25, 1832; and after three days its commander, Col. Domingo de Ugartechea, surrendered. His force was allowed to return to Béjar. Piedras was kept from getting to Anáhuac, and he was convinced to surrender. He agreed to free the captive Texans, arrest Bradburn, and appoint the next senior officer to command. Bradburn managed to escape to New Orleans and proceeded to

Mexico. Subsequently, Lt. Juan Cortina was placed in command of the fort at Anáhuac.

By the end of 1832 there were essentially no regular Mexican troops left in Texas. For several years, the Anglo Texans were able to convince some of the Mexican authorities that they were Federalists and were fighting for the leader of the Federalist movement, General Santa Anna. The colonists even named a town on the Navidad River "Santa Anna" after the man they honestly believed would support their cause. They repeatedly claimed that they were fighting for the constitution of 1824 to be upheld.

During most of his early career, Santa Anna had supported the Federalists and had fought against the Centralists. He had been able to overthrow Agustín de Iturbide and help put in power the government that enacted the liberal constitution of 1824. However, it was a constant struggle for his party to stay in power. Over time he developed the strategy of taking power and then leaving Mexico City, often claiming illness, for his hacienda at Manga de Clavo. He would leave his vice president in charge of the government until things got so bad that he would finally return to Mexico City to save the people. When this happened, he would march into Mexico City at the head of a procession as the returning hero.

In 1833, President Santa Anna left Mexico City for his hacienda and left Valentín Gómez Farías, his vice president, in charge of the government. Gómez Farías was considered a radical liberal, and along with fellow liberal Lorenzo de Zavala, governor of the state of Mexico, he started enacting laws that were very anti-military and even more anti-church. The main ways that these new laws hurt the church concerned its ability to raise money and to control the education system. When the church and the military could not tolerate these radical measures any longer, they turned to Santa Anna for support. Santa Anna made a shocking 180-degree turn in his politics. By means of the Plan of Cuernavaca in April of 1834, Santa Anna declared himself to be a Centralist and removed the liberal government from power. The constitution of 1824 was immediately repealed, as were the liberal reforms of the Gómez Farías government. The powers of the state legislatures were univocally removed. This obviously did not sit well with the Texans, and feelings of unrest and a tendency toward violence were growing in the state.

To better understand the extent of the problems of the Mexican government and army in dealing with the growing discord and lawless actions among the

Texans (more so the newly arrived immigrants than the original colonists), one need look no further than the case of Gen. Vicente Filisola in 1833.[10] His situation was a microcosm of the overall situation in Mexico. Filisola served as the military commander of the Internal States of the East. These states included Tamaulipas, Nuevo Leon, and Coahuila y Tejas.

Filisola documented his difficulties in dealing with the Federalist general Francisco Vital Fernández, who was serving as governor of the state of Tamaulipas at the time. In one of many examples, he decried the fact that Vital Fernández had appointed his own relative, N. Leal, as customs inspector (Leal had previously worked as a violinist at the church in Reinoso). As a result, Leal had become a rich man, and the army's funding from import tariffs in Tamaulipas had been reduced to nothing.

General Filisola also estimated that the strength of the units of the army had been decreased to approximately one-fifth or one-sixth of what was normal. He noted that this was attributable to war and pestilence. According to his records, one unit lost 206 men to cholera.

Filisola wrote the minister of war three times in September and October of that year to complain about the severe lack of money to make payments to the troops. He stated that the presidial troops, the only troops on the frontiers, were nine to ten months in arears for their salaries. Thus, their numbers were decreasing, and the indigenous population was not being controlled.

Because of a severe illness Filisola was replaced on November 22, 1833, by Gen. Pedro Lemus. On December 30, 1833, Filisola wrote to Lemus giving a summary of the state of conditions in regard to the command. He noted that the lack of supplies and funds was causing poor morale among the troops. He reported that several units had been disbanded in order to search for food. Ammunition and guns were found to be useless due to the humidity. Buildings and quarters were in ruins and hospitals were closed.

Filisola further reported to Lemus that he had been obliged to go to the governor of the state to obtain men and horses to chase down a group of twenty-five robbers. He also added that the Texas colonists followed their own ways and laws and paid no duties.

He explained that the company commanders would issue promissory notes to fund their needs. These notes would then be sold at 5 percent of their face value, only to be taken to the customhouses, where they would be cashed in at full value. Ample men were available to man the units, but this lack of funding prevented it.

Noting that the administration of justice was lacking, Filisola claimed this was attributable to inadequate judges and legal advisors, poor communications, and a complete lack of organization. There was a grave problem of immorality and fraud in fiscal affairs. If the government did hire an honest worker, he was soon corrupted, or some scandal was brought against him to get rid of him.

In his report to Lemus, Filisola told him that it was not his illness that had caused him to resign his position but rather lack of authority and frustration at the lack of support.[11]

Filisola's reports were obviously the tip of the iceberg when it came to the overall ability of the Mexican government to deal with the growing boldness and audacity of the colonists in Texas. The reports are, however, a good example of the immensity of the problems that would need to be overcome to save Texas for their country.

By 1834 it was becoming more and more obvious that the colonists had no intention of respecting the government that had accepted them as new citizens. It was certain that the only response that might have the desired effect would be a show of force. However, the big question was whether the government had the ability and willpower to undertake this kind of action, considering all the other national problems that existed at the time. The internal strife would have to be put aside and all resources directed to dealing with the ungrateful rebels in Texas. As will be documented in this work, sparks would fly in 1834, but by 1835 the powder keg would explode.

CHAPTER ONE

Santa Anna

It would be nearly impossible to examine the Mexican army's campaign in Texas without first examining the evolution of its oligarch, Antonio López de Santa Anna. His rise from a young officer to president of Mexico and supreme commander of the Mexican army is not only a fascinating story but gives a preview of what was to come in Texas. By 1835 Santa Anna was in such complete control of every aspect of the campaign that the influence of his style of command, tactics, supply, financing, etc. was evident in every detail. After Santa Anna's capture at San Jacinto, his absence left such a void in the Mexican hierarchy that the main focus of the campaign changed immediately from putting down the revolt in Texas to preserving the Centralist government of the Mexican Republic.

According to his baptismal register, Antonio de Padua María Severino López de Santa Anna de Lebrón was born on February 21, 1794.[1] On the same document, his parents were listed as the lawyer Antonio Santa Anna and Doña Manuela Pérez Lebrón. The future *presidente* was born in the mountain town of Jalapa, near the port city of Veracruz.

According to Mexican historian Manuel Rivera, Santa Anna was educated only in the basics and was placed by his father in a counting house at an early age. The establishment was in Veracruz and was owned by a rich merchant by the name of Cos.[2] Apparently dissatisfied with his new occupation, the young Santa Anna enrolled as a cadet in the local infantry regiment. In his autobiography Santa Anna wrote the following: "I received the consent of my parents and took my place as a gentleman cadet in the regiment of infantry, *Fijo de Veracruz*, on June 9, 1810, having previously presented them indispensable proofs of my qualifications as a gentleman which was required by them."[3] In the regiment

Antonio and his bother Manuel were said to be of a quarrelsome character and were constantly getting in fights with their classmates.[4]

This lack of a quality education defined Santa Anna for the rest of his career. Mexican historian Genaro García wrote a sketch of the life of General Santa Anna and included the following statement: "It is inferred that his education was very much neglected. He never revealed in his long life any habits of morality, nor in his numerous writings any solid instruction at all. He himself said in his manifesto of April: 'My education has been purely military and the years which I might have dedicated to cultivating the sciences, I passed in the barracks and the camps.' Unfortunately, the military career was not at that time a moralizing influence and less was it instructive. Don Lucas Alaman, who was closely associated with Santa Anna, discovered in him a man of natural talent very outstanding, but lacking in moral and literary culture."[5] Young Santa Anna cut his military teeth while campaigning with the *Fijo de Veracruz* regiment in northern Mexico and Texas. He served under and was greatly influenced by Gen. Joaquín de Arredondo, an old-school Spanish officer who was well known for his heavy-handed tactics.

Historian Walter Edgar Hancock had the following to say about Arredondo's command style: "Arredondo had many losses, but there were always plenty of soldiers to replace those who fell, and horses were abundant for the cavalry. But this wholesale method of brutal massacre and the unjust and harsh treatment which Arredondo employed in dealing with his officers and soldiers in order to stamp out rebellion, was not accomplished without many complaints from numerous sources."[6]

In 1813 a revolution arose in Texas that is referred to as the Gutiérrez-Magee Expedition. Arredondo's forces met and defeated the insurgents just south of Béjar on August 24, 1813, at the battle of Medina. In his official report, General Arredondo reported that his troops killed 1,000 of the enemy and captured 112, who were shot immediately. The Royalist troops continued to Béjar and captured 215 more rebels. The rebels from the United States, and many of the Béjareños, were also shot. Of the 850 Americans who entered the battle, only 93 were said to have returned to the United States.[7]

Gen. Vicente Filisola wrote in his in his memoirs:

> Arredondo in Béxar, stained his victory and his triumph with acts of a character truly barbarous, causing a great number of military executions among the officers and soldiers taken after the battle on the road, in the city and vicinity, and also among individuals of the city who had not taken up

> arms against the government; and, to set the seal to his cruelty, confiscated a great deal of property, and shut up in one house . . . a multitude of women, including married ladies and young girls, and made them grind materials for the composition of gunpowder, under the insolent rule of a sergeant, brutal, immoral and cruel, who, with a small detachment, in the place of protecting them, insulted and mortified them in the most vile and indecent manner. At the same time, he made himself odious by other despotic cruelties, which will never be forgotten by that unfortunate population, while there remains in it a single inhabitant, which characterizes him as a scourge of human kind, and a true type of the most savage tyranny which can put the human race to shame.[8]

Further evidence that Santa Anna admired and emulated Arredondo is given by José Luis Mora: "With these manners of proceeding and with the license that is allowed to the soldiers, their [the locals at Béjar] minds, far from being quieted, conceived a hatred of the deepest kind against Arredondo, his troops, and the cause that he defended. For this cause, there came to life the new efforts that later tended to kindle an insurrection in those provinces. In this expedition Antonio López de Santa Anna made his first military assays, who afterwards made so much noise in Mexico, and who to this day speaks with so much enthusiasm of the qualities of Arredondo as a military and political chief for exercising authority in both branches."[9]

One of Santa Anna's many biographers, Wilford Callcott, had the following to say about Santa Anna's service under Arredondo and his experience in Texas: "The whole campaign built up in the mind of Santa Anna (still a boy of nineteen, but again warmly commended in official reports of the Battle of Medina for gallant conduct under fire) two illusions that were to cost him dearly at a later date. One of these was that the way to handle Texas rebels was by terrorization, and the other was that said rebels were ineffective fighters and could be easily defeated by Mexican troops."[10]

Lieutenant Santa Anna spent the next few years fighting for the Spanish Royalist cause in the vicinity of Veracruz. He carried out many campaigns against the local insurgents, winning many battles and losing at times as well. In September 1817 Santa Anna's troops were attacked by rebels under the command of Valentín Guzmán and Marcos Benavides. His Royalist troops were defeated, and he barely escaped with his life, thanks to the swiftness of the horse that carried him. There would be several more of these mad dashes to escape the enemy in Santa Anna's future career, and one cannot help but think that he felt confident, as he fled from the battle of San Jacinto, that this was just another adventure.

He did show early signs of a tendency toward cruelty, but he was certainly not the worst of the Royalist officers in that regard.[11] Santa Anna's strength seemed to be in his daring and aggressive decisions. He seemed to have an amazing grasp of the big picture. When there was an important position to be gained or a troop movement to be thwarted, he set immediately to the task. It was also apparent that Santa Anna began to believe that speed of march and the element of surprise were far more important than numbers of troops in the outcome of a battle.

By early 1820 the Royalist army had nearly broken the spirit of the rebels. However, there was a sudden change in the status quo in March 1820, when the constitution of 1812 was restored in Spain and a liberal revolution resulted. Creoles (persons of pure Spanish blood who were born in Mexico) were no longer inclined to support the Spanish since their privileged standing was no longer secure. Now the Creoles, the indigenous elements of New Spain, and even the liberal Spanish were united in their desire for Mexican independence. This eventually led to Gen. Agustín de Iturbide and Gen. Vicente Guerrero, a commander of the insurgents, meeting and proclaiming the Plan de Iguala on February 24, 1821. The essence of the plan was reflected in the words "religion," "independence," and "union." These ideas were referred to as the three guarantees.

In March 1821 the Royalist Santa Anna was fighting insurgents at Orizaba. His forces began to desert him, and he was urged by the leader of the insurgents to join the rebels for the cause of independence. On the morning of March 29, Santa Anna took a small force and attacked some outposts of the insurgents. He captured most of the rebels, eleven horses, five loads of cartridges, and some arms. He also took a wounded officer prisoner, Manuel Prieto. Later that same day Santa Anna declared his support for the Plan de Iguala and united his troops with those of the rebel commander José Joaquín de Herrera. This sudden and dramatic change in his loyalties was certainly a foretaste of things to come.

Historian Manuel Rivera had the following to say about the significance of Santa Anna's pronunciamiento: "The adhesion of Santa Anna to the cause of independence hastened the development of events in the province of Veracruz by the extraordinary activity that the new leader displayed, communicating a new impulse to the elements that existed there, exhibiting from that time the energy and intrepidity that afterwards distinguished him during his long public career, overriding all the inconveniences and confiding the results of his enterprises to fortune, the inseparable companion of men of action."[12] Soon after his pronunciamiento, Santa Anna showed the extremes he was willing to go to achieve his goals. He had taken his troops to his hometown of Jalapa and upon arriving there pretended that he had been appointed commanding general of the province. The town leaders of Jalapa called his bluff and asked to see documentation of his appointment. He sent them two vague proclamations, the second of which stated that he should also be named political chief of the province. These proclamations, along with other complaints, eventually led to an inspection tour of the district by Iturbide. This would eventually contribute to the rift that developed between Iturbide and his former loyal supporter.

At Jalapa Santa Anna decided that the town should pay for its rescue from the Royalists. He declared that the city fathers were to give him a "loan" of twelve thousand pesos to feed and clothe his army. Forced payments were another practice that was to continue throughout Santa Anna's career and was one of his many traits that made him quite unpopular with the inhabitants of the towns that his armies marched through.

Another significant event took place at Jalapa. Among the troops that reinforced him there was a well-educated historian named Carlos M. Bustamante. Callcott wrote that Bustamante "was to teach Santa Anna to add classical references to the egotism and bombast of the day in his future proclamations."[13]

In Jalapa Santa Anna captured many arms and was able to equip and train his troops. He organized the 11th Division of the Army of the Three Guarantees. He now felt that the time was right, and in June 1821 he set out to capture Veracruz. A closer look at this action will give a great deal of insight into the extreme vacillations of emotion that Santa Anna often exhibited.

Regarding Santa Anna's swings of emotion, it is appropriate to give a quote from the Mexican historian Francisco Bulnes. Some of what he says in his evaluation of the Mexican and Spanish army of the time seems to hold true in the Texas campaign. Commenting on their behavior, Bulnes remarked that the Mexicans inherited one ridiculous vice from the emotional Spanish conquerors: "Before a battle, all the Spanish equipment was excellent; artillery, powder, bullets, fortifications, cavalry, arms, and especially the troops, the officers and the general; even the light, the clouds, the earth, the flowers and the beasts. After the defeat it is asserted that the artillery was of wood [*oyamel*], the bayonets of clay, the powder was wet, the bullets would not fit the guns; there was no artillery park or train, nor mules to move it; clouds had made it dark as night; the sun had blinded the eyes of the troops; the earth had opened and swallowed up various outfits, while the very flowers had breathed out poisonous vapors. Without such untoward developments victory would have been certain, for our gallant troops can never be defeated."[14]

Santa Anna published an impassioned proclamation prior to the attack on Jalapa. Part of the proclamation read: "Soldiers, you are going to change the face of the world and recover the most glorious name of which we have been despoiled for three centuries, which passes even among ourselves as weak and cowardly. You at last are going to cover yourselves in glory. Fight with the fury of a climate that devours men, and with the dagger of wretches that dare arrogantly to oppose your cause, trusting in their weak walls and in their little fortresses. Fools they are! Soon they shall weep for their temerity; soon you shall see them crawling before you to implore your compassion. Their pride is stupid force that will be dissipated at the breath of your courage, and with only your presence."[15]

Despite some initial successes, Santa Anna's troops were eventually forced to withdraw from Veracruz in defeat. The commander of the Royalist forces, Gov. José Dávila (previously a benefactor of Santa Anna's career), reported that Santa Anna withdrew leaving some two hundred *soldados* dead, wounded, or captive. Rivera, as Bulnes would have predicted, gave the following excuse for the defeat: "The orders of Santa Anna were not faithfully executed, for some wine shops having been opened, a number of soldiers and officials took refuge in them, for which reason an assault, which had begun so happily, failed."[16]

The defeated Santa Anna withdrew from Veracruz and marched his division to Córdova. He was apparently despondent and bent upon revenge when he issued the following proclamation, which is in direct contrast to the earlier impassioned notice: "Veracruz, Veracruz! The voice of your extermination shall be henceforth the cry of our combatants on entering into battle. In all their meetings and congresses, the vow to your ruin shall be added to their deliberations. Carthage, from whose glory you are as far removed as the gama grass from the noble oaks, ought to inspire you with the dread of her memories, and Carthage never offended Rome so much Veracruz has offended Mexico."[17]

Soon after this proclamation was issued, Santa Anna's fortunes took a sudden turn for the better. This seemed to be the norm for Santa Anna in his early career. He was generally able to align himself with the winning side, and he often went a step further than alignment by sensing when the time was right to start his own uprising—which was usually successful. It appears Santa Anna was repeatedly the recipient of the fortune that accompanies men of action, as mentioned by Rivera. Nonetheless, it happened so often that some credit must be given to Santa Anna for his special ability to sense the political and military ebbs and flows of his country.

In this case the sudden turn was attributable to a visit by General Iturbide. The general greeted Santa Anna openly with a large group of officers present. He declared that Santa Anna was a hero and that the action at Veracruz was militarily sound and heroic.

On September 27, 1821, Iturbide entered Mexico City at the head of the army of Three Guarantees. There was great rejoicing upon his arrival, and Iturbide was proclaimed the hero of Mexican independence. Santa Anna did not take part in the festivities, but as a reward for his faithful service he was promoted to the rank of brigadier general. Thus, he had risen from the rank of brevet captain to brigadier general in six months.

After a few months of unsuccessfully trying to deal with a congress that refused to cooperate, Iturbide arranged to have himself proclaimed emperor. In July 1822 he was officially crowned Emperor Agustín I. Santa Anna was one of Iturbide's more ardent supporters at the time.

Soon after, a rift began to develop between Santa Anna and Iturbide due to a botched attempt by Santa Anna to capture the Spanish fortress of San Juan de Ulúa.[18] In addition, he had been frequently accused of poor conduct and abuses of power by the local authorities. This caused General Iturbide to make a personal trip to Jalapa to investigate all the negative reports of Santa Anna. At the same time, Emperor Iturbide was making new plans for attacking the Spanish at San Juan de Ulúa. It quickly became apparent to Santa Anna that he was not being involved in the planning and had obviously lost favor with the emperor.

Santa Anna knew that Iturbide was withdrawing from him when the emperor told him he was relieving him of his command at Veracruz and requested his presence for important matters in Mexico City. Santa Anna saw the writing on the wall and immediately set out from Jalapa to Veracruz, hoping to get there before the news of his being relieved of command arrived.

With the help of minister from the Republic of Columbia Miguel Santa María, recently dismissed from Mexico by Iturbide, Santa Anna drew up the Plan of Veracruz and led an uprising against Emperor Iturbide on December

6, 1822. Santa Anna's timing was impeccable. Even though his motivation for the revolt was likely self-serving, the entire country seemed to have wearied of Iturbide's heavy-handed methods and unwillingness to work with the congress.

Santa Anna, true to form, immediately set out with his forces and attacked the government troops at Jalapa. He was soundly defeated and lost almost all his troops and arms. Iturbide ordered that all the rebel prisoners be shot with their coats turned inside out, as a sign of being traitors. The Mexican commander at Jalapa, General Calderón, ignored the emperor's order to shoot the rebels.

Once again Santa Anna had to flee from a defeat and barely escaped with his life. He was said to have encountered Guadalupe Victoria in his flight to Veracruz and suggested to Victoria that they flee to the United States. Lorenzo de Zavala wrote that Victoria instructed Santa Anna to return to Veracruz, hold his post, and to sail only when he was presented with the head of Victoria.[19]

Santa Anna was bottled up in Veracruz, and the revolt seemed to be fizzling when he had another of his many strokes of good fortune. The Scottish Rite Masons (*escoceses*), bitter rivals of the emperor, managed to talk the commander of the Mexican government troops, Gen. José Antonio Echávarri, into declaring for the revolution and joining Santa Anna. On February 1, 1823, thirty-four officers led a pronunciamiento according to the Plan de Casa Mata, a slight variation of Santa Anna's Plan of Veracruz. From this point on, the revolution spread like wildfire to the various provinces of Mexico, and Iturbide abdicated on March 19, 1823.[20]

Hancock wrote an interesting comparison of Santa Anna and Iturbide:

> There were some points of similarity in the character and careers of Santa Anna and Iturbide. Both were very ambitious, and both had a militaristic mental bend from which neither could ever free himself. They were not wholly to blame for this, for they both had only a military training. In mental capacity and intellectual training, Iturbide was Santa Anna's superior by far; but in capacity to work with the leading men of the nation, Santa Anna was superior to Iturbide. In a sense it may be said that Iturbide took himself and his task too seriously to heart, and therefore failed to adjust and adapt himself to the needs and exigencies of the fatherland. In consequence of this he became, unfortunately for Mexico, an incapable despot in spite of undoubtedly high ideals and purposes which evidently animated him. Santa Anna also became an intolerable despot, because he did not take, nor was he capable of taking seriously enough the high honors and the unusual

> powers conferred upon him so many times by his countrymen. He could not raise his ideals and purposes for any great length of time above the trivial tendencies of the vulgar nature.[21]

Santa Anna's revolt against Emperor Iturbide had barely ended when he decided to participate in a new uprising. He had decided that the triumvirate that replaced Iturbide and the same congress that existed before the insurrection was not truly a republican government. He took his 8th Brigade to San Luís to join in a new revolt but was greeted only with hatred. Apparently, his tactics there turned both the 12th Battalion and the locals against him and his troops. After many attempts to convince them that they should join him against the new Mexican government, Santa Anna finally gave up his command and went to Mexico City, where he was arrested and scheduled to stand trial. The charges against him were that he was guilty of insurrection against the government in favor of the establishment of a federal republic and that he had seized thirty thousand pesos belonging to the national government.

Before General Santa Anna could be tried, the political mood shifted in his favor and he was declared a national hero. Although his revolt had failed miserably, he had again correctly gauged the popular sentiment of the country. Partly because of Santa Anna's actions in proclaiming for a federal republic, a new congress was elected and the liberal constitution of 1824 was enacted. After eleven years of struggle, Mexico finally had its representative government. Guadalupe Victoria and Nicolas Bravo were elected president and vice president, respectively.

For the next year Santa Anna served as governor and military commander in the Yucatán, where he was quite successful in getting the rival factions to work together. He also helped create a liberal state constitution, which was adopted just after he left office. He then served a short time as commander of the Corps of Engineers in Mexico City. As would become commonplace in Santa Anna's long career, he either became tired of politics or lacked the ability to finish, and he retired to his hacienda at Manga de Clavo. Santa Anna claimed to be in poor health and in need of rest, as he would often do when he took his long sabbaticals.

It was either during his time in the Yucatán or just after his retirement to Manga de Clavo that Santa Anna married Doña Inez de la Paz García, the daughter of a wealthy Spaniard. He would eventually have at least four children by the marriage: two daughters, María Guadalupe and María del Carmen, and two sons, Manuel and Antonio (the latter died at age five). According to Callcott, there were also reports of an afflicted child who embarrassed Santa Anna to the point that he did not bring him to Mexico City when he served as president.[22]

For the next ten years the politics of Mexico started to develop into a conservative versus liberal situation. Both sides claimed to support a republican form of government, but they had different views as to the exact form such a government should take.

With the successful Plan of Veracruz, Santa Anna had started and would continue a disturbing trend in the country. Whenever the military was unhappy with the government, they could start an insurrection, and all too often they would succeed in unseating the government that was currently in power. The military continued to steadfastly support the church, primarily because the church was often one of the only sources of funding.

Santa Anna might have been able to keep his interests alive in both the Centralist and Federalist parties. He had early connections with the Centralists but was noted to be a Federalist in 1825. His brother, Col. Manuel Santa Anna, was a conservative and one of the editors of the *Veracruz Libre*, a newspaper that was a mouthpiece for the Centralists. There were rumors that Santa Anna supported his brother and was involved in plots against the Mexican government that were brewing in Veracruz. There is little doubt that his brother was involved, but Santa Anna seemed to either have had nothing to do with his brother and the Centralists or he was a master at doing so without detection.

At the same time that his brother was actively involved with the conservatives, Santa Anna subscribed to the *Mercurio*, a leading liberal newspaper. There is no evidence that he was involved in the writing or editing of the paper, but it did set him up to take whichever path seemed to be the one more likely to lead to his success.

In 1827, the Centralists staged a rebellion, called the Plan of Montaño. Santa Anna had been courted by the Centralists and was rumored to have been involved in the rebellion, but on January 2, 1828, he wrote the secretary of war, Gómez Pedraza, and General Guerrero, offering his services to put down the insurrection. Once again Santa Anna seemed to have been able to sense the will of the nation and either held off joining the revolt or truly still supported the Federalists—either way, he again enhanced his position as a national hero. After the government quickly crushed the revolt, Santa Anna was appointed vice governor of Veracruz, which effectively meant ruling the state as the governor of Veracruz was on trial at the time.

With the leaders of the Centralist party in exile and the Federalists firmly in control of the government, it seemed that calm would prevail in Mexico. Such was not the case, and, surprisingly, the opposition came from within the Federalist party itself. When the party decided to nominate the revolutionary hero General Guerrero for president, things began to fall apart. Lorenzo de Zavala gave this explanation as to what caused this unrest among the more moderate members of the party:

> From the very bosom of the Yorkists [York Rite Masons who were Federalists] came the germ of division and of the new civil war. The generals, with the exceptions we shall see, the colonels, the most notable ecclesiastics, the great proprietors, all the remains of the party defeated at Tulancingo [the Centralists],[23] and finally, the persons with any pretensions of culture and civilization all abominated the presidency of a man who was neither white, nor could alternate in the circles of high society with the freedom and naturalness that education and custom demand. The ladies of a certain class could not tolerate, nor see without hatred and envy, a family of darkest color occupy such a distinguished place among themselves. All, in fact, all the rest of those with old prejudices and repugnancies for a class of people oppressed and despised, together with the fact that the candidate could not substitute for the faults that were noticed in him with the elevation of his type, the energy of character, not any of those brilliant qualities that cover up these defects. These all combined to create a formidable party among the new Mexican aristocracy against the election of Guerrero.[24]

The moderate Federalists under the leadership of such notable liberals as Miguel Ramos Arispe, Valentín Gómez Farías, and even President Victoria proclaimed the candidacy of the minister of war, Gómez Pedraza. Much to his credit, Santa Anna and many of the state governors stayed loyal to Guerrero.

The followers of Pedraza, though smaller in numbers, resorted to all types of corrupt political tricks and worked to manipulate the small state legislative bodies. When the final count came in, Pedraza was favored by eleven of the eighteen state legislatures and was thus elected president. It is important to note that, despite all the bribery, dirty tricks, etc., this was technically a legal election under the constitution of 1824, and any action against the election would be in violation of said document.

Vice Governor Santa Anna did his best to sway the Veracruz state legislature toward electing the popular Guerrero. However, at the last minute, a captain of the 2nd Cavalry, Francisco Pardo,[25] arrived in Veracruz with a large amount of money, and Pedraza was suddenly the choice of the legislature. Santa Anna led a pronunciamiento against the election of Pedraza in September 1828.

It is appropriate at this point to examine the involvement of the governor of the state of Mexico, Lorenzo de Zavala, in this affair. Since he would become a major player in the Texas Revolution and have a direct effect on Santa Anna's actions in Texas, it is important to understand the evolution of their animosity. As stated before, de Zavala was a staunch Federalist, and thus he was an ardent supporter of General Guerrero. At this point he and Santa Anna were fighting for the same cause—Federalism.

As governor of the state of Mexico, de Zavala did everything in his power to support Guerrero, and indeed, unlike Veracruz, where Santa Anna was in charge, he was able to get his state legislature to support the general. This was not easy, however, as Pedraza was in Mexico City, and as minister of war he had a great influence over the military in the area.

When Santa Anna opposed the election of Pedraza, de Zavala's enemies took advantage of the opportunity and accused him of being part of the revolt. With the help of Pedraza and his supporters, the senate declared that there was a case against de Zavala and ordered him held for trial. De Zavala chose to flee rather than face exile and eventually became supportive of Santa Anna's uprising.[26]

When Santa Anna initially began his pronunciamiento against Pedraza, it was widely condemned, and the consensus seemed to be that it was doomed to failure. It may be that even Santa Anna felt as though he may have gone too far on this occasion. However, considering his situation and options at the time of his announcement, it seems as though he had no other choice. On September 5, 1828, the Veracruz legislature indicted Santa Anna for treason. According to letters sent to the legislature on September 4, he was only guilty of having been asked by an unruly crowd to revolt against the government. Santa Anna reportedly had refused the crowd and immediately notified the legislature of this occurrence. The legislature relieved Santa Anna of his office of vice governor and insisted that his trial proceed. Like de Zavala, Santa Anna had little choice but to stage a revolution.

The political situation in Mexico could not have been worse at the time. If Pedraza succeeded President Victoria, it appeared that military despotism would return to the nation. This would likely lead to the same situation the people had suffered under the rule of Emperor Iturbide. On the other hand, if Santa Anna and his insurrection were able to prevent the inauguration of Pedraza, it meant the end of the moderate Federalist government and the end of the constitution of 1824. It would mean that even with a federal constitution in place, the military could sweep away the government at their very whim. Of all Santa Anna's pronunciamientos, revolts, and bold proclamations, this one may have had the greatest effect on the long-term history of Mexican politics.

Hancock gave the following opinion on the contemporary situation: "The Mexican people were not at that time, or for many years to come, possessed of moderating elements in sufficient numbers to give rise to the hope that such a happy result could be expected. Given the situation then existing in the nation, with all the elements of discord, undisciplined ambition, and intense violence which, in this controversy, characterized nearly all the leaders in more or less degree, it was too much to expect that the normally safe and sound course of action would be pursued by any leader, or group of leaders, in the nation."[27]

General Santa Anna made his proclamation official in Jalapa on September 12. A similar pronunciamiento had been made in Mexico City on September 7, so Santa Anna was not the sole source of this revolt. He immediately took the fortress at Perote and held it with a force of 1,000–1,200 men.

The resulting campaign gives the reader a glimpse of what was to come in the Texas campaign. In his actions and those of his opponent, General Manuel Rincón, one can see many of the traits that were exhibited by Santa Anna and Houston in the San Jacinto campaign.

Unlike the later Texas campaign, Santa Anna was now on the defensive with a slightly inferior force. This was not the situation for Santa Anna's favorite tactics to be used. He did his best to split Rincón's forces with false marches and planted leaks to Rincón's camp. Rincón apparently was familiar with Santa Anna's style of engagement and refused to be tricked into a situation where he was outnumbered or could be surprised. Hancock gives a description of Rincón's tactics, which in many ways mirror the methods of Houston: "He [Rincón] knew that he could not cope with Santa Anna in versatility and unbounded energy, or in strategical and tactical planning and movements. He also knew that time and circumstances were working in his favor and that if he would hold on long enough his [Santa Anna's] energy was sure to succumb to the weight of the superior forces that were gathering against him. He was playing to the end of forcing Santa Anna to a fight on his own terms, and to meet his combined force in favorable conditions for them, rather than expose his not too numerous forces and weak artillery to the danger of being caught in detail by the maneuverings of his wily enemy."[28] Rincón said it well when he stated that "I wanted to provoke the impetuosity of General Santa Anna in order that he might advance his columns."[29] This is exactly what happened, as Santa Anna became aware that reinforcements were on their way to Rincón and that he had no other option than to attack.

On the morning of October 15, 1828, Santa Anna attacked the fortified force of Rincón and was soundly defeated. He lost his two artillery pieces and was forced to withdraw to the fortress at Perote. Rincón was later criticized for his failure to aggressively pursue Santa Anna and destroy his forces before he was able to reach the fortress. Santa Anna was to find himself in a similar situation on April 21, 1836, but the Texans did not fail to track down the fleeing troops and annihilate the Mexican division.

Rincón eventually followed Santa Anna, and the two opposing generals battled again just outside Oaxaca. For some reason (perhaps to save the city from destruction), Santa Anna left the cover of the city and attacked Rincón with a smaller force. The defeat was a disastrous one for Santa Anna. Hancock wrote that "he [Santa Anna] trusted to luck very often, but good luck does not always accompany such tactics. Fortune forsook him upon this occasion and proved to be treacherous to his usually charmed improvisations."[30]

Inexplicably, Rincón and his forces once again allowed Santa Anna and a portion of his troops to escape their clutches. Had they followed up the battle with aggressive tactics, the revolution likely would have ended that day. Considering the fact that Rincón reported that his forces suffered 36 dead and 59 wounded while placing the enemy losses at 750 dead and wounded, it is even more astounding that Santa Anna was able to live to fight another day.

The fates once again favored General Santa Anna when, on November 30, 1828, there was a new pronunciamiento in Mexico City: the Revolution of the Acordada.[31] At the same time, other unrelated revolts began breaking out in various parts of Mexico. The swell in the popularity of the revolution became so great that Pedraza fled Mexico City and eventually left the country for London and then New Orleans.[32]

On April 1, 1829, General Guerrero was sworn in as president of Mexico. His administration had no realistic chance of success. The national treasury was without any funds, its industries were paralyzed, and its credit was worthless. A counterrevolution had been declared in Puebla that was supported by several officers who would later serve in the Texas campaign, including Vicente Filisola and Juan Andrade. The constitution had basically been declared null and void by the success of the military revolt against Pedraza.

Perhaps the most significant development of the early period of Guerrero's presidency was the enactment of a law to expel the Spanish. When Spanish refugees started arriving in Spain, they reported to their countrymen that conditions were so bad in Mexico that the Mexican people would gladly embrace a Spanish invasion. To that aim, General Isidro Barradas invaded Mexico with 3,500 Spanish troops and six war ships.[33] The Mexicans were aware of the imminent invasion, and Santa Anna had arranged to be named as coastal commander to respond to the crisis.

When the Spanish arrived at Tampico, Santa Anna immediately sent one thousand infantrymen by sea and five hundred cavalrymen over land to that area.[34] As one might expect, Santa Anna threw himself into the fray without having a complete understanding of the situation. Luckily for him, Barradas's force was split and he was unable to take advantage of Santa Anna's exposed position. From the description of the Spanish movements in the campaign it seems likely that Barradas had no desire to battle the Mexican forces. He knew that he could not conquer the nation with 3,500 men but rather had hoped to win the will of the people and be greeted as a savior. As it turned out, fighting and killing Mexican troops was certainly no way to win the hearts of the populace.

On this occasion Santa Anna received help from the fates of nature. On September 9, 1829, a severe hurricane landed in the Tampico area and caused devastation to both armies. Certainly, this was worse for the Spanish as they had no way to recover their loss of men, munitions, etc.

General Santa Anna had no qualms about fighting the Spanish. He had been waiting for a chance to secure a great military victory and he had no intention of letting this opportunity pass. On the night of September 10, he held a council of war. Reportedly the enthusiasm of his officers and his troops was so great that he felt compelled to attack. He enlisted the aid of Gen. Manuel de Mier y Terán and undertook a daring night attack on Veracruz. Mier y Terán was against this move, but the aggressive nature of Santa Anna was not to be dampened. The attack began at 1:45 a.m. and lasted until nearly daybreak. After suffering large numbers of dead and wounded, Santa Anna was more than willing to parlay with the Spanish, and he accepted the capitulation of Barradas under the same terms that had been proposed by Barradas the morning before the battle.[35]

In evaluating the quality of Santa Anna's leadership during the Spanish invasion, one must consider several aspects of the action. The greatest benefit of his leadership was his rapid arrival in Tampico, which left Barradas no opportunity to spread any dissent or enlist any aid from the locals. Considering the popular pressure on the Mexican government to expel all the Spanish from Mexico it seems unlikely that Barradas would have had any success, but the fact remains that Santa Anna's quick actions left nothing to chance.

Otherwise, Santa Anna likely would be given poor evaluations for military tactics. He aggressively attacked the Spanish while they were in a fortified position when a delaying action would have greatly weakened them. They were holed up in Tampico without the possibility of resupply, with poor morale, no local support, and mounting numbers of sick. They were in the process of trying to recover from the strong hurricane. Mier y Terán advised the conservative approach but Santa Anna went forward with his plans for a frontal attack. His troops suffered a great number of casualties and they failed to take the city.[36] After this failure he accepted the capitulation of Barradas under the same conditions that he could have had the day prior to the battle, making all the loss of life unnecessary.

Hancock gave the following evaluation of the campaign:

> Santa Anna and Terán now became the heroes of the Mexican nation. Santa Anna was promoted to the grade of Division General on August 29th, and Terán received the same promotion a short time later. There were those then—and have been since that time—who would minimize the success of this hazardous expedition. Some have attributed the success of the attack to the supposedly superior military ability of Mier y Terán over that of Santa Anna. Others have minimized the strength and resistance of the Spaniards. Santa Anna has been criticized for attacking, for the sake of personal glory, a sick and almost defenseless body of soldiers, while they were pleading for mercy, thus adding cruelty and reckless inconsideration to unbounded ambition. Not a few have severely condemned Santa Anna for not accepting on the 10th of September, practically the same terms which he accepted on the 11th, by which he would have avoided a useless sacrifice of victims on both sides—occasioned by the otherwise heroic and brave conduct displayed in the engagement by the contending forces. The last criticism seems to be the only one that merits consideration. It seems obvious that Santa Anna gained nothing by allowing himself to be carried away by the enthusiasm of his subordinate officers and soldiers and by his own impetuosity. It would have been just as glorious a military achievement to have accepted Barradas' proposals before the heroic attack and the useless sacrifice of human lives on the 10th as it was to do the same thing

> on the 11th after leaving the field of battle strewn with hundreds of dead and wounded. There seems to be no good explanation for not accepting General Terán's advice to postpone the attack until the following morning; there is less reason for any attack at all, in view of the offer of capitulation just a few hours before the attack was made.[37]

The student of Texas history cannot fail to see the eerie similarities between this action and the storming of the Alamo. The council of war and ignoring the advice of his experienced generals; the early morning attack on a fortified position; the devastating casualties suffered by both sides; and the apparent lack of any true military gain in the action, as both Tampico and the Alamo were sure to capitulate in due time.

The short-term result of vanquishing the Spaniards was especially important to Santa Anna and the nation. He sent the terms of capitulation to Guerrero along with the words "Veni, vidi, vici." There was, as a result, supreme joy in the streets of the capital. There were skyrockets, ringing bells, cannonades, and repeated cheers for Guerrero, Santa Anna, and Terán. Santa Anna had given the country a burst of patriotism and pride, something that had been essentially missing since the inauguration of Emperor Iturbide.

When Santa Anna returned to Veracruz, he was received "with great enthusiasm by the inhabitants, who crowded together along the docks and nearby points, in order to celebrate his victorious entrance. He was borne way in the arms of the people to the city hall."[38] This experience may well be one of the events that began to shape the personality of Santa Anna. This exaltation and adoration seemed to be one of the cravings that he would acquire along with all his success.

As mentioned above, it was predictable that Guerrero's government would engender discontent almost immediately after he took office. One of the first problems was his choice for minister of finance, de Zavala. The latter had no experience in financial affairs and was immediately accused of all types of graft and misappropriation of funds.

It did not help that Guerrero and de Zavala were friends of and supported by Joel Poinsett, the American minister to Mexico. Poinsett had helped the Federalists in every way he could and was almost as unpopular in Mexico as the Spanish. The pressure became so great on Guerrero that de Zavala resigned as finance minister and Poinsett was sent back to the United States.

These resignations did little to quell the unhappiness of the populace, and Santa Anna's victory over the Spanish distracted them for only a short time.

A revolution broke out in Yucatán in favor of a unitary state government (a centralized government). Vice Pres. Antonio Bustamante led a group that announced an insurrection in Jalapa on December 4, 1829.

Santa Anna was immediately asked to join in the revolt, but he quickly declined. His response was a masterpiece. Given his background of revolutionary movements, the following letter showed a great deal of reason and, at the same time, irony. Notice that Santa Anna seemed to straddle the fence and appeared agreeable to the demands of the revolt but against the methods.

> Let us not be unmindful of that which the experience we have acquired in many long years teaches us. Revolutions are real evils of fatal consequences. Whether this party or the other wins, the nation suffers grave injuries. They may be started with the sanest desires, but no one can determine exactly what course they will take, or what their precise conclusions will be. I am speaking from experience and therefore I am resolved—yes, fully resolved—to never again head a revolution. No sooner has the news regarding the pronunciamiento of Campeche [Yucatán] been received by the extraordinary [mail] than one is formed in this state by the "Army of Reserve," without having any connection with the former. What will the foreign nations say about this? What will our national enemies say? Our judgment will be discredited because they will consider that we are in a state of perpetual revolution. Is it possible that in moments in which we might be using reason in the steps we take to recuperate our credit—we shall sacrifice it, and thus pollute our glory? In such a case our glorious triumphs in Tampico against the invaders would be unfruitful and null the advantages that they should bring to us. These considerations do not merit contumely.[39]

This was an interesting statement from a general who had started several revolutions against the established Mexican governments since the time of Iturbide.

Santa Anna's failure to join the revolt by Bustamante was one of the rare occasions in his early career that he joined himself to the losing side. His loyalty to Guerrero was admirable, but politically it was harmful. Santa Anna was appointed governor and military commander of Veracruz by the state legislature. He gathered his troops and proceeded to Perote and Jalapa to fight the revolutionaries. Before he could accomplish anything, word arrived that Guerrero had resigned, and Bustamante was in control of the capital. General Santa Anna had little choice but to resign his position and go into retirement at Manga de Clavo. He remained there for the next two years.

The Bustamante administration enjoyed no more time to prove itself than Guerrero's had. By March 1830 there was a growing revolt in the south of Mexico. Guerrero quickly came out in support of the insurrection. Santa Anna refused to do so. He went so far as to send his invitation to join the revolution to the Mexican government. This time Santa Anna's instincts were correct, as the revolt was put down and Guerrero was tried and executed in February 1831.[40] Santa Anna made a last-minute appeal to Bustamante to try to save Guerrero's life, but the letter had no effect.[41]

By January 1832 General Bustamante's rule was already weak and unpopular. On January 2, Col. Ciriaco Vásquez gathered a group of twenty-four officers in Veracruz and formulated a pronunciamiento. Their first action was to invite General Santa Anna to lead the new government. Despite his previous stance against the constant rebellions, on January 4 he was in Veracruz to take command of the revolt.

The Mexican government sent Gen. José M. Calderón and 4,000 men to Jalapa to put an end to Santa Anna and the revolution. Santa Anna was able to raise an army of 1,700 men and met Calderón on March 3, 1832, at the Hacienda de Tolome. Santa Anna and his troops took a terrible beating in this battle. They suffered 80 dead and 68 wounded. In the rout, 432 soldiers and 32 officers were captured, along with a large supply of arms and ammunition. Once again Santa Anna was barely able to escape the battle with his life.

As was the case with Rincón in 1828, Calderón seemed to be in no hurry to follow up the victory with a vigorous pursuit of Santa Anna. Calderón slowly advanced on Veracruz and finally arrived on March 18. It was nearly another month before a siege was begun.

Santa Anna was now on home ground, and he had successfully defended Veracruz against government troops nine years before. Calderón was no match for Santa Anna's varied, unexpected strikes and his rigorous defense against any attacks. To make matters worse the government troops were hit so hard by disease that up to one thousand of his men perished from illness. General Calderón lifted the siege on May 11, but unlike Calderón Santa Anna was highly active in his pursuit of the retreating troops and was successful in capturing a great number of men and supplies.

Initially there seemed to be no support for the revolution in the rest of the country. Another effect of the delayed movements by Calderón was that support for the revolution had time to spread. One of the first to join Santa Anna was Don Francisco Vital Fernández, governor of the state of Tamaulipas.[42]

Declarations for Santa Anna were soon announced in Tampico, San Luís Potosí, Zacatecas, Jalisco, and Guadalajara. The consensus now was that Pedraza was the legally elected president and should be reinstated until 1833, when his term would have ended.

Bustamante's cabinet resigned on May 17, 1832. Meetings were held between Santa Anna and the government to try to settle the matter peacefully. During these meetings Santa Anna again denounced the use of revolutions as a means of political gains. He stated that the revolution that he had started in 1828 was a prime example of injustice. He claimed that he could help correct this by recalling Pedraza from exile to finish his term.

During the next few months, Santa Anna was at his best in his offensive role. He defeated the government troops twice and made a rapid march on Mexico City. He then made one of his famous forced marches and arrived at Puebla before Bustamante could unite his forces.[43] By this time Pedraza had arrived, and he and Santa Anna united to defeat Bustamante in a bloody battle on the morning of December 7, 1832. After this defeat it was obvious that the government had no chance of victory, and Bustamante resigned as president.

Santa Anna was able to obtain the presidency for Pedraza, his former archenemy. With this outcome he became known as a president-maker. For the next few decades, the politics of Mexico were to revolve around either Santa Anna or whomever he decided to allow to rule in his place—that is, when he was not in exile.

On January 3, 1833, Pedraza and the leader of the army of liberation, General Santa Anna, made a triumphal entry into Mexico City. There were four huge floats, the first three of which were to honor Santa Anna and the fourth, Gómez Pedraza. There were great celebrations and the customary zeal for a new beginning, but, as had become the norm, there was no hope of stability for Mexico.

Santa Anna, playing the role of the modest military man, retired to Manga de Clavo after the celebration ended to await the results of the upcoming election. Never one to sit idly by, he published a public proclamation on January 19, 1833, pleading for "indulgence with mistakes of opinion, an end to hatreds, and the erasure from memory of the word, 'vengeance.' Thus, you will attain the object of your desires and sacrifices, long and happy days for the republic, durable happiness for all. If my dedication and sacrifices for liberty are worth anything, respond to my pleas. My whole ambition is restricted to beating my sword into a plowshare. If any hand should again disturb the public peace and constitutional order, do not forget me. I shall return at your call, and we shall again show the world that the Mexican Republic will not tolerate tyrants and oppressors of the people."[44]

It was a given that the national hero, Santa Anna, would be elected president in the election of 1833. He easily won, receiving the votes of sixteen of the eighteen states. There were still concerns among the liberals in Mexico that Santa Anna, despite his history of supporting Federalism, had strong ties to the Spanish, the army, and the Centralists. In order to allay these concerns, the Federalists ran a well-educated, very liberal civilian for vice president, Valentín Gómez Farías. He was elected by votes from eleven of the sixteen states.

At this point Santa Anna seemed to pull off a master political maneuver. He was aware of his shortcomings as a politician and knew all too well the outcomes for the last several generals who had assumed the presidency. His decision was to temporarily remain on the sidelines. On March 16 he wrote letters to President Pedraza and to Vice President elect Gómez Farías stating that his health would not allow him to take office at this time but that he had every confidence in his vice president to assume the executive power.

Gómez Farías immediately pushed for the enactment of an extremely liberal slate of reform laws. Radical changes were made in limiting the powers of the church and the army. The government enforcement of tithes to the church was discontinued, and monks and nuns were legally allowed to leave the church and return to secular life. Reforms were made to weaken the influence and size of the army and the number of officers.

In November 1833 Santa Anna returned to Mexico City and turned his attention to an old problem that had been nagging Mexico for several years—the territory of Texas and specifically the Anglo colonists from the United States.

Apparently, his attention span was poor, because in December Santa Anna asked the congress for a six-month leave of absence owing to his ongoing illness. He once again retired to Manga de Clavo. At this point it seems very likely that Santa Anna was either beginning to have serious doubts about Mexico's ability to function as a republic or he had decided to show himself as the true conservative that circumstances had kept him from revealing all those years. It is also possible that his lust for absolute power had finally gotten the better of him.

During the first few months of 1834 both Santa Anna and Gómez Farías worked vigorously for their now divergent plans of action. The latter was receiving pressure from all directions, including Santa Anna, to moderate his aggressive liberal tendencies. There seems to be little doubt that Gómez Farías's radical changes were too much too soon. These changes were totally unacceptable to most of the leaders of Mexico, who were still more worried about retaining their power and fortunes than attending to the concerns of the common man. Santa Anna seemed to sense this change in the tide of the political will of the country and was busy communicating with leaders of various states about revolting in favor of centralism.

While Santa Anna was a prisoner in Texas in 1836, Joel Poinsett, the former US minister to Mexico, sent him a message. In regards to his apparent sudden change of heart in favor of Centralism, Mr. Poinsett wrote the following: "Say to General Santa Anna that when I remember how ardent an advocate, he was of liberty ten years ago, I have no sympathy for him now, that he has gotten what he deserves." Santa Anna's reply gives us an idea of how his thought processes may have developed during this sudden about face: "Say to Mr. Poinsett that it is very true that I threw up my cap for liberty with great ardor, and perfect sincerity, but very soon found the folly of it. A hundred years to come my people will not be fit for liberty. They do not know what it is, unenlightened as they are, and under the influence of a Catholic clergy, a despotism is the proper government for them, but there is no reason why it should not be a wise and virtuous one."[45]

It is difficult to say for sure when Santa Anna started to have this change of heart. The history of his pronunciamientos and political decisions seems to show that circumstances always favored his leanings toward, at least in appearances, liberalism. For the most part his actions seemed motivated by what was best for him rather than by any underlying ideals. The tide had finally changed, and now his desire to advance and have near absolute power was better served by the conservative Centralists.

Santa Anna was not alone in his concerns regarding federalism in Mexico. Even the very liberal and well-educated Lorenzo de Zavala had serious doubts about the Mexican people's ability to self-govern: "What can be expected of Mexicans, where half of the population lives in indigence, a third part expects to receive from the presidential candidates employment or commissions for its support; where the customs of slavery make of the victors, oppressors, and of the defeated, rebels; where the interest of being superior is not a mere point of honor in having a superiority of opinion, and even less in desiring the triumph of principles, but only that of ambition, and what is worse, that of vengeance?"[46]

Gómez Farías was aware of Santa Anna's communications and plan to oust him as vice president. In May 1834 Santa Anna returned to Mexico City, and the acting president resigned his office immediately. He went into exile in New Orleans, where he and José Antonio Mejía began to act in favor of Federalism and supported the Texans' call for the return to the constitution of 1824.

Santa Anna immediately set to work undoing the laws that his vice president and the liberal congress had enacted. At the same time, several Mexican states with whom Santa Anna had been in contact declared for Centralism, demanded the church reform laws be rescinded, and called for Santa Anna to be elevated to complete control with special powers. Basically, this meant that Santa Anna did not need to have a congress, but for the sake of appearances he appointed his handpicked supporters. The new congress made sure that every law he proposed was dutifully passed. Antonio de Padua María Severino López de Santa Anna de Lebrón was now effectively, if not officially, dictator of Mexico.

By January 1835, the liberal reforms had been wiped out and the new subservient congress was seated. As had often been the case in the past, Santa Anna seemed to tire of politics and once again took a leave of absence to Manga de Clavo. In his place he left Gen. Miguel Barragán as acting president.

At this point dissent began to arise in the state of Zacatecas. This state was a center of liberal thinking and a place where Gómez Farías had been immensely popular. Santa Anna loved being a soldier as much as he hated being a politician. He immediately returned to Mexico City, and, having raised an army of 3,500 men, he left for Zacatecas on April 9, 1835.

The ease of Santa Anna's victory in this battle probably had a great influence on him and his army in the Texas Revolution. These troops had just finished the Zacatecas campaign when they were ordered to march to Texas to put down the uprising there. As will be documented in a later chapter, some of the Mexican officers seriously doubted that the Texans would fight when confronted by the veteran Mexican army. It is highly likely that overconfidence was rampant in the Mexican units.

Two major differences would become readily apparent when Santa Anna undertook the Texas campaign, and both were a disadvantage to the Mexican army. The first significant problem was that Texas was far more isolated and required a great deal more effort regarding troop movements and providing supplies.

The other variant was the fact that Zacatecas was a rich state due to its silver mining. Santa Anna was able to satisfy his officers, soldiers, and financial backers with the captured Zacatecan silver.[47] This promise of loot was one of the

Silver coin minted in Zacatecas in 1834. This coin was excavated at the San Jacinto battleground and was part of Santa Anna's treasury.

major enticements Santa Anna used when he mounted his Texas campaign, but the wealth of Texas was its crops, livestock, and lands, which were not going to satisfy his army's desire for plunder.

Two other characteristics possessed by Santa Anna should be mentioned as they influenced the outcome of the Texas Revolution. Both behaviors were discussed by Adjutant Insp. José Juan Sánchez Navarro in his memoirs When he discussed the gathering and organizing of the Mexican army for their march to Texas in late 1835. His first point had to do with delegating authority:

> There are many troops and much noise being made in the particulars. However, I do not notice that there are good political, military, and administrative systems. His Excellency [Santa Anna] himself dispatches all the matters, whether large or the most trivial. I see with astonishment that he has assumed the faculties and attributes of the Major General (who is the General Juan Arago, who has been gravely ill . . .), of the quartermaster, of the commissaries, of the brigadier generals, of the colonels, of the captains, down to the firing chiefs of the artillery, purveyors, muleteers, and cart drivers, etc.

Wouldn't it be better if His Excellency let go of such cumbersome work, which takes away his time when he needs it most for the performance of the high functions of his job? This will keep each individual of the army in full exercise of their capacity. . . . What will become of the army and of the nation if His Excellency the President dies?[48] Confusion and more confusion because only His Excellency truly knows the springs that move these masses of men called the army.[49]

Another character flaw pointed out by Sánchez Navarro was Santa Anna's attitude toward money. He noted, "It is generally said that His Excellency is very economical, even avaricious. Those who are at his side assure that if one wants to make him uncomfortable, request a peso from him. They add that he would rather give a colonel's commission than ten pesos."[50]

This thriftiness, or more likely greed, was to play a major role in the outcome of the Texas campaign. Santa Anna's brother-in-law, Ricardo Dromundo (not Cos), was quartermaster general of the army. From multiple sources it is obvious that he was given that position to profit Santa Anna. As will be seen later in this work, Santa Anna made several major campaign decisions based on finances rather than the best option militarily.

In studying the career of Santa Anna prior to the Texas Revolution, it is easy to describe his methods. His tactic of choice in a campaign or specific battle was sheer aggressiveness. He invariably tried to attack the enemy as quickly as he could, assuming that surprise would be on his side. Forced marches were a part of his plan and he did not seem to worry about the condition of his men during the march or at the time of attack. These tactics were often successful but on many occasions led to disastrous defeats. Casualties did not seem to factor into his decision-making as he had little concern for the fate of his men.

Santa Anna is usually painted as evil, treacherous, and bloodthirsty. That was often the case, but one must be careful not to judge him based purely on modern-day morality. Many of his behaviors were common among the men who trained him in the art of warfare. At times he could also be surprisingly generous in aiding people whom he trusted or who had helped him in the past.

The inability to delegate authority was a major flaw that caused major setbacks in his long and exceptional career. There is no record of his subordinates being well informed or competently making their own decisions when he was unavailable. One gets the feeling that nearly all the major decisions in the Texas Revolution were directly made by him or came through him. He was also very prone to counteracting his own orders shortly after issuing them.

There seems to be little doubt that he was a bit of a megalomaniac and may have been at his happiest when marching into Mexico City at the head of a triumphant parade in his honor. It does seem somewhat fitting that he died in poverty, a shadow of his former self, unrecognized by the people whom he had so long ruled.

It also needs to be kept in mind that the politics in Mexico City were a huge distraction to Santa Anna while he was in Texas. He was much more concerned about what the Federalists were plotting in Mexico City than the actions of the Texans. It appears that the rebellious Texans were a nuisance who had to be dealt with, but he was very anxious to get back to Mexico City where he could quell the ongoing political strife. A significant political shift occurred in March 1836, just after the fall of the Alamo, when Santa Anna received word of the unexpected death of the interim president Migel Barragán. To make matters worse, Santa Anna was not happy with the congress's appointment of José Justo Corro to fill the position. From this point on the commander in chief was even more politically distracted.

In October 1835, the last vestiges of Federalism were dissolved. Santa Anna was now dictator. Acting president Barragán enacted a law, surely at Santa Anna's direction, that all state governors were to be approved by the national government. All state legislatures were disbanded and replaced with five-men councils that had to have the approval of the national government. All state offices would be appointed by the governor with the approval of the national government. A new constitutional convention was called, but the new constitution was not finished until late 1836, after Texas was, for all practical purposes, lost.

CHAPTER TWO

The Ever-Widening Chasm

AUSTIN'S ARREST

In October 1832 and again in April 1833, delegates from the various departments of Texas came together for political conventions. During the second of the two they had the audacity to write their own constitution. This obviously did not sit well with the Mexican government, but as a result of the actions at Anáhuac and Nacogdoches in 1832 there were essentially no Mexican troops in Texas to do anything about it.

Another task undertaken by the convention was to draw up a document requesting that the federal government grant the separation of the state of Coahuila y Tejas into two separate states. Three delegates were appointed to take this request to Mexico City, but only Stephen F. Austin made the trip.[1] He arrived in July 1833 and immediately presented the document to the government, along with other matters of concern to the Texans. By October, with no action having been taken on his requests, Austin became aggravated and informed Vice President Gómez Farías that if the government did not remedy these problems the Texans would take matters into their own hands and the tranquility would be broken. This was considered a threat by Gómez Farías and the government.[2]

On October 2, 1833, Austin wrote the following letter to the city council (*ayuntamiento*) of Béjar:

> In the letter that I sent to Your Lordships, dated the proximate past 14th of August, I expressed the opinion that the matters regarding Texas would have a favorable result. Since then there have been very few sessions of the congress due to the Cholera. The events of the civil war

have also impeded all the public negotiations in a way that up to now nothing has been done. And I am sorry to say I have the feeling that, in my opinion, nothing will be done. It is difficult to form an idea as to the result of the civil war.

In this state of things, I recommend that all the city councils of Texas communicate with each other without delay, for the purpose of organizing a local government for Texas in the form of a State of the Mexican Federation, based on the law of May 7, 1824. And having everything prepared to do so in union and harmony, after it is learned that the General Congress has rejected it.

This step is an indispensable necessity as a preparatory means as there is already no doubt that the future of Texas depends on itself and not this government. Neither is there [doubt] that if the inhabitants of Texas do not take their matters into their own hands, that country is lost.

And I am firmly persuaded that the course I recommend is the only one that can be adopted to save us from anarchy and complete ruin. With that notion I hope that Your Lordships will not lose a moment in sending a communication to all the city councils of Texas, urging them to gather for the purpose of organizing a local government independent of Coahuila, although the general government denied its consent.

God and Texas Mexico [City]. Oct. 2, 1833
Esteban Austin[3]

On October 16, Austin wrote the city council in Béjar a second letter (see appendix 1). This time he was more positive. He felt that the civil war in Mexico was likely coming to an end. He stated that the Mexican government was working on the law of April 6, 1830, "which had been so harmful to Texas." However, he still felt that the issue of separate statehood for Texas was not going to be addressed and encouraged the Béjar ayuntamiento to continue to encourage the formation of their own state government without the approval of the federal government.[4]

As instructed by the ayuntamiento of Béjar, the interim political chief of that city, Manuel Jiménez, forwarded a copy of Austin's letter of October 2 to the Mexican government. Along with it they sent their reply to Austin, dated October 31, which read as follows:

The illustrious ayuntamiento of this city, being advised of the document that you have sent to it with the date of the 2nd of the month just passed, has seen with the greatest regret and surprise the exciting plea that you made to them that not a moment be lost in sending a communication to the rest of the departments, and meeting with them in order that Texas separates from Coahuila and a local government be established, even though the general government denies consent. It is certainly very lamentable that you breathe such contrary and opposing sentiments to those of any good Mexican, whose constitution and laws prohibit in a very strict way these kinds of proceedings, as you well know, and when the ephemeral support that you believe to be in the general law of May 7, 1824, is entirely destroyed by the most average capacity of the politicians of the country. Thus it is that this corporate body, neither can, nor should, nor even wishes to follow the aforementioned suggestion. It begs that you stop writing to it regarding this matter. As you well know that these communications compromise the obeying of the orders and laws of the state that must be obeyed, and those, that up to now, there is no reason to disobey in the brusque manner that you propose. There is lacking any reasonable support that could be sustained once the endeavor is started.

Much has already been said in what has been written in regard to the separation of Texas from Coahuila, and much more that you have heard here personally, making it clear to you that we have none of the elements that we need to sustain, physically and morally, this local government. In the same light it is already outside of any doubt that this project neither can, nor should be undertaken by any Coahuiltejano who knows the interests of his country and even of himself.

In conclusion, finally this corporate body entreats you, in as much as the state of revolution, which the colonies of this department, especially that [colony] of which you are the empresario, have been placed since last year, seems about to be terminated by the lenient and prudent measures that the supreme government of the state lately has put into effect, that you rethink this and do not provoke a new motive for disturbance. That upon careful examination, it will be more injurious to the colonists, and especially to you, than anyone else. We desire that this country progresses: we wish it for ourselves and for our collaborators in its attainment, the colonists established in it. However, we desire that it

> is obtained by legal and peaceful means that will not compromise the tranquility of the department and that will assure us and our children forever in the possession of the properties that we acquire in it. No doubt that the method that you propose is too adventurous.
>
> ***God and Liberty Béjar October 31, 1836***
> ***[To] Citizen empresario Stephen F. Austin***[5]

Soon after this time Austin was allowed to meet with President Santa Anna. He eventually was able to convince the Mexican government to repeal article 11 of the law of April 6, 1830. This was the article that outlawed any further immigration of colonists from the northern boundary. Austin, thinking that no more would be accomplished, left Mexico City on December 10 to return to Texas.

Things were not going to be that easy. His October 2 letter to the city council of Béjar and their reply of October 31 reached the Mexican government, and both were published in *El Telegrafo* on December 30. By this time Gómez Farías had already received said documents and had issued an arrest order for Austin. He was taken into custody in Saltillo on January 3, 1834, and was returned to Mexico City for incarceration.[6]

LEONA VICARIO VS. MONCLOVA

The matter of the political struggles between the cities of Leona Vicario (Saltillo) and Monclova that involved the state government of Coahuila y Tejas is far too complicated and extensive to thoroughly examine in this work. However, a brief summary of the events is warranted to understand the worsening of the relationship between the inhabitants of Texas and the Mexican government.[7]

Leona Vicario, the capital of the state of Coahuila y Tejas, declared in favor of Santa Anna's conservative Plan of Cuernavaca in 1832. Due to its Federalist leanings, the state congress removed itself to Monclova in March 1833 and enacted several liberal laws regarding military and commercial issues, which greatly upset the people of Leona Vicario. A bitter rivalry developed between the cities, especially after the state legislature enacted multiple laws that were beneficial to Texas. Both cities established their own state government and appointed their own governor.

Santa Anna returned to Mexico City as president on April 12, 1834. Nearly all the liberal laws that had been enacted by his previous administration under Gómez Farías were repealed. The national congress was dissolved, state legislatures and city councils were disbanded, governors were removed from office, and conservative, Centralist supporters of Santa Anna filled these positions. Effectively, these actions gave Santa Anna dictatorial powers over all of Mexico. This was a worst-case scenario for the Federalists.

On October 5, 1834, Santa Anna held a meeting to discuss the situation in Texas. The meeting was attended by four secretaries of state, three generals, three representatives to the national congress from Coahuila y Tejas, Lorenzo de Zavala, and Stephen F. Austin. After the meeting Santa Anna resolved (1) that he would mediate the repeal of the eleventh article of the law of April 6, 1830, and if not opposed, he would uphold the repeal (this would allow immigration from the northern border to resume); (2) that a corps composed of cavalry, infantry, and artillery, four thousand strong, should be stationed at Béjar for the protection of the coast and frontier of the country, to be under the command of General Mejía; (3) regular mails were to be established in Texas and obstacles to agriculture and industry were to be removed; and (4) Texas must remain united with Coahuila as it did not have the elements to warrant separation.[8]

Matters in Coahuila were only worsening, and by late 1834 the situation was threatening to become violent. A compromise was reached to allow Santa Anna to be the arbitrator, and in December 1834 he made his decisions and called for new elections. For the short-term there was calm in the state. Agustín Viesca was elected governor but would not take office until April 1835.[9]

In March 1835, the congress of the state of Coahuila y Tejas, apparently desperate for money, enacted the following law regarding sales of lands in Texas:

Special Commission

Bill of Law

Article 1. It empowers the Government to sell public lands of the state in the quantities considered sufficient to cover the public needs that currently exist.

Article 2. The sale of these lands is to be regulated under the bases and considerations deemed appropriate without regard to what is provided by the law of 26 March of the past year.

Article 3. When the objective stated in the first article is completed the Government will give accounts to the congress for its knowledge.

Article 4. The Government will dictate the necessary measures to collect such amounts coming to the state regardless of their origin and provenance.

> Monclova, 11 March 1835, Its discussion the 12th day of the present month
> Grant,[10]
> Donston [Johnston?]
> Tigerina[11]

At the time this law was passed, the military commander of the Internal States of the East was Gen. Martín Perfecto de Cos. Cos was a loyal Centralist and was doing everything within his power to impede the Federalist congress of Monclova. When the law of March 11 was passed, Cos responded to the leaders of the congress with a letter that included the following passage:

> A proposed law has arrived in my hands that was presented to that Honorable Legislature on the 11th of this month. It is for the disposal of the public lands of the state. As I see it, an obligation is imposed upon me that is charged by public office, to inform the Honorable Congress of the evils that will occur if such a proposition is taken into consideration. For its second article to be contemplated in the Senate in the broad sense in which it has been presented, it will be contrary to the 12th [article] of the law of 18 March 1824. I hasten to write to Your Lordships in order that you might inform the legislature that this General Command cannot be a cold spectator as transgressions are being made against the general laws and therefore [the General Command] will prevent the implementation of any decree that is contrary to the Federal Constitution or resolutions of the sovereign congress of the union.[12]

The letter does not specify that the passage of this law and the sale of the land was a much bigger issue than it appeared to be on the surface. The money obtained from these land transactions was to be used by the state to support their militia. The need for the stronger militia was to oppose Santa Anna and his Centralist troops. There can be little doubt that this law and the subsequent land sales were a major spark in igniting the Texas revolution.

Cos's letter probably had an influence on the congress, as the law was later repealed, but in the meantime a large amount of land was sold for next to nothing. Eleven-league parcels were the standard, but in March 1835 four hundred leagues were sold in one transaction for only thirty thousand pesos. The sale of massive amounts of land in Texas did not sit well with the colonists, as this was land that was highly sought after by new arrivals. The Mexican government was highly displeased as well, and by April 25 it had declared all these land sales to be nullified. However, it was not until September 3 that Cos finally sent orders to all the departments of Texas to quit granting land to foreigners.[13]

In response to threats of rebellion, especially in the states of Zacatecas and Coahuila y Tejas, on March 31 the federal government passed a decree requiring that the states reduce their militias to one soldier for every five hundred inhabitants. They were also ordered to surrender any surplus arms to the government.

General Cos got word that the congress in Monclova was calling up its civic militia to try to enforce its will on Leona Vicario. He decided to send a company of presidial troops to take control in Monclova.[14] Viesca was finally installed as governor on April 14 and immediately understood the precarious position he was in. He elected to send home the civic militia, and Cos's presidial company was permitted to enter the city without bloodshed.

For a short time, there was relative quiet, but the hard feelings between the two towns persisted, and Viesca called out the civic militia once again. This time, he summoned not only the local civic militia but those throughout Coahuila y Tejas. On April 27 Col. José Domingo de Ugartechea wrote Cos from Béjar and informed him of orders from Monclova to also call up the militias in Texas:[15]

> General Command of the State of Coahuila y Tejas
>
> This morning a special dispatch from Monclova was directed to the Political Chief of this department. It informed him that one hundred men of the civic militia should march to that capitol [Monclova] as quickly as possible.
>
> As this request is also addressed to the Chief of the Department of [San Felipe de] Austin, from where the same number is to march, I hurry to inform Your Excellency of this occurrence. Consequently, you can let me know if you want me to oppose this march of the militia considering that I only have ninety men from the Béjar and Alamo [presidial] companies. I have had no news from the Morelos battalion.
>
> The same message has reported that retired Lt. Col. Mateo de Ahumada is Inspector General of the Civic Militia of the state. According to my information he has not committed to accept such a position.
>
> In the colonies there is much excitement over the occurrences of the decrees concerning the alienation of the lands. Thusly, if Your Excellency cannot help me with resources, it might be impossible for me to fulfill the many orders to avoid the enactment of such a decree, or even to preserve the order and tranquility.
>
> ***God and Liberty Béjar 27 April 1835 Domingo de Ugartechea***[16]

On May 11 Cos replied to Colonel Ugartechea and wrote that the legislature of Monclova was doing the work of anarchists under the capricious pretext of weakening the department of Saltillo. He notified Ugartechea that the federal government had ordered him to completely adhere to the general law about the reduction of the civic militia. He ordered him to impede, at all costs, the departure of the one hundred militiamen from Bèjar.[17] At the same time Cos directed a broadside to the people of the Internal States of the East in an attempt to dissuade them from supporting the various acts of opposition (see appendix 2).

The legislature in Monclova adjourned on April 21, but before they did so they gave the governor the right to choose a new seat of government. Viesca elected to move the government to Béjar, where he would be even further from the Mexican government. On May 25 he set out from Monclova with 150 militiamen and about 20 Texans. Upon hearing of this action Cos wrote Secretary of War Tornel and included the following in his note: "When the Morelos battalion arrives or the rest of the force that I have requested from the President—these ungrateful foreigners will know that the Supreme Government has the power to reprimand them and that they have to obey our laws or leave the country."[18]

Capt. Manuel Lafuente, the commander of the presidial company at Laredo, wrote Cos on May 23 and informed him that he had received word from Capt. Juan José Galán, commander of the presidial company of Agua Verde, regarding the march of the officials of the state along with an escort of about three hundred civic troops. Galán was requesting troops from Lafuente to help arrest these leaders from Monclova as they attempted to flee to Béjar. Part of the reply from Cos to Lafuente was as follows:

> Every time this General Command gets more facts, I am convinced that if we do not stop the march of said authorities, it is sure that there will be an uprising in Texas. In order to avoid everything, Samuel Williams marched rapidly toward San Felipe de Austin without passing through Béjar.[19] The colonists have scared the customs employees in Galveston, resisting with force the payment of customs on their imported goods. Even those who bring their goods through Matagorda, where they have previously paid, now are refusing to do so. It will not be long before their audacity is repressed as sufficient troops are now on the march.
>
> For everything that has been expressed, and as this General Command is in the end responsible for the public peace and integrity of our territory,

> I repeat to you the orders that I have given with authority, that whenever the authorities of Monclova arrive at those presidios, maintain them under arrest and disarm their escort.[20]

Viesca was on the march for only a day or so before he got cold feet and returned to Monclova. Soon afterward, along with a small party, he set out for Texas once again. On June 1 Vicente Arreola, military commander at Monclova, notified Cos that Viesca had set out for Texas a second time. He opined that it would be hard to apprehend Viesca and his small contingent as they would be guided by citizens from Béjar who were very familiar with the scarcely populated areas.[21] As it turned out, Arreola was wrong, and Viesca and his party were captured at Naba, near San Fernando. The Mexican military archives has a list of the following men that were captured with him:

> **General Command of the Internal States of the East**
>
> **List of the individuals who have been apprehended**
> Governor Agustín Viesca
> Retired Colonel José Mar.o Yrala, Secretary
> James Grant, Permanent Deputy
> two foreigners
> Mariano Garcia, Chief of the Department
> Vicente Aldrete, Commissioner from Texas
>
> ***San Fernando, June 6, 1835***
> ***Juan José Galán***[22]

In the process of being transported to prison, Viesca and the others managed to escape and eventually made their way to Texas. They were aided by the Federalist Col. José María Gonzalez, who had, along with his unit, rebelled against Santa Anna and the Centralists.

All the decrees that had been enacted by the last session of congress were annulled. Any members of the state congress who remained were arrested and banished. On June 9 Cos wrote to Tornel that things had calmed in Coahuila and in Monclova. He reported that he was ready to focus all his efforts on Texas, the more important objective.

On June 15 Ugartechea informed Cos that his spies had returned from the Texas colonies. The spies informed him that the Texans had started to organize in order to march their militias to Monclova, but when they heard of the troops that were being gathered to oppose such a movement, they changed their minds.[23]

The issues of scandalous land sales and the failure of the state of Coahuila y Tejas to reduce its civic militias to the required size were causing the Mexican government and military to have less and less trust in what the Texans reported. A good example can be seen in an August 11 letter from Henry Rueg, the political chief of Nacogdoches, to Cos, which the latter forwarded to Tornel (see appendix 3). Rueg was trying to explain the situation in Texas and to justify the failure to disband the civic militia. It is obvious from Cos's comments to Tornel that he did not buy it.

Rueg wrote Cos that two-thirds of the population of his department were Mexican natives and adopted citizens who were honorable and peaceful. They were not causing any unrest nor participating in the revolution. He argued that the other third were men without country, morality, or occupation, and that therefore they had nothing to lose in a disturbance. Rueg wrote that without the militia there was no way to control these factions. He also threw in the added threat of an Indian uprising as another excuse for not dissolving the militia. In his final comment to Tornel, Cos wrote that he felt this was all a pretext for keeping the militia under arms.

NACOGDOCHES: MURDER AND NATIVE AMERICANS

Considering its vast distance from Mexico City, it is not surprising that trouble would arise at Nacogdoches. The closest colony to the United States and the gathering place for newly arrived, land-hungry immigrants, Nacogdoches was a favorable location for dissidents to foment rebellion, which is exactly what happened. The fact that Col. José de las Piedras, who had been stationed at Nacogdoches with approximately three hundred troops since the Fredonian Rebellion in 1827, left the colony in 1832 to stabilize the uprising in Anáhuac, made things even worse. There was no Mexican military presence to keep order or to punish those who encouraged rebellion.[24]

On January 12, 1835, Ugartechea notified Cos of trouble in Nacogdoches. He informed Cos that he received daily news of many immigrants entering the town and of the poor order kept by the authorities there. Ugartechea had been told that the authorities were capriciously using random laws from the United States in their legal system. He also knew that the few Mexicans who lived there were being disgraced by the outsiders.

Ugartechea was obviously upset by another piece of tragic news that he passed on to Cos. This was the murder of five individuals, including the Guadalupian monk Fray Antonio Días.[25] Cos passed this information on to the secretary of war, Tornel, who notified the president of the republic. On January 24, Tornel wrote to Cos and instructed him to gather five hundred men. In the coming spring, Colonel Ugartechea was to take three hundred of the men and restore order in Nacogdoches. Ugartechea was to make sure that only the laws of Mexico were enforced. He was also instructed to make sure that the national honor was respected.[26]

Another issue that became a major point of division between the colonists and the Mexican leaders was the status of the indigenous tribes who lived in Texas. This involved not only the tribes who were native to Texas but also those who were being forced out of the United States owing to the demand for land. From early on the Spanish and later the Mexican people had conflict with the Native Americans in Texas. The Mexicans relied mainly on their presidial troops to protect the people from this danger. As has been mentioned already, the presidial units in and near Texas were becoming less effective after 1830, owing to lack of pay and supplies.

In November 1834 Ugartechea notified Cos that due to the lack of arms, uniforms, and pay, the troops on the border were not able to prevent the indigenous tribes from carrying out robberies with impunity. He stated that they continued to harass the frontier posts and their Mexican neighbors. Ugartechea also mentioned that the Americans had sent a commissioner to give the tribes considerable gifts and obligate them to agree to a peace treaty among themselves. To document the fact that the Native Americans were forming alliances, he sent a list of the tribes that had made peace with the Comanches, broken down by their place of origin:

> Commanding General of Coahuila y Tejas
>
> News of the tribes of Indians that have made peace with the Comanches according to reports.
>
> **<u>From North America, the following</u>**
> First The Tluasas tribe
> Second The Chicasa tribe [Chickasha]
> Third The Aguajes tribe [Skidi Pawnee]

Those that have immigrated to Texas
Fourth That of the Charaquís or Saraquí [Cherokee]
Fifth That of the Saguanos
Sixth That of the Quicapías [Kickapoo?]

Those that already exist in Texas and have newly ratified the peace that they maintain
The Cadó [Caddo]
Quichas [Kichai]
Nadacos [Anadarkos?]
Tejas
Aínay [Hainai]
Corara [Cosara?]

Béjar December 15, 1834
Ugartechea[27]

Cos sent the Ugartechea dispatches on to Tornel and added some thoughts of his own in a note of December 29. Cos seemed to be wary of the idea that all the indigenous tribes might be united and at peace with one another. He wrote that they had never seen all the barbarians united among themselves. He pointed out to Tornel that the people of Mexico still remembered the grave evils they had suffered about twenty years ago when some of the more aggressive tribes united and made an incursion all the way to Matamoros, Mier, and places north of Tamaulipas. Cos stated that the presidial troops were more inclined to act at that time than they were at the present and added that despite the growth in population on the frontier the indigenous population would be more of a problem now. He concluded with the warning that the Native Americans had changed in the last twenty years, as they were more skilled in the use of all kinds of weapons.[28]

Apparently, the Mexican officials felt that giving gifts to the Native Americans would be a good idea for them as well. In a document from Cos to Ugartechea, dated May 8, 1835, Cos instructed him to continue giving gifts to the tribes, especially the Comanches. Either this approach of buying the Comanches' friendship with gifts did not work, or the Mexican officials decided to approach the problem from both sides. On July 11, Cos wrote Tornel and requested him to obtain President Santa Anna's approval for gunpowder to be purchased and given to the friendly tribes for use against the Comanches.

Because of the westward migration of Native Americans from the United States, and the fact that it was simple for the Americans to interfere in Mexican matters so close to the border, many of the "Indian problems" were taking place in the vicinity of Nacogdoches. On April 21, Col. Pedro Elis Bean,[29] the military commander at Nacogdoches, wrote Ugartechea a letter that included the following comment: "I have just received news that a party of traffickers from the United States have set up a house of commerce in the old village of the Tahuallàses [*sic*; Tahauyases or Taovaya] along the banks of the Red River of Natchitoches, about fifty leagues [approximately 131 miles] inside Mexican Territory. As a result of this, as I understand it, the barbarians with whom we are at war, will do great damage to this frontier. The sale of stolen livestock to those traffickers provides them with goods for making war."[30]

On May 8, the political chief of Nacogdoches, Henry Rueg, in a letter to Ugartechea, gave more details on what seems to be the same incursion by Americans into Mexican Texas. These details were even more disturbing to the Mexican officials as there was information on a possible attack and the news that the Native Americans were being influenced to fight the Mexicans:

> I have just received news from a Hueco [Waco] Indian, one of the principles of this tribe. He arrived here in the company of a few Quiches [Kichai] who are living in the village that he is from. [He reports] that the Tahuayaches and the lower Comanches have been stirred up by the counsel of an American who has established an extensive trade of munitions of war in the village of the Tahuayaches. It [the trade] is sustained with a force of twenty to twenty-five men of his own country. They are going on a campaign this next month, heading against Béjar and la Bahía, and considering this news as certain, it is communicated to Your Excellency for your government.
>
> I have dispatched this same Indian to dissuade these [Indian] nations from following the pernicious counsel of this stranger. He has assured me that he will be able to do so with the Huecos and Tahuacanos [Tawakonis], who are disposed to make peace, but not with the Comanches and Tahuayaches who consider this American to be a sorcerer. I wanted to encourage this same Indian because in the company of other peaceful Indian tribes they would be learning much more from said American which is a fear that terrifies one of such a thing. This same Indian has declared to me that this cited American has gathered the leaders of the Ouaches [Ouachita or Wichita], the Comanches, the Chawataw [Choctaw?] and various other tribes and they have made peace only to later make war together against

> the Mexicans. In order to undo this evil as much as I am able, I am going to take the quickest and most energetic measures to apprehend the counselor and his people.[31]

It is obvious that Bean and Rueg felt that this intrusion into Mexican Texas by the Americans was a serious issue, and apparently their superiors felt the same. However, the amount of time spent forwarding this important news, as well as the method of dealing with the problem, is a good indication of the difficulty of getting a response in Texas. There also seemed to be a lack of independent thinking in the chain of command, as the various commanders seemed hesitant to act until they had been instructed to do so by a superior. The meetings between the Americans and indigenous tribes were reported to Ugartechea on April 21 and May 8, 1835. We can follow the trail of Bean's April 21 letter through archival documentation. Ugartechea forwarded the document from Béjar on an unknown date. The letter reached Cos at Boca del Rio, and he forwarded it to Secretary of War Tornel on May 26. Tornel apparently received the letter on June 16 and forwarded it to Secretary of State Bonilla on the same day. Bonilla, in turn, informed the president of Mexico, probably Santa Anna, if he happened to be in Mexico City at the time. Finally, on July 15, Bonilla wrote to Tornel and told him that the president was going to instruct the governor of the state of Coahuila y Tejas (technically there was no governor, as Viesca had been arrested) to take suitable measures to avoid the sale of arms and munitions to indigenous tribes. Thus, it took four months just to get a response from Mexico City, and obviously the dispatch to the governor would take weeks to arrive in Monclova and any action that he would dictate to the authorities in Texas would have arrived an additional several weeks later. There is no known documentation as to whether the governor was able to act on this issue, but with all the other matters that were going on at the time it seems unlikely. Based on the extant documentation, it seems the normal procedure for dealing with many of these issues was to forward them to a superior or another department and hope they could do something about the problem.

On August 11 Bean forwarded Ugartechea a letter from Rueg. In this note Rueg claimed to be upset about the fact that Santiago Bovvi (*sic*; James Bowie), at the head of a few individuals, had seized by force a few of the nation's muskets stored in a warehouse under Bean's control. Rueg added that owing to not having any forces at his disposal, and the civic militia still not being organized, he felt that they were in a position of having to act with great prudence to avoid any pretexts that would result in an insurrection. Bean added a personal note to Ugartechea that as a result of unsettled feelings on the border, no efforts for compromise or peace had been able to move forward. He also made an interesting observation about newcomers in Texas. He stated that these new arrivals had lost hope of being able to enjoy the fruits of their labor, which they had set their sights upon. To close his letter, he added that these newcomers received no support from the inhabitants of the frontier, who lived in peace and were strictly dedicated to obeying the supreme government and that of their department.[32]

One week later, Bean sent Ugartechea another dispatch. He reported that a petition had been started in town to form a faction of men who wanted to recruit the local Native Americans in their fight against the Mexican government. They also wanted to seek funding in New Orleans to fund the revolution. Bean added a very interesting note that, once the petition was adopted, the people backing it wanted to pass an order that all the people who didn't participate in the rebellious plan would lose their property, leaving these lands to the benefit of the faction. This would certainly be consistent with the fact that the newly arrived immigrants were struggling to meet their hopes of success in the new country and were anxious to get the lands of the local Tejanos. Bean wrote that he was worried that this situation would lead to bad things happening to the local inhabitants, especially the Mexicans. He asked for rapid garrisoning of the frontier and emphasized that a significant number of troops were required to meet the purpose. Bean further requested that he be given one month's leave to travel to Béjar to meet with Ugartechea in person. Some dispatches had been opened in San Felipe, so he did not feel comfortable in sending everything he had to say in writing.[33]

Bean became so upset with the Indian troubles in his department that, as superintendent of Indians and as military commander (he held both offices at the same time), he wrote Pres. Andrew Jackson on September 11. He protested the daily incursions of indigenous people into his department from the United States, and he reminded Jackson that both countries had signed a treaty that required them to prevent such dangerous intrusions into each other's territory. He pointed out to Jackson that many of the Native American parties were obliged to travel past Fort Jessup in the United States and nothing was being done at that outpost to prevent this. In closing he politely requested that Jackson take the necessary action to solve this issue.[34]

J. B. Miller, political chief of the department of the Brazos, sent a dispatch to Cos on September 28 notifying him that more than three hundred armed men were walking in the wilds of the Brazos River bottoms in pursuit of four tribes of "barbaric Indians" that had congregated and formed alliances in order to attack the inhabitants of his department. Miller was confident that the colonists would be rewarded with victory and the "savages" defeated and chastened because of their cowardice. The combination of this letter and Bean's letter to Jackson suggests that the attempts by the Texans to unite the indigenous tribes to fight against the Mexicans was unsuccessful.

It had to be difficult for the Mexican officials in Mexican Texas and in Mexico City to be completely at ease having two Anglos serving in the two most important positions of the department of Nacogdoches, especially with all the disturbances already discussed. On July 8, Rueg sent out a broadside to the citizens of his department that would have confirmed all their fears. After this document was printed and distributed, there was no doubt as to where his loyalties lay. Calling outright for a revolution, Rueg intentionally stoked the ill will between the Texans and the Mexican peoples:

> **The Political Chief of the Department of Nacogdoches to its Inhabitants**
>
> Citizens: A few days after having returned to take charge of the political command of this department I found the aspects of our political business in such a state that I think it my duty to inform you of the particulars.
>
> By accepting the responsible position that I fulfill, I did it with great confidence and with the most vehement desire to perform the duties that are attached, for the greater benefit to the country. This has been the principle that has regulated my official conduct, and believing, as I do, that we have great reasons to fear dangers of a very serious nature, I think it my duty to make to the people a short and simple account of the facts, most of which have not come to my knowledge by official reports but by rumors. It seems from everything that I have heard that rapid changes have been made in our form of general government and that hostile means have been taken, of a violent character, in order to demand obedience to these changes. Large units of troops, of whose intentions we are satisfactorily informed, have entered into the borderlands

of the state, whose Governor, along with some of the representatives of the congress, have been imprisoned under the orders of the military commanders. Our mails are intercepted, or what amounts to the same, we do not receive one word of official news from the interior.

This situation should produce great uncertainties and restlessness in the soul of each one of the citizens in Texas. We cannot know how many dangers of great implications are nearing us. In such circumstances it is our first duty to organize ourselves and be prepared for everything that could happen to us.

We established ourselves in this country due to the promises of protection of our property and rights and we have sworn obedience to the constitution of our general government. Consequently, we cannot observe any other conduct than that which these institutions prescribe.

We have been tranquil and peaceful; we have avoided the complaints and revolutions that have shattered the republic. Our policy would have been to conserve in this state quietude and peace all the time that the constitution [of 1824] would have been in force among us. However, while our duty is to do it thusly, there is also another [duty] that we owe to ourselves, to our country, to our God, and to the cause of the freedom of man in all the world, which is that of being prepared to defend our rights and liberties until the final extreme.

I am sorry that the Government of this state has provided a pretext for these hostilities; selling four hundred leagues of land.[35] It is a very sensitive matter for me to have to criticize the behavior of any government employee, but justice obligates me to say that there is no way that I can justify the way in which said sale was verified. I believe that it is our duty to separate ourselves from all these controversies.

I will take all the means that circumstances demand, and I do not need to reinforce to the citizens of our department the absolute need to organize the militia as quickly as possible. I will advise them of the convenience of forming volunteer units and of cooperating with the city councils to carry out the orders that can be communicated by this department.

I have already given previous orders to the city councils of this department that the civic militias be placed under arms immediately. As required by law and as required by the current state of affairs, I hope

> that no one falters in completing their duty to themselves as well as to their country, using as many means as are within their capabilities to achieve that end.
>
> ***God and Liberty Nacogdoches July 8, 1835 H. Rueg***[36]

For some time, the Texans seemed to be under the impression that they could get away with basically any behavior if they justified the actions as adherence to the constitution of 1824. On August 17, Cos advised Rueg that the Mexican officials were not buying into this thinking. He clearly responded to the above document by telling Rueg, "The projects of the troublemakers of Texas are well known to this general command. It is therefore in vain that they want to be connected by a hypocritical adhesion to the constitution of this country. The one [constitution] that governs all Mexicans is the one that the settlers of Texas must obey, whatever the form of principles that establish it."[37]

ZACATECAS

It might be argued that the rebellion in the state of Zacatecas had little to do with the rebellion in Texas other than some similarities in the causes of their rebellions. There is no doubt, however, that the Zacatecas rebellion did influence the Texas Revolution and the frame of mind of the Mexican military as they marched for Texas.

The battle for Zacatecas was fought on May 11, 1835, at Guadalupe, near the capital city (of the same name as the state). Santa Anna, at the head of an army of over 3,600 men, quickly routed a force that he estimated to have comprised 5,000 well-armed civic militiamen. One of Santa Anna's officers wrote that the general had undone in two hours what the Zacatecans had been building for seven months.

Santa Anna wrote a report to Tornel on the campaign that demonstrated his usual bluster in feeling that he was unbeatable (see appendix 4). There is little doubt that this rapid, one-sided victory over a numerically superior force gave Santa Anna and the Mexican army a sense of personal superiority over these untrained state militias. They would bring this same bluster and lack of respect into Texas, and it would end up costing them dearly.

The Mexican military did suffer some casualties in the conflict, but Santa Anna documented that there were fewer than one hundred dead and wounded on the Mexican army's side. This may have had a small effect on their ability to fight against the Texans, as many of these same units would soon be marching north. However, it is more probable that the experience they gained, and the artillery and munitions they captured, outweighed the losses. A list of the captured goods at Zacatecas made after the battle illustrates this point: among other things, there were sixty-four cannons of various sizes, 3,347 muskets, 937 bayonets, 1,115 cannon balls, and 8,331 cans of canister.[38]

What might have had the greatest effect on the Texans was what happened in Zacatecas after the battle. Apparently, Santa Anna had taken note of what General Arredondo had allowed to take place in Béjar after the battle of Medina in 1813. The aftermath of Zacatecas was just as troubling: there were reports of executions, rape, and plundering. Evidence that word of this behavior got back to the Texans can be found in a letter from the alcalde of Victoria, John Linn, to the alcalde of San Patricio, Thomas Henry. The letter was probably written on October 10, 1835, and noted, "And we *Irishmen* know how to appreciate a despotic military government; therefore, I will deem it derogatory to your known character to offer you any other motives in order to arouse your known patriotism. All that you *can* do, *to aid us,* I am confident you *will* do, in order to drive from the soil of Texas the marauders and butchers of Zacatecas; whose yell, on entering that devoted city was, '*death to all foreigners.*'"[39]

Another example of the colonists' perception of what had occurred in Zacatecas, as well as other states in Mexico, is found in an address by Robert McAlpin Williamson on June 22, 1835, at a meeting in San Felipe. He gave a very inflammatory address that included the following comments: "Your republican form of Government is broken down, your state authorities have been driven by the military from the exercise of their constitutional duties, and the Governor of your State, who was your choice, is detained in custody. Not only in Coahuila y Tejas has this arbitrary and despotic course been pursued, but other states of the Federation mourn the loss of their constitution and their liberties. At this moment, the proud, gallant, and republic State of Zacatecas mourns the loss of two thousand citizens, slain in battle by the troops of Gen. Santa Anna, and the survivors now endure the galling chains of military rule.—Durango and other states have also fallen beneath the rule of military power, and every state and province of the Mexican Republic (excepting Texas) has submitted to the Dictator."[40]

As it turns out, the reports spread in Texas were gross exaggerations. An article published in the *American Monthly Magazine* in July 1837 by a foreign resident of Zacatecas, Grace Grafton, provides a description of what took place.[41] She describes the battle on the plains of Guadalupe and notes that Santa Anna tricked the Zacatecas militia by leaving the campfires burning in their camp and quietly taking up new positions near the militia. By the time it was light, the Zacatecans fled in a panic with little fighting. Her estimate of dead was approximately sixty Zacatecans and a handful of Mexican troops.

Grafton did note that there were cries in the streets of "Death to Foreigners" and "Death to the English." She also witnessed a few incidences of mistreatment of civilians, especially the English, but commented that these were not common and that the Mexican officers did a fairly good job of controlling the troops. Looting was quite widespread, but molesting or killing civilians was rare. Most of the violence was committed by what Grafton described as the "riffraff" of the army, who brought up the rear in utmost disorder.

Included in her description of the events of that day were the following comments: "With all Santa Ana's [*sic*] vices, he had never been considered a sanguinary man; and the only lives taken by his soldiers in Zacatecas were the Englishman and his gentleman's servant before mentioned. . . . The officers were quartered on the inhabitants; nor were foreigners exempt from the charge of entertaining them; nor did they wish to avoid it as the presence of two or three captains or colonels was felt to be protection in those perilous times. . . . [A particular officer] had never fought with Santa Ana before, but had often been in engagements against him, and spoke rather disrespectfully of "Don Antonito" as they called him. . . . In Zacatecas Santa Ana made a large addition to his warlike supplies; for it appeared incredible the quantity of cannon and military stores of every description that he found and carried off." The distribution of these rumors, as exaggerated as they were, throughout Texas surely helped to forge opinions regarding Santa Anna and to strengthen the resolve of the Texans. They were made to believe that the Mexican army under Santa Anna was not likely to be merciful in surrender or defeat.

LIBERALS FLEE TO TEXAS AND ORDERS FOR ARRESTS

With Santa Anna's sudden conversion to the Centralist party in 1833, the prominent liberals in Mexico were in a bad position. Under Spanish rule and even in the early days of Mexican independence it was not unusual for a politician or insurgent to suffer death at the hands of his captors. At best they could expect imprisonment. Some were exiled to other countries, and if their party happened to regain control of the government they were welcomed back.

Santa Anna's own vice president, Gómez Farías, obviously felt insecure and eventually made his way to New Orleans. While in New Orleans he and several other liberal Mexican leaders who had fled Mexico became part of what was called the Amphictyonic Council.[42] This term stemmed from an ancient Greek tradition represented by a word that meant "league of neighbors." This council included Gómez Farías, José Antonio Mejía, and Manuel Lorenzo Justiniano de Zavala y Sáenz, as three of the more prominent Mexicans, along with many well-known Louisiana capitalists who were interested in lands in Texas.[43]

Mejía had served as secretary for the Mexican legation in the United States from 1829–31. During that time, he also served as an agent for the Galveston Bay and Texas Land Company. This group of New York land men had bought out three empresario contracts, including that of de Zavala. After his return to Mexico, Mejía rejoined the military, rose to the rank of brigadier general, and became a strong supporter of Santa Anna. He went to Texas in 1832 to help calm the first Anáhuac disturbance. After Santa Anna's conversion to Centralism, Mejía participated in a failed uprising in Jalisco while serving as a senator from the state of Mexico (there is a state of Mexico in the country of Mexico) and was exiled by Santa Anna. He came to New Orleans determined to reinstate the Federalists as the ruling party in Mexico.

De Zavala was a highly educated priest and doctor from the Yucatán. He was a lifelong liberal who served on two separate occasions as governor of the state of Mexico. Due to his political views, he was exiled to New York in 1830, and at that time he transferred his interest in his colony in Texas to the New York land men. He did, however, continue to be a major stockholder in the company. As an ally of Santa Anna, in 1833 he was appointed to serve as minister of the Mexican legation in Paris. Upon learning of Santa Anna's political about-face, he resigned the position in France. Ignoring Santa Anna's order for him to return to Mexico, he traveled to New York and then on to New Orleans and Texas. Santa Anna apparently never forgave de Zavala this insult and his grudge against him ended up playing a major role in the Texas Revolution.

In a secret meeting in New Orleans, held on September 4, 1835, Gómez Farías, Mejía, de Zavala, and thirty-seven others agreed on a plan whereby the former three men would serve as "the supreme directors of the enterprise for the regaining of supremacy by the Federalists, and the installation of an eminently liberal government in Mexico." Gómez Farías was to oversee general operations, Mejía was to command the troops, and de Zavala was to arm Texas colonists to distract the Mexican government while Mejía attacked the port at Tampico.[44]

The New Orleans capitalists and Mejía raised the funds. About one hundred "troops," mostly Americans, left New Orleans on November 6, 1835. After running aground on the bar at Tampico and poor timing by the troops who were to support Mejía, the expedition failed. Some of Mejía's men were captured and later executed, while Mejía and the rest of his troops sailed to Texas, arriving on December 3. He was not embraced as a leader by the Texans and returned to New Orleans after a short stay in Texas. After his failed attempt, the Mexican commander at Santa Anna de Tamaulipas, Gregorio Gómez Palomino, wrote a broadside to the people about the Mexican victory there (see appendix 5).

Obviously, this incident did not please the Mexican government and what was particularly galling to them was the fact that the expedition was organized and funded in the United States. Secretary of War Tornel later wrote a treatise on the relationship between Texas, the United States, and the Republic of Mexico. After describing the failed attack, he added:

> Whose blood does not boil in his veins if he is a true Mexican as he contemplates the fact that this expedition was made ready in a port of a nation that calls itself a friend, in order to come and murder our fellow countrymen, to sack our property, and to upset everything? If laws exist in the United States that prohibit this bearing of arms against friendly nations, it is a breach of trust not to have demanded that they be obeyed. If such laws do not exist, that is one of the most dangerous societies on the globe because no nation can consider itself safe from attack that neither prevents nor condemns public power. Very worthy of note is what a newspaper of the United States THE COMMERCIAL HERALD has written concerning this and similar aggressions with a spirit of independence that does true honor to the editor:
>
>> "What would be thought," he says, "of a gathering of men that organized a junta and proceeded openly to raise and equip a body of troops in the United States and send them with arms and equipment to Ireland with the declared purpose of aiding the Irish to declare themselves independent of England? Or to give a stronger example of the support of which we speak—what would be said if in Haiti a junta was formed to make the offer to arm and equip a body of troops to send them against us with the purpose of aiding our Negroes to throw off the yoke of slavery?
>>
>> "We will go even further. What feeling of indignation would not be aroused among us if we were to read in one of the diaries of Canada the proposal to raise a body of troops to send to the aid of the Cherokee Indians and to help them to defend their territory against the attacks by Georgia? Placing ourselves for a moment in the place of the Mexicans, we should likewise conceive

> how we would look upon the conduct of our fellow citizens in the United States that are making efforts to raise troops to aid those in the provinces that are in a state of rebellion."
>
> There is nothing that can be added to these equitable and illuminating observations.[45]

In early June Cos ordered Capt. Manuel Sabariego, the commander of the presidio de La Bahía (Goliad), to arrest José María Jesús Carbajal.[46] Carbajal was wanted for the part he had played in the four-hundred-league land deal as a deputy in the state legislature at Monclova. At the same time there was an order to apprehend and interrogate Juan Sambrano (Zambrano), who also was involved in the land dealings of the state government.[47] Ugartechea was later informed, in two separate documents, that Carbajal was hiding at the ranch of Don Silvestre de Leon and Sambrano was to be found at the ranch of Carbajal.

By the end of July, the "wanted" list had greatly expanded. Ugartechea wrote to the political chief of the department of the Brazos and instructed him to arrest Lorenzo de Zavala, who had landed at Brazoria and was said to be in Columbia. He was also ordered to apprehend the following individuals: Frank W. Johnson,[48] Robert McAlpin Williamson,[49] William Barret Travis,[50] Samuel May Williams,[51] and Moseley Baker.[52] It is obvious from the archives that the Mexican leaders were also anxious to get their hands on Jim Bowie. In June he was reported to have escaped from Goliad and was in San Felipe. In August he was identified as one of the individuals who had stolen government muskets in Nacogdoches. That August, in a separate document, John H. Moore, a colonist who was very outspoken against the Mexican government, was added to the list of those to be arrested.

The arrest of these individuals seemed to be a major concern for Cos, Ugartechea, and other Mexican officials. There were at least forty dispatches, and probably many more, sent to various commanders, political chiefs, etc. regarding the location of these persons. Often, the responses explained why the local leaders could not arrest them. Looking at these documents it appears that de Zavala was the individual whom the Mexicans were most interested in finding. Seemingly he should have been the easiest to arrest, as he was variously in Brazoria, Columbia, and San Felipe. If the Texans had had any interest in arresting him, they could have easily done so. On August 8, Cos wrote to Ugartechea commanding him that if the political chief of the Brazos, Wyly Martin, did not arrest de Zavala, Ugartechea was to march his troops to achieve the intended purpose, even at the risk of losing all his cavalry.

Several of the letters containing vague excuses as to why these individuals could not be arrested were written by Captain Tenorio from San Felipe. He was positioned at the heart of the Texas colony where these men were surely to show up on occasion, yet he failed to take meaningful action. It is known that he had some of his troops from Anáhuac there with him, whom he surely could have deployed in the task. However, he seems to have favored the Federalist cause, or perhaps he realized that the odds were against him and he was in no position to carry out the arrest orders without great risk to himself and his men.

On November 5 Cos wrote to Tornel from Béjar, where he and his troops were under siege by the Texans. He noted that he had previously written about the flight of the principal insurrectionists. Now, in the center of the colonies, the insurrectionists were working as much as possible to preserve the criminal disorder and revolution that they had ignited. Cos informed Tornel that de Zavala was at San Felipe directing a political meeting, called a "convention," while other leaders of the sect were part of the force that was camped about one mile from that city.

OTHER FACTORS

There were many other factors that widened the gap between the Mexican people and the Texans. The underlying suspicion that the United States and Pres. Andrew Jackson were desperate to add Texas to their country was certainly in play. There is no doubt that the Mexican nation was aware of Jackson's desire. A well-known publisher and abolitionist wrote Col. Juan Almonte, who was serving as a land commissioner in Washington, DC, on September 15, 1835, and informed him that:

> he designs which some of my slaveholding and insatiable countrymen cherish of wresting from your country the noble and beautiful province of Texas are villainous. The Hon. Hutchins G. Burton, of North Carolina, has bought 40,000 acres of land in Texas, and week before last he was in Philadelphia and declared to a near relative residing there (a respectable man and an earnest obolitionist [*sic*]) that the reason of his making said purchase, was that Texas was soon to be annexed to the United States, that President Jackson had declared to him at the city of Washington on the occasion of calling as he passed through that city about three weeks ago, that we must have it either by negotiation or force; that if 10,000 men would not do, 100,000 should, and that it was his intention to make said Burton first governor of the new Territory. Jackson has made the same declaration to two other persons within the past few weeks.[53]

Almonte became so fed up with the actions of the colonists in Texas and with the failure of the United States to do anything to stop them that he wrote the following to Mexican Secretary of Foreign Affairs Bonilla on October 2:

> The newspapers that I am sending separately will inform you of recent events in Texas. The audacity of those colonists is now intolerable, as is the protection given them by the authorities in New Orleans, where they have taken the national schooner-of-war *Correo* as a prize.—It is necessary for the Government to assume all the vigor sufficient to repress the excesses of these adventurers and to severely criticize this [US] Government, whose treacherous conduct I am confirming more each day. If it were declared, or we discovered beyond a doubt, that [President Jackson] is secretly protecting the revolution in Texas, we would have more than enough means to defeat it, seeking support in France—with whom they still have not made a deal, as you will see in today's paper—and causing the uprising of the two million slaves and the 300 or 400 thousand Indians whose land they have taken. What we would need is money, and I am sure that for this war we would find it soon in foreign trade and even in France itself.—Far from believing that we should avoid the encounter [with the United States], I say we should seek it. On the sea we fear nothing because we have nothing to lose. On land we are equal if not superior.—We just need activity, and I believe that we have enough to salvage our honor and preserve our status as an independent nation to which we have risen by our own efforts.[54]

Another example of the Mexicans being told of the involvement of the United States in the uprisings in Texas was Secretary of War Tornel, arguing in October 1835 that the Texas revolution was a US plot and that Mexico needed to react severely. He appeared before the Mexican congress on October 29 and acknowledged that a state of war existed in Texas and he needed appropriations to win it. He mentioned that the rebels had accomplices in Louisiana.[55] Tornel, having served as minister to the United States from 1829–31, was aware of American designs on Texas. As early as the spring of 1831 Tornel had written his foreign secretary and warned him that the American newspapers were preoccupied with the subject of Texas. He noted that when debating about the acquisition of Texas they failed to consider the rights of Mexico. Tornel also warned that the new US president was bent upon acquiring the colony.[56]

Two American representatives to Mexico, Joel Poinsett and Anthony Butler, were very ineffective in serving the interests of the United States while in Mexico. Both tried vigorously to buy Texas and other parts of Mexico with no success. Butler was especially irritating to the Mexicans with his use of bribery and constant interference in the internal affairs of Mexico. He was described as arrogant, vulgar, and calculating, a man completely lacking the qualities of a diplomat. He was never popular in Mexico and was disliked by most Texans as well. After threatening to cane or whip the secretary of war, the Mexican government insisted that Butler be recalled.[57]

The constant rumors and reports from the Mexican consul in New Orleans, Francisco Pizarro Martínez, that armed volunteers were sailing from that place for Texas, obviously caused nervousness in Mexico. The many conspiratorial meetings that have been touched on previously in this chapter were considered illegal by the Mexican authorities, and the fact that the meetings were often called "committees of public safety," a refence to the violence and chaos of the French Revolution, could not have helped.

As the number and diversity of the committees in various towns grew, a proposal started to circulate that the Texans needed to gather representatives for a statewide consultation to try to iron things out. On September 17, Lorenzo de Zavala wrote Stephen F. Austin from Lynchburg, Virginia, regarding the proposed meeting. He observed that the Texans, while they had individual patriotism and would defend their private rights until death, had no *unified* patriotism and did not realize the need for cooperation. He predicted that at the convention, two parties would arise. One would maintain that the group had the right to legislate and would immediately demand the absolute independence of Texas. The other party, he opined, would restrict itself to the literal title of consultation and would consider its mission accomplished by drafting three or four reports. Both parties would be dangerous and the second fatal.

De Zavala felt that the Texans could not continue to support the constitution of 1824. He felt that they could make a declaration in support of the federal basis of the constitution of 1824 but nothing more. It seems as if de Zavala was very astute at sensing the situation in Texas at the time. His last thoughts on Santa Anna and a possible war with Mexico were amazingly on point:

> Do not forget that besides the army Santa Anna can count on the support only of the priests and a few undependable rich men; bayonets can support him only for a time. His whole army scarcely numbers 20,000 [scattered throughout Mexico]. . . . [Of these there is] a flying column of three thousand for urgent necessities and two thousand for the eastern provinces.
>
> . . . An uprising may occur at any time that will make him tremble; but the present attitude of Texas is his certain death. If, out of desperation, he sends two or three thousand men here, or should he come himself, his fall

will only be hastened. The rivers, forests, deserts, rifles, the scant sympathy the invading troops will find in the area, the ignorance of the language and above all American steadfastness will bring Santa Anna and his satellites to a quick end. Today, in my opinion, there is no cause for alarm. Santa Anna fears Texas more than all the rest of the country because he instinctively fears that it will cause his overthrow.[58]

CHAPTER THREE

Tenorio, Tariffs, and Trouble in Anáhuac and San Felipe

Finances were a huge problem for the nascent United States of Mexico. As previously mentioned, nearly three hundred years of the Spanish draining the country of anything of value had taken its toll. Tariffs were the primary method of funding the government and the military. The colonists had been forgiven taxes on imports and exports for six years, but that time had expired, and they were expected to start paying their fair share.

After giving up his command of the Internal States of the East, General Filisola wrote that most of the ills of the desperate financial situation of the presidial troops were due to embezzlement by the commissaries and paymasters of the troops. He noted that if this had not been the case, the customhouses at Anáhuac and Galveston would not have been taken over in 1832 and the colonists who attacked Fort Velasco would have been punished.[1] Moreover, there would not have been such a rapid and offensive increase in the jumbled masses of vagabonds and malcontents who flooded in from the borders of the United States.

Trying to establish tariff income, the Mexican government had resolved to open the customhouses in Texas. Cos sent a detachment of troops under the command of Capt. Antonio Tenorio to Galveston aboard the national ship *Moctezuma*. They arrived there after twenty-three days of sailing, but because of the ill will with which they were received by the colonists there, they soon moved to Anáhuac and established the customhouse there. Even though the customhouse continued to be called the "Maritime Customs of Galveston," many of the documents added the phrase "residing in Anáhuac." Therefore, the customhouse was never physically located in Galveston.

On January 20, 1835, Cos informed Tornel that he was appointing First Adjutant Mariano Campusáno as the new military commander at Galveston. To this report he attached a list of seventeen specific instructions:

> Instructions that 1st Infantry Adjutant Don Mariano Campusano should follow in carrying out the mission that has been entrusted to him as military commander of the port of Galveston.
>
> 1. The main purpose for which you are being stationed at the port of Galveston is the security of the employees of the Treasury, so that they can collect the duties on the goods that are brought in through that port.
> 2. At the indicated island of Galveston there are three buildings belonging to the Federation. You will occupy one of these for lodging the troops under the immediate command of Captain Don Antonio Tenorio, who will be subject to your orders so that you might fulfill your mission. Mr. Choehel,[2] who lives on said island, cares for the buildings that will serve as the customhouse, warehouse, and garrison.
> 3. The force that will comprise the detachment will have, in addition to the salary that will run out in the month that it embarks, two [salaries] in advance so that it will not find itself reduced to starvation, and this general command will see that they are sent assistance before what they are now taking runs out.
> 4. For the acquisition of provisions, you will appoint a sergeant or officer whom you trust to visit the dwellings that are along the San Jacinto and Trinity Rivers to obtain provisions from them, at the same notifying the alcalde [mayor] of the village of Liberty of your arrival, so that the citizens who so wish might go with their provisions to the island, and [you] will see that they are paid religiously.
> 5. In order that the troops might carry better provisions and obtain them at a moderate price, you will insist that they be fed with all the pickets [i.e., squads] together.
> 6. You will not permit the slightest laxity in the discipline of the troops, and despite their being assigned a barrack, you will encourage the soldiers to till the land and to erect their own dwellings [*jacales*] when they are not employed in matters of the service, causing them to help each other mutually in this work, without obliging them to do so on the lands of officers.
> 7. In order to carry out the preceding article, you will present yourself to the señor commissary general of Tamaulipas before making your departure, for the purpose of learning who possesses the most teams of oxen and other farming implements that should remain in the settlements closest to Galveston.

8. When you arrive at Galveston, you will arrange with the customs officer to post a small detachment of 8 or 10 men with a good sergeant at the mouth of the river of Los Brazos de Dios, in order to support the treasury office that will be established there, and in the meantime to oblige all vessels that enter there to pay their duties to the customs of Galveston.
9. To lodge the aforesaid detachment, you can occupy the buildings that exist at the afore-cited river mouth, which also belong to the Federation.
10. You will apply every measure that prudence suggests to reestablish better harmony and good friendship between the settlers who are established there and the persons who form the detachment under your command, making a special effort so that the difference in customs does not give rise to rivalries, because there should be none if all are members of the same nation, who live under the protection of the same laws and government. You will take care most especially that no soldier takes part in acts of the civil jurisdiction, nor that on the pretext of providing assistance, they involve themselves in judicial procedures.
11. As soon as you arrive at your assigned post, you will report to the alcaldes of the nearby settlements that you are going to be posted [there], by order of the Supreme Government, in order to protect the settlements, guard the coast, cause the laws to be observed, assist the authorities, and promote the prosperity of the region. [You should] invite them to do the same to the citizens for the purpose of their bringing their provisions for the subsistence of the detachment.
12. The immediate authority to which you should report is the commandancy general of the state, headed by Sr. Colonel Don Domingo Ugartechea, who resides in the city of Béjar and whom you will notify immediately upon your arrival.
13. For the continuous communication that you must maintain with the aforesaid commander, and with this commandancy general, you will make use of the mail that departs from Brazoria for San Felipe, unless after your arrival you learn of another one from which you can forward your correspondence.
14. Above the Trinity River, the Cuchaté [Coushatta] tribe is located in two or three villages. They live in complete independence on their industry of farming and hunting, and you will establish communication with their chiefs, making them understand that the Mexican troops stationed there hold everyone in their tribe in the highest regard.
15. On the Trinity River live the citizens Juan Will[i]ams,[3] Gorje [Jorge] Orr,[4] and José M[arí]a Coronado; to the east of the Barra del Pescado, Juan M. Smith;[5] six miles from the military post at Anáhuac, Don

Santiago Telajuay; and four [miles?], James Camel. These individuals have maintained friendship with the Mexican officials stationed there, and it would be useful for you to get to know them for the news and resources they can provide to you through their positive dispositions.

16. With the designation of the ships that should sail regularly from Galveston Bay to Matamoros, the most urgent communications that arise can be sent to you with them, and with regard to subsequent salaries of the troops, you will arrange with the director of the customhouse, who will cover them with its proceeds.
17. Finally, you will report to me on all the particulars that occur, so [I] can report with greater precision to the Supreme Government on the effect that its orders have had on such important objectives, to whose success you and all your subordinates will contribute, having the occasion now to garner special merit, which will be justly rewarded by the most excellent señor president of the Republic.

Leona Vicario January 17, 1835 Martín Perfecto de Cos[6]

Studying these instructions carefully suggests that General Cos was anxious to ensure that these troops did everything possible to start the process of collecting tariffs on imports as gently and peacefully as possible. After all, the federal government was enforcing a law that was already in place. It also was an issue that the colonists were aware was coming, as they had agreed to these terms when they migrated to Texas and swore to uphold the laws of the country.

Filisola wrote that when the customhouse was established the colonists did everything in their power to convince the soldiers to desert. He noted that when the first ship put into harbor, the guard who had been on duty was poisoned by the colonists so the goods could be unloaded and the duties avoided. The second boat was successfully unloaded under the supervision of the customs officers, and the goods were placed in a warehouse, but the colonists broke into the warehouse and removed the items, once again avoiding the duties.

At about this time the new administrator of the customhouse, Gen. José González, had arrived from New Orleans. When he tried to start collecting tariffs, "he was told to his face by all the colonists living there that they were determined not to pay one cent, even though he should try to make them do so by force, and that they would resist to the end."[7]

González's stay at Anáhuac was short-lived since he had insufficient forces to stand up to the colonists. He apparently did not want to suffer the same indignation as Ugartechea in 1832, who had even more troops. Tenorio wrote

Ugartechea on May 18 that on May 2 González, the inspector (Martín de Alegría), the interpreter, a corporal of receipts, and two guards had departed Anáhuac. They all planned on eventually returning to Mexico City. Tenorio stayed on as the commander of the troops stationed at Anáhuac, and he appointed Antonio Gil Hernandez, the captain of the customs guards, to oversee the customs office.[8]

The same day that the customhouse was abandoned by most of its officials, Tenorio wrote a dispatch to General Cos. It is interesting that he went over the head of his immediate commander, Ugartechea. This letter is insightful in understanding the Mexican soldiers' views of the Texans, and it is particularly telling in that it is written by an officer who was living among and dealing with the colonists on a daily basis:

> **Commander of Anáhuac**
>
> With the date of the 23rd of the last month [April] I expressed to the commanding general of this state [Ugartechea] the liabilities that I had due to the colonists preventing me from satisfying the orders. At the same time, I also made known to another gentleman that one of the causes was that the neighbors of this village claimed that the rich businessmen in Brazoria are not paying José González, administrator of the customs, more than tonnage on the ships.[9] However, they claim to be ignorant of the causes because Señor González has not communicated with them. Yet on the same day that I dispatched the communication with the soldiers sent by the commanding general, Señor González arrived. In conversations we had, he told me that the reason he had not come before was his inability to find a boat or a horse. Thus, he was not able to carry out his official duties for a period of four months. Only by using a lot of money and work was he able to come. The reason that he had not been able to collect taxes except on the tonnage was because the colonists openly refused to use other methods. They said that giving this [the money for tonnage] was only so that the employees would not starve to death; not because we had the right to demand it. Since we had no physical force it was foolish to confront men who were determined to maintain their interests, even against force. As we did not have any [force], it was decided, after suffering mocking and numerous threats to said person [González], to give an account to the Supreme Government. This had been done recently, looking at the difficulties

that had been suffered here in regard to the cargo of the Schooner *Mary Jane*. When it was ready to depart, an account was given to the Supreme Government as well that Martín Alegría and various individuals of the guard left the Commander of the Guard, Gil Hernandez, in charge with the register. As a result of the limited abilities of this individual, I think that he was going to jeopardize the force that he commanded or, because of weakness and lack of tact in handling matters that he does not understand, place the Supreme Government in ridicule. The colonists, seeing the disorganization of the office, do not want to satisfy their obligations that they have pending. These few employees, which have three or four guards, gravitate to the National Customs without providing any advantage whatsoever. If no help is given, they will find themselves expecting no collections. For one thing all the ships will go to the Brazos. In addition, the one who is left in command, not knowing how to handle the office, will have a difficult time operating it according to the laws, even assuming sufficient force exists to enforce them.

I have expressed to the Commanding General to let Your Excellency know that my presence at this post if of little value, however I much prefer it because this is where the inhabitants are more peaceful, even with the difficulty of those that come from Brazoria. These are more indolent and have artillery. They have more armed forces emboldened by the triumph they achieved over the troops at Fort Velasco in 1832. At this fort [Velasco] exists a 24 pounder gunnade that was from the Brigantine *Santa Anna*.[10] Also, there are another two [cannons] in Brazoria that they say came from the same ship and left for the colonists by General Mejía when he was at that place. The colonists had at most two carronades of a smaller caliber in their equipment.

I know the inhabitants of this district are forming a company of volunteers with the pretext of Indians, who are not hostile. Some honest inhabitants who are faithful to the Supreme Government have not wanted to sign the list, and not thinking well of the formation of the company, they have refused. The landowners only talk of the cultivation of the land, despite the suggestions and threats of the businessmen, who are the ones who are most interested. Thus, there is no order in Texas. Those [businessmen] have at their service many lost men who have nothing to do but hunt like savages and have nothing to lose in opposing the Government of the Republic. Just in case they do not obtain the victory, they cross the Sabine, moving everything with them in a caravan.

> Certainly, the business class is numerous in Brazoria but a respectable force not only will impose but also will guarantee the security of the inhabitants that have a love of the law of the Republic that has demonstrated its good will. Those who did [those who support the Mexican Government] when the troops left in 1832 have suffered prejudices and hostilities. Some of them have had to abandon the country and their poor families have faced misery.
>
> There are honest inhabitants who want the laws to be upheld in order to have the security that has not been enjoyed by any authority. They want action to contain the many vagrants who exist who are always drunk, cursing, and provoking the good men. They [the rebels] would challenge the legal system to be more in the style of the United States. They are inclined to fight as they have nothing to lose, not family nor friends as it has occurred in Brazoria just a few days ago.
>
> I persuade Your Excellency that only the duty of my service makes me tell Your Excellency such pitiful news and I implore you to disseminate it after reading it.
>
> ***God and Liberty Anáhuac May 2, 1835 Antonio Tenorio***[11]

Upon their arrival at Matamoros, Cos had two of the officials who had abandoned Anáhuac deposed to discover why they had left without orders. De Alegria testified that he had been threatened by the colonists with pistols and daggers. He added that in Brazoria a committee had been formed whose purpose was to go to Anáhuac to kill the administrator, González. He also noted that mail from Mexico to the customhouse was read or withheld as it passed through Brazoria so they did not trust that they would get any orders from Mexico. Apparently, someone named Morgun (James Morgan?) reported him to the authorities in Liberty as an intruder and thief. According to his testimony the colonists were indeed encouraging the Mexican troops to desert and were protecting them when they did so. Thus, by the time they left Anáhuac there were only twenty-eight soldiers there to enforce the laws.[12]

In his explanation of his departure, González cited "the brazen refusal of its [Anáhuac's] inhabitants not only to pay the established duties for the maritime tariffs but also to comply with even the least that is required of our laws that prevent them from opposing with arms and attacking completely those that support their adherence."[13]

As of May 2, Tenorio was left as commander of the twenty-eight soldiers in Anáhuac. His main job was to protect and enforce the actions of the customhouse. The administrator of the customs, the inspector of the customs, the commander of the guard, and several of the guards had left. This left only three or four regular employees of the customhouse. To make matters worse the new commander of the guard was Antonio Gil Hernandez, who was also functioning as the administrator, and Tenorio did not trust him to be able to fill that role.

Two days after González left, Tenorio wrote a note to the commissioner of Anáhuac. He reported that the colonists had burned the lumber that was to be used in the reconstruction of Fort Davis. He chastised the commissioner for allowing disagreeable drunks, such as a man named More (John W. Moore?), to remain in the community and asked that the commissioner enforce the laws against citizens carrying short arms. Tenorio added that the disturbance had been promoted by drunk and scandalous citizens but he was also worried that other residents, for whom he had a high regard, had taken part.[14] He wrote General Cos again the same day and reported what had happened in greater detail. He was obviously very emotional about his situation as he had no recourse in dealing with the colonists, and he ended his letter with the following: "I beg Your Excellency that if an expedition is formed with the purpose of punishing and subduing the pride of these colonists, send me, even if it is in the class of a simple soldier, for I have the greatest desire to battle these true enemies of the fatherland."[15]

Anáhuac was not the only customhouse in Texas. As mentioned above, there was trouble at the customhouse in Brazoria as well. In addition, the administrator of the customhouse at Matagorda, Juan Zenteno, was having major difficulties in performing his duties. On May 23 Cos wrote a dispatch to Tornel in which he included a letter from Zenteno written on May 17. It was obvious that he was having the same sort of problems as were plaguing the administrators in Anáhuac and Brazoria. Cos added his obviously heartfelt feelings on trying to save Texas:

> **Most Excellent Sir**
>
> The administrator of the maritime customs at Matagorda [Zenteno], in the official dispatch of the 17th of this month, which I received by special courier, tells me the following:

The smuggling that is being done at the bar of the Paso del Caballo is scandalous, in terms that I have positive news that in the villages of Matagorda, Santa Anna, and Gonzales there exist considerable merchandise and other foreign goods for which no duties have been paid to the public treasury.

After having taken all the measures that are in my powers to avoid the fraud, [it is shocking] what has happened lately in a meeting between the colonists in line with the merchants who introduce those effects, and the counter of this customs, the commander of the guard, and two guards exercised their duties with two ships that arrived at La Vaca. They threatened force, mocking these Federal employees, have taken almost all of the cargo without paying the just duties, without them [the customs employees] being able to avoid it. For everything, I implore to obtain from Your Excellency rapid aid to avoid the continuation of the defrauding of the public treasury and increasing the shortages of the treasury.

It seemed appropriate for me to communicate this to Your Excellency by special courier, so much [more] so [after] this very day I have been given notice that five ships have left the bar at Matagorda without any of them having made the least presentation. I am informing you that with this same date I am requesting aid of force from the principle commander of this state [Ugartechea] to see if with it the capture of some of these charges can be achieved.

I have the honor of transmitting it to Your Excellency so that you might serve to make His Excellency the President aware, making it clear to him that on the part of this commanding general various measures have been dictated with the purpose of containing these evils, but these never can be of the realm that is needed and that are solely dependent on the High Government. Deign Your Excellency to extend your sight to Texas, which calls very seriously. There is still time to remedy her evils. Admit in the meantime the sincere protests of my respectful consideration.

God and Liberty Matamoros May 23, 1835
Mtín. Perf.to de Cos[16]

As time passed it became more and more obvious that the colonists were going to do everything possible to avoid paying any duties to the government. Smuggling was becoming commonplace. The smattering of Mexican soldiers were not being paid, as the funds in the accounts of the customhouses were lacking. The conditions were ripe for producing violence and this occurred on June 12. A Mexican corporal and four privates were resisted by three Texans, and a fight broke out on the bank of the lagoon at Anáhuac. One of the Mexicans, Pedro Fabre, was slightly wounded in the neck. Responding to this, one of the Mexican privates shot and seriously wounded one of the three Texans.[17]

The other two Texans were arrested and placed in the stockade, and their cases were turned over to a judge, who set them free on bond.

One thing that the Mexican officials did seem to be aware of was the fact that the colonists were becoming more and more divided as the aggression of the Texans increased. This seems to be one of the reasons that the Mexicans delayed in dealing with the Texans in a timely manner. Many of the Mexican officials were convinced that a good number of the Texans were loyal to their oaths to the Mexican Federation and did not want independence from Mexico. A letter to the political chief of the department of the Brazos from General Cos on August 1 documented that the supreme government and Cos's general command had always made a distinction between the Texans who were faithful to their oaths and the laws and those adventurers of bad faith. He noted that the latter had nothing at risk and spent all their time in things that disrupted the public order. He went on to talk of the scandalous actions of the colonists at Anáhuac.

A dispatch from Ugartechea to General Cos, dated June 29, provides another example of the Mexican officials noticing this division among the Texans. Ugartechea noted that his spies had recently arrived from San Felipe de Austin. He was informed by the spies that meetings were going on at both places and that the committees and adventurers wanted to assemble a force and attack Béjar. He added that the owners of the habitations and the landowners were opposed to such an action. Ugartechea did add that both sides were opposed to any introduction of Mexican troops. Ugartechea added that, by the same sources, he knew that a councilman from San Felipe had left with some forces to attack Anáhuac in response to a sentinel at Anáhuac killing a foreigner who tried to enter by force in defiance of the sentinel warning him not to do so.[18]

Another piece of information was added: "I have been informed that the foreigner, Bui [*sic;* Bowie], who escaped from there [Anáhuac] has gone to the Mississippi with the objective of recruiting adventurers. I have sounded the alarm on that individual as the depraved intentions of these people should have the attention of the Supreme Government."[19]

In addition to the information from the spies, Ugartechea also informed Cos that he was attaching a note from a corporal with whom he had sent a correspondence for Tenorio at Anáhuac. Although the note is no longer with the letter, there is a short dispatch in the collections of the Archivo General de la Nación that is likely to be the mentioned note. It reads as follows:

> I must notify the greatness of Your Lordship that as soon as I arrived at this village of S[an] Felipe de Austin, I received reliable news at the house of a Mexican [resident], Don Antonio Mancha. From the reports that I received on the way, it was necessary for me to arrive at a late hour of the night. And I was given a sure reason, and it was that a gathering of Americans was taking place, and that they were determined to go and attack you at that city of Béjar, about which they know the number of officers and troops there. I remain here awaiting orders from the greatness of Your Lordship, not having sent the correspondence because of the uproar, and I have been unable [to do so] for the reason that three hundred men have gone to attack Anáhuac, and another force of two thousand men is on the way to capture the greatness of Your Lordship at that post of Béjar. June 25, 1835[20]

Obviously not everything that is included in these documents can be taken as fact. For instance, the Mexicans had documented that Tenorio had been shot and killed by a pistol-wielding Texan. This turned out not to be the case. Similarly, the claim of two thousand Texans headed to Béjar was a blatant exaggeration or rumor. On the other hand, it must be noted that there was underlying truth as to what the Texans were plotting, and it should be stated that these dispatches, even if only partly true, must have had a great effect on the psyche of the Mexican government and soldiers.

Things in Anáhuac came to a head on June 27. Tenorio sent Ugartechea the following dispatch from Harrisburg on July 7:

> The 27th day of the current [month], a force of colonists from this department arrived at Anáhuac aboard the sloop *Ojallo* [Ohio] with two pieces of cannon. They made their landing, which was not possible to prevent, at three in the afternoon. They gathered with all the armed population. Seeing that there was no defense in the houses I retired to a thicket, where I remained during a part of the night until I had a meeting with Mr. Julian Barret Travis, who revealed to me that the purpose of their march had been to force the civic militia to surrender their arms, [so] that the permanent troops should not have them; that he and all of the Texans had decided to oppose the reform laws of the Current Sovereign Congress; and at the same time to liberate the Governor of the State [Viesca] and establish the Governor in San Felipe or some other place where he could be protected from attacks of the military forces. I consulted with a council and they decided, in light

of the difficulty and futility of a defense, that a capitulation would be made under the following articles: (1) that the troops surrender their arms, except for 12 that are of good service; (2) Captain Travis agrees to provide the troops the necessary assistance to pay fair prices until they arrive at the interior of the republic; (3) the commander and the troops will not take part in the current struggle under which condition they will give the necessary aide; (4) that as soon as the authorities give the relevant aid the troops will begin their march. It was signed on the day of the 30th. Consequently, in the same sloop he proceeded to this point where he remained from the 2nd, giving a delay in the assistance that I had requested. I awaited those, for I have some useless soldiers, but I am decided that if tomorrow I do not know if they will aide me, I will march by the means possible. The lack of time does not allow me to give details in answering that which I give quickly to Your Excellency but it will have to be done by me as quickly as possible considering, as I have said to you, an attack was given by the colonists from San Felipe. They have marched so that there is no hope of any aid, however if they could provide me with sufficient arms to fill 32 *homores* [?] it would be very good.

Since the night of the 29th three privates have deserted me, one who upon hearing a cannon shot fired by the enemy, abandoned his post. The other two [deserted] from the road, one that is actually missing.

God and Liberty Harrisburg [Harciburgo] July 7, 1835
Antonio Tenorio[21]

A list of the armaments, munitions, and soldiers present at Anáhuac on April 23, 1835, are found in appendix 6. The items from the first list were likely captured by the colonists when the fort was surrendered.

An informant passed a hint of the capitulation of Tenorio and his troops to Ugartechea in Béjar on July 13. The informant had come from San Felipe, and he reported that the day he left that place an American came into town sporting a cartridge belt and arms from an infantryman who had surrendered at Anáhuac.

The informant also made Ugartechea aware of an incident that, at the time, seemed much more important than the chance of trouble at Anáhuac. The informant let him know that military couriers carrying documents to Tenorio at Anáhuac had been apprehended by the Texans near San Felipe. In what

Artist's conception of the meeting between brevet Capt. Antonio Tenorio and William Barrett Travis on June 27 in a thicket at or near Anáhuac. Drawing by Manuel Hinojosa.

Ugartechea described as criminal conduct, the sealed documents were opened by the colonists. The couriers were stripped of their arms, horses, and saddles and remained prisoners at San Felipe.

This incident had been reported by the political chief at San Felipe as early as July 2 (the incident took place on June 21). For some reason, like Tenorio in some of his earlier dispatches, James B. Miller chose to send the information directly to Cos instead of Ugartechea at Béjar. Certainly, this could have been to buy time, as Cos was much further away and would have had to then send his instructions to Ugartechea. Another indication that Miller was intentionally trying to stall is that this document was sent to Cos nine days after the event. In his letter of July 2, Miller noted, "I report to Your Excellency that a few individuals inspected the bearers of the dispatches that came from Your Excellency for the commander at Anáhuac. There was an accompanying document from Col. Ugartechea. This correspondence was opened and has been the cause of the alarm that is reigning. I have the honor of including to Your Excellency a copy of the resolutions that have been adopted at a significant meeting of the inhabitants of this department. These resolutions show the sentiments of the majority of those same [individuals]. Your Excellency could make all the forces possible available to maintain order and you could order a commission to explain all that has happened."[22]

In order to understand the seriousness of the capture of these documents, one needs to examine their contents.[23] The first was a dispatch from Cos to the political chief of the department of the Brazos dated June 12. In it he advised Miller of the capture of Viesca and noted that he, as political chief, would now be in charge of keeping order in his department, particularly with the governor gone and the legislature not yet in session. Cos sent a similar document to all seven departments in Coahuila y Texas.

The second is an extract of an undated letter from S. M. Aguado to an unknown recipient. In this document he stated that the action at Zacatecas had ended and that there was nothing preventing the Mexican government from addressing the issues in Texas. He reported that the government had embarked six hundred troops, including four hundred infantrymen, for Texas.

The third captured document was apparently one of the rare 1835 personal letters mentioned in the introduction. It is written by someone named Mariano, seemingly from Matamoros, with no date. It is addressed to "my very dear friend, Don Antonio Tenorio" and informs him that within days six vessels, carrying the Morelos battalion, would be leaving Matamoros for Texas.

The fourth document that was opened by the Texans seemed to be another personal letter and was from Ugartechea to Tenorio, dated June 20:

> **Captain Antonio Tenorio**
>
> *My esteemed friend*—Do not fail to communicate whatever intelligence you may have, and whatever you may think proper in relation to the public affairs, in your section of the country. In a very short time, the affairs of Texas will be definitively settled, for which purpose the Government has ordered to take up the line of march, a strong division composed of the troops that were in Zasatecas [*sic*] and are now in Saltillo.
>
> ***Take care of yourself and command your friend, etc.***
> ***Domingo de Ugartechea***
>
> P.S. Friend—as the commandant General is not acquainted with your coast, he does not know that the soldiers will die of fever if they do not have mosquito bars, for want of sleep. You will make for them such as I had at Velasco, as it is known the Colonists are on the march from Pecan point across the Colony. Nothing is heard but God damn St. Anna, God damn Ugartechea. These Revolutionists will be ground down, and it appears to me we shall very soon see each other, since the Government takes their matters in hand.

The fifth and last message confiscated from the Mexican couriers was written by Cos, addressed to Tenorio, dated May 26. He noted that the dispatches that Tenorio had sent to him allow him to "see to what an extreme the impudence of some strangers [foreigners] [had gone], for they appear to have persuaded themselves that the ports of the Republic appertain exclusively for the purpose of carrying a criminal and clandestine commerce." He notified Tenorio that he had arranged for the Morelos battalion to march from Ciudad Victoria to Matamoros to embark for Cópano. From there they would proceed to wherever needed.

The content of the five documents that were confiscated from the Mexican couriers leaves little doubt as to why Miller, in his July 2 letter to Cos, talked about the alarm that was reigning among the colonists. The news that large numbers of Mexican troops were headed to Texas, with the purpose of grinding down the colonists, could not have been welcome to the people of Texas. No doubt word spread quickly, and by June 22 the colonists held a meeting of in San Felipe de Austin. There were two documents written at this meeting. Robert M. Williamson chaired the meeting and Moseley Baker served as secretary. The first of the two documents was a long diatribe against the change in the government and the dissolution of the constitution of 1824. It documented eight specific actions carried out by the Mexican government that justified the taking up of arms by the Texans. These actions included the arrest of Governor Viesca, the dissolution of the local militia, and the creation of a dictator (Santa Anna) with absolute power who was only controlled by his own will and whim. The Mexican authorities were aware of this declaration, as a copy, in Spanish, is found in the Mexican military archives (see appendix 7).[24]

The second document from this meeting is dated June 22 as well, but was apparently printed on July 4. This inflammatory document was much more specific regarding actions that must be taken by the Texans in response to the news of the Mexican troops who were coming into Texas:

> For what, Fellow Citizens, are they coming, in the name of God say not [land] speculation: they are coming to compel you into obedience to the new form of Government; to compel you to give up your arms, to compel you to have your country garrisoned; to compel you to liberate your slaves; to compel you to swear to support and sustain the government of the Dictator; to compel you to submit to the imperial rule of the aristocracy, to pay tythes [*sic*] and adoration to the clergy. . . .
>
> . . . Inhabitants of the frontier—your situation will [be] deplorable; instigated and protected by the Mexicans, the Indians will be your constant enemies; they will be the continued ravagers of your country and destroyers of yourselves. If you drive them from your neighborhood, they will seek refuge and protection under the troops of San Antonio and will retire only to return with renewed violence and destruction. You will hear around your habitations the Indian yell, mingling with the Mexican cry, and the shrieking of your murdered wives, rousing the slumbers of the cradle, from the midst of your burning buildings, will tell you, when too late, of the error to your policy in permitting San Antonio to be garrisoned by Mexican troops. Fellow Citizens, depend upon it, your policy is wrong and the danger great. If you would save the country and protect the frontier San Antonio must be taken; already has Anáhuac fallen, already has [*sic*] the spies [couriers who were captured at San Felipe] of the country been arrested and the correspondence examined—already have you proceeded too far to retreat—already are the troops of the Dictator on the march against you, and you have to fight, surrender or run away.[25]

It is interesting that the document refers to Texas as "your country." Cos had written in one of his documents that the colonists already felt like they owned the place, and this certainly seems to confirm his statement.

This statement repeatedly calls for the taking of Béjar by force before the Mexican force there was so strong that it could not be done. It also appealed to the newcomers in Texas by stating that 75 percent of the colonists who had arrived in Texas had not yet gotten their land. The only way they could do so was to drive the Mexican forces from Texas and allow the vice governor, Ramón Múzquiz, to resume giving land grants to immigrants.[26]

In response to the meeting in San Felipe, General Cos wrote to Ugartechea that it seemed funny that the fate of the republic rested on the will of half a dozen wretches. He admonished Ugartechea, "Do not legalize, with your acquiescence, those tumultuous meetings, that under the name of convention, or whatever, do nothing more than promote disorder and disturb the public tranquility. The towns of Texas have their respective authorities, and through them they can make legal writs about what the laws permit, but never the means that have been verified to have been used in San Felipe."[27] On July 7 Cos informed Ugartechea that he was not to try to disarm the good citizens. However, Ugartechea was to expel all foreigners who have "no property save a gun and no occupation save hunting."

As a result of the news obtained from the stolen documents, another meeting of colonists was held on June 28, in Columbia, to address this issue. Miller also mentioned this meeting in his July 2 letter and sent a copy of the resolutions that were drawn up. A July 4 article in the *Texas Republican* reported on the meeting and detailed the resolutions (see appendix 8).[28]

Being aware of Mexican troops coming to Texas, the Columbia committee seems to have attempted to write a conciliatory document. On the surface, it seems that this meeting and its resolutions might have reassured the Mexican government that the Texans truly did want to remain a part of Mexico and obey the constitution and laws of the land. They called out the Texans who were the aggressors at Anáhuac and decried any actions by individuals that would cause a conflict between the federal government and the citizens of Texas. This and other reassurances from political and military chiefs mollified the Mexican officials for a short time. On the other hand, as will be discussed later in this work, Cos was in no hurry to act in any case, as he had no troops to marshal against the colonists who had caused the disturbances at Anáhuac and San Felipe.

Reading between the lines of the minutes from the meeting likely exasperated the Mexican officials. The meeting itself was probably seen as an act of defiance. There was no constitutional provision to hold public meetings as the Texans were wont to do. The committee also specified that it objected to a minority of the colonists disturbing the peace, but that if a majority of the people were in favor of a certain action it would be acceptable. The Texans wanted to declare their own political chiefs as the executive power of the state and give them the authority to suspend further orders until a consultation of all the departments in the state could be held. Making the political chiefs the executive authority was actually Cos's idea, but he certainly had not said anything about suspending orders. Possibly the most infuriating part of the declaration was the call to arm the civic militias to fight the indigenous tribes. Immediately after discovering that large numbers of Mexican troops were bound for Texas, it seems odd that the colonists were worried about the native population.

One last item that Miller added to his July 2 note to Cos was the idea that Cos might want to try to explain to the Texans why Mexican troops were needed. Cos did exactly that on July 12 by writing a circular letter to the three political chiefs in Texas. He talked about the introduction of many men into Texas who had no country, morality, or employment and who thereby had nothing to lose in fanning the flame of discord. He argued that these types of people would claim that the movement of Mexican troops to that state would be the beginning of military subjugation. Cos added that sending troops to Texas was no different than sending them to Oaxaca or Vera Cruz and that if they were needed in Galveston they should be received without resistance. He stated to the political chiefs, "You will please make the honest residents of this department understand that so long as they remain attached to the government and the laws they have nothing to fear; as an armed force is sent to no part of the Republic with any other object than to maintain the peace and security of the nation." He did add that he would be obliged to proceed against anyone who would overturn the peace that the country now enjoyed.[29]

It seems highly likely that the persons responsible for capturing the Mexican couriers Cpl. Juan Ximenes and Pvt. Santos Flores and opening the official dispatches listed above never did come to justice.[30] Filisola wrote that one of the four individuals responsible was José María Carbajal, but the Mexican officials had already been unsuccessfully trying to arrest him. By August 5, six weeks after the crime was committed, the Texans were still not cooperating with the Mexican authorities. On that date, Wyly Martin, the interim political chief of the department of the Brazos (J. B. Miller had resigned in mid-July), wrote to Ugartechea:

> By the regular mail I received your attentive note of about the persecution and apprehension of the individuals who intercepted the military mail in this village. I had received another before about the same matter by special courier. Before I was in charge of this leadership, the reckless attack was committed that is mentioned in the expressed notes. It certainly deserves worthy punishment. However, it has not been practical to apprehend those delinquents as they have dispersed and left the department that I lead. However, I have ordered that a dispatch be formed regarding this embarrassing occurrence, as it is too sensitive [for regular mail]. As soon as it is completed, I will send it to the competent authorities so that the guilty might suffer the appropriate penalty for such a horrible crime.
>
> This council does not need the help of the armed force that you have offered, since this department now enjoys a complete tranquility and all the people have shown a most decisive resolve to conserve order and the public peace and to adhere to the Mexican nation and support the local authorities in exercising their duties and compliance with the laws.[31]

The military archives are rife with similar examples of Anglo administrators giving lip service to the Mexican officials and always having convenient excuses as to why they were unable to carry out the instructions they had been given. Another great example of this behavior is seen in the attempt to punish the leaders of the men who attacked Anáhuac. Cos wrote to Martin on August 1 and informed him that initially the authorities in Béjar were informed that the scandalous, criminal action at Anáhuac was committed under the direction of the political chief of the Brazos (it is unclear if he was referring to Miller or Martin). However, on July 17 Ugartechea received many letters from inhabitants in San Felipe "in which they explicitly declare their feelings of reprobation about those events and they renew their assurances of obedience to the laws of the Republic." Cos demanded that they immediately arrest Travis, the leader of the action, and send him to Béjar. He noted that this would prove the loyalty of the colonists. Cos also wrote to Tornel on August 4 and informed him of the action at Anáhuac and the denial of the colonists in San Felipe of having been involved. He informed Tornel that he had ordered the arrest of Travis. He ended the letter with "if they are sorry for their attacks, they need to show it with actions and not words." Martin failed to act on this demand.

By August 12 Cos was apparently losing trust in most of the colonists of Texas. Even though he was trying to keep the peace until he was reinforced and could take action against them, he wrote the Mexican consul in New Orleans, Francisco Pizarro Martínez, regarding the fact that the colonists did not like the changes in the Mexican government. He stated that they had small numbers and occupied only a small part of the country. Cos informed Pizarro Martínez that the final recourse for the Mexican government was to force the foreign colonists to obey the new laws. If not, they could move to another country where they could live in the extravagant independence that they desired.[32]

Meanwhile, the colonists took Tenorio and some of his troops to San Felipe. After consulting with Ugartechea in Béjar, Tenorio informed the colonists that they would need to return the muskets and armaments that were taken from his troops by Travis and his men at Anáhuac.[33] While in San Felipe he wrote the leaders in the city to thank them for the aid they had given him to support his troops (this was one of the conditions of his surrender). On July 24 Tenorio wrote to Béjar and assured Ugartechea that he was not being held in San Felipe by force but that the colonists believed it would be a testimony to their loyalty to the supreme government if he remained there of his own free will. Even though Ugartechea had ordered him to return to Béjar, he responded that he was going to wait in San Felipe until the arms that had been taken from his troops were returned. Regarding the action at Anáhuac that led to his surrender he gave the following information to Ugartechea: "About the events at Anáhuac, a great part was due to my isolated position. The troops were seduced, which was verified with an offer of an open protection to the discontented [troops]. The force scattered and some troops abandoned their post when they heard a cannonade. None of these were known cowards. One of the dispersed left with everything and his musket, as I have informed you already in my report. Of the rest of them, almost all, have deserted from Harrisburg; I did not want to report this because it is very shameful, but if the news leaks out it will show that the presidial troops are not very good."[34]

Tenorio remained in San Felipe for quite some time and seemed to have developed a good relationship with the colonists there. When it came to politics, he seemed to have a Federalist leaning but was honest in his opinion about the loyalties of the residents of San Felipe. He informed Ugartechea on August 4 that in his opinion, "The change of governments announced in the interior of the nation has disgusted them to a man and I think that all will support the opposition of the government of a dictator or emperor. They say in their papers what is to be established and have quite a few ideas on what to maintain."

By August 14 Tenorio was still in San Felipe, and only eighteen of the sixty-three muskets had been returned, six of them broken. Interestingly, Tenorio requested leave so that he could visit his family in Matamoros. Tenorio finally arrived at Béjar on or about September 8 and reported to Ugartechea that the colonists had told him that Mejía was in the United States and had gathered a force of 1500 men, presumably with the knowledge of the US government. Rather than being allowed to return to Matamoros, Tenorio ended up participating in the siege of Béjar.

CHAPTER FOUR

Gathering an Army

In mid-November 1834, Col. Domingo Ugartechea notified General Cos, commanding general of the Internal States of the East, that he had arrived in Béjar to take over the duties of the military commander of the state of Coahuila y Texas. He wrote Cos that he felt it his duty to inform him of the state of public opinions in the department as these were the conditions under which the presidial companies were forced to function. He was concerned by the evils that would result if his recommendations were not acted upon by Cos and his superiors.

According to Ugartechea, the political convulsions between Monclova and Leona Vicario (Saltillo) had animated many of the towns neighboring Béjar, notably Goliad, to join with the other colonists in championing the cause of the separation of Texas from Coahuila. In his opinion, if they did not accede to their requests the colonists would use armed conflict to further their purpose.

Ugartechea observed that the presidial companies of Monclova, Ríogrande, Aguaverde, Bavía, Béjar, Bahía (Goliad), and Alamo de Parras had been without salaries for months, and as a result they were short of troops.[1] With the shortages at each presidio, including uniforms and horses, it would be impossible for them to carry out their duties. While he seemed to be most concerned with these companies being unable to respond to the incursions of "barbaric Indians," he did add that strengthening the presidial command would also be a deterrent to the pretenses of the colonists and the North Americans.[2]

Cos passed this information on to Tornel, so Tornel was aware of the poor condition of the presidial troops when he wrote to Cos on January 24, 1835, and told him to gather five hundred presidial troops in Béjar. Three hundred of these men were to march, under the command of Ugartechea, and restore order in Nacogdoches. In early February Cos responded to Tornel that the march of the 2nd active battalion of Nuevo Leon and the company of Lampasas would be delayed. Even after they arrived, he did not believe that he could gather the requested five hundred presidial troops. In late June Tornel put Cos in command of all the presidial troops in the area and ordered him to "improve them and put them in a brilliant state." The problem was that Cos was provided with no men, supplies, or funds to do so.

Tornel (possibly under the direction of Santa Anna) opted to send permanent Mexican troops to Texas rather than to try to shore up the presidial units. The permanent battalions of Mexican troops composed the regular army of Mexico. They were full-time soldiers and for the most part were experienced, as the Mexican people had been fighting amongst themselves constantly since Mexico gained its independence in 1821.

In 1832 the Mexican army changed from numbering each permanent battalion to naming them after famous insurgents and heroes of the independence movement (Matamoros, Morelos, Jiménez, etc.). After 1838, they returned to numbering the units. The uniforms of the Mexican army were redesigned in 1832 after a long directive about the new units was published (see appendix 25).

When at full strength, a permanent battalion was composed of eight companies. The grenadiers were the veteran troops. Their company was often deployed last in a battle to make sure that the regular infantry companies in front of them did not retreat in the face of enemy fire. There was also one company of light infantry, or *cazadores,* in each battalion. This company would occasionally be armed with rifles, if available, and would be deployed as sharpshooters. These two companies were referred to as "preferential units." The other six companies were composed of regular infantrymen. For the most part the regular infantrymen were armed with .75-caliber East India–pattern Brown Bess muskets. On occasion they would use other patterns of Brown Bess muskets or muskets from other countries.

There were also battalions in the Mexican army referred to as "active units." These could be compared to the National Guard troops of today. They would be called to duty in times of need, and these battalions were named after their place of origin (San Luís, Querétaro, Tres Villas, etc.).

The cavalry at that time was organized into regiments. The regiments were named after famous battles in Mexican history (Dolores, Tampico, Cuautla, etc.). The cavalry units were also designated as permanent or active regiments. For the most part the cavalry was armed with carbines (shortened .75-caliber muskets). There were also some squads of lancers in the cavalry; these were considered the most effective in battle and the most feared by their enemies.

Morelos battalion cross-belt plate from the Sea of Mud. This plate was used to connect the two leather straps that crossed the chest of the soldado.

On February 11, 1835, Tornel sent orders for two permanent Mexican battalions to march for Texas. The first of these was the Morelos battalion. They were to start the march from San Luís Potosí to Tampico de Tamaulipas on March 10. These units were instructed to arrange their own financing until the end of the month.

That same day Tornel informed General Cos that the Morelos battalion would be embarking in Tampico on April 1 and would be disembarking at Matagorda in Texas. Cos was to prepare the needed baggage and transportation for the march of the Morelos from Matagorda to San Antonio de Béjar. He also was to prepare the roads between the two cities since they were to bring four pieces of artillery with them.

Tornel also wrote the commanding general at Jalisco on April 11 and ordered him to send the permanent Guerrero battalion to San Luís Potosí on March 1. He did not say specifically that the Guerrero was headed to Texas, but it seems likely. On February 19, after having received his order to march to San Luís, the commander of the Guerrero battalion, Col. Francisco Berdejo, responded to the commanding general with a dispatch that was quite informative as to the readiness of the Mexican army to move against Texas:

General Command of the State of Jalisco

Permanent battalion of Guerrero—I am informed by the dispatch from Your Excellency dated today, which I answer, in which you serve to transmit to me the superior orders communicated by the Minister of War in the dispatch of the 11th of the current [month]; that the battalion under my command march precisely on the day of the 1st of April with 15 days of supplies, for San Luís Potosí. I tell Your Excellency for your knowledge and so that you can inform the Supreme Government [of] the situation that exists and the obstacles that are presented in carrying out said superior order. Your Excellency can then see with your own eyes the current condition of the troops and be informed of all that is happening as mentioned above.

The battalion under my command has, as of this date, 334 men. Of these, not 60 are fit for service, half of them being recruits whose uniforms are completely destroyed. The rest of the 334, not counting the sergeants and the band, are recruits in instruction and accused criminals. As soon as those recruits, who are from this state, have been trained and begin to understand the march, I am certain that they will desert. This has been verified, without this motive, by nearly 300 men, taking their uniforms and some their arms. With this there do not remain more than 30 reliable men. This is not enough to escort the criminals and recruits, nor guard the arms, pay box, paper bin, stores, and equipment.[3] For these reasons, Your Excellency can see that the Supreme Government would not approve this march for the lack of soldiers with which they can complete your orders. It would also expose the pay box and the arms to being robbed. . . .

This battalion in the past revolution and in all the scarcities it has had, has not received the budgeted items and has had many expenses in its continuous marches, and these continuous movements do not allow for any creation of funds. In the past month of December, they were reduced to a budget of three thousand five hundred and some odd pesos for the clothing, which was given on credit, and even two hundred of the budgeted should be budgeted for starters for January and February and more to the amounts to be invested to buy the goods and utensils of the battalion. They had done without them in the revolution with a few missing and others lost. Now I will say to Your Excellency with the situation in regard to the troop: 65 privates whose uniforms are so destroyed that it is an indecency to the service, as Your Excellency has seen in the enlisted men. The remainder, except the sergeants and the band, are absolutely stripped, and the majority of them only have the sack clothes that they had been given to cover themselves, the condition of which Your Excellency can see whenever you want if you come to my headquarters. So few have shoes, of all in general, and the arms that I have given them all are unusable, which is the reason for all of the instruction that I give inside the barracks, so that the units of the army do not detract from their status and [incur] the mockery of the peoples. I hope that it serves Your Excellency to present this to the Supreme Government, which on this date I [also] do separately, so that it [the government] serves to resolve what is good and without deceit the armed forces can use, and that their decisions have the needed success, because this is not a lie about imaginary things and what-ifs.

I have the honor to inform Your Excellency of this according to your related note.

God and Liberty Guadalajara February 19, 1835 Francisco Berdejo[4]

Cos gave some more details on the artillery to be sent to Texas when he wrote to Ugartechea on February 21 and informed him that he had requested the commander at Veracruz to send bronze cannons to Texas, two of a caliber of six and one of four.[5] However, by March 19 General Cos notified Ugartechea that these cannons would not be coming and that the troops would now disembark at Cópano. Instead of the cannons being shipped, the director of artillery suggested that he send some artillerymen with the Morelos battalion and they could mount some of the loose cannons that were at Béjar on gun carriages.[6]

The commander of Tampico, Gregorio Gómez, did respond to Cos about the expected arrival of the Morelos battalion.[7] He wrote that he had been notified of the embarkation of the Morelos by Cos, but that up to that point he had had no orders from the Mexican government. These changes and omissions are a good example of the constant adjustments that were being made in the planning of the Mexican army's march to Texas. Notice that the changes were usually made for lack of money, men, supplies, or means of transportation.

As was often the case, there was still a glitch in the plans. At Goliad, commanding officer Manuel Sabaríego informed Col. Ugartechea that he was occupied escorting newly arrived families destined for the new village of Dolores. The thirty horses and six teams of oxen that were needed for the Morelos battalion, along with the four pieces of artillery (apparently, he had not yet been notified that the artillery was not coming), would have to be paid for in advance, and he did not have the funds. As it turned out, all of this planning was for naught; on March 31 Tornel sent orders to the commanding general at Tamaulipas that the march of the Morelos battalion was to be put on hold and they were to be situated in Horcasitas and Buenavista. No reason was given for the change in plans.

Prior to learning of the cancelation of the march of the Morelos battalion, Cos wrote the following dispatch to Tornel, giving an emotional plea for sending more troops to Texas. Little did he know that, for at least the short-term, the plan was to send fewer troops.

> **Your Excellency**
>
> With the date of the 23rd of the past month [March], Colonel Domingo Ugartechea, Principal Commander of this state, reported from Béjar the following:
>
>> Señor Vicente de la Garza has just arrived from Brazoria and has informed me that Austin's colonists have not recognized the Administrator who was to be established at that port [Brazoria], and the same if another worker comes to Boca del Rio.[8]
>>
>> The same individual has made me aware that other colonists were not only against fulfilling the rights but also that they had decided not to permit any detachments of troops. To prevent this, they will take up arms, even the youths.
>>
>> The above verifies clearly what I said in my previous communications to you about how insignificant it was to place such a small detachment there, when there is an urgent need to put a respectable force there to make the authorities comfortable, whose orders are otherwise deceptive.
>>
>> This occurrence and the introduction, since last month to the present, of more than 250 families to the department of Nacogdoches, calls for, in my opinion, the attention of the Supreme Government. This is why I rush to inform Your Excellency. With those that arrive daily there might be 50,000 souls in the Departments of Austin and Nacogdoches. This will cause the few Mexicans that are found there to be pressured to do what the foreigners want and to this degree the local governments are favoring the smugglers.
>>
>> In view of all that I have expressed, Your Excellency will arrange the orders that you feel opportune and they will be carried out on my part to the letter.
>
> I have the honor to inform Your Excellency, to enable you to inform His Excellency, the President of the Republic, making it clear to him at the same time, that in my opinion, not many days should be allowed

to pass without serious attention to Texas being given by the Supreme Government. From what I have seen, the measures that have been recommended by this Headquarters to prevent evils have not been as efficacious as I would like. I do not have sufficient infantry and resources have been lacking to the extreme. I informed Your Excellency of this in my dispatch of the 2nd of this month. This [lack] is by virtue of the administrator of the customs of Matamoros having prevented payments and paying by preference all the checks written in that capital. They [the Supreme Government] should garner all the funds raised for at least two months as a result of the fact that the troops of these states have not yet been paid their wages from last month.

I also need to inform you of another matter. The Morelos battalion has suffered much desertion in its march. [To the degree] that they would sail from Santa Anna [de Tamaulipas] with [only] a cadre of officers, sergeants, and some privates. I would persuade Your Excellency that nothing can be done if the Supreme Government does not decide to send at least two battalions of 600 men each, with a corresponding train of artillery, to Texas immediately. And above all, [send] everything needed to supply this force as well as the Presidial troops [that are here currently]. The majority of these cannot be used to work together at some point as they need to be used exclusively in guarding the borders from incursions of the savages.

God and Liberty Leona Vicario April 6, 1835
Martín Perfecto de Cos

In the margin of this letter, Tornel added a note, dated April 14, 1835, with the response that was to be sent to Cos: "That the Supreme Government occupy itself seriously and send a force to fix the problems in Texas. These should take place when the disturbances in Zacatecas are finished."[9]

On April 16 Cos finally got the news that the Morelos battalion's march had been halted and that they would remain in the state of Tamaulipas for the present. Cos immediately responded to Tornel in what was obviously a very heartfelt dispatch:

I have been informed by the commanding general of Tamaulipas that the Morelos battalion, which was destined for Texas, has countermarched by superior orders. I cannot excuse myself for protesting

> to Your Excellency that this measure is absolutely detrimental to the Republic, which has abandoned its boundaries in the most interesting part. Whatever dissensions that are being suffered in the interior of the nation, their consequences will be inferior to the positive evils that we could experience. It would not be unusual if the colonists of Texas took advantage of our dissent in order to put into effect their ancient practices of separation, and it is necessary to acknowledge that they not be forgotten. The lack of infantry troops to guard the ports and places of interest is a motive to start producing disorder in the most interesting area of the Republic. I am responsible for the tranquility of these states. I cannot in the least agree with Your Excellency about the countermarch of the Morelos battalion. I plead for it to be sent from Santa Anna de Tamaulipas. If it is not, the frontier will continue to be abandoned, in which state it has remained until now. It is up to the commanding general to remedy this.
>
> ***God and Liberty Monterrey April 19, 1835***
> ***Martín Perfecto de Cos***[10]

When he received the above dispatch on April 29, Tornel responded to Cos that once the situation in Zacatecas had been resolved the government would send no fewer than two thousand troops to Texas to definitively fix those problems.

On April 30 the American schooner *Leonides* arrived at the port of Matamoros, carrying fifty men of the Morelos battalion. These men had been allowed to continue their movement toward Texas while the rest of the battalion countermarched. According to Cos, that "picket" of men was worthless. He was confident that his previous dispatch to Tornel would convince the government to send the rest of the Morelos to Cópano as previously planned and wrote that he had already prepared for their arrival: "The first [of the carts] are hired [at a rate] of one peso per day. I have ordered as many carriers as supplies that remain there. I am making such an expenditure because I am persuaded that the Supreme Government by my reasons will determine to send the referred Morelos battalion to embark soon at Santa Anna de Tamaulipas."[11]

It seems that Cos's confidence was well founded, as on May 19, after conferring with the interim president, Tornel was given permission to proceed with arrangements for the Morelos battalion's march to Texas. It was stated that this order could not be countermanded. Cos was relieved upon learning of the government's intention to send a large force to Texas after the rebellion in Zacatecas was resolved. He recommended that the first troops be sent to garrison Galveston, Brazoria, and other locations where shipments of great value were being introduced. He added that, "this [smuggling] is destroying completely the commerce of the republic."

The fiasco of the alternating orders for the Morelos battalion did not end there. Apparently, Santa Anna got involved and ordered the Morelos to Leona Vicario. Tornel met with the interim president about the matter, but Cos had already ordered the Morelos battalion to Matamoros and on to Cópano.

This book will not go into as much detail in discussing all the units that comprised the army of operations against Texas as it has regarding the Morelos battalion. However, all these details allow the reader to understand the complexity of organizing this march. Remember that Tornel and Cos were dealing with the interim president Miguel Barragán as well as Santa Anna, who was lurking in the background from his hacienda at Manga de Clavo.

A June 8 letter from Tornel to Cos provides excellent documentation of the multiple issues that were at play in regard to Texas:

> I have thoroughly advised His Excellency the president of the dispatches from you of the 28th, 29th and 30th of May as well as the documents that accompany them. As a consequence, he has asked me to answer Your Excellency that he approves the embarkation of the Morelos battalion to the Port of Cópano, charging to make totally sure that the orders are received and verified. They are to take two pieces of campaign artillery with them, making it more formidable. They are also to assure that this meritorious unit has supplies for at least one month until a permanent solution is obtained.
>
> His Excellency the Interim President is aware of the bad faith and perfidy of the authorities of Monclova. [He knows] of the projects they pursued in order to rebel against the supreme government and even to attack the integrity of the national territory. He has disposed that the Guerrero battalion, today garrisoned at San Luís Potosí, march and situate itself in Tula de Tamaulipas, to act at Your Excellency's orders. In view of this, the communication is repeated and sent by special courier, instructing the Dolores regiment to be ready to move from that city as soon as the government has a need. This will be determined later when Your Excellency advises me by special courier when this force of cavalry is needed. With these measures and the activities and energy that

Your Excellency has given, it will be sufficient to correct the maladies announced. Meanwhile His Excellency the President of the Republic, General Antonio López de Santa Anna, arrived at this capital. He will evaluate everything in order to command a formal expedition against Texas. That will ensure the fate, forever vacillating and precarious, of that department.

All the measures that Your Excellency has suggested for the apprehension of the Governor and other rebel authorities of Coahuila y Tejas merit the approval of His Excellency the interim president. Although the measures of conduct that have been observed are sufficient, I should add that the general congress has expedited a decree declaring the election of the rebellious authorities null and void. Consequently [their congress] will cease to function legally and any further actions will be their individual responsibility. His Excellency the interim president has also instructed that the ex-governor, ex-deputies, and the rest of the refractories, whose presence will be harmful in those states, be apprehended and sent to Veracruz as prisoners at the disposal of that commanding general.

In respect to Valentín Gómez Farías, His Excellency the Interim President approves Your Excellency's [decision] to have him march to Matamoros with the corresponding escort, allowing his embarkation and verifying it as soon as possible.

Matters will be arranged so that Your Excellency is credited with 80,000 pesos per month in Matamoros. Since the time has come to act, it is indispensable that you do not lack resources. . . .

I am particularly satisfied to tell Your Excellency that I reiterate my old and sincere affections.

God and Liberty Mexico June 8, 1835 Tornel[12]

On July 2, 1835, the Morelos battalion sailed from Brazos de Santiago (the entry to the port for Matamoros) on the schooners *Anna Maria* and *Josefa*. Their strength report (see appendix 9) shows that 146 officers and men departed. No mention of any artillery was included in the strength report, however. On July 27, the Morelos battalion was reported by Cos as having arrived at Béjar.[13]

Cos, meanwhile, decided that he needed to be more visible in Texas, and on August 31 he announced his plan to march there. He left Matamoros on

September 17 and traveled to Béjar by way of Rancho Viejo, Lipantitlán, and Goliad with a party of presidial lancers.[14] He arrived in Béjar on or about October 10.

When one considers that the initial order for the Morelos battalion to march to Tampico and then sail on to Matagorda was issued on February 11 and that the unit sailed from Matamoros, destined for Cópano, on July 2, it can be seen that the operation of the Mexican army in 1835 wase severely lacking in planning and efficiency. Furthermore, at full strength a Mexican infantry battalion would be expected to number four or five hundred men. As can be seen from the above numbers the Morelos battalion was woefully undermanned.

On September 2, José Juan Sánchez Navarro, adjutant inspector for the states of Tamaulipas and Nuevo León, was chosen by Cos to lead approximately four hundred replacements for the Morelos battalion to Texas. He and the reinforcements were to be escorted to Béjar by the Guerrero battalion. After the February 19 dispatch from Berdejo regarding the inability of the Guerrero battalion to march as ordered, there is little mention of this unit in the military archives until the June 8 letter from Tornel to Cos copied above. In that note Tornel reassured Cos that the Guerrero battalion was at his disposal for use in Texas and that the Dolores regiment cavalry would be made ready and would march as soon as Cos deemed it necessary. In early July Cos "begged" that the Guerrero battalion be sent to Texas so that he could secure the customhouses at Anáhuac, Brazoria, and Matagorda. Weeks later, in response to Cos's request for the Guerrero battalion, Tornel notified him that he could not commit to said battalion being available for use in Texas.

On August 21, the commander at San Luís Potosí, Felipe Codallo, informed Tornel that reinforcements from the states of San Luís and Zacatecas had arrived and were ready to march to bolster the Morelos battalion. He also noted that he had only been able to get twelve thousand pesos, of a promised twenty-seven-thousand-peso loan, from Cayetano Rubio. Thus, only the Guerrero battalion, escorting the Morelos battalion replacements, would be able to march from that place to Leona Vicario. The Dolores regiment cavalry would have to stay in San Luís Potosí.

Cos was still under the impression that both the Guerrero battalion and the Dolores regiment were coming to Texas on August 24 when he wrote and thanked Tornel for making these units available to him. He was also concerned that both units would arrive undermanned due to desertion on the march (the Guerrero battalion was also starting the march with only 280 men). He requested that Tornel have them reinforced immediately and make sure the new recruits received instructions in a timely manner.

As it turned out, Cos had bigger problems than the strength of the units when they arrived in Texas. On September 5, Tornel suddenly and inexplicably ordered the military commander of San Luís Potosí to instruct the Guerrero battalion to countermarch from Leona Vicario and the Dolores regiment cavalry to remain at San Luís Potosí. The new commander of the Guerrero, Col. Agustín Peralta, was ordered to use the picket of cavalry that had marched with him and forty men from the unit at Leona Vicario to escort the reinforcements for the Morelos battalion to Matamoros.[15]

As would be expected, Cos did not take this news well. He argued that the Guerrero battalion, being a small force, would have no impact in San Luís, but that its absence in Texas would weaken what little authority he had. Not only did Cos make his feelings known to Tornel, he also wrote Peralta at Leona Vicario and told him that the military commander of San Luís Potosí could not order the countermarch (he acted as though he was unaware that the original order had come from Tornel) and that the Guerrero battalion was not to leave Leona Vicario until they received further orders. Despite this order the Guerrero battalion, after a short delay for Peralta to request clarification from Tornel, began the countermarch.

This movement by the Guerrero was an important turning point of the Texas revolution. Had the Dolores cavalry and the Guerrero battalion proceeded to Texas in a timely manner to join the Morelos battalion, it is very possible that the Mexican force in Texas would have been sufficient to put down the uprising before it got out of hand. On the other hand, it should be noted that in the notebook he kept during the Texas campaign, Sánchez Navarro wrote that the Guerrero battalion, at the time they turned back toward San Luís, was tired, nearly naked, poorly trained, lacking in force, and short of discipline. Yet he still did his best to convince Peralta and the Guerrero battalion to continue the march with the Morelos replacements.[16]

In his memoirs, Sánchez Navarro wrote the following entry, from Monclova, on February 14, 1836, as the Mexican army was marching to Texas: "I saw Lt. Col., brevet Colonel Agustin Peralta and I said to him, you see how the 'channel takes out the rogue [*chorrera saca bandido*].' . . . It was indiscretion; but I already am and will be convinced that because the Guerrero battalion and the Dolores regiment, the first commanded by said commander and the second by Senior Ventura Mora, did not march in time, that [Béjar] was lost and who knows how much more."[17]

Because of the countermarch of the Guerrero battalion, Adjutant Inspector Sánchez Navarro was forced to lead the Morelos battalion replacements on to Laredo with only a small picket of men from the Guerrero battalion, under the command of Capt. José Ramón Berra. At El Venado another ninety men of the active cavalry company of Coahuila were added to the force. Filisola described these men as a hindrance, as they were greenhorns who had just enlisted, without saddles or horses. They were under the command of 2nd Lt. Rafael Aguirre. A few days later another group from the presidio company of Lampasas joined them at the same village. This group was under the command of Lt. Santiago Navaira and was composed of a sergeant, three corporals, and twenty-seven men. Just ten days after Peralta abandoned Sánchez Navarro, Captain Berra did the same.

After delays caused by supplying the troops with shoes, food, etc., Sánchez Navarro finally set out for Laredo with his ragtag force of replacements on October 21. During his march north, he received word that another 186 replacements were marching to join his force. These men were eventually incorporated into his unit on November 4.[18] He was also able to acquire a 4-pounder iron cannon while on the march. His force reached Laredo on November 17, where a few days later he was joined by a unit of cavalry under the command of Capt. Manuel Hernández. This force included twenty men, nine dragoons from the Veracruz regiment, two sergeants with ten artillerymen, and a five-and-one-half-inch howitzer (*obus*).[19] They brought thirty six-inch, unloaded howitzer shells and twelve thousand pesos. Accompanying this force were Capt. Pedro Navarrete and five men of the military health corps who were proceeding to Béjar to set up a hospital.

The same day Col. Domingo Ugartechea arrived at Laredo with a force of presidial soldiers to escort Sánchez Navarro and his force to Béjar. The strength of Sánchez Navarro's force, as they left Laredo on November 26, was 10 officers, 47 infantrymen of Morelos, 14 artillerymen, 17 dragoons, and 454 replacements for the Morelos battalion. They brought the 4-pounder cannon and the howitzer, pulled by oxen and mules, but left the howitzer shells as they were larger than what could be fired from the howitzer. That very night, fifteen men, armed and mounted, deserted.

Ugartechea was slowly gathering presidial troops to comply with the orders of Tornel, Cos, and Santa Anna to defend Béjar. Earlier he had been ordered to take three hundred men to march against Nacogdoches, but as that would have been counter to his orders to stay on the defensive and hold the line of Béjar to Goliad to Cópano, he never undertook that mission.

On June 17, Ugartechea wrote Cos that he had been told by an honorable and truthful man named Esmit that the colonists were gathering forces at various places for the purpose of attacking the garrison at Béjar.[20] As a result of this information, Ugartechea ordered the commander at Goliad, Manuel Sabaríego, to send forty men from his presidial company to march to Béjar, leaving only forty soldiers in Goliad. He also ordered twenty-five soldiers from the cavalry company at Aguaverde and the company of Ríogrande to march to Béjar.

The Bexar Archives contain strength reports from several of the presidial units of that department dated around September 30. Some of these strength reports also give inventories of arms, horses, uniform pieces, etc. Most of these also document the different statuses that the men were assigned, including guards, ranchers, barracks cleaners, sick, and prisoners.

On September 28, the 1st active company of cavalry of Nuevo Leon reported 77 men, but it noted that 38 of the men had gone to Gonzales. The 2nd active cavalry company of Nuevo Leon reported that they had 50 men and 45 horses, including 15 men and 30 horses in Gonzales. The 1st permanent company of Tamaulipas documented that on September 30 they had a strength of 42 men and 72 horses, of which 32 men and horses were in Gonzales. The presidial company of Béjar had 89 men and 240 horses on September 1. The presidial company of Ríogrande was in the village of Guerrero on October 1, but they did document that they had 7 men in Béjar. The permanent Morelos battalion strength report dated October 1 (see appendix 10) reported a strength of 195 men, not counting officers.[21] This does not account for all of the Mexican soldiers in Béjar at the time, because there are no strength reports from the companies of Alamo de Parras or Laredo. However, from the strength reports that exist, it is known that in late September there were, at a minimum, 450 Mexican soldiers in Béjar or Gonzales (85 are documented to have gone to the latter).

There was one other attempt to bolster the strength of the Morelos battalion. It is likely that this was not a serious attempt to help Cos and the Morelos but more of a way to get rid of some troublemakers in Veracruz. On October 15, the commander at Veracruz, Ciriano Vasques, wrote Tornel that he was transporting thirty-two inmates on the national ship *Bravo* to Matamoros to reinforce the Morelos battalion. He attached a list of the names of the men, which included thirty-four individuals, one of whom was listed as deceased, one sick, and three destined for the Californias (see appendix 11).[22] No record has been found to date as to the fate of these inmates.

In late October, Santa Anna apparently had finally had enough bad news from Texas. He wrote Tornel from his hacienda at Manga de Clavo that it was time to take action. He mentioned the attack on Tenorio's men and the taking of Goliad but also seemed to be aware of Cos's situation in Béjar. His dispatch to Tornel in Mexico City read as follows:

> **Army of Operations Your Excellency**
>
> By the message from Your Excellency of the 23rd of this month and copies that were attached, I have learned with great disgust of the actions of the insurrectionist colonists of Texas at La Bahía del Espíritu Santo [Goliad]. This should result in detriment to the Supreme Government, which has made assurances in the official newspaper that nothing new has taken place in that part of the Republic. [Also embarrassing is] the escape of the adventurers who surprised the detachment at Anáhuac commanded by Captain Tenorio and [then the] reporting that there was nothing to fear in these areas and everything was secure, etc. These reassurances had even persuaded me that uniting our troops at Leona Vicario [Saltillo] was unnecessary. Before this I had felt that doing so would be needed as I did have doubts about the good faith of these adventurers.
>
> Now the remedy must come with the timelessness and accuracy that this case demands so that the arms of the Nation will not suffer any more disgrace from these damn foreigners. To that effect it seems appropriate and indispensable that General Joaquín Ramírez y Sesma march with the permanent Jiménez and Matamoros battalions to Leona Vicario with six pieces of artillery of 8, 6, and 4 [pounders], along with two howitzers with their respective detachments [cannon crews], one hundred cases of musket cartridges, with 4,000 flints [*piezas de chispa*]. Instruct him to march double speed as soon as possible and when he arrives there, he will take command of the division of operations. . . .
>
> . . . As well as the Matamoros and Jiménez battalions it will be necessary to march the active battalion of San Luís Potosí and the permanent regiment of Dolores [cavalry] to Leona Vicario. Both units should be

at full strength, conducting two pieces of campaign artillery with their corresponding detachments of artillerymen and munitions, and fifty cases of musket cartridges with two hundred flints to cover the garrison at San Luís. The Guerrero battalion should have returned to that capital. The commanding general of San Luís can proceed with the formation of the active regiment of cavalry from that state, strengthening as much as possible the Guerrero battalion, which is in that city.

It would be opportune for the active battalion of Querétaro to march to San Luís Potosí to reinforce the garrison there or march to where it is appropriate. The 2nd active [battalion] of Mexico [City] that resides in that capital should leave for Querétaro as a replacement for the garrison that left for San Luís. . . .[23]

. . . It will be advantageous that the Brevet General Vital Fernández, who should be found in that Capital, return to the post of Ciudad Victoria, making it easier for him to recruit the necessary forces and march with them to become part of the Division of Operations. The commander of the Division can march the necessary officers from the great surplus that exists in that capital. He will remit to Matamoros the arms and equipment needed by the active companies.

The Commander of the Port of Matamoros should fortify it so as to avoid any surprise [attacks].

It is important to advise General Cos of the march of the Division commanded by General Ramírez y Sesma, of the units that compose his corps, and of the arms and munitions that he is transporting. He [Cos] is to remain on the defense at S. A. de Béjar and fortify that community by the best means possible until the arrival of General Ramírez y Sesma.

This is what I think about the measures that can be issued at the moment, in light of the sad picture presented by the Army of the Republic, the diversity of attentions that must be covered, and the care that must be given to the anarchists who work without rest to destroy order and peace. The lack of money is no less an obstacle for recruiting the best forces. Even before now I have been in favor of the formation of an army that can operate successfully against the considerable portion of foreigners who have arbitrarily taken control of our territories in Texas. But neither can the Republic, in the condition that it finds itself, gather 6,000 to 8,000 troops, nor can the Government easily provide the one million pesos that would be indispensable to achieve the objective.

There is nothing more than to wait until the Nation finishes constituting itself to see if we can change the present situation. In the meantime, we need to cover the frontier of Texas, in the line of S. Ant.o de Béjar, as I have indicated repeatedly to General Cos. I even warned him in my last communications that he needed to gather as many troops as possible in Béjar, to fortify that town and to establish his headquarters there. . . .

. . . You know well, Your Excellency, that the Fortress of Veracruz and the Fortress of Ulúa are completely abandoned due to the lack of troops to man them. In spite of what I have declared to Your Excellency in a private letter you have not sent a single replacement. This leaves the unhappy soldiers who serve as sentries 15–20 days of the most precise guard duties. Therefore, as there is no hope for replacements, it is going to be necessary that the Aldama battalion garrison Veracruz before the start of winter, thus avoiding an accidental fall of the Fortress of Ulúa into the hands of foreigners, which would be very difficult to recapture.

Besides what is already said, there are no ships in the port to charter, and even if there were, the cost would not be a small sum, being the most exposed, embarking troops in the current season of northers. A shipwreck would add to our loses and sentiments. Even if such a nuisance is avoided the need that they have for troops in Matamoros would not be remedied. Without a doubt two hundred men from said battalion [Aldama] will not arrive as this Corps is [short of men] as are all the others. Those who remain are assigned without any effective means of gathering replacements in the numbers that are needed to complete the units with the forces that they need: [These are] urgent measures, which the Government should not, even for a moment, stop from putting into practice. With what has been expressed I have the honor of said note from Your Excellency, repeating my consideration and appreciation.

God and Liberty Manga de Clavo Oct. 26, 1835
Antonio López de Santa Anna[24]

Santa Anna addressed several issues in the above document that merit discussion. First, he instructed Tornel to make sure that Cos was aware of the plan to march the division to Béjar and that Cos should stay on the defensive, fortifying Béjar by the best means possible until Ramírez y Sesma arrived. On

July 27 Cos, in his response to Tornel's instructions of July 8, replied that he was aware of his order to remain on the defensive for the time being, preserving the line of defense of Béjar, Bahía de Espíritu Santo, and the port of Cópano. Later in the letter Santa Anna wrote that he had "repeatedly" indicated to Cos to hold the expressed defensive line. It is interesting that after the fall of Béjar Cos was to be criticized for taking the offensive at the battle of Concepción.

Another issue that Santa Anna addressed was funding. As has been previously noted, financing was by far the greatest problem facing the Mexican officials in organizing the Mexican army and marching it to Texas. There seem to be far more documents in the Mexican military archives regarding lack of money and supplies than any other subject. Loans at outrageous interest rates and forced loans or contributions were common. Once a portion of the Mexican army had passed through an area, the troops who were trailing them would receive little or no support from the locals as a result of their treatment by the troops who had previously been there.

Another subject addressed in the dispatch was the fact that the coastal cities, especially Veracruz and the fortress of San Juan de Ulúa, were susceptible to invasion.[25] It must be admitted that Santa Anna's instincts were accurate. Albeit not in Veracruz, General Mejía executed his mission against the Centralists in another coastal city, Tampico, just a few weeks after this document was written.

Santa Anna also briefly discussed the issue of whether to send troops to Texas by land or by sea. He mentioned lack of ships, excessive cost, exposure to the storms that were active at that time of year, possible shipwrecks, and being unable to move large numbers of troops, as reasons that he would be sending the army by land. Unfortunately, General Santa Anna did not give his reasoning for entering Texas through Béjar instead of through Goliad and Victoria. Since Béjar would not fall until December 10, the idea that Santa Anna was trying to avenge the taking of Béjar does not hold up.[26] It is more likely that as the division to relieve Cos at Béjar had already started to march, he considered it more efficient to use the same trail. In addition, the cost of leasing ships (the Mexican navy had very few ships at the time) was likely a major obstacle because, as previously pointed out, Santa Anna was thrifty to a fault.

Gen. Francisco Vital Fernández was ordered by Santa Anna to raise a force of one thousand men in Nuevo Leon and Tamaulipas and take it to Matamoros. This unit was to be named "Volunteers of the Country." He did go to Matamoros in 1835 and was named military commander of that place, but there does not seem to be evidence that he ever gathered sufficient troops to aid the army of operations against Texas. As a staunch Federalist, it is possible that his effort to support Santa Anna and the Centralist army was not 100 percent.

Fernández did, however, respond to Tornel that he needed materials for uniforms for the force that he was to raise. He planned to gather six hundred infantrymen and four hundred cavalrymen. In a document dated November 11, Fernández wrote: "For better compliance with the supreme order that Your Excellency served to communicate to me in your superior directive of the 7th of the current [month], it is indispensable for me to beg you to have the goodness to direct that in Querétaro 5,150 bars of cloth be prepared in the colors and following terms: 1500 of indigo [*turquí*] to make one thousand pants: eight hundred of sky blue [*seleste*] for four hundred cavalry frock coats [*casacas de caballeria*]: 1950 for six hundred infantry greatcoats [*capotes á la infanteria*]; and eight hundred of red [*de encarnado*; blood red], for trimming [*vivos*], stripes [*varras*], facing [*vueltos*; cuffs?], collars [*cuellos*], and fringes [*franjas*]."[27]

On October 29, Santa Anna ordered the Tres Villas battalion, which had been at Jalapa Pass, to gather its standards at Perote and prepare to march when ordered.[28] On December 18, they were ordered to march double-time to Querétaro and were to march for San Luís on January 3. They were to be under the leadership of the commanding general of Querétaro, José María Rincón.

The same day Santa Anna was notified by the war department that his request for one million pesos had been forwarded to the national congress, and they had approved the authority to negotiate loans for that amount by the best representatives available from the villages. There is no archival evidence found that suggests that funds anywhere near this amount were ever received. There are multiple documents that state that the payments on previous loans exhausted most of the funds that were designated for the use of the army.

In the following statement, General Filisola noted the fact that the Mexican army's plans to march to Texas were continuously made public and thus were well known to the Texans:

> But what we do know is that from the month of April 1835, when General and President Don Antonio López de Santa Anna was preparing to march at the head of respectable division on the State of Zacatecas . . . it had been made public in the waiting rooms of the palaces of Mexico City and Tacubaya and in the most popular cafes and gatherings that at the beginning of the following year 1836 a similar expedition would be repeated against the Texas colonies, not only to bring them to submit to obedience to our laws but to punish them, to exterminate them, and to throw them far

> beyond our borders.[29] And from what was seen later there is no doubt but that was the way it was agreed upon in the cabinet.
>
> Whether this lack of secrecy, of circumspection and of prudence was contrary, or not to politics, to the national interests and to the success of the undertaking that was being planned needs not be said. With it notice was given to [the] enemy with advance knowledge of almost a year's time of the storm which was threatening so that they would be able with that time to ward it off or to prepare themselves against it in the best manner possible. Especially when their principal errand boy and agent for the colonies, Stephen Austin, was in Mexico City.[30]

With the October 26 orders from Santa Anna, Tornel and the Mexican government decided to get serious. Tornel quit worrying about getting individual units to Texas and followed Santa Anna's orders for a division of operations to be formed. The purpose of this division was to march to Texas and relieve Cos at Béjar. Tornel sent the following order to General Cadallos at San Luís Potosí and copied the dispatch to Santa Anna and to Cos:

> The ungrateful colonists of Texas, abusing the benevolence with which they were availed in the Republic, are trying to separate a precious part from it. The supreme government, in order to castigate their boldness and to conserve the decorum of the nation that it represents, has seen fit to arrange for the permanent battalions of Matamoros and Jiménez, the active [battalion] of that city [San Luís Potosí], and the Dolores regiment, to form a division of operations. Also, it should take two four-pound pieces [of artillery], two six-pound pieces and two eight-pound pieces, with their respective crews, one hundred cases of musket cartridges, and 8,000 extra musket flints. This division is entrusted to General Joaquín Ramírez y Sesma.[31] The necessary measures have already been facilitated for its movement. To communicate this measure to Your Excellency I contacted His Excellency the Interim President, recommending that he send orders for the active battalion of that city to prepare to march to join with the troops that General Ramirez is conducting from Zacatecas. This unit will take out from that plaza fifty cases of musket cartridges, and to do this, with the same date, inform that commanding general of Querétaro to come with them [the cartridges] immediately to that city. Equally, he orders Your Excellency that along with the indicated unit there should go two campaign

pieces [or artillery], besides those that General Ramirez y Sesma is conducting.

Finally, His Excellency directed me to say to Your Excellency that 10,000 pesos are going to be situated in that city for the purpose of assuring the movement of the cited active battalion of that city. I have the honor of communicating all this to Your Excellency for your intelligence and appropriate purposes.

God and LibertyOct. 31, 1835
[Tornel's rubric][32]

The choice of Ramírez y Sesma to command this division was remarkably interesting. As will be shown in the second volume of this work, when Santa Anna sent a vanguard of troops ahead of the main body, in order to chase down the enemy or make a surprise attack on them, he would either personally take command or make Ramírez y Sesma the commander. This was odd because it seems obvious from the archival records that many of the Mexican officers considered Ramírez y Sesma to be a poor commander. In 1836, after the fall of the Alamo, Sánchez Navarro wrote that when Santa Anna ordered Ramírez y Sesma to take the vanguard division and chase Houston toward the Colorado River, "Everyone says that he will not pass [the river] unless he is aided by the most excellent president or whichever of the other generals."[33] More examples of his failings as a commanding general will be documented in the second volume of this work.

Santa Anna's choice of Ramírez y Sesma to be his preferred commander for important missions makes one think that he was not necessarily hoping for Ramírez y Sesma to succeed. As was noted in chapter 1, Santa Anna may have had an addiction to glory. A comment made by Sánchez Navarro, after Santa Anna refused to delay the storming of the Alamo until more troops and heavy artillery arrived at Béjar, provides another hint of this trait. Sánchez Navarro wrote: "It has been decided for the assault. Why is it that Señor Santa Anna always wants his triumphs and defeats to be marked with blood and tears?"[34] It seems likely that Santa Anna was unwilling to share the glory with others and thus preferred to use a general who was least likely to succeed.

Ramírez y Sesma left Zacatecas on November 8. He reported that, for the units to move rapidly, he had left the wounded, criminal prisoners, and stores. He reached San Luís on November 17. On that day he informed Tornel that the San Luís battalion (under the command of brevet Col. Juan Morales), a squad of the Dolores Cavalry (which was on foot because of the lack of horses), and two 8-pounder cannons had left San Luís for Leona Vicario. In the margin of this dispatch Ramírez y Sesma gave the strengths of the units that were in San Luís at the time. San Luís battalion—500; Jiménez—380; Matamoros—380; Querétaro—350; Dolores regiment—300. There was a more detailed strength report from the active battalion of San Luís, which included the number of men by rank. It also detailed the number of men who were ready to march, those who would join them on the march, and those who would be left behind (see appendix 12).[35]

Ramírez y Sesma also reported that he had ordered hardtack (*galleta*) to be made for the troops. He wrote that this food was needed for his command to survive the wilderness on the way to Béjar and beyond. Lastly, Ramírez y Sesma stated that he would try to unite with as many cavalry troops as possible since that branch of the military was the most important for operations in Texas.

A flurry of orders started coming out of the office of the secretary of war in November. Santa Anna had decided that the army would rendezvous at San Luís Potosí. The division under Ramírez y Sesma was to march on from that place to Leona Vicario (Saltillo) and then on to Laredo, where they would get news of Cos's situation in Béjar and march to his relief if indicated. The rest of the units would be organized and would begin the march, under the command of Santa Anna, to San Antonio de Béjar.

The active Querétaro battalion had been ordered by Tornel on October 31 to march immediately to San Luís. The military commander of that city, Eugenio Tolsa, responded on November 7 that despite various financial difficulties the unit would soon march.

The Tampico regiment cavalry was ordered to march from Puebla to Mexico City on November 16. After two days rest in Mexico City, they were to proceed from there to San Luís.

On November 18, Tornel issued orders for the Zapadores battalion to march to San Luís immediately.[36] They were instructed not to enter Mexico City on their march. On this same day, he also sent orders for the active regiment of Guanajuato to march to Querétaro on November 26, and to remain there awaiting further orders.[37]

On November 19, Tornel was notified that the permanent Aldama battalion would be marching for San Luís Potosí starting November 23.

Cos and Ramírez y Sesma were notified on November 18 that Santa Anna would be marching. In this dispatch Tornel was able to paint Santa Anna as a martyr:

> Leaving domestic repose, without regard to the state of broken health, and only to serve the country in the cause of the interest of the integrity of the Mexican territory, the propriety of the military and the wellbeing of all the citizens, His Excellency, President of the Country, Antonio López de Santa Anna marches to place himself at the head of the army of operations that must act against the rebels of Texas. As of this time the corps that will compose it are already moving so I must advise Your Excellency of this for your knowledge.
>
> ***God and Liberty—November 18, 1835***
> ***[Tornel's mark]***[38]

He also sent dispatches to Gen. José Urrea, the commanding general of Chihuahua;[39] José Joaquin del Calvo; and the military commander of New Mexico, Col. Alvino Pérez, notifying them that Santa Anna would be marching at the head of ten thousand men from San Luís to San Antonio de Béjar. From there he would begin operations against the Texans once the winter had passed.

During this time, Tornel, Santa Anna, and his aides were organizing the army. Ramírez y Sesma and his division would be designated as the first division (also called the vanguard division). The second division was to be composed of the 1st and 2nd infantry brigades. There was also a cavalry brigade and a separate corps under the command of Urrea. The artillery was to be split among all these forces, apart from the cavalry brigade.

Santa Anna needed a second-in-command, and Gen. Vicente Filisola was chosen to fill that position. Lt. Col. Juan N. Cuevas was to serve as his aide-de-camp. Filisola wrote in his memoirs that Santa Anna instructed him to proceed to Béjar to take command of the forces of both Cos and Ramírez y Sesma. Filisola documented that Santa Anna advised him that when Ramírez y Sesma arrived at Béjar, "certain differences might arise concerning the chief command of those forces gathered there because of the equality of the rank of the principal leaders. It seems prudent in extraordinary and dangerous circumstances to avoid by all means arguments or unpleasantness." Santa Anna added that Filisola was to start work on the fortifications there and "keep the enemy on alert until my arrival so that we may do battle with certainty of success." This seems to be another example of Santa Anna trying to ensure that he would be the recipient of the glory that would accompany the victory.

The next step was to organize a general staff for the army. Gen. Manuel F. Castrillon, another aide-de-camp to Santa Anna, drew up the first list of men to serve on the headquarters staff. This original list (it would later see many changes) was compiled in Tacubaya and released on November 23.

> List of the General Commanders and officers who compose the staff of His Excellency the General President and those of its secretaries[40]

Branch	Brevet[41]	Rank	Rank Names
infantry	General	Colonel	Manuel Fernández Castrillon
	Lt. Col.	Captain	Juan Dias
		Another	Mag.l Bachiller
		Lt.	Anastacio Covos
		1st Adj.	Eusevio Flores
cavalry	Col.	Lt. Col.	José Batres
	Id.	Another	Juan Maria Bringas
	Id.	Another	Manuel de la Portilla[42]
	Id.	Another	Estevan de la Mora
		Lt. Col.	Pedro Francisco Delgado
	Lt. Col.	Captain	Marcial Aguirre
		Another	Manuel Badillo
infantry			
Aldama battalion		Cazadore	Juan Alvarez
Tampico regiment		1st Corporal	Valentin Gil
Iguala regiment		Dragoon	Justo Garcia

Tacubaya Nov. 23, 1835
Manuel F. Castrillon[43]

Another task Santa Anna addressed was the gathering of the unattached officers who would be marching with the army. These officers were to be assigned to a specific unit once they reached the army of operations. One such officer, who will be a prominent character later in this work, was brevet Lt. Col. José

Enrique de la Peña. It is interesting that Filisola, after the Texas campaign had ended, claimed that one of the reasons that the Mexican army was defeated in Texas was that there was an excess of officers in the army (see appendix 13 for a list of a few of the unattached officers who were instructed to join the army for the Texas campaign).

Filisola and Santa Anna arrived at San Luís on the same day, December 5. General Ramírez y Sesma marched for Texas on December 7 with the vanguard division, including the eight pieces of artillery mentioned by Santa Anna in his dispatch of October 26, to do battle with the Texan besiegers. A summary of the instructions given to Ramírez y Sesma by Santa Anna follows:

1. When you arrive at Laredo, incorporate the replacements who have been sent to the Morelos battalion, arm them, and distribute them among the units of the division. If they are already on the road from Laredo to Béjar, order them to stop until you have joined them.
   [The replacements, as will be discussed later, arrived at Béjar on December 9, before Ramírez y Sesma was able to stop them.]
2. When you pass through towns on the march, make use of their enthusiasm and incorporate capable citizens who know how to handle arms into your ranks.
3. From Laredo observe the enemy so that you will know their positions, force, the number of cannons they have, and, if possible, the operations that they are thinking of executing. At the same time send trusted convicts, well experienced with the terrain, to General Cos to let him know when you will approach the enemy camp. When you do approach, if there is artillery fire between his forces and that of the besiegers, you will know the battle has begun, and make a sortie with all the force that you can.
4. Proceed from Laredo to Béjar with the utmost caution so as not to be surprised by an ambush. During the night in your camp make sure that guard duty is carried out according to the strictest laws of the military.
5. If the enemy comes out to offer you battle, examine the position they have taken. If it is so advantageous that you would not want to fight them, avoid attacking them and maneuver to get them to fight in another place, perhaps by marching toward Béjar by one of their flanks, or simulating a retreat for one or two leagues. If this does not work and you must fight them in that position, use the artillery first, especially trench mortars. Then make a slight skirmish to delay them so the General Cos can attack them from the rear.

6. If the enemy presents for battle in the open, try not to lose a moment in the formation of the lines so that the fire and movements are anticipated by your men. Use the artillery first. The cavalry will be in two columns and will attract the attention of the enemy on the flanks or in the rear. They will take advantage of any carelessness or weakness to do battle as the result will be certain if the enemy cavalry faces ours. Upon noticing the slightest disorder or indecision in the enemy's ranks, rapidly order a bayonet charge. Leave two forces of reserves, one to support the artillery and the other to support the infantry charge with bayonets. Once that action has begun, all vacillation is dangerous. "Victory is obtained by the one who, with more order, swiftness, and valor, knows how to attack or resist his opponent, without once losing hope of victory."[44]
7. If the enemy entrenches itself in the Missions of Espada and Concepción, the first division will not attack. Do not take the main road and go by the missions, take a short detour to Béjar to be able to carry out the order of attack with a greater effect. If the enemy sees that it is facing an attack at the fortified places of Laredo [It is obvious Santa Anna meant to say Mission Espada here] and Concepción, and it dares to attack, information to this effect will be sent to General Cos and battle shall be offered in the manner already stated in article 6. The locality or some other reason might make changes in these movements necessary. The least disorder must always be avoided, even that which is sometimes produced by the enthusiasm of the soldier.
8. If the enemy were to remain in one of the missions named, or in some other place that they might have fortified, try, before attacking, to examine it well until there is no more doubt about its condition. Nothing will be undertaken if there is no certainty of a successful outcome, which is a decisive defeat. Any upset will be irreparable in those lands so distant from aid. For the same reason, nothing should be left to fortune.
9. The foreigners who are making war against the Mexican nation, violating all laws, are not deserving of any consideration, and for that reason no quarter will be given them. This order will be made known to the troops at an opportune time. They have, with audacity, declared a war of extermination of the Mexicans, and they should be treated in the same way.`

Not being able to foresee all the situations in which the General of the first division might find himself, it is up to his valor and skill to prepare for them, charging him above all not to undertake any action whatsoever, without being certain of a successful ending. However, if the enemy, due to carelessness or cowardice, presents an opportunity, he should take advantage of it.[45]

This lengthy set of orders reinforces some of the previously discussed tendencies and thoughts of Santa Anna. The fact that the orders are so thorough and repeatedly caution Ramírez y Sesma to take no action unless he is sure of victory reinforces the conclusion that Santa Anna did not trust in Ramírez y Sesma's ability as a commander. It also makes one believe that Santa Anna was, once again, hopeful that no action would be taken until he arrived on the scene and, as a result, he would be the one who would get to ride at the head of the triumphal parade that marched into Mexico City.

Of great interest is the information included in article 9. Secretary of War Tornel issued a decree on December 30 stating that all foreigners caught under arms on Mexican soil would be considered pirates and would be dealt with according (i.e., executed). It is interesting that this decree was issued several weeks after Santa Anna had notified Ramírez y Sesma to execute any prisoners. It is also of interest that Santa Anna claimed that the Texans were waging a war of extermination against the Mexican people when they had released all the Mexican prisoners up to this point and did so again after the surrender of Cos at Béjar, six days after Santa Anna wrote the orders to Ramírez y Sesma. It is important to note that it is likely that the Texans were not aware of the decree until it was published in the *Telegraph and Texas Register* on March 9 and 12, 1836. This was after the fall of the Alamo and just before the capture of Fannin and his men at Coleto Creek. Despite his stated strong objections to executing prisoners, Urrea, under orders from Santa Anna, did execute some of the Texan prisoners captured at Refugio and Agua Dulce as he marched toward Goliad. Thus, it is possible that word had reached the Texans earlier that "no quarter" was to be the standard for the Mexican army.

Emotions were riding high at this point among the Mexican people and the Mexican army. The Texans' actions had brought the country together in a common bond, even among the Centralists and Federalists. Many examples of documents from Mexican officers to their troops exist in the archives. One such example was written by Gen. Luis Quintanar, military commander of Oaxaca, on November 13 (see appendix 14 for the original):

> Luis Quintanar, Division General and Commanding General of the Department of Oaxaca, to his subordinates.
>
> Soldiers: A miserable portion of adventurers and hypocrite settlers in Texas have dared to set foot hostilely in some of the towns of that

territory. In these [towns] the magnanimous Mexican nation with liberal hands gave hospitality to those same monsters who today attempt to subjugate it and usurp one of the richest parts of its richest ground.

Is it the case that those ingrates have forgotten it was the Mexican soldiers who knew to destroy the Spanish armies and make them bite the dust? They [Mexican soldiers] are as numerous and disciplined as in 1821, when we achieved our independence and unquestionable rights. In these [their independence and rights] have we appreciated life when dealing with these valuable objects? Those miserable people! What a short reign they are hoping for! To pulverize them we know to abandon everything, leaving the Supreme Government to surely turn them in front of its fearful bayonets. We will jump their weak barriers, in the manner that in Tampico, predicted by the Immortal Santa Anna, our valiant troops did it against a more war-like enemy.

Soldiers of the Homeland: I feel the fire of indignation running in the blood of your veins, much more so if we do not occupy the first file in combat.

Companions in arms: the 9th of this month, wielding these, we have solemnly sworn to sustain the constitutional bases sanctioned by the general congress. Let us also swear, before the creator of the universe, to die in defense of the Supreme Government, sustaining our sacred rights.

Since I have the satisfaction of sending you, I have seen you march on the path of honor. You had been inflexible in order to conserve the order; moderate and generous between both parties: far from you has been personal vengeance, as owned by vile and precarious souls. This conduct has gained you universal estimation and mine particularly. Follow as up to here: forget times and resentments: Let us all for the fraternal column in which the machinations of the anarchists and outside enemies crash: that in the Department of Oaxaca there cannot be heard any other voices but the following: long live independence! Long live the union! Long live the Supreme Government! This will be our motto and the banner with which your old friend and comrade will be gladly sacrificed.

Oaxaca Nov. 13, 1835
Luis Quintanar[46]

There were also many documents from the commanders of various units volunteering their units for action in Texas. One such document was sent by Isidro Reyes from Morelia:

> **Most Excellent Sir**
>
> Attached to Your Excellency are the records of the garrison of this department, in which it is requested that the Supreme Government does not deprive it [the garrison] of the glory of marching to Texas with the purpose of vindicating the national honor, castigating the perfidious [residents] who have dared to make an attempt against the integrity of the territory of the republic. For my part I beg Your Excellency to interpose your high respects so that it is deferred to such a noble desire.
>
> I protest to Your Excellency my singular appreciation and respect.
>
> ***God and Liberty Morelia Nov. 6, 1835***
> ***Isidro Reyes[rubric][To] Most Excellent Minister of War and Navy***[47]

This document is interesting in light of the fact that Tornel accepted their request and ordered four companies of the Morelia battalion to proceed to join the army. Apparently, problems arose, and despite their plea to participate they never did join the army of operations against Texas.

In December Santa Anna was still organizing his army. He sent orders on December 8 to Gen. José Cosme Urrea to march from the department of Durango with 250 well-mounted dragoons. Each dragoon was to have a reserve mount to make sure the unit could move rapidly. Initially he ordered Urrea to Laredo, where he was to await further orders. Interestingly, Santa Anna also instructed him not to copy any more of his orders from the army of operations to the government. This suggests that Santa Anna was not anxious for the supreme government to know what he was doing.

CHAPTER FIVE

Arming the Army

On October 29, 1835, Secretary of War Tornel sent a dispatch to the director of artillery, José Antonio Moro, directing him to prepare the following items to be ready to march when ordered: two hundred cases of musket cartridges with ball and one hundred cases of artillery cartridges for 4-, 6-, and 8-pounder cannons and 6½-inch howitzers (twenty-five for each caliber).[1] In later dispatches, Moro made it clear that these armaments were to be manufactured in Mexico City.

Moro's response reflected the ongoing lack of resources to properly support the army. He wrote Tornel on November 3 that the commander of the artillery had notified him of the following:[2]

> In accordance with the superior orders that Your Excellency served to write to me in statement No. 608, we are diligently working with all possible rapidity in all the workshops in this arsenal of the foundry section of munitions. After I gave them my provisions to boost their work for more than two months, the chief smelter declares that work is complicated by the scarcity of molders. Yet I believe these inconveniences can be cut short with Your Excellency's support.
>
> To complete the goals of the service I think that it is indispensable that Your Excellency have the condescension to solicit from the high Government the purchase for the commissary of 1,000 qq [*quintales;* about 110 tons] of lead for musket balls and one hundred packages of buntine [*lanilla,* a thick woolen material] for cannon cartridges. The gunpowder factories should provide 1,000 qq of powder to those workshops for muskets, in order to meet the continuous orders of the corps and foreign places.[3] Bronze and copper that is unusable for coinage should be requested from the mint to place in those workshops, which make me understand

> extra-judicially, that this aid will greatly advance the casting of plain balls for 4-pounder cannons, of which there is a great shortage. This will also help with [the need] for canister for the same caliber as well as for 8-pounders and 6½-inch howitzers. I have the honor of informing Your Excellency of this for your subsequent orders.[4]

By December 6, the request for the one hundred bundles of cloth for cannon cartridges and the one thousand *quintales* of lead for musket balls had still not been filled. Moro reported that the army was short of musket cartridges as a result of this lack of materials.[5] On December 15 Moro reported to Tornel that he had gotten the bronze from the mint but still needed the copper for constructing solid and hollow projectiles. On January 20, 1836, one hundred cases of cloth finally arrived at the foundry.

Soon after, the workshops informed Moro that there were one hundred cases of musket cartridges ready to transport. These cartridges would have been paper cartridges for a .75-caliber English Brown Bess musket. They would contain a lead (or on a rare occasion, copper) ball of seventeen or nineteen *adarmes* (about one ounce; one *adarme* is equivalent to one-sixteenth of an ounce) and a measure of gunpowder in a paper wrapper. The smaller ball (seventeen *adarmes*) could be loaded more quickly, as it was easy to ram down the barrel. However, it was looser in the barrel and thus less accurate. It was noted that each case contained 1,200 cartridges. Several documents and inventories make it clear that the paper cartridges were often tied into bundles of about ten cartridges, called a "reload" (*parada*).[6]

The artillery commander in Mexico City also notified Moro that he had twenty cases of cartridges for a 4-pounder. There were twenty projectiles per case. Ten of the cases were canister projectiles and ten were solid cannon balls of copper or iron. The canister projectiles were cans or cloth bags filled with lead or copper balls. Based on the artifacts found by the Houston Archeological Society in the Sea of Mud, the Mexican canister came in two sizes, light and heavy. The light shot measured 0.8–1.1 inches in diameter and weighed on average 2.2–2.3 ounces. The heavy canister shot was found to be 1.2–1.4 inches in diameter, with an average weight of just over 5 ounces.[7] Canister projectiles for a French 4-pounder in the Napoleonic era would have contained about sixty light canister shot or twenty-eight heavy shot.[8] The canister cans or sacks and the solid balls would be attached to a charge of gunpowder so it could be loaded in the tube in one piece.

Fragments of intact cans of cannister (*botes de metralla*) excavated by the Houston Archeological Society in the Sea of Mud.

The artillery commander wrote that he had one hundred grenades and fifty cans of canister for the 6½-inch howitzers. The grenades are technically not cannon balls but shells. The Mexican grenades were mostly made of copper or bronze and were about 6¼ inches in diameter. These shells, weighing from twenty-four to twenty-eight pounds, were hollow and packed with gunpowder. Each grenade had a fuse hole with a lead plug in the hole when they were being transported. When the grenade was to be fired, the lead plug would be removed and a wooden fuse placed in the fuse hole. The wooden fuse was hollow and packed with a special mixture of gunpowder and alcohol. The artilleryman would cut the fuse to the length that was needed for the shell to explode at the desired distance. When the shell was fired from the tube of the howitzer it would ignite the fuse.

The Mexican army used four howitzers in the Texas campaign. They were shorter than a traditional cannon and used less gunpowder for each shot. Due to their short length, they were able to fire shells at a higher trajectory and were good for bombarding fortresses. The Spanish term for howitzer was *obus*. On occasion this has been translated as a mortar, but a mortar fires at a higher and fixed trajectory, while a howitzer's trajectory can

A bronze howitzer shell, six and one-half inches (seven *pulgado*) in diameter, with unknown marking and fuse hole, excavated in the Sea of Mud.

be adjusted. Two howitzers that were captured in the Mexican-American war (one at Matamoros) are on display at West Point. There is an excellent chance that these two howitzers were two of the four that were used in Texas by the Mexican army.

One other issue that the artillery commander mentioned was the problem of transporting the artillery park. He estimated that ninety-four animals would be needed and noted that requests for these had been sent. He did not designate whether he had requested mules, oxen, or horses.

Arms and equipment were being collected from all parts of the country. On November 5, Tornel ordered the director of artillery to make ready two 4-pounders, two 6-pounders, two 8-pounders, and two 6½-inch howitzers in Mexico City.

On October 5, Cos wrote Tornel that the ammunition and artillery that had been conducted from Veracruz on the national brig *Veracruzano* was already in Béjar. On November 5 Cos notified Tornel that the brig *Veracruzano* had landed at Cópano and a load of supplies and ammunition had been unloaded. Whether this was a second load of goods or whether it had only just gotten through to Béjar through the Texans who were laying siege to the town is unknown.

On November 8, Manuel María Muños, the interim commissioner of artillery for the state of Veracruz, made an inventory of the arms, munitions, and other effects from that department that were entrusted to 1st Lt. Blas Godines of the navy for transport to Texas. This was an extensive list and included artillery firing devices, English muskets with bayonets, cavalry carbines, sabers, backpacks, musket cartridges, gun flints, and cartridges for 4-pounders (both solid balls and canister). The cartridges for the 4-pounder cannon were said to have one pound and five ounces of gunpowder per cartridge (see appendix 15).[9]

On October 26, Santa Anna ordered Ramírez y Sesma to march from Zacatecas with two 4-pounders, two 6-pounders, two 8-pounders, and two howitzers. On November 8 Ramírez y Sesma responded to Tornel, giving a list of the cannons, munitions, and equipment that he was taking with him as he marched for San Luís. He cautioned Tornel that there were only two 4-pounders and two 6-pounders in Zacatecas. He requested that two howitzers be assigned to him because of the utility of elevated rounds in certain cases. He reported that there were no 8-pounders in Zacatecas and notified Tornel that he only had two artillery crews for the four cannons that were to march (see appendix 16 for the inventory of the equipment that was transported by Ramírez y Sesma's division).[10]

In response to the news from Ramírez y Sesma, Tornel sent orders for two 8-pounders and two 6½-inch howitzers to be made ready at San Luís. He also instructed them to have two artillery crews organized for the two 4-pounders that were coming from Zacatecas without crews. The next day, Moro answered that he was able to prepare the two 8-pounders and two 6½-inch howitzers but that there were no artillery crews in Mexico City.

On November 19, Moro reported to Tornel that the artillery and corresponding supplies from Mexico City were nearly ready for the march to San Luís and on to Texas:

> Today [I have] given the corresponding order to the commanding general of this department that the twelve pieces of artillery that are named in the above dispatch of today, be made ready to march;[11] as well as 1,594 serviceable muskets [from] those that are in the warehouses, 1,000 swords and sabers, and 50,000 gunflints. Not so the 1,000 carbines, as there are no more than thirty-one in the general armory, nor the five hundred cases of musket cartridges. Of those, three hundred cases can be ready by Saturday of this week. Their construction will continue until the completion of the indicated number.
>
> In addition, I have commanded that three loose carriages for different calibers, loose wheels for others, two carts of munitions, and two [cannon] covers be prepared to march. This is all for the purpose of having the artillery division, which should be assembled at San Luís, better equipped. Also, be aware that eight workers of different professions are marching.
>
> I report all of this in response to Your Excellency's cited note for the knowledge of His Excellency the Interim President.
>
> ***God and Liberty Mexico Nov. 19, 1835***
> ***José Ant. Moro***[12]

On November 20 Moro documented that two 8-pounders and two 6½-inch howitzers would be leaving Mexico City for San Luís. It is unclear if these four artillery pieces were a part of the twelve pieces mentioned in the letter above. On November 21 two 6½-inch howitzers left San Luís to join Ramírez y Sesma's division.

That same day, five pieces of artillery were ordered to be taken from Jalisco to San Luís under the command of Subaltern (*Alférez*) Ygnacio Segura. In a letter dated December 1, the director of artillery in that city stated that "every soldier will carry his shako [*morrion*] with cover [*funda*] and canteen [*cantinploma*] for water: that the cannons are being painted and the ammunition park is such that each [cannon] has two hundred rounds of balls and canister." The director concluded by saying that said cannons comprised two 8-pounders, two 4-pounders, and a 6½-inch howitzer that he had commanded to be ready. However, just after these artillery pieces had marched, Santa Anna decided that these pieces were needed in the state of Guanajuato and they countermarched back to Jalisco.

Regarding the twelve pieces of artillery that were to be sent to Texas from Mexico City, there were problems, as usual. Moro wrote three dispatches to Tornel about these twelve pieces on November 24. The first concerned salaries. He noted that the artillery officers had not been paid since June and the troops had also not received pay. He felt that if both groups were given backpay for three months of salary they would be able to pay their debts and would be willing to march.

The second letter that he wrote that day concerned the need for 425 mules to pull the pieces and carry the equipment. He did promise that if fewer than that proved to be sufficient, he would return the rest so that only those needed would be paid for.

The third note stated that only half of the detachment of gunners who were coming from Puebla and Oaxaca had arrived. The remaining twenty-nine gunners did arrive in Mexico City on November 30 and were sent to catch up with the artillery.

On December 24 Tornel informed Moro that the interim president had ordered one hundred English Congreve rockets (*Cohetes á la Congrev*) to be sent to the army of operations. Moro responded that, prior to sending the rockets as directed, he had had them tested to see if they were still functional. The report of a committee of officers who tested the rockets follows:

> Congreve rockets, which have been used for a while by the English, particularly to attack fortified points, have been given major importance. However, in the opinion of the classic authors, they have more effect in the imagination than on the objects that they have been used against. It could be that the authors are partial due to their nations being anti-English, as those that we know of are from Bologna, Copenhagen, Huningue, and Algiers, in the course of the war of Spain. However, more particularly, they [the rockets] were employed with success in the Battle of Leipzig where the genius of war [Napoleon] was defeated. But it has always been necessary to use this projectile in large numbers by entire squadrons of English.
>
> These rockets came to the Republic about nine years ago and the General Director [of artillery] feels that they might have suffered some

deterioration during their transport and storage in different climates that influence their quality. He arranged with the General-in-Chief of the [artillery] school, and assisted by other individuals involved, to make some simple experiments to determine their real condition, verifying it on the afternoon of the 28th. In accordance with the Commanding General, three rockets and everything necessary to fire them were taken to the shelter at San Lazaro as circumstances required to achieve this operation. The results were that the first rocket, as it exited the tube in which it was placed, left its trajectory because of the elevation that it was given. While in the air the fire burned with such a fast velocity that it finished its course at a distance of twenty *varas* [56 ft]. The same happened with the second [rocket]. The third advanced up to fifty *varas* [140 ft] but none of the three grenades, which were in their heads, exploded. One had its tail broken off and the tubes of all three were destroyed.

By what is reported we deduce that, in the present condition in which the other rockets are found, not only are they useless, but more dangerous to use for the men who fire them than the enemies who are targeted. Noting that all their parts have been deteriorated by time and the atmosphere, [and] that the fuses of the grenades have surely deteriorated, it is indispensable to declare the other rockets to be in a state of complete uselessness.

Also, those who request them do not have experience in the use of such projectiles that are employed in considerable numbers in the attack and defense of posts, nor in the pitched actions mentioned that have occurred in the events where the English have had great success. This is principally attributed to the great number of rockets directed at the objectives. At Copenhagen they fired more than forty thousand shots in less than 24 hours and in the same proportions in other cases.

Due to these results and particular reasons reserved to the Supreme Government, and not for us to investigate, the exercise could be of use for this means of attack against the enemy. It would be indispensable that other rockets be constructed according to the concepts of individuals who have the honor of belonging to the Mexican artillery. There is sufficient knowledge to effectively construct perfect rockets, if the Supreme Government determines so and provides the means and money necessary, which we cannot work without. If it is decided to do this project it needs to be done on a grand scale, as one hundred or two hundred rockets would not have the activity or potential to cause the desired effect. Considering all the opinions that have been written and the rest of the particulars that exist in this case, it should be necessary to order at least three thousand of

> the expressed rockets of different calibers. This is the minimum to which they would reduce it for now, in their judgment. The cost would be approximately 75,000 pesos, plus the time necessary to make them. . . .
>
> **Mexico Dec. 30, 1835**
> **The Interim Committee José Maria Contreras José Manuel González José Maria Arrieta Pedro Valdez**[13]

That same day Tornel responded to Moro that the interim president was now aware that the Congreve rockets held in the general armory were useless. He did not specify whether to cancel the order to send them to the army but based on this information and the fact that there was no further mention of them, it seems likely they were not sent.

Most of the army did not march until the new year, so the composition of the different divisions, brigades, etc. will be discussed in volume 2 of this work. It does, however, seem appropriate to document the artillery that marched with the army at this point.

In his memoirs, Filisola wrote that the 1st division, under General Ramírez y Sesma, had eight pieces of artillery, comprising two 8-pounders, two 6-pounders, two 4-pounders and two 6½-inch howitzers. These were likely the two 4-pounders and two 6-pounders that Ramírez y Sesma brought with him from Zacatecas, along with the two 8-pounders and two 6½-inch howitzers from San Luís. Filisola also documented that sixty-two artillerymen, under the command of Capt. Mariano Silva, accompanied the division.

The 1st brigade of the 2nd division, under the command of brevet Brig. Gen. Antonio Gaona, brought two 12-pounders, two 6-pounders, and two 4-pounders into Texas. It is likely but not documented that these were six of the twelve artillery pieces that were sent from Mexico City to San Luís. In this brigade there were sixty artillerymen under the command of Capt. Agustín Terán.

The 2nd brigade of the 2nd division, under the command of brevet Brig. Gen. Eugenio Tolsa, had two 8-pounders, two 4-pounders and two 6½-inch howitzers. It had sixty artillerymen under the command of Lt. José Miramón. These were likely the other six pieces sent from Mexico City.[14]

The total number of artillery pieces brought into Texas by the army of operations was twenty-one: two 12-pounders, four 8-pounders, four

6-pounders, seven 4-pounders, and four 6½-inch howitzers (this total includes one 4-pounder that was brought by the section under Urrea, which will be discussed in volume 2 of this work). The army also brought six extra gun carriages.

Overall, the Mexican army had a huge advantage when it came to artillery. They not only had more cannons, but they also had howitzers. It was also an advantage that they had exploding shells and canister shot. They also had more officers who were trained in the use of artillery. One of the problems with the Mexican artillery, however, is that they had not developed tactics for the use of artillery as a separate force commanded by artillery officers. They were divided up and attached to various brigades and divisions and were under the orders of the commander of that corp. They also had not developed the strategy of mobile artillery, so their pieces were generally in fixed positions. At the battle of Palo Alto, in the Mexican-American War, the Americans and their flying artillery were so effective that the Mexican infantry and cavalry were unable to make serious advances without facing withering artillery fire.

As far as arms, the Mexican army was well supplied for the type of warfare for which they were trained. The training they received was for the Napoleonic style of open-field battles with both armies facing each other. In this style of fighting, the idea was to lay down a field of fire against the opposing ranks of the enemy, so accuracy was not important. More important than accuracy for this style was rapidity of fire. To reload and fire an East India–pattern Brown Bess musket took eighteen steps, and a soldier was expected to be able to fire three times per minute. The fact that, for the most part, the Mexican army used the smaller, 17-*adarme* musket balls did speed up the rate of fire. It is well documented that many of the soldiers in the Mexican army, especially the raw recruits and men of the active units, did not have much training in loading and reloading the muskets (some of the Mexican inventories mention cartridges without balls, however, so apparently there was some training).

One further disadvantage was the quality of their gunpowder. The Mexican soldiers were said to have used double loads of powder, which caused severe recoil. For this reason, the soldiers would sometimes fire from the hip. When considering the lack of training and the poor quality of the powder, it is understandable why the most feared part of a Mexican musket was said to be the bayonet.

There have been many reports of the Mexican army having English Baker rifles that were used by the *cazadores* (light infantry). There are rare inventories in the Mexican archives that mention rifles (*rifles*), but I have not found any that reference Baker rifles. The number of rifles on the inventory lists was generally quite low, so it seems that the use of rifles by the Mexican army was not common.

CHAPTER SIX

Maritime Affairs

At the time of the outbreak of the Texas Revolution, the Mexican navy was almost nonexistent. They did have a few warships, but even those were in poor condition. They had no transport ships and had to pay to use foreign ships to move troops and supplies. An example of this occurred on April 27, 1835, when the commander of the Internal States of the East, Gen. Martín Perfecto de Cos, received a dispatch from the captain of the port of Matamoros. He informed the general that the American schooner *Leonida* had arrived from Tampico at that port with fifty soldiers under the command of Capt. Francisco Camácho. These troops were meant to garrison the town of Matamoros. It is telling that neither the Mexican navy nor the Mexican commercial shipping industry could transport such a small force over a short distance.

INGHAM VERSUS *MOCTEZUMA*

One maritime incident occurred off the coast of Texas when the Mexican warship *Moctezuma* captured two merchant vessels that did not have the proper papers.[1] One of these two ships was the American packet schooner *Martha*. Juan Calvi wrote to Antonio Tenorio, military commander at Anáhuac, on May 7, 1835, that the *Martha* had no papers and its passengers had no credentials.[2] Some of its passengers were arrested since they had taken up arms against the troops who were sent to check its cargo.

The second captured vessel was the American brigantine *Columbia*. It was taken off the coast near Velasco for the same reasons as the *Martha*. Filisola noted that these two seizures, even though they were completely justified and legitimate, aroused the locals at Anáhuac and caused them to take action against the Mexican soldiers there.

Antonio Tenorio wrote to Ugartechea on June 25 that "they [the colonists from San Felipe], by reason of the capture of the sloop, *Columbia*, are very much excited, and I have been informed that they are arming a sloop for the purpose of fighting the *Moctezuma*."[3]

The *Moctezuma* arrived at the port of Matamoros from Galveston on May 21, with two Mexican customs officials escorting several American citizens locked in its hold. Cos documented that he would organize a summary judgement to investigate the matter.[4]

There is a long document in the Archivo Histórico Militar that is a transcription of an article from the *New Orleans Commercial Bulletin*.[5] The article is a copy of a letter written to the editor of the paper in June and published on June 15. The author of the letter is not named, but it seems to have been an American, probably living in Matamoros. The author stated that it was probable that there were various exaggerated reports about the attack between the United States cutter *Ingham* and the Mexican ship of war *Moctezuma*.[6] He claimed to have been an eyewitness to the conflict between the two ships.

The witness stated that the *Ingham*, an American ship under the command of Capt. Ezekiel Jones, had been cruising along the Mexican coast to suppress the slave trade. While this ship was anchored near the mouth of the Brazos, Jones was visited by some locals who reported the capture of the *Martha* and the arrest of some American citizens. These reports were verified at Matagorda by John Bartlett, who had been on board the *Martha* when it was captured. Jones decided to sail to Matamoros to find the *Moctezuma* and free the Americans.

The *Ingham* was spotted on June 14 about five miles from the *Moctezuma*, which was anchored outside of the bar at Brazos de Santiago.[7] At first sight of the *Ingham*, the Mexican ship raised anchor, headed directly toward the American cutter, and opened fire on it. The *Ingham* then raised its colors and discharged a few rounds at the Mexicans. In response the *Moctezuma* started running at full speed, fleeing its antagonist. The author noted that by this time the sand dunes in front of the port were covered with American citizens "whose hearts felt at this time the greatest of satisfaction."

For the next six hours, the two ships tried to maneuver, and the Mexican ship took courage and twice tacked around the *Ingham*, which immediately pressed the attack. As soon as the *Moctezuma* perceived these attempts by the Americans, it would take sail and escape. The commander of the port did reinforce the *Moctezuma* with thirty men, and they were instructed not to disgrace the national colors.[8] The author and the Americans with him expected an action, but surprisingly the *Moctezuma,* against an insignificant enemy, grounded itself on the reefs.

The *Ingham* then sent a boat ashore with two lieutenants, Harby (*sic*) and Moore. They found the captain of the *Moctezuma* and gave him a letter from Jones requesting the release of the American citizens. The two officers then went to the home of Gen. John J. Mason, an American citizen. They had not been there long when they were warned by Captain Boylen of the American brig *Pheros* that a body of soldiers and armed rabble, under the command of the captain of the *Moctezuma,* were headed to the *Ingham* to take the ship and crew. The lieutenants of the *Ingham* ran back to their boat, swords in hand, and warned the crew to arm themselves. One of the crew, William Peterson, took the American flag and jumped to the ground, exclaiming, "This is my protection." This movement caused the Mexican soldiers and the scoundrels to restrain themselves. Eventually the captain of the port intervened, and violence was avoided. Apparently, the American captives had already been freed the day before, and the author wrote that several American citizens there at the scene confirmed to him that this was the case.

The author reported that the *Moctezuma* was a much larger ship than the *Ingham* and had a superior battery. It had over fifty men aboard, while the smaller American ship had but twenty-four. The Mexicans were indignant that the captain of the *Moctezuma* fled after having fired on the *Ingham.* They reported him to the authorities, and the author believed he would be forced to leave the navy. He ended his statement with the following: "I conclude saying that Capt. Jones, his officers, and crew deserve the most cordial of thanks of all Americans residing in Mexico. The passengers that have been referenced are Mr. Thos. J. Early, Mr. Francis S. Early, sons of the Governor that was from Georgia, N. G. Thomas of Courtland Alabama, and Mr. Rufus Turnage of Memphis Tennessee."

SAN FELIPE VERSUS *CORREO DE MEXICO*

Another Mexican ship of war, *Correo de Mexico,* was sailing off the Texas coast in the summer of 1835.[9] It is interesting that its commander, Thomas M. Thompson, was British but had become an American citizen in New Orleans in the early 1830s. He seized the opportunity for a quick command and became a lieutenant in the Mexican navy in 1835. On July 25 Thompson's ship was stationed at Anáhuac in response to the attack on the Mexican garrison there. On that date he wrote Tenorio at San Felipe and requested that he return to his post at Anáhuac. He assured Tenorio that the people were friendly and that it was safe to return. On July 28 Tenorio responded and politely declined Thompson's invitation. As an excuse he reported to Thompson that he had orders to march to Béjar as soon as he was done at San Felipe.

Thompson issued a proclamation to the citizens of Anáhuac on July 26 that included the following:

> Having seen by advertisements posted in front of the principal stores in this city signed by Judges Williams and Hardinge under the pretense of having received orders from the Political Chief of these districts, and having in my possession a copy of a document purporting to be signed by H. S. Huey, dated Nacogdoches July 2, 1835, ordering the inhabitants of this place and its vicinity to meet and elect officers for the purpose of organizing a militia all of which are contrary to the law of the Government. Be it therefore known that I, T. M. Thompson commander of the Mexican United States schooner of war *Correo*, now at anchor in the port do warn all good citizens from attending such meetings and that none may plead ignorance hereafter do hereby publish and declare in the name of the Mexican Nation, all such meetings to be illegal, dangerous, unnecessary and contrary to the Constitution. The General Congress has passed a law which is now in force ordering every state to disband their Militia and I here find that in defiance of the Government you are organizing and arming yourselves and have forcibly seized upon the arms of the Mexican Nation. They tell you of dangers that do not exist—all Mexico is at peace and will continue to be so, if your own rashness does not lead you astray. Citizens of Anahuac [*sic*], Beware! Listen not to men who have no home, who have no family, who have nothing to lose in case of civil war and who by merely crossing the Sabine, can put themselves out of the power of the Mexican Nation, leav-ing yourselves, wives, and children a prey to the infuriated Soldier, without protection and without friends. Citizens of Anahuac [*sic*], remain at home occupy yourselves in your daily avocations for the maintenance of your family, have confidence in the General Government and all will yet be well. With due respect and confiding fully in your good judgement, I subscribe myself your esteemed friend and fellow citizen—
> on board.
>
> **God and Liberty July 26th, 1835**
> **Thomas M. Thompson**[10]

On September 18, a small sloop (*balandrita*) carrying two Americans and a Mexican sailor arrived at Brazos de Santiago. The first of the two was Edward Cooper (spelled "Couper" in some Mexican documents). In his deposition, taken by the captain of the port, Guillermo Wyse, he noted under oath that he was a native of the United Sates of the North and that he was a house butler by trade. He informed Wyse that the sloop belonged to the commander of the small schooner *Correo de Mexico,* Thomas M. Thompson. Cooper noted that the sloop left Galveston Bay with the *Correo* on August 31, but they were separated at the mouth of the Brazos River on September 1.

When they arrived at the Brazos, there was an American brig from Pensacola anchored there, loaded with wood. He and three other men were ordered to board the brig and move it near the *Correo.* Before they could do so, a steamboat, the *Laura,* came out of the river. Fearing that an armed force could be on the steamboat, they abandoned their task of moving the brig and returned to the *Correo* with the steamboat pursuing them and firing upon them. Thompson answered with his cannons, and while setting sail they noticed another ship to the leeward. The steamboat headed to the new arrival and gave it tow.

About 2:00 p.m., the new ship, the schooner *San Felipe,* anchored near the brig. Thompson tried to approach the two ships, and as he did so the steamship started to receive cargo from the *San Felipe.*[11] At sunset, the brig moved closer to land and anchored. During the evening prayer, the steamboat entered the river.

Thompson then ordered Cooper, three sailors, a corporal, and four soldiers to take the sloop and take possession of the brig. As they were starting to sail to the brig, the *San Felipe* began to sail toward the *Correo,* and the men in the sloop returned to advise Thompson of this development. As the *San Felipe* neared the *Correo,* Thompson directed his fire at it, making various tacks, to which the *San Felipe* answered with musketry and cannonade. Cooper and the men on his sloop also fired on the *San Felipe* with their muskets. The firing lasted about twenty minutes, and during that time the sloop was separated from the *Correo* and made for shore.

From the protected, shallow water, they started sailing down the coast toward Matamoros. Three days later they encountered the Mexican brig *Veracruzano,* which had lost two anchors, in front of the bar at Aransas. They boarded the ship for about a day, and then Cooper, his companion William Morrison, and a third sailor from the *Correo,* named Benjamin, boarded the sloop and guided the *Veracruzano* to Matagorda. At that place Benjamin deserted them. After one day in port, they set sail and arrived at Brazos de Santiago on September 8.

Cooper stated that he knew the schooner was the *San Felipe* because he had lived at the bar of Brazoria for about six months and was familiar with it. He also declared that the last time he saw the *San Felipe* it was not armed but that he had heard its owner, Mr. McKinney, say that he was going to arm it in New Orleans because one of his ships had already been seized by the *Moctezuma*.

He stated that he had come on board the *Correo* as a passenger and that Thompson had offered him passage from Galveston to Brazoria, where he was headed. Cooper also informed Wyse that, even though he was a house butler, he did have experience as a sailor in the past. He reported that various persons on land had reported to him that Thompson had purchased the small sloop at Anáhuac from a Mr. Truman. Cooper was unaware of the fate of the *Correo*, but he thought that it was firing as long as he could see it. He stated that he was twenty-nine years old and what he said was the truth, as sworn by the oath that he made.[12]

William Morrison also gave his deposition to Wyse. He reported that he was from the United States of the North and that he was a sailor. His deposition was very similar to that of Cooper, but he did give a few additional details. He noted that Thompson had the captain of the brig from Pensacola come to the *Correo* with the ship's papers. He also called the *San Felipe* a fore-top-sail schooner (*goleta de velacho*).

Morrison mentioned that the rest of the men who were on the sloop were brought aboard the *Veracruzano* after Benjamin deserted. He reported that they had lived on water and pumpkins until they got supplies from the *Veracruzano*. He testified that he knew the man in Anáhuac who had sold Thompson the sloop, as he himself lived in Anáhuac. Morrison added that Thompson had promised to help get him a position in the navy for helping to get the sloop to Matamoros.

When asked about the arms of the *San Felipe* he replied that they were composed of many muskets and two cannons on the side. By the roar of one of them he believed it to be a caliber of six, while the other was smaller. He was asked about the sails that the *Correo* and the *San Felipe* were using when they were firing at each other. He reported that both had their main sails and jibs, nothing more. He noted that his age was thirty-six, and he signed his deposition.

A third deposition was taken from the Mexican sailor who remained on the small sloop with Cooper and Morrison. His name was Felipe Antonio Himenez (*sic*) and he testified that he was a sailor and a native of Campeche. He boarded the *Correo* as an escort for the 4th battalion on its way to Cópano, and his rank was boatswain.[13] After the troops disembarked at Cópano, the *Correo* sailed to Galveston to take Lieutenant Ocampo there, but he could not find his troops. After leaving there [Galveston], Himenez noted that they were fourteen days with no power to sail, so they turned to go to Galveston.

Himenez agreed that the captain of the brig at Brazoria came aboard the *Correo* and added that the papers he presented lacked the manifests, so Thompson decided to take the brig as a prize. He added that as the *Correo* left Galveston they had one barrel of medium salted meat from the north and a half barrel of pork, also from the north, and that they lacked crackers. The rest of his lengthy deposition was, for the most part, in agreement with the depositions of Cooper and Morrison. He gave his age as twenty-three, and, not knowing how to sign, he made a cross.[14]

The Mexican consul of New Orleans, Francisco Pizarro Martínez, notified the US attorney for the district of Louisiana, Henry Carleton, on September 16 that he had just been informed of the *Correo de Mexico* being brought into the port of New Orleans by the captain of the American schooner *San Felipe*. The crew and captain of the captured vessel were confined as prisoners. He filed a complaint with Carlton regarding the outrage committed against the Mexican flag by a citizen of the United States and demanded the immediate release of the ship, captain, and crew.

Pizarro Martínez pointed out that Thompson was "duly commissioned by the Mexican government, and was engaged in the exercise of the public function that had been confided to him, when the *San Felipe*, aided by the insurgents of Texas, seized upon him and his vessel, in the waters of the republic, without commission or authority to that effect." He noted that no evidence or statements had been given that there was just cause against Captain Thompson and that the actions of the captain of the *San Felipe* were flagrant violations of the laws of nations."[15]

In response to Pizarro Martínez, Carleton reported that an affidavit had been made by Captain Hurd of the *San Felipe* before Mr. Justice Preval. He testified that on or about September 1, 1835, Thompson, by open force, violently and unlawfully attacked and set upon the *San Felipe*, with the intent to plunder or despoil the owners thereof of their property. He wrote that if the facts were substantiated, he would have to bring the case before the US court in New Orleans.[16]

Pizarro Martínez reported that the *Correo* and 2nd Lt. Thomas Thompson of the navy arrived in New Orleans on October 15. The ship was escorted by Capt. William C. Hurd of the American mercantile schooner *San Felipe*, which captured them near the mouth of the Brazos. He also wrote, "I am mortified to see that the Schooner *San Felipe* has augmented its armaments, and is being prepared to return shortly to Texas to vomit elements of destruction equal to those that it conducted in its last voyage to Brazoria, without my being able to impede it."[17]

Thompson wrote a report of the encounter between his ship and the *San Felipe* from a jail cell in New Orleans.[18] He reported that he had left Matamoros as the commander of the *Correo,* escorting the ships *Josepha* and *Ana Maria,* which were transporting the Morelos battalion to Cópano in Aransas Bay.

After that task was completed, he sailed for Anáhuac, carrying the lieutenant of *cazadores* of the Jiménez battalion, Carlos Ocampos, who was bringing supplies and two pickets of troops from the Jiménez and Abasolo battalions to reinforce the Anáhuac detachment. When they arrived there the detachment was not to be found since they had been disarmed by the rebels of Texas. As documented previously, he notified Tenorio by express courier of his arrival.

Thompson wrote that he waited for a month to hear from Tenorio, and while waiting he occupied himself mapping the coasts and bars of the rivers and particularly the general entrance of Galveston. By August 29 he had not heard anything from the messenger and feared that his courier had been intercepted by the rebels. He also needed supplies for his crew, so he set sail for Matamoros.

On September 1, at daybreak, they discovered the brig *Fremant* (*Tremont*), commanded by Silvestre and carrying wood as a cargo. They had unloaded ten thousand pesos (*sic*; likely ten thousand pesos' worth of wood) by steamboat, and the ship lacked a cargo manifest. Thompson placed eight of his men on the brig to take it to Veracruz. At that time, the steamboat came out with many men firing, along with cannons, and they were forced to abandon the brig to defend their ship.

After about fifteen minutes of exchanging fire with the steamboat, they noticed a sail to the northeast. This turned out to be the *San Felipe,* under the command of Hurd, with a double crew, muskets, powder, and munitions of all classes. It had thirty-some passengers and was armed in New Orleans for the purpose of forcing its way into Texas. Thompson believed that it was his sacred duty to block the entrance of the *San Felipe,* but because of the winds he was unable to prevent it. His details of the actions of that day are essentially the same as the depositions of the sailors, until about 8:00 p.m.

Thompson wrote that at 8:00 they exchanged fire with the other vessels for about an hour. At that time, his two cannons were dismounted by enemy fire, the majority of his people were wounded, and he had received two musket ball wounds in his legs. He therefore broke off the encounter and set sail for Matamoros.

There was little wind all night, and in the morning of the second day they saw the enemy pursuing them at full sail. By 9:00 a.m. the *San Felipe*, being towed by the steamship, was within half a cannon shot of them. He was about to be boarded, so after consulting with Ocampos he decided to capitulate. He sent Ocampos and two others to the *San Felipe* to talk to the captain. The captain informed him that his time for negotiations was already over and that in a few moments the ship would be scuttled and the men drowned. Ocampos was informed that from that moment he and the men with him were under arrest.

At the same time, the *San Felipe* sent a boat under a white flag, requesting in the name of Captain Hurd that Thompson not resist, because they were determined to conquer all types of Mexican ships. Thompson immediately gave command of the ship to the pilot of the Brazos, Captain Hawkins. The Texans then sent the crew to shore in the steamboat and Thompson, Ocampos, and four naval officers were sent to the *San Felipe*.

On day three they were anchored outside the bar at the Brazos River, and on day five they were transferred to the *Correo* and shackled without distinction before setting sail toward New Orleans. On the fifteenth day they arrived at New Orleans, where they were accused of being pirates and placed in the public jail.

Thompson wrote that the Mexican consul in that city was doing everything in his power to improve their situation and he [the consul] deserved the thanks of the government for the part that he had played for the national honor. He also stated that the *San Felipe* was now armed with four 12-pounder cannons and had a double crew.

Another deposition was taken from Lt. Carlos Ocampos at the port of New Orleans on September 21, after he was taken prisoner. He testified that he was aboard the *Correo* to deliver one thousand pesos to the detachment at Anáhuac, but by the time the ship arrived, the garrison had already been taken prisoner. Ocampos decided to return to Matamoros, but he stated that on the way the *Correo* encountered an American brig anchored near the bar at Velasco. It was hailed by Thompson by means of a speaking trumpet, and it was found to be operating clandestinely.

His description of the details of that day's encounter with the vessels operated by the Texans is essentially the same as the above witnesses. He did mention that the small sloop that accompanied them disappeared and that they did not know what happened to it. He also noted that the *San Felipe* was not able to maneuver to board them as it had lost a rudder.

Ocampos did add a few details about the surrender on the next day that Thompson did not mention. He reported that one of the other officers who came on board the *San Felipe* with Thompson was the engineer Edmond Hogan. He also reported that the Texans took everything they had, including the one thousand pesos that he was carrying, his luggage, his papers, and the sealed papers concerning his mission. The sealed papers, after examination, were returned to him later. After arriving at New Orleans, Thompson and part of his crew were taken to jail, but Ocampos was released and was told that he was free from blame.[19]

The clash between the two ships was, without a doubt, another issue that greatly irritated the Mexican officials. In response, General Cos wrote that "there is no doubt that if they remain unpunished, they will continue in a conduct so perverse as has been observed by those in that department. They would not have adopted this [behavior] if the crimes committed in the year of 1832 [the first Anáhuac incident] had been punished."

OTHER EVENTS

Another incident between the Americans, Texans, and Tejanos took place in November–December 1835. There is not a great deal of documentation in the Mexican archives, but some details can be found. On December 3, the captain of the port of Matamoros, Guillermo Wyse, sent the following document to Secretary of War Tornel:

> **Captaincy of the Port of Matamoros**
>
> **Most Excellent Sir**
>
> I have the honor of informing Your Excellency that [on] the morning of the 24th of this [last?] month the national schooner of war *General Brabo* [*Bravo*] returned from its cruise, due to lack of supplies and necessary things.[20] It has conducted fifteen prisoners, whose names I have included in a separate note. They were arrested on an American merchant ship that was loaded with cannons and pertinences of war.[21] This ship, to avoid being taken as a prize by the schooner of war, ran aground on the beaches of Texas. In this encounter we have lost, on our part, a naval cadet [*aspirante*] and eleven men who should be prisoners because they did not comply with the orders of the commander. The schooner

San Felipe, which came out to battle the schooner of war *General Brabo*, had been thrown by a strong storm onto the beach.

Today, after a thousand hindrances on these beaches, I have arranged that the schooner of war [*Brabo*] made sail in pursuit of Mr. Mejía (who left as a fugitive from Tampico on the 26th day of last month in the schooner *Halcyon*), by the order of the Commanding General of this state, Mariano Guerra.

God and Liberty Brazos de Santiago December 3, 1835
Guillermo A. Wyse

On a separate page, Wyse wrote the following list of prisoners.

Names of the individuals who were arrested by the national schooner of war *General Brabo*		
[Sailor]	José Ma. Carvajal	Mexican
[Sailor]	José Luis Carvajal	[Mexican]
[Sailor]	Fernando de Leon	[Mexican]
[Sailor]	Domingo Medrano	[Mexican]
Captain	John Chuisu	American
Sailor	J. C. Backeford	[American]
[Sailor]	William Reed	[American]
[Sailor]	Isaac F. Shulos	[American]
[Sailor]	Jimmerson Strother	[American]
[Sailor]	Thomas Pugh	[American]
[Sailor]	Elouzo March	[American]
[Sailor]	Eduard W. B. Scrugham	[American]
[Sailor]	William S. Brosom	[American]
[Sailor]	Carlos Laro	[American]
[Sailor]	Pedro Villarreal	Puerto Rican

Note: Pedro Villarreal had been the commander of the Second National Schooner of War *Moctezuma* in the year 1832. He had compromised the honor of the flag and was arrested by the American ship of war *Prampus* and conducted to New Orleans as a pirate, where he suffered two years as a prisoner.[22]

Another issue that was genuinely concerning to the Mexican government and military was the repeated rumors and reports of men, arms, munitions, cannons, etc. being shipped from the United States to Texas. Most were said to be coming from New Orleans, but there were also reports of ships coming from Baltimore, New York, and other major ports.

On August 29, the captain of the port of Campeche, Francisco G. P. Lopez, wrote to Tornel about such a report. He documented that on August 13 the captain of the national merchant schooner *Segunda Lancho*, Anastacio Careaño, reported that an eighty-ton schooner had left from New Orleans for Texas. It was said to have been laden with cannons, bullets, musketry, gunpowder, and other munitions of war. On October 3 Cos notified Tornel that this was the same ship that he had previously reported to Tornel and informed him that Samuel Williams had left San Felipe for that purpose (to meet the ship?). He warned that he could do nothing to stop these arms shipments for lack of ships to patrol the coast.

In October, a Mexican official in Philadelphia, J. M. de Castillo, wrote that a friend had received letters from Lorenzo de Zavala. De Zavala reported that the Texans had thrown down the gauntlet and were preparing to overthrow their cowardly Mexican countrymen if they dared to enter Texas, which the Texans felt was unlikely. He documented that they had six thousand riflemen who were well supplied with munitions and were animated like lions, but nevertheless they requested help urgently. They offered one thousand acres of land to any American adventurers who would come to their aid. De Zavala reported that the Texans had sent circulars to the states in the south and west to recruit adventurers. De Castillo's friend stated, "To be or not to be, let me say it again, let the devil take everything or send a force sufficient to fortify Galveston, the Brazos, and Nacogdoches, putting an end to those three smugglers' nests, and give a good lesson to those agitators." Obviously, de Zavala exaggerated the numbers of riflemen and weapons, but the Mexican government did not know what was fact or what was fiction.

The American secretary of state received notice from a Mexican official in New York, P. González, that a ship loaded with two hundred armed men had left New York on Saturday, November 25. He reported that it was to meet up with one or more similar ships and sail to New Orleans. He also wrote that another ship had left from New York to Cartagena, Columbia, and from there it would sail to Texas.

On December 13, Pizarro Martínez wrote the Mexican secretary of state from New Orleans and notified him that the brig *Durango* and the warship *Pennsylvania* had recently left for Texas with illicit commerce and about two hundred immigrants. It was also noted that when the two ships left port, without any documents from the consul, they were flying the American Flag. Pizarro Martínez also informed him that, recently, a steamboat in good condition, the *Yellow Stone*, had left for Texas.[23]

CHAPTER SEVEN

Gonzales and the Come-and-Take-It Cannon

In January 1831, Green DeWitt, the empresario of the DeWitt colony, notified Ramón Múzquiz, the political chief of Béjar, that the Tahuacano Indians were gathering in two separate groups on the Navidad and La Vaca Rivers. He hoped that the military commander of Béjar would address this issue. Seemingly as an afterthought he added that he requested that the military commander provide a cannon for the protection of the village of Gonzales. DeWitt added that the cannon would be returned as soon as it was requested.

DeWitt was notified that a cannon would be made available, and he responded, on March 4, that a freight hauler would be sent to Béjar to pick up the cannon, provided it was not too heavy for his wagon. Six days later Múzquiz wrote to the military commander of Béjar, Antonio Elozua, that there was a 4- or 6-pounder bronze cannon at the government house. He asked if this cannon might be used to send to the colony and if so, under what terms. Elozua approved the loan of the cannon and asked that they get a receipt for it. He told Múzquiz to use whatever terms he felt best in the receipt.

Múzquiz requested Green DeWitt write a receipt that included the following: "Received a reinforced bronze cannon that the commander of this department delivered to me [DeWitt] for the defense of this population against the savage Indians who are hostile. Said cannon will be maintained in the same state in which it was received. I am obliged to return it as soon as the commanding general of the military of this department requests it."

DeWitt's wagon driver, James Tumlinson, received the cannon on March 10, as shown by his signed receipt for the cannon:

> I have received from the Commander of this Department a bronze cannon to transport to the village of Gonzales. This is in response to the request of the Empresario citizen Gren D. Witt [*sic*]BéjarMarch 10, 1831[signed] James Tumlinson[1]

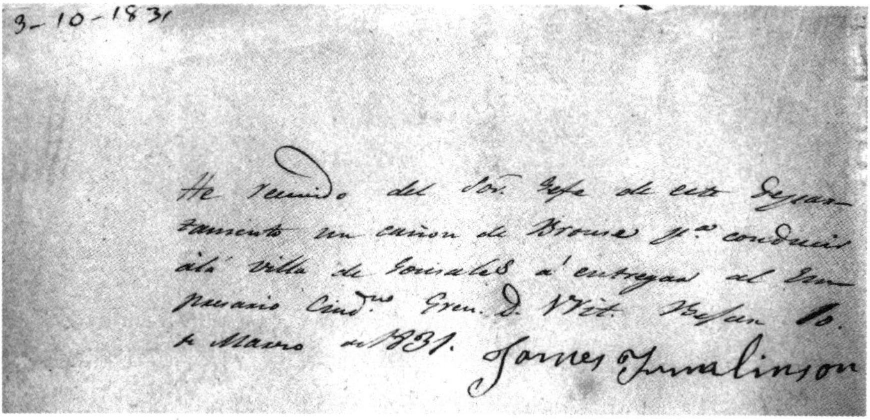

3-10-1831

He recibido del Sor. Gefe de este Departamento un cañon de Bronce p.a conducir á la villa de Gonzales á entregar al Empresario Ciud.no Gren. D. Witt. Bejar 10 de Marzo de 1831. James Tumlinson

Receipt for a bronze cannon to be taken from Béjar to Gonzales. The receipt is signed by the hauler, James Tumlinson, on March 10, 1835. Courtesy of the Dolph Briscoe Library, Bexar Archives, University of Texas at Austin.

Several items need to be emphasized about the cannon that was sent from Béjar to Gonzales as requested by Green DeWitt. First was the fact that it was a 4-pounder or 6-pounder. The tube for a 4-pounder would have weighed in the range of six to seven hundred pounds, and a 6-pounder tube would generally have weighed in the range of one thousand pounds. Thus, the fact that DeWitt wrote that hopefully the wagon was big enough to carry the cannon would be consistent with the fact that it was a 4- or 6-pounder.

It also should be noted that both Múzquiz and Tumlinson called the cannon a bronze cannon. Several other documents in this chapter will affirm the fact that the cannon that was sent to Gonzales was a bronze cannon that weighed at least six hundred pounds.

In September 1835, with all the problems that were arising between the Texans and the Mexicans, the new military chief of San Antonio, Col. Domingo Ugartechea, decided that it was time to get the cannon back from Gonzales. The political chief of Béjar sent the following dispatch to the alcalde of Gonzales, Andrew Ponton:

Political Chieftaincy of the Department of Béjar

At the founding of that colony its empresario, Mr. Green DeWitt, solicited of this Chieftaincy a cannon for the defense of said colony, the same [cannon] that this headquarters [political chieftaincy] requested from his Lordship the military commander [Elozua] of this city, who approved it. And, as his Lordship the Commandant General of this state, Col. Don Domingo de Ugartechea reclaims it, I expect that you will be served to turn it over to the bearer of this [communication], who has a commission to receive it.

God and Liberty. Béjar, Sept. 21, 1835.
Angel Navarro[2]

The commissioner that Navarro mentioned was Corp. Casimiro de Leon. He was sent with three to five privates (depending on the source), including Ysabel de la Garza, to retrieve the cannon.

Ponton responded to Navarro on September 26 and let him know that he had received an order "purporting to have come from you for a certain piece of ordnance which is in this place." With this statement, emphasizing that the order was *purported* to have come from Navarro, Ponton made it obvious that he was not going to cooperate. As unlikely as it seems, he and the entire council were, according to Ponton, absent at the time that Corporal de Leon arrived. For this reason, the men who bore the dispatch were detained until they could give an answer. Ponton gave his opinion that, to his understanding, the cannon was given in perpetuity to the town. He was advised that "deposits of this nature should be permanent." Ponton added that he would have to consult with the chief of the department (Wyly Martin) and that if, after a mature deliberation on the matter, it appeared to be the right thing to do, he would promptly send the cannon to Navarro. This document was translated into Spanish and forwarded on the Ugartechea on September 27.[3]

Navarro informed Ponton that he had information that the cannon was only lent to the deceased Empresario DeWitt and cautioned him that, since Ugartechea had ordered the return of the cannon, it would be unwise to await the recommendations of Martin.[4] Ponton was advised that Ugartechea had told Navarro that if the cannon was not returned, he would use force if needed.[5]

The fact that DeWitt had died by this time did confuse the issue, as he was the one who had agreed to the condition that he would return the cannon whenever requested to do so. On the other hand, it seems highly unlikely that no one was left in Gonzales who was aware of the terms of the procurement of the cannon in 1831.

Ugartechea also informed Ponton that he was serious about getting the cannon back. He warned the alcalde that, because the cannon was borrowed from the military jurisdiction at Béjar, he was sending Lt. Francisco de Castañeda of the Alamo presidial company with one hundred dragoons (cavalrymen) to take possession of the canon and return it to Béjar.[6] He pointed out to Ponton that the cannon had not been used since it was taken to Gonzales. He observed that the village was now more populated and, therefore, the need for the cannon was less. Ponton was notified that if there was to be any violence, he would be solely responsible.

That day, September 27, Ugartechea ordered Lieutenant Castañeda to take one hundred dragoons and conduct a cannon that belonged to his command back to Béjar. Castañeda was informed that Ponton would deliver up the cannon and that he was aware that the troops were on their way. If the piece of artillery was not delivered under any pretext, or if it were hidden, Castañeda was to use force if needed. He was to take the alcalde prisoner and return him to Béjar and to punish those who tried to resist.

Lieutenant Castañeda wrote a report on September 29 regarding his current situation. That morning he had encountered two military couriers who were escorting Private de la Garza back toward Béjar. They had found him afoot and without arms. De la Garza reported to the lieutenant that the day prior he had been with Corporal de Leon when about ten or twelve Texans crossed the river (the Guadalupe) and disarmed them. They took the Mexican soldiers in carts, as prisoners, to Gonzales. He was released by the same Texans on September 29. De la Garza reported to Castañeda that there were currently about two hundred Texans gathered at Gonzales and that more were expected that afternoon.

This number must have caused Castañeda to have doubts, as it was now clear that he was outnumbered. He stopped about five miles outside of Gonzales and sent a courier ahead with two documents for Ponton. One was from Ugartechea, and he himself had just written the other. In the letter he had personally written, Castañeda requested a meeting with the alcalde to discuss the situation. A response came from Gonzales, but not from Ponton, as he was reportedly out of town. The writer of the response informed the lieutenant that Ponton should be able to meet within three hours. Rather than wait for the meeting, Castañeda decided that it was better to write to Ugartechea with this update so he could take any necessary actions.

He added in this dispatch that there was no possibility of crossing the river in front of the town. There were canoes and a raft, but both were being guarded by the Texans on the other side of the river. All the homes on the side of the river where his troops were, opposite the town, had been abandoned. In the closing of the letter, he gave his location as "within sight of the village of Gonzales."[7]

Ugartechea received the news contained in Castañeda's dispatch of September 29 and was obviously concerned about the number of Texans who had gathered. He wrote the following to Castañeda:

> I am informed by yesterday's dispatch from you that you were not able to cross the river due to the rising water and [the fact that] the raft and canoes were on the other side under guard. This being the case, if you have had the interview with the Alcalde and have not settled the differences, and if you know positively that the combined resistance forces are superior to those [forces] under your command, without compromising the national honor, you are to retreat, giving me updates.
>
> ***God and Liberty. Béjar Sept. 30, 1835***
> ***Domingo de Ugartechea [To] Lt. Francisco de Castañeda,***
> ***Commander of the operational party.***[8]

The officials of Gonzales finally responded to Castañeda the next day, September 30, but the reply was not from Ponton. One of the aldermen (*regidores*) of the town council, Joseph D. Clements, stated that the alcalde was absent, so it fell upon him to respond to the request for negotiations regarding the demand for the cannon. For some reason Ponton's request to consult with the political chief, Martin, seemed to have been denied. Clements stated that the only answer he could give was, "I cannot and will not deliver to you the cannon agreeable to my notions of propriety." All the other members of the council were said to have agreed. The cannon was in town, and Clements stated that if it was to be taken by force, they would have to submit, as they were weak and few in numbers. Nevertheless, they would contend for what they believed to be just principles.

After having received this letter and attempting to meet with Ponton, Castañeda wrote the following dispatch to Ugartechea:

This morning I went to the bank of the river opposite the village of Gonzales for the purpose of talking with the alcalde about my commission. I was answered by a *regidor* [Clement] that he was absent, but that they had sent for him and that he should come soon. The aforesaid *regidor* assured me that by four in the afternoon I would be able to confer with the aforementioned alcalde, or in his absence with the first [the *regidor*] at that same spot, where they would go to do it. In fact, the appointed hour arrived, and I appeared at the afore-cited place, where the aforesaid *regidor,* with two others and Mr. Smith, arrived.[9] The result was they refused to let me pass as they had promised, and from the other side of the river they read to me the following communication, which I remit to Your Lordship for your knowledge.[10]

By it, Your Lordship can see that there is no doubt that these ungrateful men have acted and continue to act in bad faith. I told them there was no way they would be allowed to keep the cannon that had been loaned to them as a favor, as well as the outrage that they caused by taking the corporal and privates as prisoners. Nonetheless, they refused everything, limiting their responses to what they had said in writing.

From a Cochaté [Coushatta] Indian who came to me this afternoon, fleeing after his companion was killed after they had spent many days among them [the Texans], I learned definitely that the force they had was currently 140 men, with 300 more due to arrive that afternoon or the next morning from San Felipe and Tenoxtitlán. That is what the aforementioned alcalde was doing. All the families have been sent away, but I do not know where, and only the men are there. Mr. Smith is a prisoner like the soldiers.

I regret that I have been unable to carry out Your Lordship's orders because of the barrier of the river. It is impossible for me to do so in the vicinity of this village, because they have stationed men along the bank to impede me. Therefore, if I have not received orders from Your Lordship by morning, I will abandon this place and move up the river until I have withdrawn sufficiently to cross the river without difficulty.

God and Liberty Within sight of Gonzales September 30, 1835
Francisco de Castañeda[11]

After all the above problems had transpired, Ugartechea finally decided to make his commander, General Cos, aware of what was happening. He wrote two dispatches to Cos on September 30, one of which had copies of seven of the above documents attached. In the cover letter for the seven documents, Ugartechea informed Cos that Ramón Múzquiz was aware that the village of Gonzales had an "eight-pounder cannon of very good class."[12] Ugartechea was worried that the affair between the *Correo* and the steamboat *San Felipe* was a sign that the colonists were going to use the cannon against the Mexicans.[13] He had initially sent a corporal and five privates with a wagon large enough to carry the cannon, thinking that there would be no reason for the colonists to deny the delivery of a cannon that did not belong to the village. This dispatch ended with an emphatic declaration by Ugartechea: "I am sending this to Your Excellency by special courier because it shows in a positive manner that a declaration of war has already been served and you can decide what actions are to be taken."[14]

In the second dispatch of that day, Ugartechea stated that he did not trust any of the colonists; on the contrary, he had information that undeniably showed their bad faith. There were continuing reports of meetings in San Felipe and Nacogdoches, so, in order not to act blindly, he had sent two clever, trustworthy spies to San Felipe. At the time they had not yet returned.

He added that the action that proved the horrible views of the colonists was the refusal in Gonzales to return a cannon that was unjustly detained and that did not belong to them.[15] Ugartechea felt that the colonists should be given no more leeway and that more troops needed to come to Texas to make them respect the national honor. He noted that "the only thing that remains is that they be declared positively as enemies."

When Ugartechea ordered Castañeda to retreat if he faced superior forces, several foreigners in Béjar requested to go to Gonzales to try to prevent a conflict. Dr. Smither was instructed by Ugartechea to inform Castañeda that if a retreat would compromise the national honor he was to remain in the vicinity of Gonzales until he received further orders.

General Cos arrived in Goliad on October 1, and by the end of the day he had written four dispatches concerning the cannon at Gonzales. The first of the four was addressed to Colonel Ugartechea and was very mild. Based on the style of the letter and the information it contained, it is likely that this was the personal letter that accompanied an official letter. Unlike the other three documents that he wrote that day, this one did not include the time of day.

In this first correspondence Cos wrote that he was not bothered that the town of Gonzales was reluctant to surrender the cannon. He did not think that the Mexicans should be prideful as they still had not discovered the truth and added that it was a trivial matter. Cos did advise Ugartechea to march, as ordered in the official dispatch. No record of the mentioned official dispatch has been located in the archives, and therefore the details of the march Ugartechea was to undertake are not known. Cos also informed Ugartechea that he had not yet determined which direction (to Béjar or Gonzales) he would take, but as soon as he knew he would inform Ugartechea.

The second letter that Cos wrote on October 1 was also to Ugartechea, but this time he was far more serious. It was written at 11:30 p.m. and Cos noted that he had received the communications from Ugartechea from the day prior. Apparently, these documents had a great influence on Cos, as he changed his attitude entirely from earlier that same day:

> I am informed by what Your Excellency told me in your communication from yesterday and the consequences. Therefore, I have decided to place you at the head of 100 cavalrymen and the preferential companies of the Morelos [battalion], equalized for strength, and [command you to] march immediately to the village of Gonzales to demand and bring to that City [Béjar] the 8-pounder cannon that unduly exists there. During the march you will incorporate with the other 100 Dragoons you sent there with Lt. Francisco Castañeda.
>
> You can unite your forces more securely on the other side of the river in case the population resists another attempt [to take the cannon]. You have room to pass [the river] at some distance from the front of Gonzales, hiding your movements and taking those precautions as you would know in these cases.
>
> If you think it wise you can bring a battle cannon that will support the infantry.
>
> It is not acceptable to tolerate the scandalous conduct of the authorities of Gonzales. Therefore, you are to act in this action with the firmness necessary, but your decisions should always be thoughtful and [made with] the prudence and circumspection that the Government desires. . . .
>
> Now, on the other side of the river and in the area surrounding the town, you will advise [people] about the purpose of the march and will remit to the Alcalde the document which is included [this document is discussed below]. Give him a set amount of time to answer, in which no moratoria will be permitted of any kind. . . .

I recommend to Your Excellency very particularly and demand under your responsibility, that should they resist you with force of arms, do not allow your troops to commit excesses of any type, and to have a religiously extreme respect for properties, even those of the Captains of the rebellion. It is important for them to know that the troops of the Supreme Government are disciplined and want nothing else but that the laws are respected, and the Citizens do not place themselves above them [the laws]. Lastly, I have no doubt of your expertise and prudence and that you will completely fulfill my wishes in this operation and give honor to the Supreme Government.

God and Liberty Goliad Oct. 1, 1835 11:30 p.m.
Martín Perfecto de Cos[16]

The document that was to be taken by Ugartechea to the alcalde, Ponton, when he marched to Gonzales, was also written at 11:30 p.m. In it, Cos informed Ponton that his refusal to surrender the cannon was scandalous conduct and would result in a great deal of evil, primarily to Ponton, if he failed to hand over the cannon. If force were needed the responsibility would weigh on him personally. "You will not just be fighting with the small force that has appeared there, but with the entire Mexican nation, known for its seriousness, tolerance, and characteristic kindness."[17]

The fourth and final document Cos wrote on that day was written at 11:45 p.m. and was sent to Tornel, the secretary of war. He forwarded eleven documents regarding the cannon, including the ones he had written that day. He mentioned the disarming and arrest of four soldiers and the refusal of the Texans to surrender an 8-pounder cannon. It is interesting that he offered to march to Gonzales immediately, if that was Tornel's wish. Considering that it would likely take the mail about two months to get to Mexico City and back, he apparently was not too serious about this plan.

As Ugartechea had instructed Castañeda to retreat if the forces he faced were superior and the issue of the cannon could not be settled, he began his retreat on the night of September 30. The events of the next day started a chain reaction that would cost the Mexican nation dearly and make them pay for not addressing matters in Texas in a more timely and serious manner. The actions of October 2 would put the Mexican army on the defensive for the remainder of 1835 and gave the colonists valuable time to import more men, munitions, and supplies, as well as to organize their army.

On the afternoon of October 2, Lieutenant Castañeda wrote a very brief account to Ugartechea about the action of that morning:

> Today at five in the morning I was attacked at the habitation of la Perra by two hundred Americans, more or less. They had one medium piece [cannon] and a small piece of ordnance [*esmeril*]. So great was the superiority of the force opposing us and as per your repeated orders, I began my retreat for this city where I could give you an account of the circumstances of all that has occurred.
>
> I suffered the loss of only one Private of the 1st Permanent [company] of Tamaulipas, from a carbine ball.[18]
>
> ***God and Liberty Camp of the Carrizo October 2, 1835 1 p.m.***
> ***Francisco de Castañeda***[19] ***[see appendix 17 for original]***

Obviously, this action was not a battle and barely qualified as a skirmish. Only one Mexican soldier was killed or wounded and one Texan wounded in a fall. It is important to note that the Texans did have two cannons at the skirmish. They used both of the cannons but apparently caused no damage. The "medium piece" was obviously the only one that the Mexican army wanted to be returned. The other piece was a small cannon that would not have been any real threat to the Mexican army. It is possible that the small iron cannon that is currently in the Gonzales Memorial Museum, which weighs about sixty-nine pounds, is the *esmiril*, or small piece of ordnance. From all the documentation above, however, there can be little doubt that it is not the "come-and-take-it" cannon that was the reason for the conflict.

Filisola provides further confirmation that the Texans had two cannons at the battle of Gonzales. According to his memoirs, when Capt. Manuel Sabaríego was taken prisoner at Goliad, he and the other military officers were taken to Victoria and on to Gonzales. He wrote that they met with Stephen F. Austin, who had gathered some five hundred rebels from the interior of the colonies and two artillery pieces.[20] There can be little doubt that these two cannons were the medium piece and the *esmiril*, as there is no record of the Texans bringing other cannons with them.

The medium-sized piece that Castañeda described was taken by the Texans to Béjar and was used in the siege against the Mexican army. It was captured by the Mexicans at the storming of the Alamo on March 6, 1836. It was likely disabled and buried by the Mexicans upon their retreat from Béjar in May

Artist's conception of the battle of Gonzales on October 2, 1835. Drawing by Manuel Hinojosa.

1836. Samuel Maverick dug up several cannons on his property close to the Alamo in 1852, including four bronze cannons. It is probable that one of these four cannons was the actual come-and-take-it cannon. Currently at the Alamo there is a 4-pounder bronze cannon on display, on loan from the San Jacinto Battleground Conservancy.[21] It has good provenance for being one of the four bronze cannons dug up by Maverick. However, as a result of recent research, it is almost certain that the come-and-take-it cannon was a bronze 6-pounder that was later melted down by Sam Maverick's wife and used to cast the bell for her church.

Ugartechea informed Cos that he was unable to march immediately to Gonzales, as had been ordered by Cos. He lacked teams of horses, cartridges for the cannon, and munitions that were supposed to be coming from "that village" (Goliad?). Ugartechea felt that the hostilities that were started by the dissidents of Gonzales were a result of the conventions that were held at San Felipe and other colonies to impede the entrance of troops. He was able to verify that there was to have been a meeting in San Felipe on September 15, at which de Zavala and Mejía hoped to raise a force of two thousand men. A Mr. Smith (Smither?) heard from the commissioners and communicated to Ugartechea in a secret dispatch that one goal of the Texans was to force the Mexican troops out of Béjar. Ugartechea reasoned that it would be good to have the presidial company of Ríogrande, and other companies, as Cos saw fit, to come to Béjar to avoid this result.

Castañeda wrote his official report of the entire trip to and from Gonzales on October 4. Many of the details of his report had already been included in the previous documents, but this report gave a more detailed and thorough account of the skirmish on the morning of October 2:

> As per your order I left this city on the 27th of the past month [September] toward Rosillo, where we spent the night.[22] On the morning of the 28th we made a journey of fifteen leagues toward Carrizo. The 29th I arrived at the edge of the village of Gonzales, and in agreement with your order of the 21st of the cited month, four leagues before arriving at the village I sent the dispatch for the Alcalde of Gonzales ahead. I continued my march and two and one-half leagues before arriving at the river, I encountered the soldiers who had been sent [by me] with the mentioned documents. They were not able to get to Gonzales because they encountered the soldier of the Alamo [Company] Ysabel de la Garza who had accompanied Corporal Casimiro de Leon. They had been sent by you in advance with the carts that were to bring the cannon. They made this known to those [soldiers] that I sent: they were not able to cross the river and Corporal Casimiro [de Leon] and two other soldiers had been made prisoners the day before in Gonzales. Despite this I continued my march until I reached the edge of said village. I paused to reconnoiter for fords of the river and observed that none existed anywhere. On the opposite bank there was a raft and canoes with a guard of about 20 men on a wooden parapet they had built. I resolved to send the sealed document for the Acalde of Gonzales with the citizen Juan de los Santos Coy. He decided to pass [the river] by swimming, which he did on the 29th at about 4 p.m. With said Santos Coy I sent a letter from me as well as your official document, soliciting an interview with the mentioned Acalde. About two hours later, from the other bank, a cart driver was sent by a *Regidor* to tell me that the Acalde was absent

and that he would come soon to answer me. I waited for the response the entire night without anything new occurring.

On the morning of the 30th, seeing that the reply was delayed, I went to the pass with a soldier who spoke English. He asked the guard where the Alcalde was. They answered that he had not come yet but that the *Regidor* would come to the bank in a short time for a talk. In a little while the *Regidor* came and told me the Alcalde would need to be present because he was not able to resolve the [issue] about the return of the cannon, nor agree with me about anything. However, if the Alcalde had not returned by 4 p.m. he would pass [the river] to negotiate with me, as long as I would guarantee his personal safety. I offered him this and we were left in agreement on this and the appointed hour.

This arrived [the appointed hour] and I went to the same place where we had met and soon after the mentioned *Regidor* arrived. He refused all my suggestions on the delivery of the cannon and the prisoner soldiers. He showed me by word that only by force would it happen. This was proven by the document that I originally sent to you that very night. I was to have a soldier swim [the river] to receive it [his response].

The *Regidor* withdrew and nothing new occurred that night other than receiving orders from you. [You ordered] me not to cross the river, and if the meeting with the Alcalde had not taken place, I was to retire and conserve the horses.

On the 1st [of October], I began my march, at about ten a.m., already having retired to the habitation of la Perra, where I arrived at about twelve and stopped to pass the night and rest and graze the herd of horses.[23] When I was there a foreigner, Mr. Smitten [Smither], arrived and presented to me a pass from you. He had an official letter that told that said Smitten was to use his influence to avoid a fight and get the cannon delivered. He and I had already agreed to return to the village when we sighted three foreigners riding all the way. Smitten offered to go talk to them and I agreed. Upon returning he reported that the three foreigners wanted to reconnoiter the habitations and see if the troops had damaged them and see if I was retiring to Béjar or was camped there with the intention of staying. Those same foreigners, through Smitten, invited me and him to return to Gonzales the next day to try to negotiate the question, offering that even if we did not reach an agreement I would be allowed to return, because, before this invitation, Smitten and I had accorded them safety. We would embark the morning of the following day. The foreigners withdrew and at dusk I placed a guard at the place where the foreigners had been sighted that afternoon. From this hour until 3 a.m. nothing new happened; but then a shot from the guard was heard and I put the troop to arms. Shortly the corporal of the guard arrived and reported that the Americans had passed through the woods along the river with a cannon. As a consequence of this notice, not thinking that the point that I occupied was appropriate, I mounted the troop and proceeded to occupy a height, remaining there until daybreak of the 2nd.

The morning of that day was dark and foggy and thus I could not perceive the number of the Americans who were in ambush along the river. At about 6 a.m. they came out of the forest and immediately commenced firing with carbines. I ordered Lt. Gregorio Perez to attack them with 40 dragoons, which he began immediately. His march starting, I went to our rearguard with the rest of the troop to protect it if the action began.

At the moment they [the Texans] saw the troop charge, they fled in another direction into the forest. From there they fired a shot from a small piece of ordnance and both sides ceased fire. I returned to the height that we occupied to wait for the fog to dissipate and then act. One Private of the 1st Permanent [company] was wounded by a carbine.

After about one and a half hours the morning cleared, and it was seen that the Americans had seized the house and the point that I had abandoned. Their number was from two hundred to two hundred twenty. In a short time, within sight of both camps, a foreigner with a white flag presented himself to me and wanted to parlay. I went to where he was, and by means of an interpreter who came with him, he said that I could surrender at discretion. I said that there was no way that this was going to happen. He said that I should wait there for a short time and that he was going to confer with the Commander of the Division. He returned to his company quickly. Through his commander he reiterated to me two or three times that I surrender. Each time I refused, explaining that there was no merit to this, and I asked them what was the motive for having attacked me. They responded that it was because I was a Centralist and they were Federalists. I pointed out that it was not so and that at this date the Government of the Nation existed under this form and their aggression was unjust and that they would bear the fatal results due to their responsibility. No response was given other than to call on me again to surrender. I refused to do so and we separated. I had scarcely arrived at my camp when they fired the cannon at me and, as you ordered, a retreat was commenced without compromising the honor of the Mexican arms. This was undertaken until the vicinity of Clao, where we spent the night without any disturbances.[24]

At three in the morning I marched and arrived at Rosillo, and this morning I arrived at this city where, fulfilling my duty, I gave Your Lordship this circumstantial report because it was directed that your orders remain secret.

I believe as well that I should not fail to add to your superior knowledge that the force that was actually gathered in Gonzales must be greater than 500 men, because according to the assurances of a Cochate Indian, when the 200 plus left to attack me, more than 300 had arrived from San Felipe and others from Tenoxtitlan. There had only been about 150 men in Gonzales when I arrived at the banks of the river.

God and Liberty. Béjar, 4 October 1835. Franco de Castañeda[25]

After receiving word of the skirmish on October 2, Cos wrote Ugartechea and copied the dispatch to Tornel. This document addressed several separate matters. Cos had been contacted by a citizen, Pascasio Meza, who had left San Felipe on September 1. Meza reported that de Zavala, along with persons known as Travis, Yonce (probably F. W. Johnson), and Beca (probably Mosely Baker), was in San Felipe, but that Carbajal and Zambrano had left for Nacogdoches to go to the United States.

More importantly, he was aware that three hundred well-armed, mounted men had left San Felipe in the direction of Gonzales on the afternoon of September 1. He was not aware of any fortifications anywhere in the colonies and knew of only two unmounted pieces of artillery that were in Yrlanda (probably San Patricio, as two cannons were located there prior to being seized by the Mexican army).

Meza told Cos that all the inhabitants of the colonies wanted to break away from Mexico and that they had planned to have a meeting in San Felipe on October 5. After finding out that the colonists in Gonzales had been threatened, they decided to move the meeting to that city, where the citizens from La Vaca could come as well.

Cos told Ugartechea that, based on all that was happening, he would not recommend that he venture out from Béjar at this time, but he added that if he felt that he could acquire the cannon without any loses he should do so.

In the part of the letter that was directed only to Tornel, Cos added an interesting detail that was not true but helped explain the order for Castañeda to retreat. Cos wrote, "Knowing with certainty that at a place called Tejocote,[26] three leagues distant from Gonzales, there is gathered a force of a thousand men, I have ordered, for the time being, as had been done previously, that the troops withdraw, in order to see if I can manage with the pen, rather than with military operations, to dissuade them from the attack that they have planned, and notify them that the Supreme Government has abundant means to thwart them should they persevere in carrying out the business they have started."[27]

Two days after the skirmish, Ugartechea responded to Stephen F. Austin's letter of September 15, which is included in chapter 9. He gave a summary of the events that occurred in Gonzales. He claimed that he would be marching the next day with a force composed of all the branches, "capable of making it obvious, that the Mexicans never know how to suffer being insulted." He added the following statement in regard to the return of the cannon, "Therefore, I can assure you that by using your influence with the political chief, and delivering the mentioned cannon to me, I will return [to Béjar] with it right away from where they find me. But on the contrary, I will act militarily and the resulting consequences will be a war declared by the colonists that will be sustained by the Supreme Government of the Nation with the corresponding dignity."[28]

Ugartechea also contacted the ayuntamiento at Gonzales and informed them that he would be marching for that place on October 5 with a force sufficient to insure the recovery of the cannon. As in his statement to Austin, he informed them that if they delivered the cannon, he would immediately return to Béjar. He also made an interesting comment that if they complied there would be no further need for troops to be sent to Texas.

When examining all the above materials, it seems obvious that the Texans were nervous about the captured documents that showed that more Mexican troops were headed to Texas. It appears that their plan was to start a fight before this happened, and the Gonzales cannon provided the spark that they needed. Based on the efforts of the Mexicans to do what they could to avoid a fight and the Texans doing everything they could to provoke one, it seems that there was nothing the Mexicans were going to be able to do other than use force.

There was a major problem with the use of force: Cos, and presumably Ugartechea, had been ordered to do everything they could to stay on the defensive and hold the Béjar, Goliad, and Cópano line until more Mexican troops arrived. Cos was notified on several occasions that he was not to go on the offensive. It also appears that Cos made sure that Ugartechea did not march on Gonzales as planned because of that fact. Another likely deterrent was their well-founded suspicion that the Texans were very anxious to capture Béjar and may have had up to one thousand men available to do so.

Ugartechea did notify Cos on October 5 that he was planning on marching to Gonzales in two hours. However, he had received a letter from Stephen F. Austin that seemed conciliatory. Several colonists also informed Ugartechea that Austin had circulated a proclamation in the departments that was peaceful in its wording. He did not specifically say that he was calling off the march to Gonzales but informed Cos that if he insisted that Ugartechea carry out the hostilities he would do so with all the energy and valor of a Mexican. Cos was at Goliad at the time, which meant that Ugartechea was calling off the attack on Gonzales unless he heard otherwise.

Cos was thinking the same way as Ugartechea regarding the attack on Gonzales. Cos informed Tornel on October 5 that he had initially ordered Ugartechea to attack the colonists at Gonzales but thought better of it. He was worried that sending a small force against the Texans would put the honor of the government at risk in the case of a defeat.

CHAPTER EIGHT

Goliad and Lipantitlán

On October 2, 1835, the commander of the presidial company of San Antonio Bucareli de la Babia (Bavía), located in Coahuila near the Río Grande, wrote the following dispatch to General Cos:

> The laments heard daily from the troops of this company and their poor families, because they lack the very basics for their subsistence, and the need for me to make the efforts that humanity demands and in fulfillment of my duties, move me no less than to make known these events to Your Lordship.
>
> During the entire present year, this company has received no more than two salaries. For this reason, Your Lordship will please contemplate this for a time and determine whether during the period of nine months these poor wretches might receive their wages (I do not speak of the numerous credit balances [*alcances*] they have earned, but of the basic assistance that I have mentioned).
>
> When the paymaster [*habilitado*] of this company departs to pick up its payroll, he always takes with him two or three budgeted payments for the previous months, from which these individuals have received no assistance whatsoever, and unfortunately, he brings back only one payment. He makes this trip to the village of Matamoros, a distance of more than 150 leagues, with the result that the journey he makes takes two or three months, because it was not dispatched by that commissary, as has happened several times, especially to this [company] since the beginning of July.
>
> Another paymaster departed for Matamoros and has not returned up to now, leaving me with the regret of not having the slightest recourse

> for maintaining the aforesaid soldiers and their families, and the onset of the evils of desertion, as was just done by two privates of those detached at the presidio of Ríogrande, as the captain of that company pleased to notify me in an official letter of the 25th of the previous [month]. But I retain the hope and satisfaction that Your Lordship will not fail to attend these needs, taking, if it is to your superior liking, the measures that Your Lordship shall dictate in your superior zeal in order to prevent such ills henceforth, whose results I believe will be no other than the benefit received by greater service to the Nation and the end to the afflictions with which these families are surrounded.[1]

The above letter is yet another example of the poor condition of the Mexican military at the time of the outbreak of the Texas Revolution. It is possible that the conditions at La Bahía de Espíritu Santo (Goliad) were even worse as it was even more distant from Mexico City. Graft at the customhouses and excessive interest rates on loans that the officials were forced to take were making it impossible for the government to give even basic support to the military. Things got so bad that by mid-October it was being suggested that the payments for the warrants issued by the general treasury be suspended until the army was able to provision its troops.

The dispatch is also a great example showing that the majority of the officers seemed to care about the men and their families. The commander of the presidial company of La Babia was obviously exasperated by the conditions there and knew that if things did not change there would be mass desertions. Cos forwarded this dispatch to Tornel and added in his note, "I have the honor of transmitting this to Your Excellency for your superior knowledge and in order that the superior authority truly feels the miseries that the troops of this state experience with so much suffering." As has been noted in this work previously, Tornel was presented with such dilemmas on a routine basis. Considering that this dispatch only dealt with one commander's difficulties it is hard to imagine how much more Tornel was dealing with since there were multiple ongoing or threatened revolutions in the country at the time. Tornel predictably forwarded the dispatch to the secretary of finance and recommended that they help the troops of the eastern states.

At the time the above letter was being written, General Cos was on his way to Goliad. He came to Texas from Matamoros by way of Rancho Viejo, Lipantitlán, and then on to Goliad, which he reached late in the night of October 2.

Upon his arrival he immediately began to deal with the issue of the cannon at Gonzales.

On October 5 he wrote several dispatches from Goliad, one of which was to forward the report of Captain Sabaríego, the commander of Goliad, after that officer had completed a mission to reconnoiter the surrounding villages, especially Gonzales. Sabaríego gave his report to Cos upon his return to Goliad and informed him that he had been checking the roads to Matagorda, Gonzales, and La Vaca, and had returned to Goliad by way of Victoria. He noted that Cos had been given a report that two cannons had recently arrived in the village of Matagorda. Sabaríego notified Cos that, according to a source, there were positively three ship's carronades in Matagorda that had been there for some time, but no new cannons were there.[2]

During his expedition, Sabaríego was able to discover that there was a gathering of the rebels at Gonzales. They had not made any movements from that place as they were still waiting on more men from San Felipe and other locations. He noted that it was fifty leagues (131 English miles) from Goliad to Matagorda. With the reports that he had about the rebels and considering that there were several colonial establishments on the way, he thought it best not to put the troops at risk and turned back prior to arriving at Matagorda.

He did note in his report, "I am bringing a four-caliber cannon that existed in the village of Guadalupe [Victoria]. This piece did not give fears of being misused in the control of those colonists, but it is possible that it could have been taken by the rebels and this now has been avoided."[3] Filisola wrote that the cannon was taken from the de Leon family in Victoria, who had borrowed it for use against the "barbarous Indians" in that area. Contrary to Sabaríego's opinion that they would not have misused the cannon, Filisola reported that the de Leons had hidden the cannon under a table in order to later use it against the government troops.[4]

That day, in a separate and secret document, Cos wrote to Tornel to give his opinion about the situation in Texas. He was obviously uncomfortable being so brutally honest but apparently he felt that he had to let Tornel know exactly how he felt:

> **Excellent Señor:**
>
> In a separate note I speak about the state of insurrection that the colonists have created in Texas, and by means of this confidential letter, I believe it opportune to speak to you with necessary clarity about a matter of the greatest transcendence to the Republic.

I understand that the government of the United States of the North favors the rebellion in this precious part of the Republic, because in their ports the directors have made all the preparations for war in the presence of their authorities.

Today the population of foreign inhabitants in Texas has passed 30 thousand, of which at least one seventh can take up arms and will do it willingly, without the efforts of some rich property owners that exist there being sufficient to hinder it. It is well known that adventurers, sent and protected by an unseen hand, form the majority.

In such circumstances, this general command cannot assemble more than a thousand men to operate against the rebels, and for this, some companies of the line of presidios would need to be pulled. If the other [presidial] companies are relocated, another major evil will ensue, as the savage Indians, seeing the abandoned villages, will begin a war more fearsome than that with the colonists, because it is difficult to reach them.

In addition, there are companies at these [presidios] that have not received their pay due in May, and this delay has caused many of them to be poorly armed and dressed and even more poorly mounted, in spite of my efforts to resolve that [situation]. This is because the resources on which I depend are unsure, since the proceeds of the customs of Matamoros have diminished notably and will diminish more as a consequence of the disturbances in Texas.

The troops that I command are overflowing with courage and enthusiasm to march at this moment to the very heart of the colonies. I would determine to do so if not for the fact that I consider how much the moral strength of their government would wane if, through a misfortune, the rebels should achieve any advantage over our forces, not because they would achieve it in combat with them, but [because] they would withdraw all kinds of supplies, and we would find ourselves obliged to traverse an immense wilderness where we would have no other resources to consume than what we carried.

For all these reasons, I believe it my duty to tell that superior authority that if it does not send me the necessary forces of all branches of at least two thousand men, with the supplies necessary for their subsistence, the position of Texas is very uncertain, and perhaps soon we will feel the regret of seeing it in other hands, without the efforts of the resolute soldiers that I command being enough to prevent it.

> Your Excellency will be so kind as to make the most excellent señor president of the Republic aware of all this, overlooking my speaking to you with the frankness that I have thought necessary.
>
> I repeat to you the assurances of my constant respect.
>
> ***God and Liberty. Goliad, October 5, 1835.***
> ***Martín Perfecto de Cos***[5]

On October 6, Cos began his march for Béjar. When he left, he took some of the soldiers of the Goliad company to act as guides. This left the presidio at Goliad severely undermanned. Filisola wrote that there were scarcely fifteen men left to defend the site, though other sources report twenty-five to forty. The Texans immediately started planning a surprise attack.

The commander of Goliad, Col. Francisco Sandoval, documented another interesting detail about the events in the village. On October 8, he wrote Cos that the minister from the United States, Anthony Butler, had just arrived in that village on his way to Mexico City. He had come overland and was planning to leave Goliad two days later. Sandoval obviously was suspicious of Butler, "both for the character that he represents, and for the reflections to which his transit through the dissenting colonies give rise; the distance that he has undertaken is so long and he brings no entourage."

Cos sent this report regarding Butler to Tornel on October 10. He too was worried about what Butler might be up to. He wrote Tornel that while he was in Matamoros, he had heard that Butler was relieved of his post since he had not completed his mission concerning Texas. Cos found it interesting that Butler was making a long and arduous trip through the colonies, and it was his opinion that this was not an isolated event. He suspected some sort of hoax and felt the Americans would always do what was in their national interest. Cos felt that this occurrence reinforced what he had written about the Americans in his letter of October 5 that is included above.

According to Filisola, several of the locals from Goliad and Victoria made an agreement with the foreign colonists to surprise the presidio before any reinforcements could arrive. On the night of October 9–10, the Texans decided to host a dance and invited the commander of the Goliad presidio, Colonel Sandoval, and the other officers in order to deceive them. Several colonists, including Felipe Dimiti (called Philip Dimmit in English sources), hid in the house of Guadalupe de los Santos. They then called the administrator of the Matagorda customs, Juan Zenteno, to the house, where they captured and detained him.

Apparently, the trap set for Sandoval and the other officers did not work, as they were suspicious and left for the barracks with the few soldiers that they had. At about 1:00 a.m. on October 10, approximately one hundred Texans attacked the barracks. Filisola wrote that the fighting lasted about an hour, and after a stout defense, the Mexicans, having suffered three killed and others wounded, in addition to having run out of gunpowder, surrendered.

Zenteno also gave an account of the action of that night and the next two days.[6] He wrote that at 1:00 a.m. the plaza and barracks were taken by the Texans. Commander Sandoval, Captain Sabaríego, Subaltern Garza, the 1st officer of the customs, and himself were taken prisoner. He noted that he was the first to be taken and mentioned the firing of carbines at the opening of a door (presumably that of the barracks).

Zenteno told of doing his best to save the important papers from the Matagorda customs that he had packed in boxes prior to leaving that place. The captive military officers were sent to San Felipe on October 10. That afternoon, Zenteno was told that he also would be marched to San Felipe the next morning, under guard, along with the 1st officer of the customhouse, Francisco B. Arsamendi (Arzamendi), and the comptroller, José Manuel Rodrigues (Rodríguez).[7] Zenteno noted that he and the other two were the only officials of the customhouse who were there. He ended his dispatch by saying that he was being watched very carefully by the Americans and some ungrateful neighbors, so he could not give a more extensive report and that by sending this communication at all he was placing himself at total risk.

Other details about the capture of Goliad were given in a letter written by John Linn from Victoria. The Mexicans intercepted several letters from Victoria, and Linn's letter to his brother in Mexico was one of them. The letter was sent on to Tornel as evidence of what the Texans were plotting. Linn informed his brother that the war had been begun by the citizens of Gonzales refusing to deliver a cannon to the soldiers. In the letter he wrote that Goliad had been taken on the night of October 9 by about fifty men, after fifteen minutes of fighting. Lieutenant Colonel Sandoval, Captain Sabaríego, and Lieutenant Garza were captured; one Mexican was dead; and four were wounded. He reported that twenty-one Mexicans in total were captured. He also gave his brother advice for which roads to take on his return from Saltillo and warned him that if anyone asked, the people of Texas only wanted the federal constitution of 1824.[8]

Linn wrote another letter at about the same time to Thomas Henry, the alcalde of San Patricio, which was also intercepted and forwarded to the government of Mexico. He requested aid from Henry and the people of his jurisdiction. He emphasized that the Texans were fighting for the constitution of 1824, which they had sworn to uphold, and urged him to let his motto be federalism contra centralism. Linn noted that as Irishmen they knew how to appreciate a despotic military government.

He informed Henry that Austin, the commander of the main army of the people, had crossed the Guadalupe River at Gonzales, headed for Béjar. Also, Goliad had been taken by storm on the night of October 9 without the loss of a single man on their side and that they had been ordered to hold it at all costs. He stated that they could now do so against one thousand men.

He reminded Henry that the convention would be held on November 1 and that they should elect seven representatives from their colony. On the back of the cover page for the letter, Linn wrote a short note saying, "Tell us how many men strong and how many horses that are at Lipantitlán."[9]

Word of the action at Goliad spread quickly through the Mexican military command. On October 12, the military commander of the state of Tamaulipas, J. M. Guerra, wrote the following dispatch to the secretary of war. He gave an excellent summary of the state of affairs in Texas and the problems that Cos was facing:

> This very night I have learned from the special dispatch sent to me by the commander of the military post of Lipantitlán on the Nueces River that the rebel colonists of Texas had taken possession of the post of La Bahía del Espíritu Santo, which today is called the village of Goliad, after half an hour of fighting that began at 1:30 in the morning on October tenth, with that small garrison being taken prisoner. I refer to a letter sent with unlimited authority by infantry Lieutenant Don Miguel Zenón Truxillo, who witnessed the attack and who managed by chance to make it to Lipantitlán, from where by breaking through [*atravesía*] report of the event has been made to the señor commandant general of these states. This superior commander left Goliad for Béjar on the 6th with an escort consisting of 60 cavalry, and it is quite likely that he would have reached the aforesaid city on the 9th, unless from the village of Gonzales, which was serving as a garrison for the rebels, some force of considerable strength may have come out to attack His Lordship en route, which is 40 leagues.

Since the 5th, when this superior commander . . . had removed their [the Texans'] masks, their treachery was discovered, and hostilities had broken out, I have not received any news at all from him. I heard from a soldier who also escaped from La Bahía that he heard that another party of rebels had set out with the aim of surprising the commanding general on his march, not knowing the results.

I hasten to report this to Your Excellency by special courier for the superior knowledge of His Excellency the President. I must add for my part that I consider Gen. Martín de Cos to be in a very difficult position due to the scarcity of forces that are available in Béjar, reduced mostly to incomplete permanent presidio companies, poorly mounted and poorly armed, as well as the active [companies] in the same condition and green to combat. Also, their equipment is a joke, suitable only for a war against the savages. The permanent Morelos battalion consists of barely 200 men, with a small unit of campaign artillery without gunners and few munitions.

Neither the commandant general of Nuevo León nor I will be able to reinforce the aforesaid superior commander because everything is scarce. In addition, we are at least 130 leagues distant [from that place]. Thus, in order to send some munitions, a few gunners, the medicine chest, and surgeons, a few troops who would not amount to 100 men who could be assembled, and the small amount of money that was collected this week, I will try to learn, first of all, the whereabouts of the general. Second, it must be determined which direction they are to be sent, in view of the fact that they could be intercepted from Goliad, which is the most direct route, which [once] had a government garrison.

Another thing that I should add, which does not seem out of place, is that from the month of August, by supreme order, the revenues of the maritime customs were destined for the needs of the troops of these states. Up to now, payment orders of the supreme government issued by the general treasury have been drawn at the same office—and with greater urgency payment on notice—for more than 30,000 pesos. These have been extremely lacking for the preparations for the expedition to Texas. There has been no relief, no horses, nor armaments for 4 or 5 months for the presidio companies, which would be complete today and ready for battle. We do not have today, in the meantime, anything to collect and send to Béjar for General Cos but small amounts of money that are barely enough for daily expenses, and that is with brokering the enormous bonus of 4 percent per month in accordance with what is provided in this matter, which I also beg Your Excellency to communicate to the superior authority.

Before closing this letter, I have seen a paragraph of a personal letter from Lt. Trujillo in which he says he found it very notable that the minister plenipotentiary of the United States of the North, Mr. Butler, who went to his country last year with permission, has now returned by land and has overseen in the colonies the horrendous attacks of the rebels, his countrymen, committed against the persons of the few Mexicans who are there; that from Austin he proceeded to Gonzales, where the hostile [rebels] of the country were gathering; and that finally, two days before the event in Goliad, he appeared at that presidio, and after [him] the enemy [appeared]. He was present for everything that occurred, and he was continuing on his way to this city, where I intend to advise him not to tarry, for his own safety.

God and Liberty. Matamoros, October 12, 1835.
J M Guerra[10]

Cos finally sent his report of the action at Goliad on October 13 from Béjar. He wrote that he had first heard of the fall of Goliad on October 11 from a sergeant of the Goliad garrison, but he had waited for confirmation. Apparently, two officers who were taken prisoner at Goliad escaped from the Texans and made their way to Béjar and confirmed the information. They informed Cos that there had been about one-half hour of fighting, after which the entire town was taken by the Texans. They stated that the commander and Captain Sabaríego had both been captured and were being taken toward Gonzales to be presented to Señor Mejía.

Cos then proceeded to make excuses as to why he should not be blamed for the capture of Goliad. He wrote that when he first arrived in Goliad, he knew immediately that it was an important location. When he left, he took sixty infantrymen with him, but he added that he left a piece of artillery (probably the cannon taken from the de Leons at Victoria) to help fortify the position. Cos also added that he cautioned Colonel Sandoval that the place should be fortified immediately and that Sandoval should act with diligence and activity. As the distance from Béjar to Goliad was so great, he was unable to send any aid.

The perfidious colonists attacked the garrison. Cos stated that there were forty Mexican soldiers there (likely an overestimate to bolster his case). He claimed that the colonists had not fooled him and wrote that the supreme government had the proof that this was the case.

Cos wrote that if he had sufficient infantry, he would have sent them immediately to retake Goliad, but having only two hundred men of the Morelos battalion, he was not able to do so. He observed that Béjar seemed to be the main desire of the colonists (which was likely true) and that if he "dismembered its garrison" the colonists would look upon it as a triumph.[11]

Cos wrote another letter to Tornel the same day.[12] It primarily addressed the issue of the lack of funding from the customs and the need for troops, but Cos contradicted his other letter. He documented that upon receiving the news from Goliad he immediately gathered two hundred infantrymen and four hundred cavalrymen and set off for Goliad. However, he was soon persuaded that the action at Goliad might have been designed to draw him away from Béjar, and therefore he reconsidered and stopped the march.

In the second letter he also mentioned the lack of support for the troops and profoundly stated, "Although I am able to bring all my subordinates up to the bayonets of the enemies, I have not found, up to this day, the secret of maintaining men without requisite food."

Zenteno informed Cos on October 17 that he, Arzamendi, and Rodríguez had been sent to Gonzales. The trip took twenty-four hours and they spent the night of October 13 there. The next day they were led to the encampment of the "so-called" General Austin, which was about six miles from the town, at the ranch of Clemente de la Garza.[13] Austin treated them with the greatest consideration, pointed out the justness of the Texans' cause, and ordered them to continue the march with the Texans toward Béjar. Zenteno informed Austin that as an employee of the supreme government he would remain faithful. He also notified Austin that the customs officials would be in imminent danger if they continued with the Texan division. After several meetings it was decided that the officials would sign an oath not to take up arms against the pronunciamientos in favor of the constitution of 1824. After doing this, they were to be released to proceed to wherever they saw fit. Arzamendi, who spoke English, informed Zenteno that, because of the insults and harassments made against them, their lives were in danger, so they elected to sign the papers. They were given a passport from Austin and immediately left for Lipantitlán. Zenteno did add to his letter that he signed the statement under extreme duress.[14]

On November 14 Zenteno sent a copy of the oath that he and the others had signed a month earlier:

> Having been made prisoners in La Bahía by the Texas Division in revolt for the Constitution of 1824 and the Federal System, we are required to promise to not take up arms or take part against said pronunciamientos. [We do this] to obtain full liberty under our word of honor, and in proof that we will comply, we sign the present document. At Williams Camp along the Guadalupe River near Gonzales—Oct. 14, 1835 [see appendix 18]
>
> ***Juan Zenteno, Francisco Arzamendi, José Maria Rodríguez***[15]

On October 19 Cos notified Tornel that Zenteno had been placed at liberty and had returned from a ranch near Gonzales by virtue of a "ridiculous declaration" that the Texans had demanded he sign. Less than two months later, Cos would be forced to sign a similar document. His reaction to this document foretold the lack of sincerity that he would place on the oath that he would sign.

After his arrival at Lipantitlán Zenteno informed Cos of the strength of the Texans. He estimated that they could gather an effective force of no more than six hundred undisciplined men. The Texans were in confusion and were going to meet at Salado Creek to advance on Béjar.

After the captured military officers arrived at San Felipe, they were required to sign an oath as well. After being freed by the Texans, Sabaríego made a report to Cos and gave some details of what had happened to them. He was initially given his freedom but was imprisoned for a second time. The Texans demanded that he sign a document that he would not take up arms against those who sustained the constitution of the year of 1824. He signed the oath and was released, but Señor de Zavala warned him that he was going to be arrested again. Therefore, he left San Felipe on the night of October 23 in the company of Eusebio Cortina, who was a waggoneer for their company.

Sabaríego was also concerned about Sandoval and Garza, who were still being held at San Felipe. He believed the Texans wanted to use them for a prisoner exchange. He also seemed to be worried that Cos might not want to exchange them as they had also signed the same oath not to take up arms. Sabaríego reiterated that even though he had signed the oath, upon his return to Goliad he had recommenced hostilities against the Texans, as was his duty as a Mexican and a soldier.

On October 13, Stephen F. Austin wrote the committee on safety of San Felipe and told them of the expected arrival of the three officers in that town. He singled out Sabaríego and noted that he was a supporter of federalism and was married to a woman from Goliad. He recommended that Sabaríego be paroled and allowed to return to his home. Even though Sabaríego did not return to Goliad, he must have passed through there or spoken to someone from there, because he reported to Cos that his home had been robbed. He wrote that he had previously expected to be able to live his life at rest, but now he was going to have to continue with work. He estimated that he had lost thirty thousand pesos' worth of goods but added that he thanked the Supreme Being that he still had his arms (not weapons but his actual arms).

Filisola wrote that when the military officers from Goliad arrived at San Felipe, they had a discussion with Lorenzo de Zavala, who tried to persuade them to take part in the revolution. Sabaríego asked him, "Do you think that the revolution is only to support the constitution of 1824?" De Zavala replied, "Friends, the revolutionaries are like a mighty river, which in its onward rush cannot be directed."

LIPANTITLÁN

Upon the news of the fall of Goliad, Cos notified the commander of the 2nd Active Company of Tamaulipas, stationed at the fort at Lipantitlán, Lt. Nicolas Rodríguez, that he should take his troops to within sight of Goliad and evaluate the strength of the force that defended it. If possible, he was to attack and capture it. On the contrary, if unable to attack, he was to choose ten or twelve brave men with good horses to harass the fort every night until he received new orders.

The following is a dispatch from the commander of the state of Tamaulipas, Jose María Guerra, to Tornel, forwarding Rodríguez's report of his march to Goliad and back, as well as what went on at the fort during his absences:

> **Headquarters Tamaulipas**
> **Your Excellency**
>
> Lieutenant of permanent cavalry Don Nicolás Rodríguez, commander of the 2nd Active Company of this department [Tamaulipas] and the military post of Lipantitlán on the Nueces River, reported in an official letter dated November 5 at 9 p.m. from that point, the following:
>
> > Your Excellency: Today I have reported to the commanding general and inspector of this state [Cos] what I copy here:
> >
> > "Señor Commanding General: Have undertaken my march to Goliad on October 28 with the object of attacking or harassing constantly, as per your superior orders of October 24, I arrived in the vicinity of that village

on the 31st. I situated myself with my force, consisting of 40 troops and five citizens.[16] From there I ordered a scouting mission to inform me where the rebels might be located. Two soldier-spies who entered Goliad brought word that a party of more than forty men of the enemy had set out for the purpose of harassing this place [Lipantitlán] and San Patricio, whereupon by means of forced marches, I returned and arrived there on the 1st [of November] at 9 p.m. Having encountered nothing, I continued my march on a 2nd route toward Goliad, taking 60 men, since some citizens and ten Irishmen from San Patricio had joined us. I could not travel as rapidly as I would have liked, as a result of the enemy party that was in the area. It was necessary to find them, with my force remaining in ambush in the vicinity of San Patricio. I continued from there on the 3rd toward the Aranzasu [River], where at 2 o'clock on the morning of the 4th I received a message that the rebels were approaching this place, and I ordered a rapid countermarch. In this transit, at about 6 a.m, I observed a cannon shot that caused me to speed up my march with 30 of the best mounted men. My advance proved futile, since near this place I was informed that the enemy had crossed the river. This obliged me to hold the force that remained on the road, and obtaining it, I managed to cross above this point by swimming. Then, knowing that they had tried to withdraw, at 3 p.m. an action took place between them and our troops and just the citizens from San Patricio. I divided this force into three parts—one on foot and two mounted. The firing lasted until nightfall, at which time they retreated, pulling in[to?] the water two cannons and a cart that they took from here when they captured this position.[17]

The fort that I had prepared [Lipantitlán] was surrendered on November 3 between 10 and 11 at night, without a shot having been fired, by those who remained there under the command of Sgt. Rafael Aceves, with twenty men, both troops and civilians. This unexpected event has caused infinite harm: the loss of ammunition and various weapons, including the cannons, the burning of the quarters and the fort, the sacking of my house and that of Don José María Villarreal and of *Alférez* Don Marcelino García.[18] In the aforesaid action that I led, this officer [García] and five of the troops were seriously wounded, and Private Longoria, of this company, was killed. The enemy losses are known: four dead and three wounded. We thought that everything was over if they left for the prairie, but they did not want that, and they were greatly favored by the protection of the oak forest on the river.

This is what I consider [important] to notify Your Lordship, as well as to offer to place our daily log, or at least details of my operations, at your

> disposal. Nevertheless, I cannot fail to tell Your Lordship of the valor displayed by the troops during three hours under fire, as well as by the Irishmen from San Patricio who were accompanying me."
>
> And I report it to Your Lordship for your information.

And I have the honor to forward it to Your Excellency for the superior knowledge of His Excellency, the President, with the understanding that for my part, I have dictated the most effective measures for the purpose of recovering the cannons, and to return to the fort and surrounding town, as long as there is a force to strengthen that point, all of it depending on what the señor commanding general decides in Béjar.

God and Liberty. Matamoros, November 10, 1835.
J. M[aría] Guerra[19]

This document can be a bit confusing, but it has too many important details to try to summarize. Briefly, Rodríguez set out to Goliad from Lipantitlán on October 28, as ordered by Cos, and arrived on October 31. When he arrived, he got news that the Texans were headed to Lipantitlán to attack the fort there. He immediately withdrew and headed back to the fort. He did not encounter the Texans, as they had taken a different road to Lipantitlán. When he reached the Nueces, he ran into the Texans, who were returning from capturing the fort. They were hauling two cannons and a wagon from the fort. There was a skirmish at the crossing that was confusing as the Mexican soldiers were headed south and the Texans were headed to the north.

Guerra noted in a separate document that an officer (likely Rodríguez) who had participated in the action at Lipantitlán had retreated more than thirty leagues toward Matamoros. This officer had been informed that the troops that made up his rearguard had been captured by Viesca, Grant, and the traitor Colonel Gonzales.[20] Guerra ordered the officer to return to the vicinity of Lipantitlán and observe the rebels.

Filisola reported in his memoirs that Rodríguez lost most of his men to desertion shortly after the action at the crossing of the Nueces. Rodríguez sent one of his men to San Patricio to find out the number of enemy troops who were there. Apparently, he was recognized and taken captive. He led the Texans to the Mexican camp, and Rodríguez and the few troops who remained with him were taken captive. After a few days, they were set at liberty by Dr. Grant.

These events essentially left no Mexican troops in the interior colonies of the Texans. Rodríguez and his small force would continue to be a thorn in the side of the rebels for a few months, but other than that the only Mexican troops in Texas were in Béjar. This was important as the Texans could now move troops and matériel without risk. It also made it difficult for the Mexican couriers to carry communications.

CHAPTER NINE

The Siege of Béjar

After his release from imprisonment in Mexico, Austin returned to San Felipe de Austin. He had been there for only four days when, on September 15, he wrote to Colonel Ugartechea:

> San Felipe de Austin, September 15, 1835My Esteemed Friend:
>
> I have the satisfaction to inform you of my arrival here. I disembarked at Velasco on the 1st and arrived here on the 11th of the present month. I had the regret of finding this country in great commotion because of the rumors that have circulated regarding the march of troops to Texas. For my part, I would not be able to believe such a matter, nor that the government would adopt such an impolitic and harmful measure as to send troops to this country. Now is not the time for such actions. All of Mexico is in convulsions about the change in the government, and according to all the circulars of the ministry, the people of each part of the Republic have the right to express their opinion about such an important issue.
>
> The people of this department and that of Nacogdoches have expressed theirs in favor of supporting the Constitution of 1824 and the integrity of the territory of the Mexican Federation. In this, they are unanimous; there is no division. These people are at peace, although they do not understand the current situation of things. They have acted peacefully by means of a commissioner to make the representations that must be made to the government.
>
> My Friend, there is nothing to fear of the matters of Texas if the government itself does not press for the march of troops and other impolitic measures. The real source of difficulties here lies in the very palace in

Mexico, or rather in its military measures. These inhabitants have not failed [in their duties] as Mexicans, nor will they, but they cannot look with indifference upon the hostile demonstrations being made against them. They want peace and union with Mexico, but they do not fear war. You should leave them in peace, and all will be fine.

A schooner under the command of Thompson attacked the armed American merchant schooner San Felipe on the night of the 1st of the present [month] without prior notice or saying a word. Thompson fired three volleys against the San Felipe before the latter replied. The result was a battle. Thompson escaped in the night and surrendered the following day to the captain of the San Felipe. The latter took him with ship and crew to [New] Orleans to be tried as pirates. These are the facts. I was not aboard the San Felipe since I had disembarked on the afternoon of the 1st. This is a matter between the United States and Mexico, in which the people of Texas have nothing to do or say.

This Thompson has issued proclamations in Anáhuac as if he had the power of a commanding general and a government. I do not know if he had such authority. Among other things, he intended to incite the negroes to rebel and sowed much discord. What would you have the inhabitants [of Texas] do, my friend, when other such acts are committed against them in the name of the government?

I repeat, you should leave Texas in peace, the troops should withdraw, and these inhabitants should not be vexed in such a manner. If you do that, I will support peace in Texas. I have not failed [in my duties] as a Mexican, nor will I be found lacking. I will be the first to stake my life and interests to sustain the just rights of Texas and to oppose the entry of troops into this country in the current circumstances. This I have declared publicly, and also that I am a Federalist and a supporter of the Constitution of 1824. I have suffered for years in service to Mexico, giving my courageous efforts to a wilderness [*desierto*], and I have faithfully served my adopted country. I have served an unjust imprisonment for my efforts to obtain a local government in Texas that is so necessary to protect the interests of the nation. Do you think that, if there had been a local government in Texas, the impertinences that we have seen by the state legislature would have been committed? Or that the disorders that have been permitted would have occurred? No, none of this would have happened, because they would have avoided such disorders and would have applied radical remedies. I have been persecuted, and now Texas is blamed because there are disorders, when there is no local government to contain them. Every time the Texans take action to remedy them, they are treated as rebels.

My friend, we should be united. All of Mexico is disjointed, and it is not the fault of Texas, and not its fault that things are as they are. And this country should be left alone and not embroiled in a disastrous war.

I am honest because I am a Mexican, and because it is my duty. I want to prevent disorders and protect the interests and prosperity of the nation to which we belong.

The pronunciamientos in favor of the Constitution of 1824 and the measure of calling a general consultation were made in July and the past month, before my arrival, as you have seen by the imprints published in Brazoria. I have done no more than join with the opinion that already has been declared, with the object of giving it a system and thus preventing disorders.

I repeat, there is nothing to fear regarding affairs in Texas if these inhabitants are left in peace, without being provoked with troops and other unpolitic measures. There is a moral and healthy principle among these inhabitants that is sufficient to preserve peace, order, and the interests of the nation, but this principle cannot join any military force that comes as an invader or with hostile intentions. That is impossible. Why then, provoke a war when nothing has changed, and one that can only prove harmful to the nation? By this mail, I have written to Sr. Santa Anna, however, you can forward a copy of this letter [to him] if you think it necessary. I remain, as always, your friend W[ho] K[isses] Y[our] H[and].

Esteban F. Austin

PS: After I wrote the previous letter, Mr. Burnett came, having just arrived from that [place]. My friend let me repeat that nothing will be achieved by the march of troops here. Even if the accused individuals have done wrong, this is not the time or the method that has been adopted as the most appropriate to castigate them. Leave them, for the love of God, and leave these people in peace. Fix the government in Mexico and in the nation first, and then fix this country. In the meantime, leave the Texans in peace without provoking them to desperation.

The communications that Mr. Burnett has brought from the ministry are very good. Yet, on the other hand, what are the military measures?

> Honey in the mouth and daggers in the hand. My friend, I do not think that is the way to deal with the people. It is my duty, on behalf of openness, to say that public opinion will consider the march of troops into the colonies in the present circumstances as a declaration of war, and that neither I nor anyone else can prevent the consequences.
>
> The voice of Texas now is to maintain the integrity of the territory of the Mexican Federation. Why endanger that integrity and ignite an unnecessary war?
>
> Goodbye, my friend. Write to me with frankness and above all I beg you to use your influence to prevent the coming of troops, as the country will be saved in no other way.
>
> ***Esteban F. Austin I enclose a printed item in English***[1]

Ugartechea was remarkably busy at this time dealing with the matter of the Gonzales cannon. On October 5, he responded to Austin. He wrote an emotional letter repeatedly requesting Austin to use his influence to get the people of Gonzales to deliver up the cannon. It is interesting that, at the time, both Austin and Ugartechea were being very polite and seemed to have hope that, if the other side cooperated, matters could yet be sorted out and peace restored.

On this same day, a series of correspondences was started between General Cos, from Goliad, and Austin, in San Felipe. As was the case with the above letters, the interaction was extremely polite and formal. Cos informed Austin that the interim president Barragán recommended Austin as a man who could help Cos with all his futilities regarding Texas. Cos wrote, "For everything that I need in respect to Texas you could find it, as you are a man of wisdom and local knowledge. At the same time, you are a good citizen who looks with appreciation for your adopted country, and who knows how to employ all his influence in favor of the well understood interests of the country. Lastly, he [Barragán] told me that he is in agreement with you as to the measures that are convenient to adopt in regard to those people."[2]

Cos also commented that the Mexican consul in New Orleans, Pizarro Martínez, had recommended Austin based on the conversations they had had in New Orleans about matters in Texas while Austin stopped in New Orleans on his return to Texas.

According to Cos, things were going downhill in Texas. He felt that this was a result of the ridiculous and unjust pretentions of a few adventurers, who with their exaggerated ideas were going to make a lot of trouble for honorable

Texans. As commander, Cos stated that he was charged with bringing tranquility to Texas, and as such he requested that Austin come to Béjar to give his opinions on the matter.

Clearly Cos did not trust the Texans or Austin. On the very day that the Texans were planning a night attack on Goliad, he wrote Tornel, "It is indispensable to detach two hundred men to Goliad, a most interesting place due to its situation and military interest. I have taken some other steps to see if I can bring down the colonists, but, in my opinion, they are going to be unsuccessful because their projects seem to be planned in advance and the time in which they will try to achieve them approaches. From Goliad I invited Stephen F. Austin to come to this city with the purpose of parlaying about the status of this department. I was moved to take this step due to the particular recommendation the Most Excellent Interim President of the Republic gave me. However, today I think he is one of the main motivators of the disorder. This concept was made by me from his letter to Colonel Ugartechea."[3]

Austin replied to Cos on October 17 with two letters, one being the formal official letter and the other being a short personal note. He suggested that Cos allow him to send an officer into Béjar, under a white flag, with an escort of six to eight men. This officer would bear a communication about the disagreements in Texas. He felt that this would start the process of coming to a satisfactory settlement of all matters regarding Texas. Problems quickly arose, however, by the nature of the second, official dispatch Austin sent that day. Its heading read, "Federal Army of Texas," and the origin of the letter was given as Cibilo Creek, which was just outside of Béjar (see appendix 19).[4] The information that it contained was the same as the personal note, but these two details raised the relationship to a more heated level. Cos was obviously shaken, which is evident in his reply to Austin:

> My Dear Sir: When I wrote you from Goliad on the 5th, I did so with lavish attention to the recommendations that very respectable people gave me in your favor. I had not the slightest suspicion that you could be the main leader [*corifeo*] of the revolution. Now the disappointment surprises me, since your communications of yesterday leave me no doubt that you are at the head of the rebels, and since I have no competent authority to enter into negotiations with the partisans, it is indispensable in order to hear them for you to abandon that hostile attitude, that you pull back the people who are accompanying you, that

the Mexican soldiers that you have captured return to their posts, and that everything be reduced to petitions, and in no way to actions. In the meantime, my aforementioned invitation is now void, because it would be quite ridiculous for me to talk with you now after the events at La Bahía, etc.

I had the best intention to fix everything such that those towns would not have had to suffer the effects of a disastrous war. However, it is not my fault that you are all overconfident, and that you do not realize that you are going to crash into an entire nation, so proud that it cannot receive the law of foreigners, and that ultimately will punish the guilty. It may be true that some Mexicans, because of particular resentments or for their own convenience, or because there is the exception to all rules, will cooperate with the rebel colonists. However, the majority will fight with all their might. And it is necessary to heap scorn on anyone who does not prefer death to such an unseemly compromise.

I have not yet made the slightest step to where you or anyone can attribute less than noble intentions to me. On the contrary, one could impute weakness to me, as I have paid too much attention to the local interests of those new communities that seek to grow outstripping nature itself, like all things that when they depart from their center acquire those vices that hasten the end of their existence.

It is very strange that you put Federal Army of Texas on your official communications, which I will not answer. You realize that there is no other army in the nation than the one to which I belong, which has not attacked the established form of government nor become involved in political complications; that seeks peace, having given sufficient proof of that, but does not disdain to go to war, because that is its profession, and all the individuals that constitute it have proven since our successful emancipation that they scorn danger and know how to live with calm and spirit in the midst of bullets. From this, you will deduce that I will not admit a white flag, because that would legitimize in a certain way the existence of that rebel force, and you can from this moment (as you would have before, as well) continue in your operations if your heart is not sufficiently penetrated by the reflections that should be created in you by this communication, which will be the last one, unless, doing as I ask you, you should wish to present yourself with the peaceful character of a citizen to whom it surely matters that Mexicans not carry out in the colonies an exemplary punishment.

See how personally I can assist you, your attentive servant W[ho] K[isses] Y[our] H[and].
Martín Perfecto de Cos, Oct. 18, 1835.[5]

Even before he arrived in Béjar, Cos was preparing for the defense of that city. While he was in Goliad, he let Tornel know that he had arranged for some presidial companies to march there, as well as the replacements for the Morelos battalion, who were marching to Béjar. With these he estimated that the garrison at Béjar would number about one thousand men. He also mentioned that the munitions park and the artillery that had come on the Veracruzano had already reached Béjar. However, in his dispatch to Tornel, dated October 9, he warned that up to one-third of his troops in Béjar were sick or employed in duties that made them unavailable. The Mexican archives does contain a list of artillery and artillery stores that were in Béjar in February 1835 (see appendix 20). There is also a list of the munitions at Béjar in September 1835 (see appendix 21).

In his memoirs Filisola gave some interesting details that help tell the broader story of the siege of Béjar. According to Filisola detachments of the main body of Texans, under the command of Austin, arrived at the Cibolo (about nine leagues from Béjar) on October 12.[6] On October 19 Cos ordered all the cavalry, with thirty men of the Morelos and a 4-pounder cannon, to fire upon the rebels near a tower that stood about two thousand paces from the city on the road to Gonzales.[7] He also noted that on October 22 one hundred men under the command of Lt. Col. José María Mendoza ventured to the missions, where the Texans were rumored to be, but they found nothing.[8]

Cos described the conditions in Béjar on October 19. He noted that nothing significant had happened since his last letter. The Texans, numbering about eight hundred men and one piece of artillery, occupied the ravine of Cibolo Creek.[9] The town of Béjar and the Alamo de Parras were described as completely fortified.[10] The presidial companies of Ríogrande and the 1st Active of Tamaulipas, which had been in Laredo, were said to be on the march toward Béjar. In a note Tornel added to the margin of this document on November 14, it was noted that the government was absolutely satisfied with Cos's actions and they approved of his repulsion of Austin's offer to parlay.[11]

The governor of Coahuila and Texas, Rafael Ecay y Múzquiz, was concerned about the situation in Texas. He notified the political chiefs of the departments that the troops under Cos at Béjar were in critical need of supplies. He asked that grain and other essential needs be transported to Béjar. He suggested that a permanent force be established at the village of Ríogrande to protect those who were hauling goods to the troops. It was noted that not only would this aid transportation of goods but communications as well. The troops would also help "to attend to the part of Coahuila that is not entirely exempt from the hostile ideas of the colonists as an inevitable result of the last administration of this state [Governor Viesca]." According to Múzquiz, this force would also help to stem the tide of hostile indigenous tribes who were starting to invade the frontiers of the state.

On October 27 Cos was told that the Texans had occupied the Mission de la Espada. Reacting to this information, Cos himself led a few infantrymen and 230 cavalrymen in search of them. Later that day he was informed by two men that about one hundred Texans, under the command of James Bowie, had crossed the river near Concepción. As a result of the late hour and the fact that his men had not eaten, he returned to Béjar.

Not much happened for the first week or two after the arrival of the Texans at Béjar, but matters heated up on October 28. There are several documents in the Mexican archives, two of them by eyewitnesses to the action, that tell the story of the battle of Concepción. The first of these two eyewitness accounts was written by brevet Lt. Col. Rafael de Ugartechea, commander of a section of cavalry that was involved in the action that day.[12] He should not be confused with Col. Domingo de Ugartechea, who was the military commander of Béjar. Documentation has been found in the Mexican archives that the two were related, probably brothers.

Rafael Ugartechea gave the following account of the battle at Mission Concepción:[13]

> Commanding General [Cos]—At six a.m. I left with two hundred nine horses [cavalrymen] with the object of reconnaissance of the terrain of the Missions Road, and at the Concepción [mission] I encountered the enemy, and having blocked their way I started to fight them in guerrilla [style]. During the shooting, a sergeant presented himself to me with twenty men of the Ríogrande [presidial company] who were guarding the Rancho de Padre. I sent them back to cover their position.

> I sent the message that the enemy was under siege in the forest and at the mission. At this instant they captured nine horses and one mule from them [the Texans]. About two hours later Lt. Col. José María Mendoza arrived with an [artillery] piece and a squad of infantry. They began to battle having been reinforced by Lt. Francisco de Castañeda and two "squads" [guerrillas] of cavalry, numbering sixty men. Which officer deployed them after the infantry dispersed. Having reunited all the parties that I had advanced, I began to observe the enemy and saw that they received reinforcements at the mission. At that moment, I sent the message to Col. Domingo Ugartechea, who ordered me to fall back.—The losses I suffered on my part consisted of one corporal and two lancers wounded, two dragoons from the Aguaverde [company] and one from the 1st Active [Company] wounded, four horses dead and eight wounded. All of which I report for Your Lordship's superior knowledge.
>
> ***God and liberty, Béjar, October 28, 1835. Rafael de Ugartechea General and inspector of these states.***[14]

Filisola added that when the cavalry under Rafael Ugartechea arrived at the river crossing, they could hear the enemy in the grass, but it was foggy and only a minor skirmish took place. Even after the fog lifted, the Texans would not show themselves, so their numbers could not be determined. Ugartechea apparently got bad information that a number of the Texans were in the mission, so he sent word back to Cos that he needed a cannon.

While waiting on the cannon Ugartechea had the opportunity to question some women and a man, Antonio de León, brother-in-law of retired 2nd Sergeant Balmaceda. They informed him that Bowie and about one hundred men had passed by the previous morning, but three hundred more Texans had come to reinforce him that day. By the time a dispatch was sent to Cos with the news that the Texans were much stronger in force than previously thought, Cos had sent fifty men and a 4-pounder cannon to aid Ugartechea. Immediately after crossing the river, without consulting anyone, Mendoza, an infantry officer on the headquarters staff of Coahuila and Texas, attacked the Texans. Filisola estimated the number of Texans who were in the woods as greater than two hundred who were able to fire point-blank with great accuracy. In less than ten minutes nearly all fifty of Mendoza's force were dead or wounded, and the cannon was in the hands of the enemy. Filisola noted, "There were members of

Artist's conception of the battle of Concepción, which took place near the mission on October 28, 1835. Drawing by Manuel Hinojosa.

our troops who ran to fall at the feet of their assassins, whom, even after having several bullets in their own bodies, they sought with their bayonets, in their last moments, to avenge once and for all their lives and the insults to their country."[15] Filisola added that the total Mexican casualties for the day was twelve dead and thirty-two wounded. He also noted that the lancers gathered most of the dead, but that in the night Austin permitted the local priest, preceded by a drummer in order that the Texans might recognize him, to gather the rest of the dead.

A second report was written the same day by Lt. Col. José María Mendoza:

> Sr. Commandant General [Cos]: In fulfillment of the orders that Your Lordship pleased to issue to me to go and observe a force of the enemy that had been situated near the Concepción Mission and attack in the case that its position required me to do so, I began my march this morning with a force of sixty infantrymen of the Morelos battalion and

a light piece [of artillery] serviced by those same soldiers. I approached the aforesaid mission and found the enemy in ambush in a nearby grove [of trees]. They engaged in a light exchange of fire with the guerrillas of our cavalry who had gone ahead earlier. I was informed by them that the enemy force was small, and that it had diverted to cover the mission. Therefore, I thought an attack should be made before they could unite with the main body of the rebel colonists, which was about two and a half leagues away.

With my troops arrayed in the order that seemed to me most accommodating, I commenced to battle [the enemy] in the forest, supporting the fire of the infantry with grape shot from the cannon. They penetrated the forest with the vigor that always distinguished the soldiers of the Morelos [battalion]. However, either the enemy received reinforcements during that action, or because I was given the wrong information, a force was found there that I could calculate by their fire as being two hundred men. Having already commenced firing pistols [i.e., fighting at close range], it was necessary to continue despite such a visible inequality. We battled without pause until I had lost more than three quarters of my force among dead and wounded. Then the remainder fell back in the best order, abandoning the cannon whose custody had already cost me many solders. This retreat was supported by Captain Manuel Barragán and Lieutenant Francisco Castañeda, who with two groups of guerrillas from their presidial companies engaged the enemy while I crossed the river.

With the lists that I regretfully am sending to Your Lordship, you will see the names and ranks of the dead and wounded. Among the former is found Captain Felipe Escalante, and among the latter, Brevet Captain Antonio Tenorio and Second Lieutenants Pioquinto Gomes and Francisco Torres. These officers and Second Lieutenant Ygnacio Solís, the only one left standing, showed distinguished valor in this encounter, but especially Torres, who with great enthusiasm and resolution battled to the end despite having received two wounds from rifle bullets.

I hope that Your Lordship is persuaded that in this unsuccessful operation nothing more could be done, and if the results did not meet your wishes, it was due to the numerical superiority of the rebels and the very advantageous position they occupied. While this loss is very sad for those who perished in it, it has served to teach the enemy that

Mexicans will always fight with resolve and more energy when defending the integrity of the national territory threatened by the revolution of the inhabitants of the colonies.

I have the honor of pledging my due respect to Your Lordship.

God and Liberty. Béjar, October 28, 1835. José María Mendoza.[16]

The day of the battle the commander of the permanent Morelos battalion, Nicolas Condelle, had two lists drawn up.[17] The first list was those from the Morelos battalion who were dead or made prisoner:

PERMANENT MORELOS BATTALION STATE OF TEXAS

List of the officers and troops who died or were made prisoner in the action against the colonists at the Mission Concepción on this date.

Company	Rank	Name	
Grenadier	Corporal	José Ma. Lara	1 deceased
1st	Private	Miguel Reyes	1 deceased
4th	Captain	Felipe Gonsáles Escalante	1 prisoner
6th	Private	Ygnacio Marques	1 prisoner
Cazadores	1st Sergeant	Felipe Figueroa	1 deceased
	Cazador [Private]	José Sanson	1 deceased
	Cazador [Private]	Fran.co Martínes	1 deceased
	Cazador [Private]	Pioquinto Duarte	1 deceased
	Cazador [Private]	Abran Gutierres	1 deceased
	Cazador [Private]	Juan Lopes	1 deceased
	Cazador [Private]	José Ma. Morales	1 deceased
	Cazador [Private]	José Ma. Gonsáles	1 deceased
Attached from the Jiménez Battalion			
	Corporal	Pedro Cuellar	1 deceased
		Total	**12 [dead; 1 prisoner]**

San Antonio de Béjar Oct. 28, 1835
Condelle In charge of the detail Benito de Zenea

The list of the wounded:

PERMANENT MORELOS BATTALION STATE OF TEXAS

List of the officers and troops who were wounded in the action against the colonists at the Mission Concepción on this date.

<table>
<tr><th>Company</th><th>Rank</th><th>Name</th><th>Wounds</th></tr>
<tr><td rowspan="9">Grenadier</td><td>2nd Sergeant</td><td>Consepción Chaves</td><td>1 by a bullet shot</td></tr>
<tr><td>Cornetist</td><td>Juan Servantes</td><td>1 by a bullet shot</td></tr>
<tr><td>Corporal</td><td>José Ma. Acosta</td><td>1 by a bullet shot</td></tr>
<tr><td rowspan="6">Grenadier [Private]</td><td>Casiano Medina</td><td>1 by a bullet shot</td></tr>
<tr><td>José Esquivel</td><td>1 by a bullet shot</td></tr>
<tr><td>Fran.co Ramíres</td><td>1 by a bullet shot</td></tr>
<tr><td>Ygn.o Dias</td><td>1 by a bullet shot</td></tr>
<tr><td>Mariano Paredes</td><td>1 by a bullet shot</td></tr>
<tr><td>Juan Navidad</td><td>1 by a bullet shot</td></tr>
<tr><td>3rd</td><td rowspan="3">Private</td><td>Bartolo Bueno</td><td>1 by a bullet shot</td></tr>
<tr><td rowspan="2">4th</td><td>Alejo Alvares</td><td>1 by a bullet shot</td></tr>
<tr><td>Margarito Aldaco</td><td>1 by a bullet shot</td></tr>
<tr><td rowspan="4">5th</td><td>Sub Lieutenant</td><td>Fran.co Torres</td><td>1 by two bullet shots</td></tr>
<tr><td rowspan="3">Private</td><td>Juan Castañeda</td><td>1 by a bullet shot</td></tr>
<tr><td>José Reyes</td><td>1 by a bullet shot</td></tr>
<tr><td>Antonio Aguilar</td><td>1 by a bullet shot</td></tr>
<tr><td rowspan="3">6th</td><td>Corporal</td><td>Mariano Romero</td><td>1 by a bullet shot</td></tr>
<tr><td rowspan="2">Private</td><td>Mateo Chaves</td><td>1 by a bullet shot</td></tr>
<tr><td>Julio Gonsáles</td><td>1 by a bullet shot</td></tr>
<tr><td rowspan="3">Cazadores</td><td>2nd Sergeant</td><td>Felipe Salasar</td><td>1 by a bullet shot</td></tr>
<tr><td rowspan="2">Corporal</td><td>Simon Escamilla</td><td>1 by three bullet shots</td></tr>
<tr><td>Antonio Villagra</td><td>1 by a bullet shot</td></tr>
</table>

Company	Rank	Name	Wounds
Cazadores	Cazador [Private]	Juan Lucas	1 by a bullet shot
		Leonardo Velasco	1 by a bullet shot
		Mariano Salas	1 by a bullet shot
		Cosme Damion	1 by a bullet shot
		Secundino Osorio	1 by a bullet shot
		Vicente Zamora	1 by a bullet shot
		Doroteo Garcia	1 by a bullet shot
		Andres Tovar	1 by a bullet shot
		Bernardo Sánches	1 by a bullet shot
Headquarters	Sub Adjutant, Brevet Lt.	Pioquinto Gomes	1 by a bullet shot
		Attached	
Abasolo [Battalion]	Lt., Brevet Captain	Antonio Tenorio	1 by a bullet shot
Jiménez [Battalion]	Grenadier [Private]	Seferino Torres	1 by a bullet shot
		Total	**31 [34 if officers included]**

San Antonio de Béjar, October 28, 1835
Condelle in charge of the detail, Benito de Zenea

The day following the battle Cos wrote his action report to Tornel. He attached the reports of R. Ugartechea and Mendoza. Some of the details he gave varied somewhat from their reports:

> October 29, 1835
>
> **YOUR EXCELLENCY**
>
> Yesterday, a party of rebels approached within about a league of this city. I sent out some cavalry and sixty infantrymen to see if they could intercept them. Lt. Col. Don José María Mendoza, commander of the infantry, having received incorrect information about the number of the enemy, committed his force to battle with a fourfold disadvantage. Finally, he was forced to retire with the small force that was left, abandoning the light piece [of artillery] that he had brought, and left without the limber and munitions.
>
> At the moment I received the first reports of the encounter, I sent brevet Lt. Col. Don Benito Zenea with sixty more men of the Morelos

battalion and the 2nd permanent company of Tamaulipas, but since I was informed that the first force was retreating and that the enemy retained its very advantageous position, I ordered that [force] to return. I did not think it appropriate to expose more soldiers when it was not possible to make the enemy come out and fight in the open. Captain Don Rafael Ugartechea, who with a party of cavalry was also operating against the rebels, could not assist the infantry, because the woods that they occupied were very thick. He withdrew with some wounded.

Your Excellency will learn about the march and operations of both parties from the documents that I have the honor to enclose to you, and it would be inexcusable for me not to commend to Your Excellency the three officers of the Morelos [battalion] who were wounded, as well as the rest who fought with valor and spirit. All the families of the officers and soldiers who died in this encounter are very deserving of the highest consideration from your superior office.

I regret to tell Your Excellency that many of the wounded are dying, since we have absolutely no one who can treat. This not only goes against humanity; it greatly diminishes the spirit of the soldier. Captain Don Felipe Escalante, who was wounded in the muscle of his upper right arm, died as a consequence of being unable to stop the bleeding, something a surgeon could easily have done.

Regarding the situation in this city, nothing has been lost by this encounter. [Instead] it has strengthened the resolve of my subordinates.

The colonists, led by Don Estevan Austin and numbering a thousand men, are in possession of the Espada and Concepción Missions, but up to now they have not decided to attack the city and the Alamo de Parras, which are defended by regular fortifications.

May Your Excellency please to report all this to His Excellency, the President of the Republic, and accept the assurances of my constant obedience and respect.

God and Liberty. Béjar, October 29, 1835. M[art]ín Perf[ec]to de Cos[20]

After Tornel got word of the battle of Concepción, he informed the interim president, "with the most profound sentiment," of what he called "the disgraceful incidents" of the action that took place on October 28. As has been previously addressed, Cos was not supposed to go on the offensive, and Tornel reprimanded him for disobeying this order. He sent a dispatch to Cos on December 2 in which he chastised Cos and said that if Cos had limited his actions to the defense of the city, as he had repeatedly been charged to do, the blood of some brave men would have been spared. He reminded Cos that very respectable forces were marching to that city to aid him, and that Santa Anna should arrive in San Luís Potosí the next day.[21]

In the same dispatch Tornel notified Cos that the federal government was sensitive to the lack of surgeons and its effect on the wounded. He implied that medical help would be coming, as the brigade that had left Matamoros was continuing to Béjar.[22] It is not known if Cos received this dispatch prior to marching from Béjar.

Five days after the battle at Mission Concepción, Cos gave Tornel another update on the current situation in Béjar. In a margin note on this letter, Tornel wrote how he wanted his clerks to respond to Cos and what was to be communicated to Generals Mora and Ramírez y Sesma as well. Cos's report and Tornel's response are as follows:

> **#650 Excellent Sir**
>
> On the 29th of the month that just finished I had the honor to inform Your Excellency of the state and location of the rebellious colonists. Today I will only add that they have advanced against this city and are situated in two camps at more than two cannon shots distance. Some of their parties have advanced to exchange fire with our advanced guard. The force that they have to the north [of the city] is commanded by the Principle Commander of the allies, Estavan Austin. The other (camped to the south) by a certain Bery [Bowie] who is called Colonel.
>
> Yesterday a young man presented to me with a sealed document from the latter [Bowie] and I returned it unopened. Later a foreigner arrived below the fire of the fortifications of the Alamo who, with the security of a white flag, brought me an official note from Mr. Austin. I ordered that he countermarch, saying that I would not parley with anyone while the colonists were there with arms in hand. It seems that it bothered them, and they brought forward a piece of artillery supported by a small force of men, mounted and on foot. We fired some shots from a 12-pounder cannon that I have placed well, and the damage they received forced them to retreat quickly. At this moment I affirmed the Mexican flag

with the firing of a plain cannonball and the enemies all retreated to the forest.

Not having yet gathered sufficient forces to actively act against the enemies has obligated me to limit myself, for now, to sustaining at all costs this city, which because of its situation is of great interest to us. [The city will be of use] for quartering the troops that gather for the purpose of making the new settlers of this frontier abide by their duties and reduce their pretentious advances.

Capt. Manuel Sabaríego, who was taken prisoner at Goliad and had been at San Felipe, escaped from that village and arrived at Lipantitlán. The garrison of that establishment, united with some faithful Irish neighbors of San Patricio, has marched to harass said village of Goliad with orders to attack it and occupy it if possible.

God and Liberty. Béjar, Nov. 2, 1835 Mtín. Perf. to de Cos[To]
His Excellency Minister of War and Navy

[Margin note from Tornel] Nov. 20, 1835, Transmit this official letter to General Ramírez, instructing him that as a consequence he should continue his march to Laredo, reuniting there the battalions Jimenez, Matamoros, S. Luís Potosí, Querétaro, the Dolores Regiment, the reinforcements for the Morelos battalion, the [artillery] pieces that left from Zacatecas, and those [artillery pieces] that he should acquire in San Luís. From Laredo he should send scouts to learn the situation of the rebels, not taking one more step from that village without first agreeing with General Cos and with full assurance that he will not be beaten or weakened in his march. He [Ramírez y Sesma] is to suspend [the march] in case the security is not complete, while the 2nd division arrives. This communication will be sent to General Cos with the special courier who is leaving. This will give him an idea of the units and artillery pieces that are marching in the vanguard division of General Ramirez.

An army of 8–10,000 men will be placed in San Luís and His Excellency the President will march at the beginning of the upcoming year to take command. He [Cos] will not commit any action until the large reinforcement that is sent to him arrives.[Tornel's rubric][23]

Cos wrote another document to Tornel on November 11. He informed Tornel that, as a result of the clashes he had had with the enemy, half of his ammunition was exhausted. He requested musket cartridges as well as cartridges for 3-pounders, 4-pounders, and 8-pounders. Also, he asked that two seven-inch howitzers, along with their equipment and munitions, be sent to him.

Another problem that plagued the Mexican army at Béjar was the fact that it was difficult to get supplies and communications into and out of the city. Cos notified Tornel on November 11 that he would like duplicates of the dispatches that had been sent the fifteen days prior to October 3, as he was concerned that some had been intercepted by the Texans. He also sent Tornel copies of all the documents he had sent from Béjar between October 9 and November 2.

There was another skirmish in the vicinity of Béjar on November 8. Cos informed Tornel on November 11 that Capt. Manuel Barragán and forty dragoons managed to overtake a party of Texans. They charged the Texans before they had time to escape and seek the woods. Barragán's men killed three of them, wounded two, and captured seven saddled horses.[24]

Tornel tried to reassure Cos that help was coming in his dispatch of November 14. He reminded Cos that Santa Anna was coming to Mexico City to take charge of the organization of the army, which was going to chastise the perfidious colonists who had boldly waved the banner of anarchism. Cos was informed that General Ramírez y Sesma was already in San Luís with artillery and permanent army units ready to march to Béjar. Tornel sent Cos a list of supplies that had been gathered and notified him that the customhouse in Matamoros would use its resources for the army before paying off any notes. He closed the letter with the following: "The most accredited military men have heroically offered to fly to the defense of the integrity of the national territory. And finally, all Mexicans are watching the attack of the perfidious colonists with the indignation that it deserves."[25]

On November 15, Ramírez y Sesma wrote Tornel that he had received word from Texas. The Americans had surrounded Béjar, where the plaza was defended by eight hundred men under the command of Cos. Supplies had been scarce there since October 19 and there had been a few cases of the plague. Notwithstanding this, the besieged men defended the city with valor and the besiegers had gained no advantage although they had one thousand more men than Cos.

Cos described the conditions in Béjar again on November 16. The Texans were still within about one mile of town and were making marches and countermarches with no known purpose. They were moving their artillery closer by the day and other than the death of one dragoon, who was killed by one of their rounds, no damage had been done.

Domingo Ugartechea was sent by Cos to Laredo to meet the Morelos battalion reinforcements and escort them back to Béjar. He arrived in Laredo on November 19 and on November 22 notified the military commander at Matamoros of the desperate situation in Béjar. Supplies were dangerously low, and Cos could not write for aid from the governors of the states under his command because the communications were being intercepted. The presidial units there had practically no horses, so they were forced to fight on foot. Even if the Texans gave up on the siege and withdrew, the Mexican soldiers would not be able to pursue them and punish them as they had no mounts.

On November 19 Ugartechea wrote the governor of Coahuila y Tejas and informed him that the colonists to the front of Béjar had divided into two groups and that it was possible one of the parties was headed to the Ríogrande presidio in order to impede him. He added that he had armed some of the neighbors of those populations, to be used if needed.[26]

According to Filisola, the replacement of Stephen F. Austin with Edward Burleson on November 24 marked a sudden turn in the siege of Béjar. He noted that before that time most of the Texans fighting with Austin were landholders who were in favor of the federation or the constitution of 1824. As time went on Austin was accused by newcomers of lacking ability, of being apathetic, and of secretly dealing with the Mexican government. They were able to have him removed from command and replaced by a simple landholder, Burleson, who was incapable of understanding the "machinations" of the rebels.

Filisola wrote that Lorenzo de Zavala noted that things were turning, and being embarrassed about the state of things, he retired to his property located near Buffalo Bayou. De Zavala noticed that his influence on the colonists had dissipated like smoke, leaving his aspirations for the division of the Mexican republic without hope.

After Burleson was in command, the operations against Béjar took on a more serious nature. The number of troops was increased, and a 16-pounder cannon was brought in along with additional ammunition and arms.[27]

On November 26 there was another skirmish between the Mexicans and Texans. Texas historians have dubbed this the Grass Fight. The Mexicans were rumored to be bringing a payroll into town, but they were outside of Béjar foraging for grass for their horses. It is somewhat surprising that Cos gave so little detail in his report on the action and did not include reports from any of the others involved. On the other hand, he did seem to be wary of making any movements that might have been considered by his superiors as being offensive in nature. He included another interesting item about the Alamo in his battle report:

> Since the 16th of this month, nothing in particular has occurred except a few minor shootings in which no loses were sustained. However, yesterday, about 300–400 subversives attacked 50 dragoons who were returning from foraging. They were able to hold off [the Texans] with their limited force until the arrival of fifty infantrymen, with one piece [of artillery], which I sent to help them. [The Texans] then retreated to their camp, which was far away from the site where the shooting started. The result of the fight is one officer wounded, three dead soldiers, thirteen wounded, thirty-nine saddled horses lost, one mule, three carbines, one sword, and two muskets.
>
> The loss to the enemy is unknown to me. I will say to Your Excellency, not having seen the exit of the enemy force, that we discharged some loads of canister at a very short distance. We can infer that there was damage done to the enemy.
>
> I would also say to Your Excellency that some days ago they [the Texans] had placed, in front of the fortification of the Alamo, a barrier, in which they placed their cannons, in order to battle the garrison. Until now they have not caused any damage to my soldiers.
>
> ***God and Liberty. Béjar, Nov. 27, 1835. Martín Perfecto de Cos***[28]

It should be remembered that this was the same period when General Mejía landed at Tampico. The battle there was fought on November 15 and word was spreading regarding this event. Thus, the Mexican government and army were distracted, and their resources stretched even thinner than previously.

Filisola noted that by the beginning of December the besieging forces found themselves ready to advance on Béjar. He wrote on December 4 that there was heavy fire on the buildings and parapets, which indicated that the Texans were determined to take the city at all costs. One of the parapets was said to have been located at the entrance to the priest's house. They may have taken the city if not for the determined defense of the Mexican troops. There was only one

Mexican casualty that day: a corporal of the Morelos battalion sappers received a strong contusion from a stone that was dislodged by a bullet.

At 4:00 a.m. on December 5, 2nd Lt. Masedonio Avilés, along with a sergeant, a corporal, and four men who were manning the observation point, came into Béjar and reported that the enemy was moving against the city. The Texans moved hut to hut and house to house until they took the houses of N. Veramendi and Antonio de la Garza, which were located about one block to the north of the plaza. The houses on the plaza were defended with parapets and embrasures at the entrances to the streets. Filisola reported that as the fighting got closer to these embrasures the Mexican defenders could only fire to the front and not to the flanks because of poor planning in their construction. On that day, the firing lasted three hours and the Mexicans suffered one dead and several wounded.

On December 7 the fighting was again heavy, starting at reveille and lasting until 2:00 a.m. A wooden fence, located at the back of one of the houses, caught fire. The fire spread to the priest's house, which was one of the houses on the north side of the plaza. It became necessary to abandon the parapets and embrasures and limit the defense to the walls of the houses. Holes were made in the walls, through which muskets were introduced. Filisola wrote that these buildings were defended by only two officers and fourteen men.

With the mounting casualties there were fewer and fewer men to defend the Mexican positions. Another significant problem was the lack of artillerymen. Veteran troops from the Morelos battalion were used to man the cannons, but this took them from the front lines, where they were badly needed. To make matters worse, they were not able to effectively man the cannons. Thus, the enemy had no problem avoiding the cannon shots by staying in the houses and using the parapets to move from house to house.

At 8:00 a.m. on December 8, the Texans reached the Navarro house, which was next to the one that was being used by the Morelos battalion as its headquarters. There were a few men and officers from the battalion in that house. Each side was trying to make holes in the wall that separated the two houses, and both sides occupied both houses at various moments. After fighting all day, the Mexicans had three officers wounded as well as several soldiers.

A thorough account of what was happening on the Mexican side during the siege of Béjar is given in the journal of the adjutant inspector of Tamaulipas and Nuevo León, José Juan Sánchez Navarro. As discussed in chapter 4, he documented the organization of the Morelos replacements and their arduous trip north. His published journal resumed his documentation of the march on December 8, not far from Béjar. He wrote that at 4:30 a.m., after passing in review, the march commenced, in the middle of a continuous rain. The order of march was given as follows:

> Vanguard, Captain Barragán with the troops that he brought under his command; corps of battle, one hundred and ten infantrymen of the picket and replacements of the Morelos, which after a short while was discovered to have the howitzer and the cannon (this force was commanded in person by Señor Ugartechea), and I, to find myself by day, followed with the line, to keep order and go to the place necessary. After the armed infantry, about sixty women and children followed, then more than one hundred twenty loads of equipment, ammunition, and the provisions and stores of said battalion. With some intervals between: the cattle that remained of those taken out of Laredo to eat, the surplus mounts, and lastly the 1st flying company of Tamaulipas, which covered the rearguard, under the orders of Capt. Manuel Lafuente. The right side of the section was covered by a picket of the 1st active company of Coahuila and Texas, under the orders of its commander, Subaltern D. R. Aguirre, and the left, that of Lampasos, commanded by the subaltern of Monclova, Santiago Navaiza. Lt. José Ochorán commanded the artillery. Captain Manuel Navarrete, the infantry, together with Lt. Ignacio Ruiz. The escort of the ammunition park, Captain Manuel Hernández, with nine men of the Regiment of Veracruz. Lt. Francisco Rada and Subaltern Francisco Herrera were aides to the Colonel, and mine [his aides], of the same character, were Subaltern Bernardo Cavazos and Cadet Eduardo Hores.[29]

In his memoirs, Filisola gave the strength of this column as 47 regular infantrymen of the Morelos battalion, 14 artillerymen, 150 cavalrymen from the presidios, and 400 replacements, for a total of 600 "consumers" for whom there were no supplies.

The cornets and bugles were not allowed to play, as the enemy could be near. The column reached the Medina River at about 3:00 p.m., where a daily ration of biscuits and brandy (Sánchez Navarro noted that it was really mezcal) was distributed. After dark no one could smoke for fear of being seen by the enemy.

Sánchez Navarro gave an interesting description of the encounter with the fires that the Texans had set in the prairie:

> We soon spotted some fires in front of us. These, as we did not get closer, became more extensive, so that now we were surrounded by fire in all directions. Said fire was caused by the big fires that the enemy had made in those fields to stop us from passing through them. It would have been hard work doing so if we had not been helped by a heavy rain for more than an hour, which put us in the shelter of the fires that it extinguished. However, from the smoke and blackness that resulted from the burned branches and pastures, everything was so obscured that at ten paces you could not distinguish one man from another, unless they were mounted on white horses. So, we were concerned about ravines and cliffs, and at each step we had to make a stop because it would interrupt the order of the march. The cargo mules got tangled, and even worse, there was no good stopping place for the cannons. Their teams (mules for the howitzer and oxen for the cannon) were exhausted, as were the disarmed infantrymen, who to get by. I had them guided by ropes attached to the runners of the standards.

Sánchez Navarro told of many hardships on the road including rain, mud, lack of food, lack of drinkable water, exhaustion, and extreme cold. The troops were not dressed for the cold and he described them as being nearly naked. He had to alternate groups of dragoons every fifteen minutes to help the oxen and mules pull the howitzer and cannon. By 11:00 p.m. they had reached the vicinity of the Arroyo Enmedio, and at that point Sánchez Navarro and Ugartechea committed to finishing the march without stopping. By 2:00 a.m. they reached the Arroyo del Leon, where they were concerned that the Texans might be guarding the crossing. Sánchez Navarro wrote that he later learned that the Texans had had 190 men with a cannon at the crossing, but they had left at midnight that night.

As the column neared the city, they could hear sporadic firing. By 6:30 a.m. on December 9, they could clearly see the city, and they noticed that there was a lively fire of cannon and musket. Sánchez Navarro theorized that this fire distracted the enemy, and they were caught sleeping as his column came into town to the house of Cadet Flores and on to the plaza.

He also wrote that as the column entered Béjar they were greeted with shouts of acclamation and the pealing of bells. "We were saluted by the valiant ones, about three hundred in number, who for fifty-five days had battled day and night, working without distinction of general, commander, and officers of troops, with pickaxes and crowbars in hand."

The next line Sánchez Navarro wrote in his journal was very telling in regard to the eventual outcome of the fight for Béjar: "What bad relief we are bringing them!"

Filisola reported the arrival of Ugartechea and the column led by Sánchez Navarro at about 9:00 a.m. on December 9. At midday, the fierce fight between the two sides was suspended for some time, but the Mexican garrison had suffered several dead and wounded. Cos ordered a 4-pounder to be placed at the butcher shop, east of the city, under the command of Capt. Manuel Barragán and supported by the men of the Laredo presidial company, commanded by Capt. Manuel Lafuente. This proved to be ineffective and the entire force returned to town. By nightfall firing was stopped on both sides, "by mutual consent."

In the plaza Sánchez Navarro met Capt. Andrés Videgaray, who gave him shelter at his accommodation in the home of Erasmo Seguin, which was near the plaza where the church was. At 11:00 a.m. he met with Cos, who ordered him to reconnoiter the parapets from which they were defending against the Texans. He returned from his mission at 3:00 p.m. and reported that he had seen a lot of musket fire, and even fired some shots himself, but it was to no avail as the Texans were sheltered in covered streets and houses. Only the barrels of their rifles were seen, through small openings and embrasures. Three Texans shot at them with impunity from a fortress called Santa Anna.

After his afternoon mission Sánchez Navarro claimed to be saddened because he now understood that it was impossible to defend such an extended position with as few troops as were in the plaza. To top that off, the replacements he brought were extremely poor in quality, with no provisions and no expectations of any coming. Filisola documented similar feelings among those who were defending the city prior to the arrival of the replacements. He wrote that the troops in Béjar were dissatisfied when they realized that not only were there to be no supplies but that more men had come to help consume what they already had.

Apparently the mutually agreed-upon ceasefire that Filisola mentioned did not last long, as documented by Sánchez Navarro. (It should also be noted that Filisola was not a participant or an eyewitness; plus, he was writing his account more than ten years after the fact.) Having had no sleep and having been in the saddle for the better part of two days, Sánchez Navarro fell into such a deep sleep that evening that even the cannon fire and musketry could not awaken him. However, Videgaray, furiously shaking him that night, awoke him and warned him that all was lost because the Texans had taken the plaza. Sánchez Navarro grabbed his sword and jumped through a window facing the plaza. He joined a group of about twenty presidial soldiers and ordered them to stop retreating. The only one that he knew in the group was Lt. Pedro Rodríguez of the Ríogrande company. The commander of the Morelos, Nicolas Condelle, then arrived at the plaza, and his presence emboldened the men to the point where they repulsed the Texans three times. Filisola reported that at 10:30 p.m. the rebels surprised and took the parapet that had been constructed at the priest's house, since its exhausted guards were sound asleep. The rebels attempted to take the plaza through that entryway, but the 2nd adjutant of the Morelos, Antonio Osorio, led a fixed bayonet charge in the plaza that forced the rebels back through the priest's entrance. As they did so, the Texans immediately barred the door with logs, stones, etc. They did the same with the windows as the Mexican troops were trying to force their way in to get the enemy out of the house.

Condelle obstinately insisted on leaving the plaza to recapture the 4-pounder—the same cannon that had come with the relief column—that had been lost to the Texans. The cannon was recovered and Condelle ordered that Sánchez Navarro take command of it along with the howitzer, which was put in place by knocking down a piece of the cemetery. Filisola reported that the 4-pounder was located in the atrium of the church and that Sánchez Navarro was aided in the effort by Captain Lafuente, Capt. Antonio Tenorio, 1st Lt. Pizaña, and Lt. José María Clavel. Although there was no artillery crew, Condelle instructed Sánchez Navarro to open fire on the main door of the priest's house, where the enemy was likely to enter the plaza.

To sustain his position in the plaza, Sánchez Navarro was sent ten veteran soldiers and eighty replacements from the Morelos battalion. As the replacements did not even know how to load a musket, Condelle sent them to the rear and brought up presidial troops from the Ríogrande and Aguaverde companies.

Regarding the leadership of the officers that night, Sánchez Navarro wrote the following: "It slipped my mind to say that at the time of repelling the enemy, I heard, at various times, the voice of the Commanding General Martín Perfecto de Cos and in the most advanced post I saw him very near Lt. Col. Dionisio [Cos; brother of Martín]. They had their swords in hand, giving a brilliant example of valor. I will never forget the gallantry of Antonio Tenorio,

Lt, brevet Capt. of the battalion . . . attached to the Morelos [battalion]. This youngster was gravely wounded days ago by bullet in the bone of the right shoulder. He moved forward and stayed at the front of the danger for that entire sad night."

According to Filisola, Cos returned to the Alamo that night to make plans for the next day. As the Texans had occupied so many of the houses in the city, he decided to withdraw the troops and artillery to the Alamo. He also planned to take part of the cavalry and attack the enemy on the flanks and at their rear.

At 2:15 a.m. on the morning of December 10, a voice rang out saying that Cos was dead and that four captains, along with their companies, had fled. Those who left that night were the adjutant inspector of Coahuila and Texas, Juan José Elguezábal; Capt. Ignacio Rodríguez, commander of the escort of the general; the captain of the Aguaverde battalion, Juan José Galán; and the Capt. Manuel Barragán of the Ríogrande battalion. They were said to have left because Cos had ordered them to attack the enemy's flank. Four hundred men were said to have deserted. Filisola put the number of deserters at 6 officers and 179 men.

In the midst of the confusion, Cos began to withdraw the army into the Alamo. When daylight arrived, Sánchez Navarro noted that the replacements, the ammunition park, the artillery, many of the stores, luggage, etc. were being withdrawn toward the Alamo. In his account, Filisola wrote that by 7:00 a.m. everything was on its way to the Alamo except for the 4-pounder commanded by Sánchez Navarro, who for some reason had not been informed of the withdrawal. Filisola gave the list of things being pulled back to the Alamo as the wounded, cash funds, the munitions, nine pieces of artillery, and the mules.

> While they were in the process of dismounting the howitzer, Sánchez Navarro was approached by an aide of General Cos, Lt. Francisco Rada. He informed Sánchez Navarro that Cos had ordered him to drop whatever he was doing and report to him immediately. Sánchez Navarro replied that he was not going to do so as General Cos was dead and Condelle had ordered him to defend the plaza at all costs. Shortly afterward, Condelle notified Sánchez Navarro that he would take over command of the plaza and told him to obey the order to present to Cos, who was not dead. During the trip to the Alamo, Rada told Sánchez Navarro that there had been an assassination attempt on Cos but that it had been thwarted by a few soldiers.

Upon arriving at the Alamo, confusion and discouragement were seen to be widespread. Sánchez Navarro documented that the five hundred or so horses were so hungry they were chewing on uniform cloaks and even the brackets of the guncarriages of the cannons. Women and babies had abandoned their houses in Béjar and gathered there. Officers were heard mumbling, "All is lost" and "What are we to do?" The story of the panic at the Alamo was even more dramatic according to Filisola. He wrote that there was mass hysteria and that the women and children thought the whole garrison in the city had perished and the Mexicans had been routed. "They were overcome with such fright that they increased the confusion with their cries, tears and running about as they were doing without any purpose, wandering from one place to another, thus spreading discouragement in the troop itself." He went on to note that the people in the Alamo were crying, "Treason, they want to hand us over, we are lost." Cos tried to calm them, but because of the darkness and the multitude being in a panic, the general was trampled and mauled in a brutal manner.[30]

When he was taken to see Cos, Sánchez Navarro observed that Cos tried to sit up but was unable to do so, due to illness (or injury). Cos informed him that, as a result of the cowardice and treachery of many of their companions, all was lost. He inquired about the status of the plaza, and Sánchez Navarro reassured him that Condelle and the Morelos troops still held the plaza. Cos instructed him to "go and save those valiant men." He gave Sánchez Navarro authority to approach the enemy and negotiate a workable agreement. Ramón Múzquiz and Lieutenant Rada were named to join him on his commission. Cos forcefully instructed Sánchez Navarro to "save the decorum of our government, the honor of its arms, and the honor, lives, and property of its officers and troops who still accompany me, even if I perish."

Sánchez Navarro gave a long but interesting account of confronting first his own troops at the plaza, and later the Texans, as the commissioners tried to enter Béjar. When Sánchez Navarro notified Condelle that the plaza was to be abandoned and firing suspended, he responded that Sánchez Navarro would not be allowed to go negotiate with the enemy because the Morelos battalion had never capitulated. Several of the troops and officers nearby heard this, including Lt. Col. Juan Aguayo and Lt. Juan Tello. These men surrounded Sánchez Navarro, threatening him with weapons and rude insults. After further discussion, Condelle finally gave in and allowed the commission to proceed.

Sánchez Navarro noted that the enemy could not understand the Mexican bugle calls, so the commissioners attached a handkerchief to a stick as they approached Béjar. They were immediately surrounded by a group of colonists, among them Smith, a resident of Béjar, who asked them a thousand questions in a language they did not understand and therefore could not answer.[31] The colonists then began making some threatening demonstrations. He noted that the priest, Rafael de la Garza, joined the commissioners and was constantly at their sides.

At about 9:00 a.m., the commander, Edward Burleson, appeared, and immediately the issue of their lack of credentials proving their right to negotiate came up. Smith introduced the other Texans, Maj. Gen. N. Thompson, Major Morris, and Captain Edelt ("or something like that," according to Sánchez Navarro).[32] It was pointed out by Burleson that the Texans had tried three times to send representatives to the Mexican general under a white flag and received only cannon fire. He also noted that the day prior, one of the Mexican batteries raised a black flag. Sánchez Navarro asked Burleson under what principles they were negotiating, and Burleson replied, "Under the good faith of men who have valor and arms; and precisely under the condition that the belligerent forces strictly conserve the respective positions that they occupied when we came that morning to this city." With these kinds of comments, the Texans were said to have treated the Mexican commission with great disrespect until Rada went to the Alamo and returned with written documentation from Cos.

At one point in his diary Sánchez Navarro did point out two separate acts of kindness performed by Major Morris:

> Burleson was urging us to tell him if our General was wounded, as if we had many officers and troops in this condition. He took the delicacy of telling them that it was not simply a curiosity but the desire to be useful to us as he had excellent doctors. I gave him thanks for this kindness and I named the wounded, sharing (because friendship moved me) the bad luck of Lt. Col. José María Mendoza, who in addition to being gravely wounded, eight days ago had lost his baggage with his dispatches, clothes, jewelry, [and] money, and [hoped] when possible, somehow his luck could be alleviated. I stopped, and Morris spoke with much interest. Bringing out a small purse with six or more ounces of gold, he said: "This and all the luggage of Señor Mendoza that I took by force, I have much pleasure and satisfaction in giving back to a representative named by Señor Mendoza." And this return was carried out.

During an uneasy back and forth and several trips to the Alamo by Rada, Sánchez Navarro heard the Texans, on various occasions, mention the names "Galán" and "Barragán." As it turned out, the Texans were suspicious that these commanders had left with their companies in order to make a surprise attack on them. Sánchez Navarro was pleased with the Texans thinking this, as he thought that he would be negotiating from strength in this case. Rada ruined that perception, however, when he returned from the Alamo and told the Texans that the troops who had left were deserters.

As negotiations began, the Mexicans used N. Arsinieaga as their translator. The Texans used Smith, with James Cameron as his assistant because Smith was drunk.

The Texans initially asked the Mexicans to come up with a list of proposals. They did so and presented the Texans with a list of eight items for their approval. Burleson and his commissioners left the room and returned later with a list of their own eighteen proposals and a rejection of the Mexican articles. The first Texan proposal was that their besieging army be declared the victor, and therefore the Alamo would not be destroyed and all artillery and arms would be brought into Béjar and surrendered. The second article was that the Mexican general, commanders, and officers would remain as prisoners of war until the conclusion of the fighting. They would be conducted to San Felipe and would not be able to reclaim, for now, anything more than their lives.

After hearing only the two mentioned articles, Lieutenant Rada arose and declared with a zeal that Sánchez Navarro described as laudable but very reckless: "Not a bit of it. . . . We will shoot each other before admitting to such vile and degrading conditions." Apparently Señor Múzquiz was the calm and thoughtful negotiator on the Mexican side. Sánchez Navarro later claimed that the country owed him a debt, as "due to his prudence and finesse, he touched on points that I, as a soldier, could not remember." Sánchez Navarro noted that he was an adherent to the principle that a Mexican soldier appreciated honor more than his life. After Múzquiz left the room and met with the Texans alone, he was able to point out to them that "they had acted in contradiction to their principals, [because] they wanted to oppress and take away the honor and freedom of men who obeyed their government." Upon their return the Texans seemed to be somewhat more understanding, but both sides continued to disagree on the legality of the current Mexican government. Finally, after much discussion, Sánchez Navarro wrote, "It is amazing the pride that enters the soul of a Mexican when he sees that foreigners want to outrage him or intimidate him: I felt myself embrace a blazing fire, and getting up and addressing Burleson, I said, taking out my watch, 'Arrange your sample for mine [i.e., synchronize your watch] and remain in the intelligence, because the gentleman wants it (I pointed out to Johnson) that within three hours we commence the firing. We will prove that on not being defeated we have honor and courage. God and men judge those who cause blood to spill.'" Burleson and Múzquiz both pointed out that all six of the commissioners were brothers as they were all Mexicans, and Sánchez Navarro decided not to leave. After partaking in some coffee, wheat tortillas, and nuts, they started talking again, with the Texans focusing on all the injustices that the Mexican government had committed against them. By midnight on December 10–11 they were still debating the legality of the government, and things were getting heated once again.

Sánchez Navarro observed that he was being very careful in his choice of words because the Mexicans were aware that two hundred Texans, with an 18-pounder cannon, were making their way to Béjar.[33] He had also been informed that de Zavala and a man called Apuche were headed that way, and he had no desire to negotiate with either of them. He considered both as traitors and very evil men.

He wrote that despite their terrible situation, he did everything humanly possible not to show any signs of weakness. Sánchez Navarro theorized that the Texans finally tired of the Mexicans' endurance, and at 2:00 a.m. on December 11 they brought some propositions that seemed to the Mexicans to be rational, dignified, and equitable. The Mexican commissioners took the articles back to Cos and he made some minor alterations. Cos noted that there was nothing that tarnished the honor of the Mexicans in the agreement. Sánchez Navarro did note that two of the articles bothered him. The first was the requirement that all the officers had to pledge never to fight against any people who fought for the constitution of 1824.[34] He thought that this was not going to work because there were revolts in the central republic that were also in favor of the constitution, and the soldiers were going to obey orders. The second article that he mentioned as being unworkable was an article that said all people, military or civilian, could go with Cos's column back to Mexico or stay in Texas, and there would be no punishment. He noted that the deserters from Béjar were not going to be allowed to go unpunished.

The final agreement was signed by all the participants previously named (except Smith) on December 11 in Béjar. The final capitulation agreement did include eighteen articles (see appendix 24). Santa Anna sent on a copy of the capitulation agreement to Tornel on January 21 of the following year. He recommended that the agreement not be published.

At 11:00 a.m. on December 13, the Mexican column began its march to Laredo. Sánchez Navarro wrote that it was because "the fate of arms went against us." He also described what happened as they started their retreat: "The section began the march taking what it could, and more weapons than they brought, because even the officers, replacements, and all the muleteers carried muskets. At the beginning of the march Col. Condelle formed his troops and said, in his loudest voice, Long live the Supreme Government of Mexico! We all responded: Long live! These cries were repeated three times, and playing drum and flags deployed, we marched to San José, where we stopped, because it was assured that the enemy was coming to attack us: it turned out to be false." The Mission San José was about two miles from the Alamo. For this reason, some sources document that Cos and the Mexican troops left Béjar on December 14. They left the Alamo on December 13 and marched to the mission the first day, but technically they were outside of Béjar the night of December 13.

Several officers and troops were too sick or gravely wounded to make the trip and were left in the plaza. These included Lieutenant Colonel Mendoza, Captain Zenea, Subaltern Solís, and more than thirty individuals of the troop.[35] Lieutenant Rada, due to the insinuations of General Cos, volunteered to stay behind to aid them in any way he could. Filisola added that 2nd Lt. Ignacio Solio volunteered to stay behind as well.

The total Mexican casualties from the siege of Béjar are, for the most part, well documented. In the battle of Conception, the Morelos battalion had twelve dead and thirty-four wounded, while the cavalry under Rafael Ugartechea had six wounded.

Juan Sánchez Navarro compiled the reports from seven of the presidial companies that fought in the siege of Béjar. In the footnotes for the list, he noted that he did not have the numbers for five other presidial companies. These numbers do not include the Mexican casualties from Concepción previously given, but they might include casualties from some of the other units involved that day. Note that the list was signed by the commanders of five of the seven companies that reported their numbers. The list of the dead and wounded is as follows:[36]

List of the dead and wounded who participated in the siege of the Plaza of Béjar that lasted from Oct. to Dec. of 1835.

Company	Rank	Name	Dead	Wounded
Lampazos	Private	Francisco de los Santos	listed below as dead; no date	
	Id	Felipe Castañeda		28 October
	Id	José María de la Garza		9 November
	Corporal	Cristóbal Mendiola		28 October
	Private	Rafael de la Garza		30 September
1st Flying of Tamaulipas		Valentín de la Garza		26 November
		Antonio Jaime	15 November	
		Jesús Sánchez	25 October	
	Corporal	Juan de Jesús Avalos		8 December
		Juan Jaime		2 December
	Private	T. de Aquino Flores		26 November
		Ramón Guevara		5 December
2nd Flying of Tamaulipas		Simón Garcia		26 November
		Fulgencio Barbosa		6 December
		Pantaleón de la Garza	26 November	
		Apolonio Olivares		26 November
		Ruperto Ramos		9 December
	Corporal	Rafael Jiménez	9 December	7 December
	Private	José María del Toro		28 October
	Corporal	Candelario Guajardo		28 October
Béjar	Private	Jesús Arragaña		no date
		Guadalupe Salcido	9 December	26 November
		Eusebio Almaguey		21 October
		José María Fuentes		no date
1st Active of Nuevo León	Private	Francisco Guerrero	26 November	28 October
		Roberto Sánchez		no date

Company	Rank	Name	Dead	Wounded
2nd Active of Nuevo León	Private	Rámon Cadena	26 November	
		Juan Evaristo		26 November
Activa de Pueblo Viejo		Gregorio Ovalle [Oballos]	8 December	
		Victor García		26 November

Notes:

First. The present list does not include the names of the dead and wounded that were suffered by the companies Ríogrande, Aguaverde, Bahía del Espíritu Santo, Alamo de Parras, and the 2nd Active of Tamaulipas because their captains or commanders have not remitted the corresponding lists. [Some of these were among the troops that deserted.]

Second. The Corporals and Privates that are annotated with the sign (*) served in the Company of Lancers. [In the list in his book Sánchez Navarro did not include the asterisks].

Information of the families of the nine individuals marked as dead in the preceding list:

Private Francisco de los Santos: Mother, María Gertrudis Sánchez, residing in Lampasas.
Private Antonio Jaime: Wife, Guillerma Núñez, pregnant in Laredo.
Private Jesús Sánchez: His family should be at the presidio of Ríogrande.
Private Pantaleón de la Garza: His family should be in Carmargo.
Corporal Rafael Jiménez: His family should be in the Valley of Santa Rosa.
Private Guadalupe Salcido: His family should be in Béjar.
Private Francisco Guerrero: Sister Guadalupe in Agualeguas.
Private Ramón Cadena: Wife, Gregoria Jaramillo, with three young children in Montemorelos.
Private Gregorio Oballos [*sic*]: Wife, Gregoria Regalado, with seven young children in the Valley Nuevo de Purificación.

Lampasas, January 14, 1836 Francisco Castañeda—Juan Nepomuceno Tello—Juan Manuel Maldonado—Gregorio Pérez—Francisco Herrera

It is obvious that Sánchez Navarro cared enough about the dead men that he was anxious for the government to get aid to the families they left behind.

For the seven companies that reported their casualties there were nine dead and twenty-one wounded (we do not know if Felipe Castañeda was dead or wounded, but he is counted here as wounded as he was not listed in the notes as dead). If one assumes that the number of dead and wounded in the five companies that did not report their number mirrored the above number, these five companies would have approximately eight dead and fourteen wounded. This would give a grand total for the siege of Béjar of seventeen dead and thirty-five wounded. Adding the dead and wounded from Concepción and the siege would give an overall total, for the two and one-half months, of approximately twenty-nine dead and seventy-five wounded. It should be noted that even though there are three men on the above list who died on November 26 (the day of the grass fight), there are only seven listed as wounded from that day. Since Cos had reported one officer wounded and thirteen enlisted men wounded in that action, it seems that seven men are missing from this list, making the number of wounded possibly as high as eighty-two.

The main unknown in looking at the casualty numbers is that the number of dead and wounded of the Morelos battalion after the battle of Concepción are not given. There were 208 officers and men of the Morelos battalion documented to have arrived in Béjar. In a letter that will be discussed later in this chapter, Cos reported that after the siege was over he was left with 120 men of the Morelos battalion. Subtracting those dead and wounded from Concepción would leave about 41 dead and wounded from the Morelos battalion in the fighting over the last few days. Therefore, the number of Mexican dead and wounded in the entire October–December action is likely to be in the neighborhood of 145.

Two interesting documents are found in the Mexican military archives regarding the troops that detached or deserted from Béjar on the night of December 9–10. The first is a letter from the commander of the presidial company of Ríogrande to Santa Anna. He described the actions that were taking place just prior to the fall of Béjar and was trying to explain why he had left the city:

> **Presidial Company of Ríogrande**
> **Señor General**
>
> I have just arrived today with the company under my command, in retreat from the capital of Béjar, where I was under the orders of the commanding general, Don Martín Perfecto de Cos. The plaza [of Béjar] was occupied by the enemy on the morning of the 10th of the current month [December] after a continuous action that began the morning of the 9th.
>
> The plaza was lost, in my opinion, by some intrigue, because otherwise it would be difficult for that class of enemy to defeat us.
>
> The reasons to suggest intrigue are the following: At about seven in the evening on the ninth, the enemy fire died down, as did our own, and

about two in the morning on the following day, enemy fire began behind the plaza from the north. Being in the fortification that was under my command, I heard the voice of Señor Condelle, who was responding to [the fire] with cavalry. At that moment, I personally took half my company, along with lancers, part of the Aguaverde [company], and some infantry of the Morelos battalion, with His Lordship [Condelle] and in less than half an hour we ousted [the enemy] and recovered two of our cannons that had been taken from the plaza. At this moment I received an order communicated by Sr. Condelle to mount with all my company that was at the plaza of the Alamo and conduct a large-caliber culverin to that point [Alamo plaza]. I brought it, and because my horses were too overworked it took too long, even more so at the river crossing, where I was overtaken by other cavalry companies conducting cannons from the plaza of Béjar to that of the Alamo. Seeing that it was taking too long, I sent the lieutenant of my company to the Alamo to tell Señor Cos to please send me 8 well-mounted men from that garrison to take the piece. I stayed at that point with my company, where I encountered Captain Galán of the Aguaverde Company, coming from the Alamo. He told me that we were to return to our presidios, as the Sr. General had ordered, [and] that His Lordship was on his way to surrender to the enemy. This news was very surprising, since I understood that we had been ordered to the Alamo in order to attack the rearguard of the enemy. Just then, my lieutenant returned and told me he had found the Sr. General lying down in his room, wrapped in covers, and that [the General] told him to tell me to see if I could spike the culverin and abandon it, and for me to see Colonel Ugartechea, commander of the aforesaid plaza. Immediately I went alone and observed, as I entered the plaza, a profound silence and much darkness. When I asked some of the men I encountered where the Colonel was, none could say anything about him until, by chance, I found him resting in a campaign tent. I was very surprised at his situation in the circumstances we were in, and I could not help but rebuke him, asking him why he was in bed when the enemy was battling with Colonel Condelle. He answered me that it was no use; that I should take my company to the plaza; [and] that we were going to surrender. [He said] that our representatives, Adjutant Inspector José Juan Sánchez and Citizen Ramón Músquiz, were going to propose that we withdraw to the interior with our arms, swearing not to take up arms against the colonists. This account irritated me so much that I told him my company would not surrender their arms; that I was going to withdraw with it; and that if we clashed, [the company] would be in it to the last. He answered me that we need not clash, and that I should not worry [because] they would do nothing to us. Again, I told him no, and asked to speak with the General, which he did not permit. I left and went to where my company was, along with the Aguaverde Company. When I left, I saw all the artillery abandoned at the entrance of the wall, some unarmed men, and I heard talk that Colonel Ugartechea had surrendered the plaza to the enemy on the night of the 9th, and taken the General prisoner. I began my march for this place [Guerrero]. One of the privates from my company requested permission to remain in order to rescue his brother, which I granted. He arrived this same day and told me he had left at 3:00 in the afternoon of that day and had sent a trusted countryman to talk to his brother and tell him to come before he was captured. [He reported] that all the troops were disarmed and captured except him, and that at the first opportunity that arose, he would get out; that Señor Condelle had defended the church until 8 in the morning and had lost some men, until Colonel Ugartechea came and took him to the Alamo with the rest of the troops, telling him that the rest of [our] people were there; [and] that when he entered [the Alamo], he was taken prisoner.

The enemy do not amount to a thousand men, yet it is to those that our artillery pieces have gone, which amount to 20 pieces, though only five or six are usable and those [are] incapable of making a quick march to these places unless it were with a small force. My company is absolutely dismounted, lacking assistance for the last six months, and unable to act promptly. For all that I have written to Your Lordship, you will please, for the good of the country, to take the measures that you see fit, commanding me what to do, for I am prepared to follow my orders religiously.

God and Liberty. Village of Guerrero, December 13, 1835.
Manuel Rud[ecin]do Barragán

[To] general in chief of the division of operations in Texas wherever he may be.[37]

His account is somewhat consistent with the accounts of Sánchez Navarro and Filisola regarding the night of December 9–10, but they are all quite consistent about the rumors and chaos that were rampant that night. Barragán paints Domingo de Ugartechea as the villain and has him sleeping in a tent, arresting Cos, and surrendering the plaza, apparently all in a short time.

The second document is a similar letter written by the captain of the Aguaverde company, Juan José Galán:

> **Señor General**
>
> Now, at about three in the afternoon, I have just arrived at this presidio with the company under my command, having retreated from the capital of Béjar. There I was aiding the commanding general, Don Martín Perfecto de Cos, with the forces that were holding that plaza, which was occupied by the enemy after a continuous action that lasted from the morning of the 9th until the 10th at about 8 in the morning. At that hour, the commanding general ordered us to withdraw from the points that the garrison was holding, and that the presidial companies that were covering most of them should mount their horses and execute that right away. Another order was received right away for the companies to move the artillery to the point of the Alamo, where His Lordship was located. This came at a time when the enemy had been dislodged from those points that with the darkness of night they had managed to surprise, [and the order] caused such a sensation that I went in person to see if it were true, or what cause motivated it. I entered the Alamo looking for the señor general, and since no one would give me any certain word as to his whereabouts, I decided to threaten one of his aides to reveal to me where he was, and thus I managed to find him. I remonstrated with him about the conditions of the plaza, telling him that the infantry that was under the command of Sr. Condey [Condelle] was perishing because there was no one to provision it, because they had ordered us to withdraw with the pretext that we would move the artillery; that that was the order that had been communicated. To this he replied that he knew nothing; that the situation was hopeless; and that I should come with my company, as I have done, to the village of Aguaverde, which is my residence for the aforesaid company.

All of this I report to Your Lordship in service to my duty, making use of the conduct of the señor chief of this department, who is traveling to meet Your Lordship.

This occasion affords me the pleasure of offering to Your Lordship my respect and due esteem.

God and Liberty. Village of Guerrero, December 13, 1835.
Juan José Galán
[To] Señor General in chief of the division of operations in Texas
Wherever he is located.[38]

In reading the account of Sánchez Navarro carefully in regards to the dates and times, as well as the accounts of Barragán and Galán, it becomes obvious that the fighting in the plaza of Béjar began on the night of December 9. The next morning, December 10, is when Sánchez Navarro and his commissioners went to Béjar to parlay with the Texans. The following day, December 11, the articles of surrender were signed by both sides. Many Texas history sources place these events one day earlier, but the Mexican accounts seem to agree about the dates.

Sánchez Navarro also mentioned that the retreating column, in general, as well as several officers, were aided by Múzquiz. In addition, it was noted that the owner of Atascoso Ranch, N. Salinas, helped in any way that he could. Sánchez Navarro called Salinas a good citizen and wrote that N. Herrera was as well. Sánchez Navarro also gave a list of the commanders and officers who stayed loyal to the Mexican government and left from Béjar:

> The Commanding General and Inspector, Martín Perfecto de Cos, with his aides; Lt. Col. Dionisio Cos, Lt. Col. N. Plasencia, Captains Andrés Videgaray, Pedro Saliella, and Juan Cortina, who had functioned as paymaster; Lt. N. Resdeja; and the Cadets Antonio Videgaray and N. García Aguirre.
>
> Col. Nicolás Condelle, with all his officers and veteran soldiers of the Morelos battalion, along with some of the replacements.
>
> Capt. Manuel Hernández with six men of the Regiment of Veracruz.
>
> The company of Lampasas: Subaltern from Monclova, Santiago Navaira, with a picket of the same.
>
> 1st Flying of Tamaulipas: Its Capt., Manuel Lafuente, and Subalterns attached to it, Esteban Téllez and Remigio Pizana.
>
> 2nd Flying: Its commander and 1st Lt., Juan Manuel Maldonado, and a Subaltern who was from Mendoza, José María de la Garza, with about thirty men of the mentioned 2nd company.

Alamo de Parras: Lt. Francisco Canañeda with only three or four soldiers that followed him.

Béjar: Subaltern Francisco Herrera, with only one soldier.

1st Active of Coahuila: Commander Subaltern, Rafael de Aguirre, with the picket that commanded [serving as] the escort of the general [Cos].

1st Active of Nuevo León: Commander Lt. of the 2nd of the same state, I say Lt. of the same, Gregorio Pérez, and the Cadet from Bavía, N. Pérez Nanceros, its commander, 2nd Lt. attached to Lampasas. Juan Tello and the attached Subalterns Bernardo Cavazos and Agustín Parra.

Unattached: Col. of Cavalry, Domingo de Ugartechea; Sgt. Maj. of the active battalion of Coahuila, N. Campuzano; Captain of cavalry Rafael Ugartechea and Subaltern of the same, Luis de Ugartechea.[39]

From the corps of military health that went from Matamoros to Béjar, Mariano Arroyo and two practitioners remained in this city to treat the sick and wounded. By disposition of the commanding general [Cos], the Director, N. Moro, and two other practitioners retreated. In honor of these I will say, that of about thirty-something wounded, between officers and troops, who have come from Béjar, only one has died until today, and all are comfortable, despite the continuous marches and the weather.[40]

On December 15, from the Rancho de Salinas, Cos reported what had happened in Béjar to his commander, General Santa Anna. Sánchez Navarro documented that they spent an extra day at that ranch, once again because of reports that the Texans were planning to attack. Santa Anna passed the document on to Tornel on December 27:

Most Excellent Señor:

On the 15th, from the Rancho de Salinas 15 leagues from the city of Béjar, General Don Martín Perfecto de Cos tells me the following:

Most Excellent Señor: After fifty-six days of siege, without the slightest hope of being assisted with forces and provisions and military supplies, I have withdrawn from the city of Béjar by means of an honorable agreement.

The arrival of Colonel Ugartechea with the reinforcements at the same time that my few soldiers were battling for the sixth day, hand to hand, for the terrain of this plaza, made no difference because no use could be made of them, since they lacked training and were exhausted after having marched 23 leagues on that same day in order to arrive at the city. Rather, they only served to increase the consumption of provisions that we were absolutely lacking. Under such critical circumstances, I saw no other available option than to abandon the plaza and occupy the Alamo, which, because of its military position and [being] more reduced [in area] was easier for me to hold. I did so, taking the artillery with me, its park, and other supplies that I was able to transport, despite having been abandoned with my officers by the two presidial companies of Ríogrande and Agua Verde and a number of lancers with their captains. This event so demoralized the rest, that in dispersion almost all of them followed their example, leaving me with just 120 loyal soldiers from the Morelos battalion and a few dragoons and presidial [soldiers], because the rest of them who were fighting were dead or wounded.

The situation in which I found myself was desperate. My retreat was cut off, my troops were exhausted from so much combat, and I had no horse[s] available on which to bring in the provisions necessary to hold my position. By virtue of that, and availing myself of the lull in enemy activity, I ordered the signing of agreements, copies of which I will forward to Your Excellency as soon as I arrive at Laredo, to which I am heading, taking with me more than five hundred men, including the replacements, with their cartridge boxes full of munitions and a four[-pounder] artillery piece, with the rest of [our] armaments in possession of the rebels. I have halted today only to acquire the wagons necessary to transport the wounded and to provide to my subordinates the indispensable resources to undertake through the wilderness a march of ten days that they are estimated to have to make.

The commanders, officers, and troops have conducted themselves with their customary valor and steadfastness, and at the first opportunity I will prepare for Your Excellency the report of the firing and combat during the nearly two months that I was under siege.

And I transcribe this to Your Excellency so that you might bring it to the attention of His Excellency, the interim president. Its contents, while they do confirm the loss of the plaza of Béjar, cause the satisfaction that the majority of the garrison was saved, which was believed to have suffered a worse fate.

God and Liberty. Headquarters at San Luís Potosí.
December 27, 1835
Ant[oni]o López de Santa Anna[41]

Cos wrote to Santa Anna a second time regarding his defeat at Béjar, on December 29, after reaching Laredo. Cos seemed to be trying to minimize the results of the defeat and at the same time magnify the problems that he encountered:

Most Excellent Señor:

Fulfilling what I promised Your Excellency in my note of the 15th of this month [December], I enclose for your superior knowledge the agreements that I had to make in order to effect my withdrawal from Béjar, for even if it had been attempted by active force, I would not have arrived at this town with one fifth of my troops, due both to the poor state of that [force] and to the vast wilderness that lay between there and any other town in which to maintain myself, with no provisions to feed them.

From the documents, Your Excellency will see that the dignity of our arms has in no way been dishonored, because I derived from my position every advantage that could be desired under such circumstances, and even more than those that appear in the documents to which I refer, as Your Excellency will understand from the Report that I enclose to you.

My troops, Your Excellency, and I speak of the cavalry, were hesitating and deserting in droves, and I needed tremendous energy (despite my personal situation) to avoid worse misfortunes stemming from the disorder.

Neither the artillery nor the other supplies that remained in Béjar was I able to bring with me, because I had absolutely no mules. But notwithstanding that, I would have brought [the artillery] as well had not most of it been mounted on carts belonging to the local citizens.

Almost none of the [artillery] park fell into enemy hands because much of it had been consumed during the siege, especially during the last days of firing. I then loaded my soldiers with the cartridge boxes, and the same with the housing of the 4-inch piece, which I brought. The armaments that could not travel were rendered useless.

The force that accompanies me, including those who subsequently have been arriving, is 815 men, who, without relinquishing my direct command, I have placed under the [orders] of the Most Excellent Sr. General Don Vicente Filisola. But of all of them, only 100 infantry will be available, because the rest are raw recruits, untrained and lacking devotion to the service, and dismounted presidial companies who are incapable at present of [performing] any operations, both because of their uselessness and because of the little confidence that most of them inspire in me.

It remains to me only to assure Your Excellency that I did everything on my part to hold Béjar, and that [if] the campaign is still ongoing, there is a way for me to make up for the small setback that I suffered, as long as Your Excellency continues to provide me your special protection and affection.

Your Excellency, accept the renewed assurances of my particular loyalty and respect.

God and Liberty. Laredo, December 29, 1835.
Martín Perfecto de Cos[42]

Sánchez Navarro reported that the retreating Mexican column met up with the vanguard of the Mexican army, under the command of Ramírez y Sesma, at Laredo. He obviously was not impressed with the reception that his troops received from the advancing army, as he facetiously wrote: "Here is the beautiful brigade under the command of General Joaquín Ramírez y Sesma, who appear as Mexican soldiers; but we as Cossacks from Siberia. However, I think that their needs are more than ours, or at least they claim they are, because although they are paid superbly, well dressed, have good footwear and are very well supplied, with very fat horses, today I heard that, due to lack of shelter, they are exposed to the cold, and because of other problems, which they point out, it is an imposition to work."[43]

Filisola had reached the vanguard by this time, and he met with Sánchez Navarro to tell him that if it were in his hands, he would relieve their hunger, poor clothing, and misery. Sánchez Navarro claimed that several other worthy officers expressed similar sentiments but that in general it seemed as though his troops were despised. He believed the troops of the other units enjoyed coming to see the troops who had come from Béjar and showing off their shiny uniforms, brilliant weapons, fat horses, and beautiful luggage.

CHAPTER TEN

Conclusion

The Mexican army at Laredo included the vanguard division under the command of General Ramírez y Sesma, composed of just over 1500 troops and eight pieces of artillery. The other section of the army was the column that retreated from Béjar under the command of General Cos, made up of slightly more than 800 men, half of whom were the raw recruits (including some convicts) who were replacements for the Morelos battalion. Now that they were all together, the entire force was under the command of Gen. Vicente Filisola, who had joined Ramírez y Sesma's division at La Laja Pass on the Salado River on December 10.

Things could not have been much worse in Laredo with no shelter and, other than cattle, no food to be had. Troops were camping in the corrals, and the officers were stuffed into small huts. The distance to any surrounding town was great and no matter the direction, deserts had to be crossed in intense heat (even in December).

The army had been there only a short time when news came that three hundred rebels from Béjar had left to advance against Matamoros. There were also reports that the Federalist ex-colonel José María González was threatening towns in northern Mexico.

In addition, Filisola wrote that "there appeared in the vicinity of Laredo a horde of savages who attacked those who were guarding the horses of the presidio and killed a Corporal, wounded two soldiers and carried off the horses."[1]

Santa Anna had written Filisola on December 20 after finding out that Cos had surrendered and ordered the vanguard division under Ramírez y Sesma to march northwest to the town of Guerrero (the former Presidio Ríogrande) and await the rest of the army there. Filisola was to send a copy of the order immediately to General Urrea and tell him that instead of marching to Laredo he was to stop at Guerrero.

The next day Filisola sent a dispatch to Santa Anna trying to convince him to permit the army to use the road to Goliad instead of marching so far out of their way in going to Béjar. Santa Anna would not relent and demanded that the original order be carried out.

Santa Anna commanded the troops under Cos to march to Monclova, where they could recuperate. It is hard to imagine what the Morelos battalion had suffered in sailing (some marched) all the way to Texas, on to Béjar, back to Laredo, and then on to Monclova. This was all done through deserts and in extreme heat. Filisola documented that thirty-two of Cos's men and many women and children perished, mostly from thirst, on the trip south from Laredo.

1835 was not a good year for the Mexican army in Texas. Even though the rebellions in other parts of Mexico had calmed, to a point, things were getting much worse in Texas. There were officially no Mexican troops in Texas. The defeats at Anáhuac, Goliad, Lipantitlán, Gonzales, and Béjar had given the Texans great confidence and time to grow even stronger.

Even though the revolts in the interior were somewhat settled, the one and only man in charge of all things political and military, Santa Anna, was still greatly distracted by politics. As will be seen in the next volume of this work, he was constantly distracted by matters in Mexico City and never could turn his entire focus to Texas.

A larger and much stronger Mexican army was gathering and would be marching against Béjar soon. It is obvious that the Mexicans learned nothing about the Texans in the many defeats they suffered. Despite the setbacks the Mexican army's biggest problem was still overconfidence.

The Mexican army suffered from lack of funding, training, and supplies. They did not yet realize the conditions they would be facing in Texas, including the wide rivers, thick forests, cold weather, and muddy plains. They failed to bring pontoon bridges to cross the rivers and lacked winter uniforms to protect against the blizzards they would face.

Filisola was likely correct in his assessment that it would be much harder to advance on Béjar than Goliad as the distance was greater and the availability of provisions less. They also brought female camp followers on the campaign, which was a detriment to their ability to move quickly.

Once again, in spite of all the facts to the contrary, the Mexican officers continued to consider the Texans as riffraff with no experience in the art of war.

The officers were not even going to be paid, as they would be allowed to keep any spoils of war that they obtained as the colonists were driven out of Texas.

Often history books describe the Mexican army as poorly trained and ill-equipped Indians who did not even speak Spanish. This description is absurd. The Mexican army was, for the most part, better equipped than the Texans. They were very experienced and, from what has already been shown, tough as nails. They were, for the most part, well trained, but only in the Napoleonic style of warfare, which was not what they would experience in Texas. It is likely that the Texans' lack of training in this style of fighting turned out to be a great advantage as it forced the Mexican army to fight in ways in which they were totally unaccustomed.

1835 was definitely a bad year for the Mexican army in Texas. Due to some factors under their control, and many that were not, 1836 was going to be much worse.

APPENDIX 1

Austin to Ayuntamiento, October 16, 1833

Since my last official letter dated the 2nd of the present month the public affairs have taken a more favorable turn.

With the capitulation of Arista at Guanajuato the revolution has already been considered to be completed. The Congress has devoted itself to the great reforms that are needed to remove the monstrous anomalies that have existed in the practice and lawfulness of its administration of the government, which are so opposed and contradictory to the federal republican system.

The chamber of deputies is currently occupied with the law of April 6, 1830, which has been so harmful to Texas. The commission presented its opinion in favor of the revocation of article 11 of the afore-cited law and its discussion is scheduled for tomorrow.

The matter of the admission of Texas to the federation in the class of a state cannot be advanced until the matter of the law of April 6 has been concluded. This week I await a final resolution of all the matters of Texas.

I consider it doubtful that the question of statehood will be resolved and therefore I reiterate the opinion expressed in my last official letter, that all the ayuntamientos need to work together to organize a local government under the article of the law of May 7, 1824, as soon as the resolution of the congress on the matter is known.

God and Liberty and the Federation Mexico [City]
October 16, 1833
Esteban F. Austin
This is a copy. November 18, 1833
J. Maria Balmaceda Interim Secretary[1]

APPENDIX 2

Martín Perfecto de Cos Broadside, May 12, 1835

Brigade General Martín Perfecto de Cos, Commanding General and Inspector of the Internal States of the East to its Citizens

Fellow citizens:

Scarcely had the republic begun to enjoy, under the shadow of a paternal and just government, the peace so desired by good Mexicans, when in a corner in the south a new standard of rebellion arose anew. Such destructive principles, which scandalize even the most cold and moderate geniuses, are proclaimed by the restless Juan Alvarez.

The high government knew that the elements of discord had been reconcentrated in Zacatecas and fixed most of its attention there. Not many days passed before their fears were realized. The authorities of that state, under pretentious pretexts, break the obedience to which they are bound as the essential principle of their existences and declare themselves superior to the general powers of the Republic.

In these circumstances the Commanding General of these states painfully observed that the capital of Coahuila and Texas was piling up combustibles to use against the Supreme Government. They were alleging the same causes and apparently with the same tendencies that moved Zacatecas. It is the charge of the government, the same as the legislature, directed by the memorable decrees, that the towns resisted in the year of [page ends]

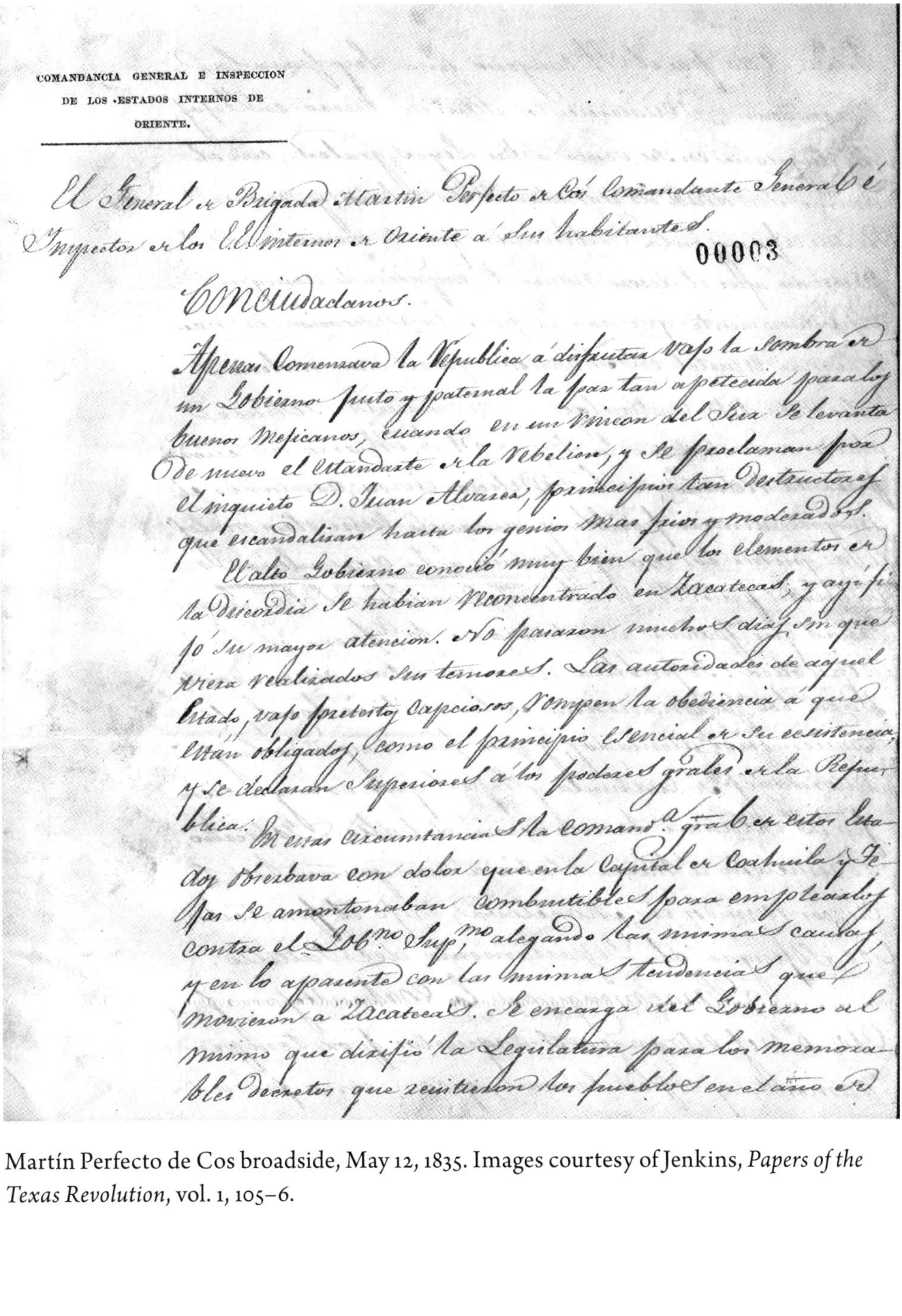

COMANDANCIA GENERAL E INSPECCION
DE LOS ESTADOS INTERNOS DE
ORIENTE.

El General de Brigada Martín Perfecto de Cós Comandante General é Inspector de los EE. internos de Oriente á sus habitantes.

00003

Conciudadanos.

Apenas comenzaba la República á disfrutar bajo la sombra de un Gobierno justo y paternal la paz tan apetecida para los buenos Mexicanos, cuando en un rincon del Sur se levanta de nuevo el estandarte de la rebelion, y se proclaman por el inquieto D. Juan Alvarez, principios tan destructores que escandalizan hasta los genios mas frios y moderados.

El alto Gobierno conoció muy bien que los elementos de la discordia se habian reconcentrado en Zacatecas, y así fijó su mayor atencion. No pasaron muchos dias sin que viera realizados sus temores. Las autoridades de aquel Estado, bajo pretextos capciosos, rompen la obediencia á que estan obligados, como el principio esencial de su existencia, y se declaran superiores á los poderes grales. de la República. En estas circunstancias la comand.a gral. de estos Estados observaba con dolor que en la Capital de Coahuila y Tejas se amontonaban combustibles para emplearlos contra el Gob.no Sup.mo alegando las mismas causas y en lo aparente con las mismas tendencias que movieron á Zacatecas. El encargado del Gobierno del mismo que dirigió la Legislatura para los memorables decretos que remitieron los pueblos en el año de

Martín Perfecto de Cos broadside, May 12, 1835. Images courtesy of Jenkins, *Papers of the Texas Revolution*, vol. 1, 105–6.

[. . .] 1833: a law was given by the honorable congress for the transference of 400 *sitios* of land in Texas, without complying with the general laws in its sale. Without a doubt [this was done] to please the colonists and it will be of service to the forces that intercede in the uprising. It was intended to disrupt the national decorum, although unsuccessfully, as a troop of the federation entered Monclova and took the barracks, as the troop was bothered at its site by the behavior of the sentinels. It [the congress] had flaunted its disobedience to the law of the previous March 31st to reduce the civic militia, arming the greatest number possible. Also, this was causing, among other evils, the removal of precious manpower from the nascent agriculture of the country. Mr. Gómez Farías is hiding in Monclova as he travels to embark for places outside of the Republic. A threatening initiative for the permanence of the local militia has been published. Other attacks are being committed, and finally, the authorities of Coahuila and Texas, believing that it was time to get the attention of the high government, resolved to make the campaign by the militiamen united in Monclova, under the pretext of subjugating the Department of Monclova.

To the disgrace of the Coahuilotexanos, two or three restless foreigners, by temperament and speculation, and with a little [page ends]

833: Se da por el H. congreso una Ley para la enagenacion de cuatrocientos sitios de tierra en Tejas, sin sugetarse en su venta á las Leyes grales., con el animo sin duda de agradar á los colonos, y servirse de sus esfuerzos en la sublevacion que se meditava: Se pretendió ajar el decoro nacional, impidiendo aunque infructuosamente que una tropa de la Federacion entrase á tomar cuartel en Monclova, pues eran molestos á su vista estos centinelas de su conducta: Se hace alarde de desobedecer la Ley de 31. de Marzo anterior para la reduccion de la Milicia civica, armando el mayor numero posible y causando entre otros males el de quitar los brazos precisos á la agricultura naciente del pais: Se oculta en Monclova al Sor. Gomez Farias que pasava á embarcarse p.a fuera de la Republica: Se publica una iniciativa amenazante para la permanencia de la milicia local: Se cometen otros atentados, y por fin creyendo las autoridades de Coahuila y Tejas que era ya tiempo de llamar la atencion del alto Gobierno, se resuelven á hacer salir á campaña los civicos reunidos en Monclova, vajo el pretesto de sojuzgar al Departamento del Saltillo.

Para mengua de los Coahuiltecanos, dos ó tres estrangeros, inquietos por temperamento y especulacion, y con una poca

[. . .] liveliness for their maneuvers, are those who have enflamed the state. They believe that it is possible to make views as crooked as they are difficult, pretending to involve in their attempts the honest colonists of Texas, who by inclination and convenience have always remained steadfast to the Supreme Government.

To seduce these new settlers, their situation is exaggerated and they are made to believe that in the nation there does not exist power enough to defeat them in case of an uprising. How wrong they are!

The commanding general, who contemplates the revolution of Coahuila as being of one single character because it involves sights that are new and offensive to all Mexicans, tried from the beginning to avoid its consequences with precautionary means, which somewhat confused the works of those who were directing the movement.

Afterwards I represented to His Excellency the Governor the reflections conducive to avoid the evils that threatened the state, but by some trick of fate reasoning did not answer, and he wanted to carry forwarded the meditated revolution. I will work with weapons to combat the recklessness of those who have strayed. The troops of the Supreme Government that have been placed under my orders, never forgetting their oaths, and always determined to maintain the national decorum, will also do their duty at this time.

I will not forget the villages [page ends]

00004

de rivera para sus Maniobras, son los que han metido en combustion al Estado, y crén posible realizar miras tan torcidas como dificiles, pretendiendo embolver en sus tentativas á los honrados colonos de Tejas, q.e por inclinacion y combeniencia han permanecido siempre adictos al Supremo Gobierno.

Para seducir á esos nuevos pobladores se les exagera su situacion, y se les hace creer que no hay en la nacion la potencia bastante para reducirlos en caso de un trastorno. ¡Cuanto se equivocan!

La Comandancia Gral. que contempla de un caracter singular la revolucion de Coahuila, porque embuelve miras nuevas, y ofensivas á todos los Mexicanos, procuró desde un principio evitar sus concecuencias, con medidas precautorias que en algun tanto desconcertaron los trabajos de los que dirigen el movimiento.

He hecho posteriorm.te al E. S. Gobernador las reflecciones conducentes á evitar los males que amenazan al Estado, pero si por una fatalidad no se atiende la razon, y se quiere llevar adelante la revolucion meditada, obraré yá con las armas p.a combatir la temeridad de los extraviados. Las tropas del Supremo Gob.no que se han puesto á mi ordenes no olvidan jamas sus juramentos y siempre decididas á mantener el decoro nacional, harán tambien su dever en esta vez. No perderé de vista á los pueblos

[. . .] of the frontier that to me merit more consideration than to their local authorities, and, whenever it is necessary, to move some force from the line of presidios, which will ensure its security in regard to the savage tribes.

Inhabitants of the states of the east! These are the occurrences that have recently called your attention. The simple story that I have recounted to you is enough for you to form a complete judgement about the matters of Coahuila, which ostensibly show no more than the uniformity with the projects of Zacatecas but in reality are other views. Be warned then to discard the insidious suggestions of the wicked. Look with the scorn that is deserved on those who attempt to seduce by painting a picture of ideal happiness. Always count on the particular esteem that your fellow citizen and friend professes toward you.

Martín Perfecto de Cos
Matamoros, May 12, 1835

de la frontera que me merecen mas consideracion q.e
á sus autoridades locales, y siempre que sea preciso
mover alguna fuerza de la linea de presidios, se hará
consultando su seguridad por lo que respeta á las tribus
salvages.

Havitantes de los Estados de Oriente! Estas son
las ocurrencias q.e han llamado ultimamente vuestra
atencion. El sencillo relato que os he hecho, es bastante
para q.e formeis un juicio cabal de los asuntos de Coa-
huila, que aunque en lo ostensible no manifies-
tan mas que uniformidad con los proyectos de
Zacatecas, en realidad son otras las miras. Estad
pues prevenidos para deshacer las insidiosas sugestio-
nes de los malvados: mirad con el desprecio devido á
aquellos que os pretendan seducir con pinturas
de una felicidad ideal, y contad siempre con la
particular estimacion que os profesa vuestro
conciudadano y amigo.

Mtin. Perf.to de Cos.

Matamoros Mayo 12. de 1835.

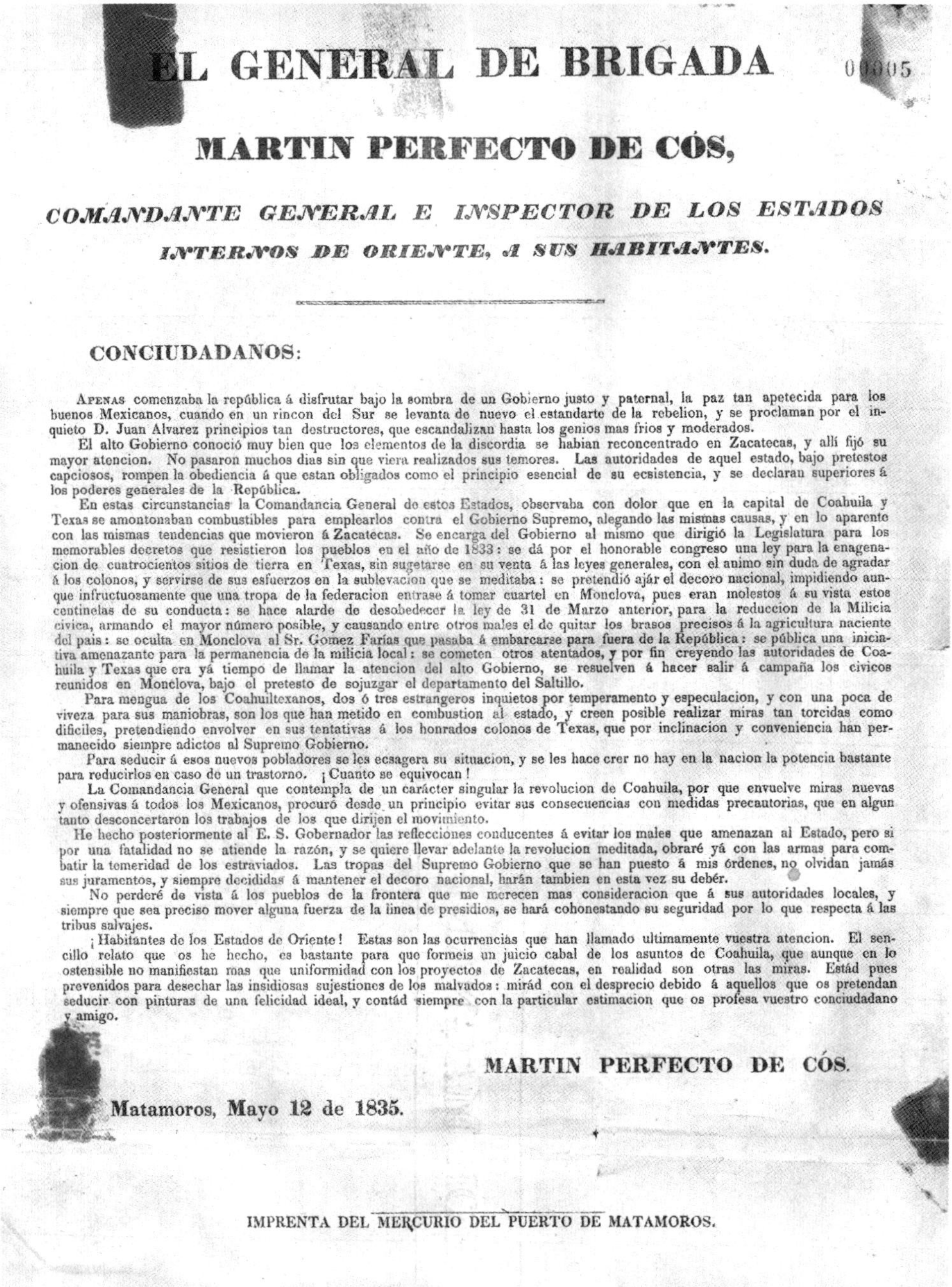

EL GENERAL DE BRIGADA

00005

MARTIN PERFECTO DE CÓS,

COMANDANTE GENERAL E INSPECTOR DE LOS ESTADOS INTERNOS DE ORIENTE, A SUS HABITANTES.

CONCIUDADANOS:

Apenas comenzaba la república á disfrutar bajo la sombra de un Gobierno justo y paternal, la paz tan apetecida para los buenos Mexicanos, cuando en un rincon del Sur se levanta de nuevo el estandarte de la rebelion, y se proclaman por el inquieto D. Juan Alvarez principios tan destructores, que escandalizan hasta los genios mas frios y moderados.

El alto Gobierno conoció muy bien que los elementos de la discordia se habian reconcentrado en Zacatecas, y allí fijó su mayor atencion. No pasaron muchos dias sin que viera realizados sus temores. Las autoridades de aquel estado, bajo pretestos capciosos, rompen la obediencia á que estan obligados como el principio esencial de su ecsistencia, y se declaran superiores á los poderes generales de la República.

En estas circunstancias la Comandancia General de estos Estados, observaba con dolor que en la capital de Coahuila y Texas se amontonaban combustibles para emplearlos contra el Gobierno Supremo, alegando las mismas causas, y en lo aparente con las mismas tendencias que movieron á Zacatecas. Se encarga del Gobierno al mismo que dirigió la Legislatura para los memorables decretos que resistieron los pueblos en el año de 1833: se dá por el honorable congreso una ley para la enagenacion de cuatrocientos sitios de tierra en Texas, sin sugetarse en su venta á las leyes generales, con el animo sin duda de agradar á los colonos, y servirse de sus esfuerzos en la sublevacion que se meditaba: se pretendió ajár el decoro nacional, impidiendo aunque infructuosamente que una tropa de la federacion entrase á tomar cuartel en Monclova, pues eran molestos á su vista estos centinelas de su conducta: se hace alarde de desobedecer la ley de 31 de Marzo anterior, para la reduccion de la Milicia civica, armando el mayor número posible, y causando entre otros males el de quitar los brasos precisos á la agricultura naciente del pais: se oculta en Monclova al Sr. Gomez Farías que pasaba á embarcarse para fuera de la República: se pública una iniciativa amenazante para la permanencia de la milicia local: se cometen otros atentados, y por fin creyendo las autoridades de Coahuila y Texas que era yá tiempo de llamar la atencion del alto Gobierno, se resuelven á hacer salir á campaña los civicos reunidos en Monclova, bajo el pretesto de sojuzgar el departamento del Saltillo.

Para mengua de los Coahuiltexanos, dos ó tres estrangeros inquietos por temperamento y especulacion, y con una poca de viveza para sus maniobras, son los que han metido en combustion al estado, y creen posible realizar miras tan torcidas como dificiles, pretendiendo envolver en sus tentativas á los honrados colonos de Texas, que por inclinacion y conveniencia han permanecido siempre adictos al Supremo Gobierno.

Para seducir á esos nuevos pobladores se les ecsagera su situacion, y se les hace crer no hay en la nacion la potencia bastante para reducirlos en caso de un trastorno. ¡Cuanto se equivocan!

La Comandancia General que contempla de un carácter singular la revolucion de Coahuila, por que envuelve miras nuevas y ofensivas á todos los Mexicanos, procuró desde un principio evitar sus consecuencias con medidas precautorias, que en algun tanto desconcertaron los trabajos de los que dirijen el movimiento.

He hecho posteriormente al E. S. Gobernador las reflecciones conducentes á evitar los males que amenazan al Estado, pero si por una fatalidad no se atiende la razón, y se quiere llevar adelante la revolucion meditada, obraré yá con las armas para combatir la temeridad de los estraviados. Las tropas del Supremo Gobierno que se han puesto á mis órdenes, no olvidan jamás sus juramentos, y siempre decididas á mantener el decoro nacional, harán tambien en esta vez su debér.

No perderé de vista á los pueblos de la frontera que me merecen mas consideracion que á sus autoridades locales, y siempre que sea preciso mover alguna fuerza de la linea de presidios, se hará cohonestando su seguridad por lo que respecta á las tribus salvajes.

¡Habitantes de los Estados de Oriente! Estas son las ocurrencias que han llamado ultimamente vuestra atencion. El sencillo relato que os he hecho, es bastante para que formeis un juicio cabal de los asuntos de Coahuila, que aunque en lo ostensible no manifiestan mas que uniformidad con los proyectos de Zacatecas, en realidad son otras las miras. Estád pues prevenidos para desechar las insidiosas sujestiones de los malvados: mirád con el desprecio debido á aquellos que os pretendan seducir con pinturas de una felicidad ideal, y contád siempre con la particular estimacion que os profesa vuestro conciudadano y amigo.

MARTIN PERFECTO DE CÓS.

Matamoros, Mayo 12 de 1835.

IMPRENTA DEL MERCURIO DEL PUERTO DE MATAMOROS.

Broadside from Cos to the Citizens published in a Matamoros newspaper on May 12, 1835.

APPENDIX 3

Cos to José María Tornel, September 28, 1835

Your Excellency

The political chief of the department of Nacogdoches, in a dispatch dated the 11th of the past [month of] August, among other things, tells me the following:

Your Lordship is not unaware of what types of inhabitants constitute this frontier. Two-thirds of the population consists of Mexican natives of the country and the adopted citizens, honorable and peaceful, who have been introduced according to the laws. They are occupied in their tasks without participating in revolution, having no other view than to work in peace the lands they have acquired by the generosity of the government. The other third consists of some men without country or morality or an occupation to sustain them, and consequently they risk nothing in a disturbance. The latter, of course, are always well armed, and are entering [the territory] each day [page ends]

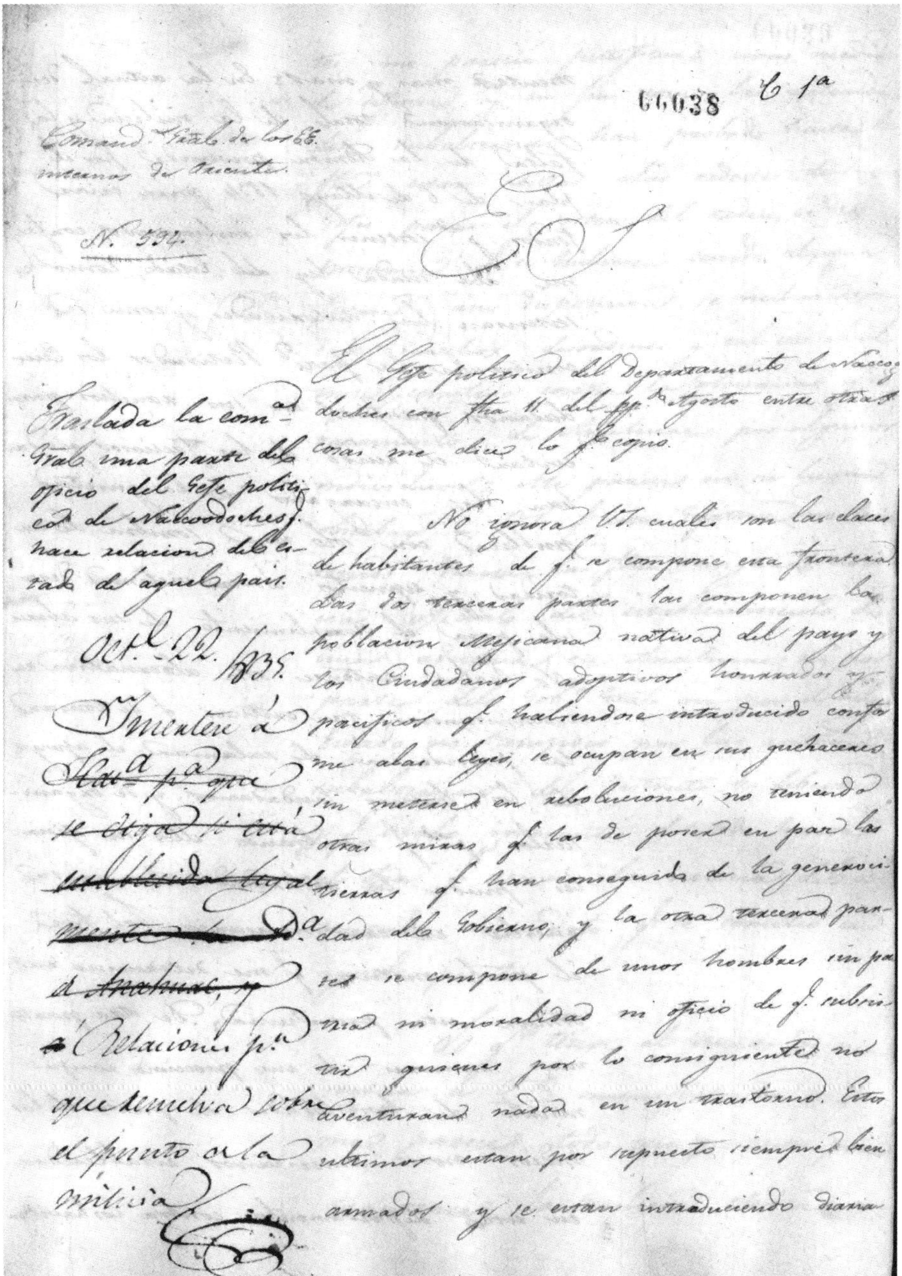
66038 C 1a

Comand.a Gral. de los E.E. internos de Oriente.

N. 594.

E. S.

Traslada la com.a Gral una parte del oficio del Gefe politico de Nacogdoches q. hace relacion del estado de aquel pais.

Oct.e 22. 1835.

Enterese [illegible]

[illegible] Relacion. p.a que resuelva sobre el punto de la milicia

El Gefe politico del Departamento de Nacogdoches con fha 11 del pp.do Agosto entre otras cosas me dice lo sig.te copio.

No ignora V.S. cuales son las clases de habitantes de q.e se compone esta frontera. Las dos terceras partes las componen la poblacion Mexicana nativa del pays y los Ciudadanos adoptivos honrados y pacificos q.e habiendose introducido conforme a las leyes, se ocupan en sus quehaceres sin meterse en revoluciones, no teniendo otras miras q.e las de poseer en paz las tierras q.e han conseguido de la generosidad del Gobierno, y la otra tercera parte se compone de unos hombres sin patria ni moralidad ni oficio de q.e subsistir quienes por lo consiguiente no aventuraran nada en un trastorno. Estos ultimos estan por supuesto siempre bien armados y se estan introduciendo diaria

Martín Perfecto de Cos to José María Tornel, September 28, 1835, XI / 481.3 / expediente 1101, fojas 63–66, Archivo Histórico Militar.

[. . .] more and more.

With the current total disorganization of the militia and the lack of the administration called for in the plan of May 6, 1834, in order to raise funds for the support of the militiamen according to the afore-cited state law, how are we to sustain the authorities, and how are we to preserve the peace?

When the peaceful citizens retreated to their ranches in order to avoid the noise of the factions, those who were in charge of public order were left with only a shadow of authority, at risk to falling victim to their [own] zeal in carrying out their duties. There was no alternative, then, in such critical circumstances than to take measures to reclaim the support of the good citizens and to organize them to appoint their own officials so that the authorities could call on their help if necessary. That was the reason that caused me to take this measure. For another thing, rumors of an impending breakout of hostilities against the inhabitants of this department on the part of the North American Indians settled here , [page ends]

mente mas y mas. En la actual desorganizacion total de la milicia y la falta de la Admon prevenida por el plan de 6 de Mayo 1834 para criar fondos p.a sostener los milicianos conforme ala citada ley del Estado, como se sostenian las autoridades, y como se conservaba la paz? Retirados los Ciudadanos pacificos en sus ranchos para evitar el ruido de los facciosos, quedaban los encargados de la quietud publica con solo una sombra de autoridad y expuestos á ser victimas desu celo para el cumplimiento de sus deberes. No habia entonces otra alternativa en circunstancias tan criticas q. de tomar la providencia de reclamar el apoyo de los buenos Ciudadanos y de organizarlos p.a q. nombrando ellos sus oficiales pueda la autoridad reclamar su auxilio en caso necesario. Tal fue el pral motivo q me determinó en tomar esta providencia. De otra parte unos rumores de un proccimo rompimiento de hostilidades de parte de los indios norte americanos establecidos en este departamento contra los havitan

[. . .] for me justified more defensive measures. Finally, since the local authorities have proven to date to be compliant with the orders of their leaders to maintain order, presumably, if they had had any force at their disposition, much disorder would have been prevented, as well as, perhaps, the outrages committed by some individuals against the customs office and detachment at Anáhuac.

I think it appropriate to tell Your Lordship that, up to now, this political office has had no official news of the establishment of a customs office in Anáhuac, either on the part of the Supreme Government, or by the state or local authorities of the district of Liberty. It [the political office] was unaware of everything up to the date that I received the report of the unprecedented attack that was committed at that place.

I have the honor to attach it [the report] for Your Excellency, stating that I believe it is all a pretext for keeping the civil militia [page ends]

00039

tes, me pareció justificar unas medidas de defensa, y en fin como las autoridades subalternas han probado hasta la fha estar adictas a las ordenes de sus Gefes para el sosten del orden, es de presumir q. si hubiesen tenido alguna fuerza a su disposicion se hubiese evitado muchos desordenes, y tal vez el ultrage cometido contra la Aduana y destacamento de Anahuac por algunos individuos.= Me parece en su lugar observar á V.S. q. esta Gefatura no ha tenido hasta la fha ninguna noticia oficial del establecimiento de una aduana en Anahuac, ni por parte del Gob.o Gral, ni por el del Estado, ni tampoco por las autorid. subalternas del distrito de Libertad, y q. estubo ignorante de todo hasta el dia q. recivió la noticia del atentado inaudito q. se cometio en aquel punto.

Lo q. le tengo el honor de insertar á V.E. manifestandole q. me parece todo un pretexto para mantener la milicia civica so-

[. . .] under arms.

God and Liberty. Lipantitlán, September 28, 1835.
Martín Perfecto de Cos

[To] His Excellency, the Secretary of War and Navy.

bre las armas.

Dios y Libertad Lipan-
Lipantitlán tlan Septbre. 28 de 1835.

Mn. Perf.to de Cos

Exmo. Sr. Secret.o de Guerra y Marina

APPENDIX 4

Santa Anna's Account of Zacatecas, May 24, 1835

Army of Operations

Number 1

Most Excellent Sir

To detail the account of the glorious and decisive action of the 11th of this [month] I deem it convenient to precede it with a relation, although brief, of the situation of the army at my arrival in Leon and of the movements that were successfully executed by the corps that composed it.

I arrived in Leon on the 24th of last April and the following day I directed the Active Battalion of Querétaro, [the Battalion of] Public Safety of Mexico, and eight pieces of artillery to Lagos. [At that point] Col. Fernando Franco was located with the Allende Battalion, the Veracruz Regiment, and four cannons. On the 29th the Zapadores Battalion; the First Active of Mexico [City]; the [Active Battalion] of Guanajuato, to which was attached two companies of auxiliaries from Leon; 100 men of those from Irapuato, who voluntarily requested to come on the campaign; and the Regiment of Iguala and four pieces of artillery arrived at Leon.

Be aware that many of these troops, such as those from Lagos, advanced toward Aguas Calientes, where it was indispensable that they remain some time, so that [page ends]

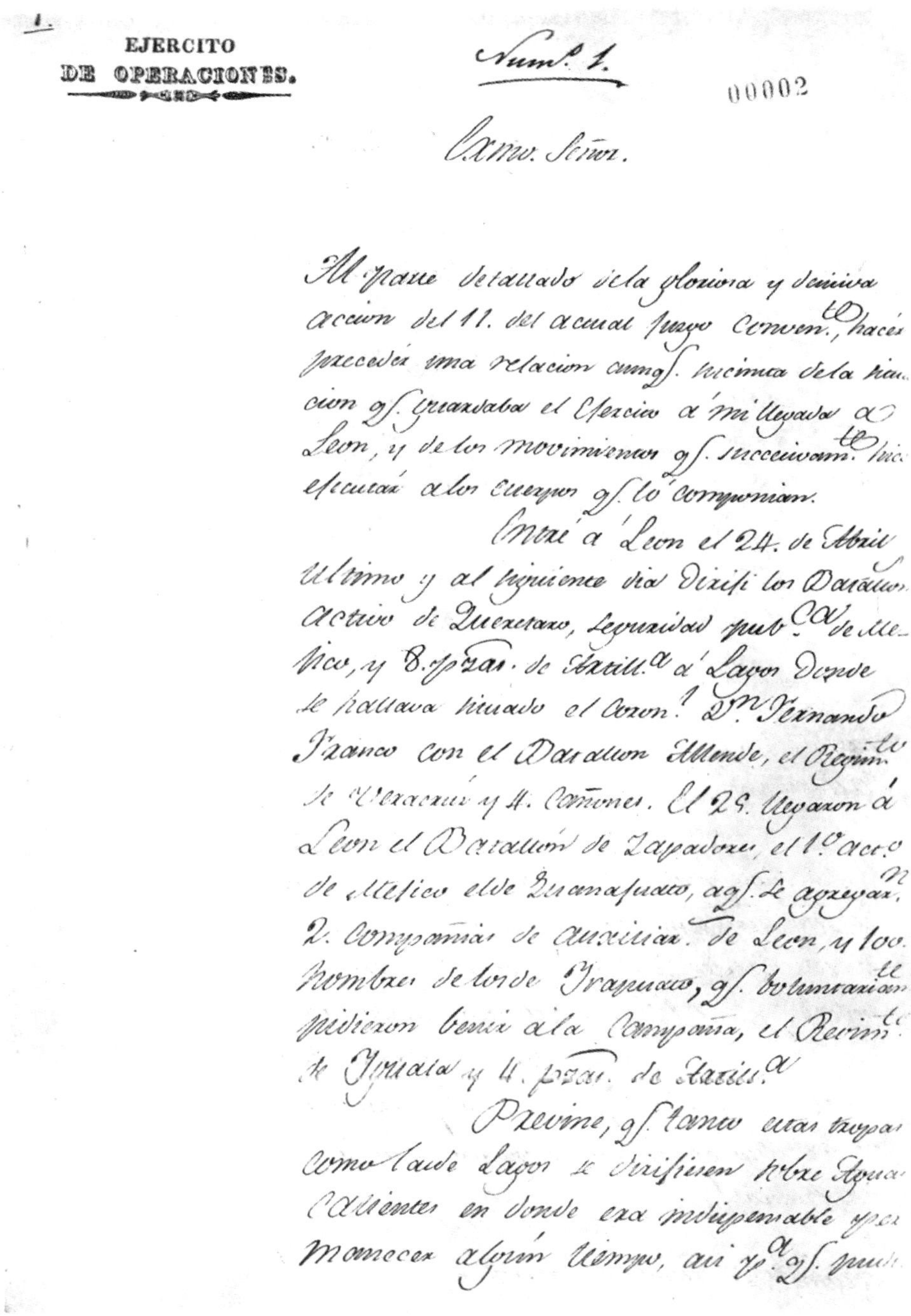

EJERCITO
DE OPERACIONES.

Num.° 1.

00002

Exmo. Señor.

Al parte detallado de la gloriosa y decisiva accion del 11. del actual juzgo conven.te hacer preceder una relacion aunq.e sucinta de la situacion q.e guardaba el Ejercito a mi llegada a Leon, y de los movimientos q.e sucesivam.te hice ejecutar a los Cuerpos q.e lo componian.

Entre a Leon el 24. de Abril ultimo y al siguiente dia dirijí los Batallones Activo de Queretaro, Seguridad pub.ca de Mexico, y 8. pzas. de Artill.a a Lagos donde se hallaba situado el Coron.l D.n Fernando Franco con el Batallon Allende, el Regim.to de Veracruz y 4. Cañones. El 29. llegaron a Leon el Batallon de Zapadores, el 1.° Act.o de Mexico el de Guanajuato, a q.e se agregar.n 2. Compañias de auxiliar. de Leon, y 100. hombres de los de Irapuato, q.e voluntariam.te pidieron venir a la Campaña, el Regim.to de Iguala y 4. pzas. de Artill.a

Previne, q.e tanto estas tropas como las de Lagos se dirijiesen sobre Aguas Calientes en donde era indispensable per manecer algun tiempo, asi p.a q.e pud...

Santa Anna's Zacatecas account, May 24, 1835, XI / 481.3 / expediente 1133, fojas 4–13, Archivo Histórico Militar.

[. . .] the First Division from San Luís Potosí, which was located at the Hacienda de la Parada, could be reunited. [Also] the small forces that they were waiting for from Guadalupe. This was to give the army a definitive organization.

The movements of these troops and the transportation of the [ammunition] parks presented some difficulties due to the absolute lack of mules. Therefore the units arrived from Aguas Calientes with no more musket cartridges than what the soldiers carried themselves in their cartridge boxes. Soon those problems were overcome due to the active cooperation of His Excellency, Division General, Luis Cortasar, and all the ammunition was reunited at the headquarters of Aguas Calientes.

My delay at said city, far from producing prudent reflections in the inexperienced leader of Zacatecas, as was imposed, entirely blinded him, persuading him that the army organized there was powerless to begin a serious attack against his capital. Senseless! How soon he received the terrible disappointment of his crazy confidence!

The Matamoros Battalion and the Tampico Regiment arrived on the 2nd of the [page ends]

sin reunirseme la Division de Sn. Luis Potosi q. estaba situada en la Hacda. de la Pa-xada, y las cortas fuerzas q. esperaba de Guadalaxa., como pa. dar al Exercito una organizacion definitiva.

Los movimientos de estas tropas y la conducion del parq. presenta-ron algunas dificultades por la falta abso-luta de mulas: asi es, q. llegaron los Cuerps. de Aguas Calientes sin mas cartuchos de fu-sil q. los q. llevaban los soldads. en sus car-tucheras. Pronto fueron vencidas aquellas por la cooperacion activa del E. S. Genl. de Division Dn. Luis Cortazar, y todo el Parque fue reunido en el Cuartel Gl. de Aguas Calientes.

Mi demora en dha. ciudad debio de producir prudtes. reflexions. en el espiritu del inexperto caudillo de Zacats., como era de suponerse, lo cegó enteramte. persuadi-endole, q. el Exercito alli organizado era impotente pa. emprender un ataque serio sobre su Capital ¡insensato! ¡cuan pronto recibio el terrible desengaño de su loca confianza!

El Batallon de Matamoros, y el Regimto. de Tampico llegaron el dia 2. del

[. . .] current [month] at headquarters. On the 5th the Division from San Luís presented, which was composed of that Active Battalion [from San Luís Potosí], the Dolores Regiment, and two pieces [of artillery]; and the section from Guadalupe with the force of 180 men from its Active Battalion, and a small picket of cavalry of public safety.

I decided at that time to commence the military operations. The army received orders to march on the 7th. It was not unknown to me that the leader of the militias of Zacatecas had, without a doubt, some spies in Aguas Calientes. By these he was informed of the exact force, brilliance, and enthusiasm of the army. The day of the 6th was used for a general review [of the troops], which was viewed by the entire population of that city. The force [of the troops] was 172 *Zapadores* [sappers], 2200 infantrymen, 1100 cavalrymen, and 18 pieces of artillery served by 140 artillerymen.

I thought for a moment that the disillusioned authorities of Zacatecas would listen to the voice of reason, and directed by prudence they would announce to me their entire submission to the law! Vain hope! The time to humble these militias would be bestowed. Their destinies would be completed.

The army marched on the 7th with three divisions of infantry, and one of cavalry [page ends]

corr.te al Cuartel Gen.l, y el 5. lo berificaron la Division de S.n Luis q.e se componia de aquel Bat.n activo, y el Regim.to de Dolores, y 2. piezas; y la Seccion de Guadalaj.a con la fuerza de 180. hombres de su Bat.n activo, y un corto piquete de Caball.a de seguridad publ.ca

Decidi al mom.to dar principio á las operacion.s militares: el Ejercito recibió ord.n p.a marchar el dia 7.– No se me habia ocultado q.e el caudillo de las Milicias de Zacatecas tendria sin duda algunos espias en Ntras Filas.; y p.a q.e estos pudieren informarle con exactitud de la fuerza, brillantez y entusiasmo del Ejto., dispuse p.a el dia 6. una revista general, la q.e se berificó á presencia de la publacion entera de aquella ciudad, y con la fuerza de 172. Zapadores 2 Cuer. Infant., 1 Cuer. Caballos, y 18. piezas servidas por 140. Artilleros.

Crei un mom.to, q.e desengañadas las autoridad.s de Zacat.s oirian la vóz de la razon, y dirigidas de la prudencia, me comunicarian su entera sumision á la Ley! Vana esperanza! La hora postrera de estas Milicias habia sonado; sus destinos debian cumplirse.

Marchó el Ejercito el dia 7. en tres Division.s de Inf.a, y una de Caball.a q.e

[. . .] that took the vanguard and on the 10th at 9:00 a.m. we sighted Guadalupe. Immediately the enemy was in position supporting the left of its line of battle against the town and its convent, whose tower was garrisoned with small cannons [*esmeriles*] that protected it with their fire. They were well protected by the immediate hills, which are cut at every turn with awkward canyons. Another canyon situated to its rear defended it in its concept. Its front and right, where the major part of its forces were located, was sustained by 22 pieces [of artillery] and 180 small cannons, persuading without a doubt that both points would be those of our attack. The force that presented to our sight was about 5,000 men of all branches, well equipped, with regular discipline. If some military talents had accompanied the presumption of the leadership of Zacatecas, the position that they occupied was formidable and its location provided immense advantages of which they did not avail themselves. At first glance I knew that the enemy had little skill. Later this foreshadowed their sure and quick defeat. However, before giving the destructive signal for combat, I wanted to provoke prudent reflections [page ends]

tomó la Vanguardia, y el 10. á las 9. de la mañana avistamos á Guadalupe. En la llanura imediata estaba en posicion el enemigo apoyando la izquierda de su linea de batalla sobre la población y su Combento, cuya torre guarnecida de tiradores la protegia con sus fuegos, siendo ademas resguardada p.r las lomas imediatas q.e estan cortadas á cada paso, con incomodas barrancas. Otra barranca situada á su retaguardia lo defendia en su Concepto; y su frente y derecha en donde se hallaban la mayor parte de sus fuerzas se sostenian p.r 22. p.zas de Artill.a y 180. tiradores persuadidos sin duda q.e ambos puntos serian los de nuestro ataque. La fuerza q.e presentaron á la vista seria de 5000. hombres de todas armas bien equipad.s y con regular diciplina; y si algunos talentos militares hubiesen acompañado la presuncion del arbitro de Zacatecas, la posicion q.e ocupaba hubiera sido formidable, pues la localidad le proporcionaban inmensas ventajas q.e no supo aprovechar. Un primer golpe de vista me hizo conocer la poca destreza del enemigo, y de luego á luego presagié su segura y pronta derrota. Sin embargo, quise antes de dar la destructora señal del Combate provocar reflexiones

[. . .] in these exalted: all was in vain. An arrogant response [*deg.*], directed so much in my official account, was given to the intimation that this government did [?]: the arms would be used to decide the question, and to me there was no doubt of success.

My plan of attack was conceived rapidly in the morning and was rectified with the reconnaissance of the enemy positions made at five in the afternoon. In this act [*recon*] shots from the small pieces of ordnance were directed toward me, and the aggressors in this fight had been those whose lives, on the following morning, were spared, thanks to the generosity of the Mexican Soldier, always devastating in combat, constantly humane in victory. I communicated the plan of attack to the senior generals and commanders of the army, and being well informed as to which each one should execute, they will make their final dispositions. At two in the morning the troops moved from the encampment of Laguna de Pasillas to go to the point that each division had been assigned.

The enemy never suspected what was to be involved at sunrise. [page ends]

2

EJERCITO
DE OPERACIONES.

00004

prudentes en esos exaltados: todo fue en vano.
Una respuesta altanera deq. dirigi en tono
en mi parte oficial, se dio ala intimacion
q. hize a ese Gob.no: las armas hiban ya
es a decidir la cuestion, y pa. mi no era du-
doso el exito.

Mi plan de ataque concebido con
rapidez en la mañana, se rectificó con
el reconocim.to q. hice dela posicion enemi-
ga alas 5. de la tarde. En este acto hicieron
fuego de Canon sobre mi, y los agresores
en esta lucha han sido aquellos cuyas vi-
das en la mañana sup.te fueron conser-
vadas, merced a la generosidad del soldado
Mexicano, siempre terrible en el combate,
constantem.te umano en la victoria. Comu-
nicado el plan de ataque alos Señores
Generales y Gefes del Exercito, y bien im-
puestos de loq. cada uno debia executar se
hicieron las ultimas disposicion.s, y a las
2. dela mañana se movieron las tropas
del Campam.to dela Laguna de Carillas,
pa. dirigirse al punto q. cada Division
tenia señalado.

El enemigo debia sorprender-
lo encontrarse envuelto al amanecer?

So indeed it happened; and in such a situation there was no more recourse than to die or surrender at discretion. Two divisions of infantry supported by a battery of ten pieces attacked by its left flank, preventing at the same time any hope of retreating to Zacatecas and to defend its line of fortifications. The cavalry charged valiantly against the rearguard and the right flank. Also across from the reserve infantry division was presented a wall of fire and of [steel or sword? *acero* or *ayero* or *azero*?]. The army had good order and after two hours of combat the most complete triumph had been obtained.

The movements that were assigned to the Generals of the Divisions and Brigade were executed with a rare precision and my instructions were followed with timely decisions and fearlessness.

To make the victory more complete I headed with part of my forces toward Zacatecas and managed, with a rapid march, to possess all of their strongholds. I gave a command for each one to surrender, and their garrisons were perplexed and frightened and surrendered their arms to me and begged for clemency. I disarmed them at the time and granted them [page ends]

asi sucedio en efecto; y en tal situacion ya
no le quedaba mas recurso q. perecer ó
rendirse á discrecion. 2. Divisiones de Inf.a
sostenidas por una bateria de 10. pzas.
lo atacaron por su flanco isquierdo qui-
tandole al mismo tiempo toda esperanza
de poderse replegar á Zacat.s y defender
su linea de fortificacion.s. La Caball.a
le cargó balerosam.te por retaguardia y
flanco derecho, y asi frente la division
de Inf.a de reserva le presentaban un muro
de fuego y de azero. El Exercito tenia ord.n
de vencer, y á las dos horas de empezado
el combate, el mas completo triunfo se
habia obtenido.

Los movim.tos q. previne
á los Generales de las Division.s y Brigad.
se efectuaron con una rara precicion y
mis instruccion.s fueron seguidas con puntu-
alidad decicion é intrepidez.

Para hacer mas completa
la victoria, me dirigi con una parte
de mis fuerzas sobre Zacat.s, y logré
con mi rapida marcha posecionarme
de todas sus fortalezas. fui intimando á
cada una rendicion, y los q. las guar-
necian perplejos y asustados me rendian
las armas é imploraban clemencia. Yo
los desarmaba al mom.to y les concedia

[. . .] their freedom. The same was granted to all the neighbors who defended some of the buildings of the city, nevertheless stopping the fire against the soldiers who presented themselves in the street. In this mode the capital of the state was left in our possession.

The Senior Generals, Commanding Officers, and troops of this small but very gallant army have left nothing for me to desire. Its behavior is worthy of praise no less than the considerations of the Supreme Government. As far as the operations of each Division and each Brigade that formed them, they were executed at the sight and under the direction of their respective generals. To them [the government] I have the pleasure of relating and designating those individuals whom I consider most deserving of particular recommendation. For this reason, I am including for Your Excellency the original accounts that the expressed generals have remitted to me, so it is set out in detail what they did in the glorious action, and they will be given well-deserved publicity.

It remains now that I recommend to the consideration of the government my aides-de-camp, Col. Manuel Fernandez Castrillón, Brevet Cols. José Batres and Manuel Portilla, Lt. Cols. José M.a Garmendia and Mariano [page ends]

00005

la libertad. Lo mismo verifiqué con todos aquellos vecinos q.s defendian algunos edificios de la ciudad, no obstante haber roto el fuego sobre mis soldados al presentarse en las calles. De este modo quedé tambien en posecion de la Capital del estado.

Nada me han dejado q.s desear los Señor.s General.s Jefes oficiales y tropa de este corto pero muy bizarro Exercito. Su comportam.to tan digno de elogios no lo es menos de la consideracion del Sup.o Gob.o: y como las operacion.s de cada Division y Brigada en esta jornada, fueron ejecutad.s a la Vista y bajo la direccion de sus respectivos General.s a ellos dejo el placer de relatarlas, y de designar a los individ.s q.s considero mas dignos de una particular recomendacion. En tal virtud acompaño a V. E. los partes originales q.s me han remitido los espresados Generales, y asi se pormenorizarán los hechos de aquella gloriosa accion, y se les dará una bien merecida publicidad.

Restame ahora recomendar a la consider.on del Gob.no a mis Ayudant.s de Campo, Coron.l D.n Manuel Fernandez Castrillon, coron.s graduad.s D.n Jose Batres y D.n Manuel Portilla, y Tent.es coron. D.n Jose M.a Sarmendia y D.n Mariano

[. . .] Jaime, whose activity in communicating my orders in the middle of fire is commendable. To the most Excellent Señor General of Division Joaquin Parres and to the General of Brigade Felipe Codallos, who at the head of their respective divisions led with the honor that distinguishes them. To the General of Brigade Juan Arago, who filled the position of Major General of the Army to my satisfaction in what he was entrusted, and as he has been known to do what I have witnessed with valor. To Brevet General Adrian Boll [*sic;* Woll], who after serving the functions of Quarter Master General was at my side in the moment of danger and complied exactly with what he was assigned. To Brevet General Joaquín Ramírez y Sesma, who with the cavalry that was placed under his orders complied with my needs, making a bold charge against the enemy until reaching the batteries of the opponents. With this a line of battle was disorganized. To the Brevet Generals Mariano Paredes, Eugenio Tolsa, Ventura Mora, and Cols. José M.a Heredia, Manuel Antonio Cañeda, Fernando Franco, and José Urrea, who were placed at the head of their respective brigades that conducted themselves with glo- [page ends]

Jaime cuya actividad p.a comunicar mis ord.s en medio del fuego es digno de elogio. Al Exmo. S. Gen.l de Division D.n Joaquin Parres, y al S. Gen.l de Brig.a D.n Felipe Codallos quienes ala Cabeza de sus Division.s respectivas la condujeron con el honor q.e los distingue. Al Gen.l de Brig.a D.n Juan Arago q.e como mayor gen.l del Exercito lleno á mi satisf.on cuanto le fue encomendado, y como ha sabido hacerlo siempre q.e he sido testigo de su bizarria. Al Gen.l graduado D.n Adrian Woll q.e despues de desempeñar las funciones de cuartel Maestre g.l estubo á mi lado en el mom.to del peligro, y cumplio exactam.te con cuanto le previne. Al Gen.l graduado D.n Joaquin Ramirez y Sesma q.e con la Caball.a q.e puse á sus ord.s lleno mi deseo dando una atrevida Carga a los enemigos hasta llegar á las baterias de los contrarios, con lo q.e desorganizó su linea de batalla. A los Gen.s graduados D.n Mariano Paredes, D.n Eugenio Tolsa, D.n Ventura Mora, y Coron.s D.n José M.a Heredia, D.n Manuel Antonio Cañedo D.n Fernando Franco, y D.n Jose Urrea, q.e puestos a la Cabeza de sus brigadas respectivas las condujeron con glo-

[. . .] -ry and showed a good example for their subordinates. To the principal commander of artillery, Col. Tomas Requena, and his second-in-command, Lt. Col. Pedro Ampudia, who directed with such accuracy the battery situated on the left flank of the enemy. To Captain (brevet Lt. Col.) José Ortega, who commanded the pieces of reserve, which operated to my satisfaction. I should equally recommend Lt. Col. Pedro Garcia Conde, commander of the section of engineers, and last but not least the adjutants of cavalry, Pedro Fran.co Delgado and Andrés Bosero, who although employed in my secretariat, they complied on that day with the missions that I confided to them on the field of battle. All, in the end, have been deserving [of the thanks] of the country; all are deserving of just recompense.

To perpetuate the memory of an action so brilliant in the accounts of the Mexican Army, I request a distinguished medal to those who have had the glory of attending it, but consider that [in] the civil wars such insignia [*siro.*] always [serve] to ingrain the hatred that [page ends]

3.

EJERCITO
DE OPERACIONES.

00006

ria y dieron ejemplo á sus subordinados. Al Com[te] Principal de Artill[a] Coron[l] D[n] Tomas Requena, á su segundo Tte. Coron[l] D[n] Pedro Ampudia q[e]. dirijio con tanto acierto la bat[a] q[e]. situé en el flanco izquierdo del enemigo, y al Cap[n] grad[o] de Tte. Coron[l] D[n] Jose Ortega q[e]. mandó las pzas. dela reserva, y operaron á mi satisf[on]. Debo igualm[te] recomendar al Tte. Coron[l] D[n] Pedro Garcia Conde Comt[e] dela Secc[n] de Ingenieros, y por ultimo, álos primeros Ayud[tes] de Caball[a] D[n] Pedro Fran[co] Delgado y D[n] Andres Dorero, q[e]. aunq[e] empleados en mi Secria. cumplieron en ese dia las comision[s] q[e] les confie en el campo de batalla. Todos enfin han bien merecido dela Patria, todos son acreedores á justas recompensas.

Para perpetuar la memoria de una accion tan brillante en los fastos del Ejercito Mexicano, hubiera consultado una condecorac[n] q[e]. distinguiera á cuantos han tenido la gloria de concurrir á ella; sinó considerara q[e]. las guerras cibiles tales insignias sirven siempre p[a] arraigár los odios q[e]. de-

[. . .] we must seek earnestly to make disappear from among us. This not being convenient, the supreme government can decide what kind of reward it considers should be due the army.

The widows and families of those who died gloriously should receive the well-deserved payments from the supreme government pensions for creditors and for those that [*pref.a*] are recommending.

The results have been incalculable from such a signal victory. One hundred and fifty commanders and officers [are] prisoners; 2443 individuals of the troop; arms, cannons, munitions, fortifications: everything has fallen into our power, as the following will express. The well-supplied storehouses of arms and ammunitions that exist in this city and the attached inventories make a list of them. They have served to supplement and improve the armaments of the corps of the army. To some have been allocated some other uniforms of those militias. I have sent a quantity of arms and munitions to Guadalajara, San Luís, Guanajuato, and Queretaro, [page ends]

debemos procurar con empeño hacer desaparecer de entre nosotros. No siendo pues esto conven.te, el Sup.o Gob.o resolverá q.e clase de premio considera deberse conseder al Ejercito.

Las viudas y familias de los q.e murieron honrosam.te recibiran de la consideracion bien merecida del Sup.o Gob.no las pensiones q.e son acreedoras, y p.a las q.e de just.a las recomiendo.

Incalculables han sido los resultados de tan señalada vict.a siendo cincuenta Gefes y oficiales prisioneros, 2443 individ.s de tropa, Armam.to, Cañones, Parque, fortificacion.s todo ha caido en nuestro poder segun ba espresado, y los bien provistos almacen.s de Armas y municion.s existentes en esta ciudad, y de q.e hacen relac.n los adjuntos inventarios, han servido p.a completar y mejorar el armam.to de los cuerpos del Ejercito, a quienes se ha repartido a demas algun vestuario de estas milicias. He remitido cantidad de armas y municion.s a Guadalaj.a, S.n Luis, Guanajuato y Queretaro,

[. . .] and the rest will be remitted successfully to that capital and to the internal states of the east and of the west according to their needs; a sufficient [amount] will remain in this city for the troops of its garrison.

The losses of the army, although always terrible, are small and do not amount to one hundred men according to the notices of the attached lists. That of the opponents has not been, due to the humanity of the conquerors and to the rapidity of the triumph, as significant as would be supposed. Those who could flee are presenting [themselves] to the civil and military authorities of the various points of the state; and only the instigating ringleaders of such criminal resistance, many wandering by the deserters, loaded by the weight of their remorse for the evils that they have caused with their conduct, but already cannot be reproduced [i.e., their actions cannot be undone].

I have reported already that two thousand four hundred forty-three individual soldiers [who were] prisoners were placed at liberty by considerations that I expressed in that note, and I have not hesitated that this act of clemency merits the [page ends]

00007

y el resto se hizo remitiendo succesiva-
mente a esa Capit.l y a los Estados internos
de Oriente y Occid.te, segun sus necesidad.s,
quedandose lo suficiente en esta ciudad
p.a las tropas de su guarn.on

La perdida del Exercito, aunq.e
siempre es sensible es corta pues no
llega a cien hombres segun se advier-
te por las relaciones adjuntas: la de
los contrarios no ha sido, gracias a la
humanidad de los vencedores y a la ra
pidez del triunfo tan considerable como
era de suponerse. Los q.e pudieron fugar-
se van presentando a las Autoridades
civiles y militares de los diversos pun-
tos del Est.o; y solo los cabecillas pro-
movedores de tan criminal reincidencia
siguen vagando por los desiertos, carga-
dos del peso de sus remordimientos
por los males q.e han causado con
su conducta, pero q.e ya no se repro-
ducirán.

He participado ya q.e los dos
mil cuatrocientos cuarenta y tres indiv.s
de tropa prisioneros, fueron puestos en
libertad por las consideraciones q.e en
aquella nota expresé, y no he dudado
q.e este acto de clemencia merezca la

[. . .] approval of a kind and just government, which can decide about the commanders and officers of these militias, whom I felt compelled to send to that capital at its [the government's?] disposition.

If it pleases Your Excellency, report everything to His Excellency the Interim President and congratulate anew for a success that assures, perhaps forever, the order and peace.

God and Liberty Headquarters of Zacatecas May 24, 1835
Antonio Lopez de Santa Anna

[To] Most Excellent Secretary of
War and Navy Mexico

aprovacion de un Gob.no bondadoso y justo, quien podrá resolver acerca de los Jefes y oficiales de esas Milicias q.e he creido deber dirijir á esa Capital á su disposicion.

Sirvase V. E. ponerlo todo en el conocim.to del E. S. Presid.te interino aquien felicito de nuevo por su suceso q.e asegurará quiza p.a siempre el ord.n y la paz.

Dios y Libertad, Cuartel general de Zacatecas Mayo 24. de 1835.

Ant.o Lopez de Santa Anna

Exmo. S. Secret.o de la Guerra y Marina. — Mexico.

APPENDIX 5

Gregorio Gomez Broadside, November 28, 1835

GREGORIO GOMEZ PALOMINO

Colonel of the Active Battalion of Tres Villas and Military Commander of this city

The imminent danger that threatened this plaza by the timid flight of foreign pirate invaders captained by the exiled Antonio Mejía and Martín Peraza has ceased. The fort of the bar was occupied by a faithful and valiant garrison, completely proving the fidelity, honor, and patriotism of this community. Being next was the aid from the Supreme Government in avoiding whatever other outrage that would be capable of compromising the decorum of the nation. Consequently, the extraordinary actions dictated by the danger of the invasion and assault that the plaza suffered are unnecessary. I have come in declaration, and I declare:

1. The proclamation of the 17th of this month is not in effect regarding the declaration from the site of this plaza and its consequences.
2. All the authorities are unobstructed in the use of their respective powers.
3. Everything returns to the state that it had before the invasion. For everyone to get the news I order it to be published by declaration in Santa Anna de Tamaulipas on November 28, 1835.

Gregorio Gomez

Imprint of the *Gaceta de Santa Anna de Tamaulipas* 1835

00036

GREGORIO GOMEZ PALOMINO

Coronel del Batallon Activo de Tres Villas y Comandante militar de esta ciudad.

Habiendo cesado el inminente peligro que amenazaba à esta plaza por la vergonzosa fuga de los piratas estranjeros invasores capitaneados por los proscriptos Antonio Mejia y Martin Peraza, y ocupado por una guarnicion fiel y valiente el Fortin de la barra; plenamente satisfecho de la fidelidad honradez y patriotismo de este vecindario, y estando procsimos los aucsilios del supremo Gobierno para evitar cualquier otro atentado que sea capaz de comprometer el decoro de la nacion, y siendo en consecuencia innecesarias las medidas estraordinarias, que dictó el peligro de momento, en la invasion y asalto que sufrió la plaza he venido en declarar y declaro:

1º Queda sin efecto el bando de 17 del actual en órden à declaracion de sitiò de esta plaza y sus consecuencias.

2º Todas las autoridades estàn espeditas en el uso de sus respectivas atribuciones.

3º Todo vuelve al estado que tenia antes de la invasion. Y para llegue á noticia de todos mando se publique por bando en Santa-Anna de Tamaulipas à 28 de Noviembre de 1835.

GREGORIO GOMEZ.

Imprenta de la Gaceta de Santa-Anna de Tamaulipas.——1835.

Gregorio Gomez broadside, November 28, 1835, XI / 481.3 / expediente 1111, foja 52, Archivo Histórico Militar.

APPENDIX 6

Anáhuac Munitions and Troop Reports

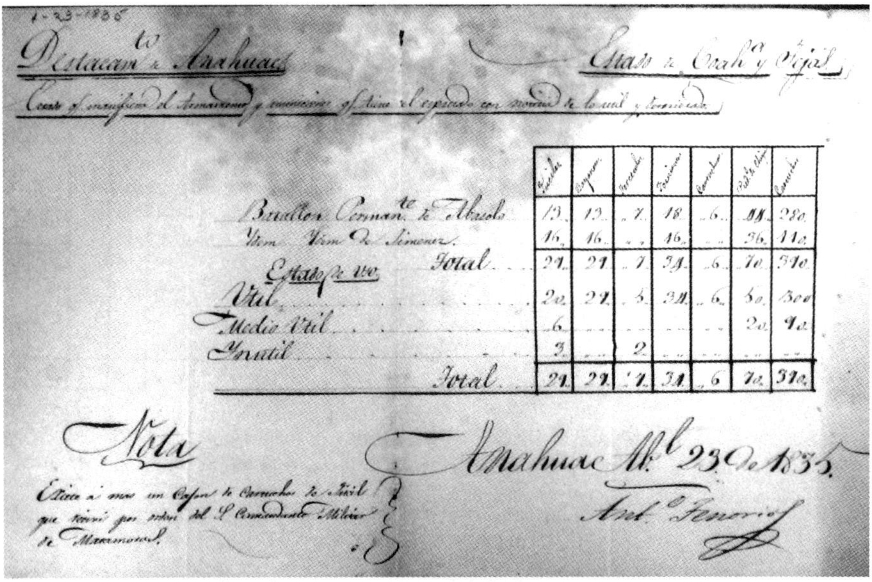

Anáhuac munitions and troop reports, box 2S315, Bexar Archives, Dolph Briscoe Center for American History, University of Texas at Austin.

DETACHMENT AT ANÁHUAC
STATE OF COAHUILA Y TEJAS

Declared state of the arms and munitions that are given, with the news of their usefulness and deterioration.

		Muskets	**Bayonets**	*Tercerolas*	**[illegible]**	**Cartridge boxes**	**flints**	**cartridges**
Permanent battalion of Abasolo		13	13	7	18	6	44	280
Permanent battalion of Jimenez		16	16	---	16	---	36	110
Total		**29**	**29**	7	**34**	**6**	**70**	**390**
State of usefulness								
	Useful	20	29	5	34	6	50	300
	Medium useful	6	---	---	---	---	20	90
	Not useful	3	---	2	---	---	---	---
Total		**29**	**29**	7	**34**	**6**	**70**	**390**

Anáhuac April 23, 1835

NOTE

There exists a case of musket cartridges that was received by order of the Sr. Military Commander Ant.o Tenorio of Matamoros.

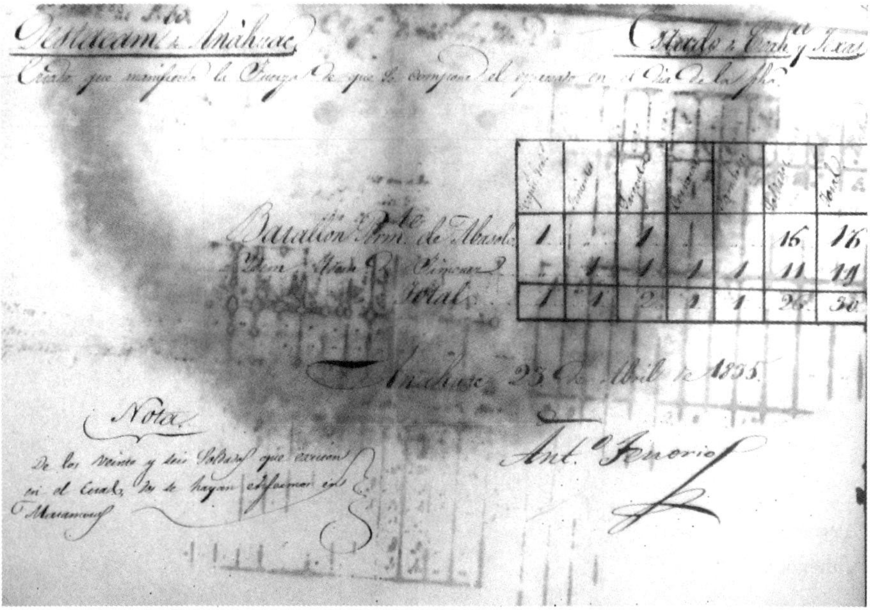

DETACHMENT AT ANÁHUAC
STATE OF COAHUILA Y TEJAS

State that composed the expressed force [detachment] on the date given [below]

	Captain	Lieutenant	Sergeants	buglers	drummers	privates	Total [less officers]
Permanent battalion of Abasolo	1	---	1	---	---	15	16
Permanent battalion of Jimenez	---	1	1	1	1	11	14
Total	**1**	**1**	**2**	**1**	**1**	**26**	**30**

Anáhuac April 23, 1835
Ant.o Tenorio

NOTE

Of the twenty-six privates in the force two are sick in Matamoros.

APPENDIX 7

Citizens of San Felipe to Citizens of Coahuila

The citizens of the jurisdiction of Austin, gathered in a public meeting, directed to the citizens of Coahuila and Texas and every republican everywhere, what is said:

Citizens, this jurisdiction sincerely deplores the present disgraceful situation of the Mexican Republic. Together with all lovers of freedom we lament to see the sad prostration to which the federal republican principle has been reduced and the creation of the government of a dictator over its ruins. It is lamented that the hopes of the patriots and the yearning of many people, who have scarcely been freed from the horrible oppression to which they were subjected by the Spanish despots, have been frustrated so suddenly and unexpectedly, and that a system equally despotic has been newly placed on them. The population of Texas long has observed and felt the advances of the General Government and has long since been convinced that the tendency of the Government has been the destruction of the constitution, and the establishment of a different form [of government]. But being such new residents and citizens only by adoption, and taught from childhood to revere and respect the national legislature, they have watched in silence aggressions that cannot be justified and usurpations that have revealed danger. They have been content to live without complaining and even without enduring the unconstitutionality of such measures. It is left to the [*cebados nativos*] and to the men and citizens of the country the right to protest and the duty to oppose. Even now the voice of complaint would not have been raised had it not been for the usurpations and measures advanced by the General Government that [page ends]

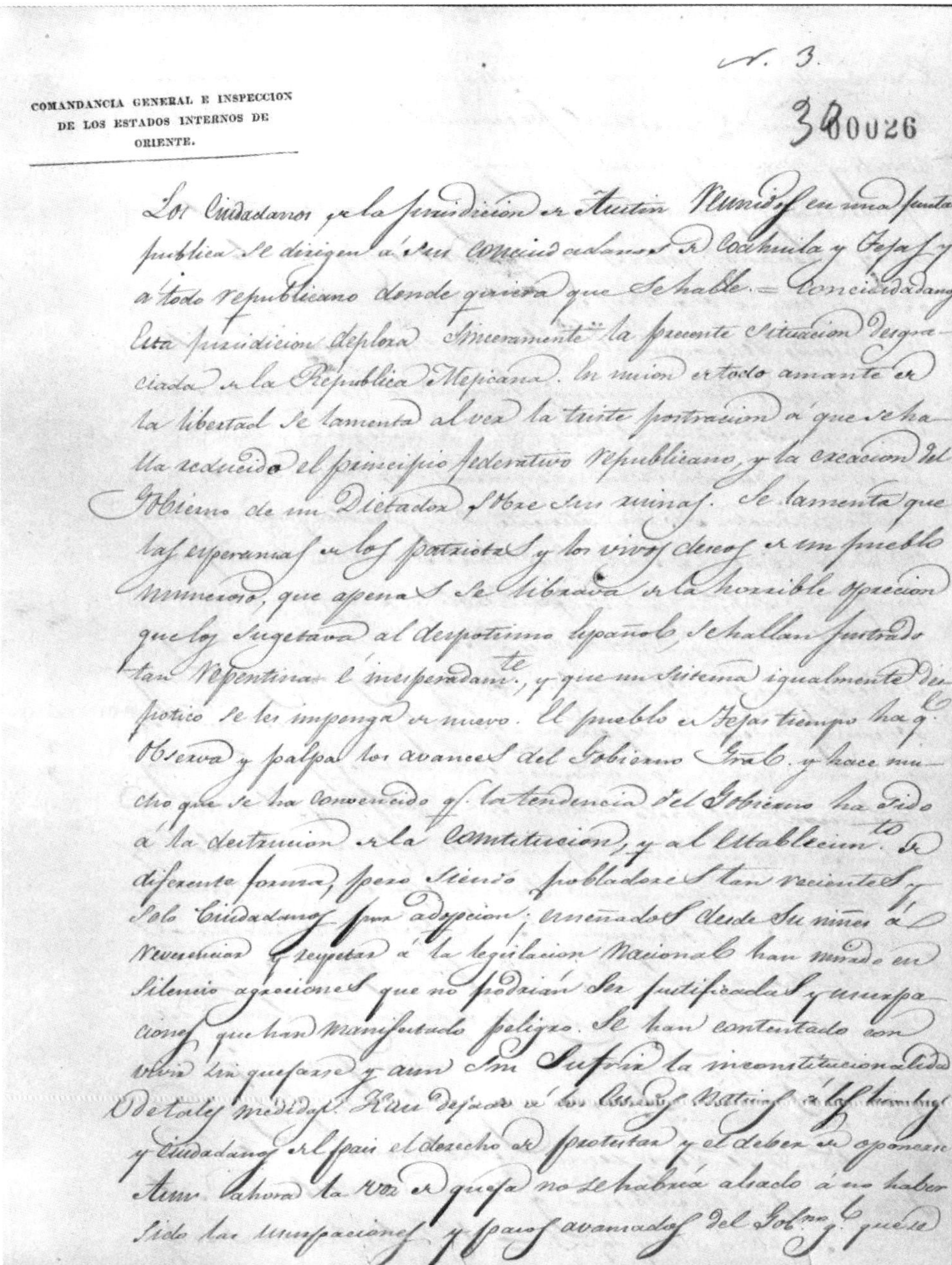

N. 3.

COMANDANCIA GENERAL E INSPECCION DE LOS ESTADOS INTERNOS DE ORIENTE.

3 00026

Los Ciudadanos de la jurisdiccion de Austin Reunidos en una junta
publica se dirigen á sus conciudadanos de Coahuila y Tejas y
á todo republicano donde quiera que se halle = Conciudadanos
Esta jurisdiccion deplora sinceramente la presente situacion desgra-
ciada de la Republica Mejicana. Su union de todo amante de
la libertad se lamenta al ver la triste postracion á que se ha-
lla reducido el principio federativo republicano, y la ereccion del
Gobierno de un Dictador sobre sus ruinas. Se lamenta que
las esperanzas de los patriotas y los vivos deseos de un pueblo
numeroso, que apenas se libraba de la horrible opresion
que los sugetaba al despotismo español, se hallan frustrados
tan repentina é inesperadamente, y que un sistema igualmente des-
potico se les imponga de nuevo. El pueblo de Tejas tiempo ha q.
observa y palpa los avances del Gobierno Gral. y hace mu-
cho que se ha convencido q. la tendencia del Gobierno ha sido
á la destruccion de la Constitucion, y al establecimto. de
diferente forma, pero siendo pobladores tan recientes, y
solo Ciudadanos por adopcion; enseñados desde su niñez á
reverenciar y respetar á la legislacion Nacional han mirado en
silencio agresiones que no podian ser justificadas, y usurpa-
ciones que han manifestado peligro. Se han contentado con
vivir sin quejarse y aun sin sufrir la inconstitucionalidad
de tales medidas. [illegible]
y Ciudadanos del pais el derecho de protestar y el deber de oponerse
Aun ahora la voz de queja no se habria alzado á no haber
sido las usurpaciones y pasos avanzados del Gobno. Gl. que se

Citizens of [San Felipe de] Austin to citizens of Coahuila y Texas, June 22, 1835, XI / 481.3 / expediente 1814, fojas 42–50, Archivo Histórico Militar.

[. . .] have extended to the state of our adoption and even threatened our personal destruction. Our feelings, our thoughts, and our views have been the subjects of mistakes and bad interpretation among our Mexican brothers. We have never been enemies of the Mexicans nor opponents of the constitution. Always we have adhered religiously to the constitution, as we still do. We will always continue doing so as long as memory reminds us of the integrity of its passion. In the disgraceful present state of things this will be our conduct. There is no incentive great enough to induce us to depart from our clear line of duty and there is no sufficiently formidable force that can stop us from a free and independent expression of our feelings. We believe that the general government and the respective states are some independent sovereignties in the areas respectively assigned to them by the constitution. We believe that the states agree in a social pact of their own and free will to more effectively assure the enjoyment of the freedom that they have gained, and to move forward with more harmony and prosperity the operations of the government. We feel that the general government was created for entirely exterior reasons and that to the states remains the regulation of their internal businesses.

An invasion by whatever power on the rights of another is equally dangerous and likewise should [not?] be forwarded. Such an invasion has been committed by the government against the sovereignty of the state of Coahuila and Texas:

1st—In the persons of the [page ends]

han estendido hasta el Estado de nuestra adopcion y aun amenazado
la destruccion de nuestras personas. Nuestros Sentimtos.
nuestras nociones y nuestras miras han sido materia de
equivocaciones y malas interpretaciones. Entre nuestros her-
manos mexicanos: jamas hemos sido enemigos de los mexi-
canos ni jamas opositores de la constitucion. Siempre nos
hemos adherido religiosamente a la constitucion como la halla-
mos. Siempre continuaremos haciendolo asi mientras la
memoria nos recuerde su merito y la integridad de su
valor. En el presente Estado desgraciado de cosas esta será
nuestra conducta. No hay aliciente tan grande que nos pueda
inducir á apartarnos de la linea clara de nuestro deber y no
hay fuerza suficientemente formidable que nos pueda cortar
una libre é independiente espresion de nuestros sentimientos.
Creemos que el Gobno. gral. y los respectivos Estados son unas
soberanias independientes en las esferas que respectivamte. se
les asigna por la constitucion, consideramos que los Estados
convinieron en el pacto social de su propia y libre voluntad
a fin de asegurar mas eficazmente el goce de las libertades
que habian ganado y para llevar adelante con mas armonia
y prosperidad las operaciones del Gobierno consideramos
que el Gobierno gral. fue criado para objetos enteramte.
esteriores y que á los Estados se dejó la regulacion de
sus negocios interiores = Una invasion por cualquiera
poder de los derechos de otro es igualmente peligrosa
é igualmente se debe resistir. Tal invasion se ha
cometido por el Gobierno gl. contra la soberania del
Estado de Coahuila y Tejas. = 1o. En las personas de los

[. . .] representatives of the National Congress who were prevented by military force from performing their duties of its employment.

2nd—In the decree of the President ordering a new election of representatives in opposition to what had been constitutionally done.

3rd—In the decree of the congress that destroyed the civic militia and required the delivery of their arms.

4th—In the law of congress that halted the right of the state of Coahuila and Texas from giving the constitutionally granted letters of citizenship to its colonists.

5th—In the arrest, by the permanent troops, of Agustín Viesca, the constitutional Governor of the state.

6th—In the recent decree that the congress had the right and the power to alter the constitution according to its feelings without subjecting itself to the prescribed restrictions of its sacred instrument.

7th—In the creation of a dictator with absolute power who has no other rule to direct his conduct than his own will and whim.

8th—And lastly, in other numerous acts, all manufacturing a total forgetfulness of the rights of the states and a determination of the current authorities who dominate the nation to totally destroy the Federal Government System.

Against all of these acts and violations, all of these abuses and usurpations, the people of Texas solemnly protest and resolve not to ever succumb to them, believing that it is our duty to make this declaration to the government and appeal to the people.

This population supports the general constitution and the constitution of the state of Coahuila and Texas as originally adopted and now existing.

It will hold at all hazards to the government of the state and all [page ends]

31 00027

representantes del congreso Nacional cuando se les evitó con la
fuerza militar del desempeño de los deveres de su empleo.= 2.º
En el decreto del Presidente ordenando una nueva eleccion
de empleados en oposicion á la que se habia hecho constitu-
cionalmente. = 3.º En el decreto del congreso q.e que destru-
ye la milicia civica y requiere de los Estados la entrega
de sus armas.= 4.º En la ley del congreso g.l en que quita
al Estado de Coahuila y Tejas un derecho constitucional p.a
dar cartas de ciudadania á sus colonos.= 5.º En el arresto
por las tropas permanentes de D. Agustin Viesca el
Gobernador Constitucional del Estado = 6.º En el reciente
decreto que declara tiene el congreso g.l derecho y facultades
para alterar la Constitucion segun le paresca sin suge-
tarse á las restricciones prescriptas en su sagrado instru-
mento = 7.º En la creacion de un dictador con poder
absoluto el cual no tiene otra norma para dirigir
su conducta q.e su propia voluntad y capricho. = 8.º y
por ultimo en otros numerosos actos todos manifestando
un total olvido de los derechos de los Estados y una determi-
nacion de las presentes autoridades que dominan a la
nacion de destruir en su totalidad el Sistema Federal
Republicano.= Contra todos estos actos y violaciones todos
estos abusos y usurpaciones el Pueblo de Tejas solemnem.te
protesta y remedio como esta á no sucumbir jamas á ellos
á creido de su deber hacer esta declaracion al Govierno y
esta apelacion á los Pueblos.= Este pueblo sostendrá la cons-
titucion gral. y la Constitucion del Estado de Coahuila
y Tejas segun se adoptaron originalmente y ahora exis-
ten.= Sostendrá á todo trance al Gobierno del Estado y todos

[. . .] the rest of the officials in dispensing their duties.

In these two resolutions all the duties that should exist as a citizen are embraced in their concept. In them is contained no more than the feelings that all lovers of constitutional freedom in the state should have. In the support of this declaration, the same as our parents in the revolution, we offer, each of us, our lives and our fortunes and our sacred honor. We will only abandon the strife when we have destroyed the most inferior weeds that grow in our land and spilled the last drop of blood that flows in the veins of the last man of our Texas.

Adopted citizens of Texas: the voice of freedom that comes from the ruins of our constitution calls us to the defense of the violated constitution and the trampled sovereignty of our state calls us to obey our oaths in its defense and support. It is made known in terms of nothing wrong that our [caricimos?] rights are involved in the fight: that our Governor is a prisoner in the hands of the military and that our congress is persecuted by them. That at this moment we are without a government except that of a dictator and the military. And not only this; it is said that the dictator is already concentrating his forces to march against Texas and the people of Texas, in whom rests [page ends]

los demas empleados en el desempeño de Su deveres.— En
estas dos resoluciones Se abrazan en Su concepto todos
los deveres que se les podria exigir como Ciudadanos
y en ellas no se contiene mas que aquellos Senti-
mientos que deveria tener todo amante de la libertad cons-
titucional en toda la Republica. En el sostenimiento de
esta declaracion lo mismo que nuestros padres en la re-
volucion nos ofrecemos á cada uno nuestras vidas y nuestras
fortunas, y nuestro sagrado honor y solo abandonaremos
la contienda cuando hallamos destruido hasta la hierva mas
inferior que crece en nuestra tierra y derramado la ul-
tima gota de Sangre que circula en las venas del ulti-
mo hombre de nuestro Tejas.— Ciudadanos adoptivos
de Tejas la voz de la livertad que sale de las ruinas
de vuestra constitucion os llama á Su defensa la cons-
titucion violada y la hollada Soberania de vuestro
Estado os llama á obedecer vuestros juramentos en su
defensa y sostenimiento. Se os hace saber en termi-
nos nada equivocos que vuestros carisimos derechos es-
tan embueltos en la lucha: que vuestro Governador es
prisionero en manos de los militares y por ellos es
perseguido vuestro congreso; y que en este momento
estais Sin gobierno exceptuado el de un Dictador y el mi-
litar. Y no solo esto, tambien se os dice que el dictador
está yá concentrando Su fuerzas pª marchar contra
Tejas y contra el Pueblo de Tejas en que descansa

[. . .] the last hope of the freedom of the republic.

If you hesitate or fear for a moment, the contention will be totally lost. If you march to meet the enemy with our accustomed firmness, our country can be redeemed.

Plant the standard of the sovereignty of the states and swear to hold it and victoriously march against all the difficulties, overcoming all opposition and freeing our constitution and our officials. Doing more than all of this, it will awaken the energies of all the liberals of the republic and animate those valiant and gallant Mexicans in the entire country and [secure] the freedom of the constitution from the prison in which the enemy now has it.

Citizens of Coahuila, the noblest contest in which the men have entered together is the contest for freedom. The entire world has seen with pleasure the heroic resistance that has been made against the despotic Spanish [by] a free and sympathetic people who are to be congratulated in that time or [to be] implore[d] in this turbulent epoch to again shake off the yoke and newly meet the enemy. From a new revolution they will be free or perish, and give freedom to our constitution and our government. It [the people] only has to declare that it [freedom] is what they want. Only an intrepid and united force will be able to bring about our victory. [page ends]

COMANDANCIA GENERAL E INSPECCION
DE LOS ESTADOS INTERNOS DE
ORIENTE.

la ultima esperanza de la libertad de la Repub.ca Si
titubeais ó temeis p.r un Momento la contienda todo
se pierde. Si marchais á encontrar al enemigo con
vuestra acostumbrada firmeza vuestro pais será re-
dimido. = Plantad el estandarte de la Soberania de los
Estados y jurad sostenerlo y marchareis victoriosos sobre
todas las dificultades, quitareis toda oposicion y liber-
tareis á vuestra constitucion y á vuestras autoridades.
Hareis mas que todo esto, despertareis la dormida ener-
gia de los liberales de la Republica y animareis á
los valientes y bizarros Mexicanos en todo vuestro
pais y la libertad y la constitucion se libraran de la
prision en que los tiene el enemigo. = Ciudadanos de
Coahuila la contienda mas noble en q.e jamas se ha entra-
do el hombre es la contienda por la libertad. El mundo
entero ha visto complacer la resistencia heroica que
habeis hecho contra el despotismo Español. Un pueblo
libre y simpatizador que os congratuló en aquella
vez os implora en esta epoca turbulenta que de
nuevo sacudais el yugo, que de nuebo encontreis al
enemigo, que de nuevo resolvais ser libres ó morir y
q.e emancipeis á vuestra constitucion y á vuestro Gobernad.r
Solo teneis que declarar q.e asi lo quereis. Solo un
esfuerzo intrepido y unido teneis que hacer y la victoria

It only has to resolve for freedom and the goddess will rest on our standard. Our fellow citizens of Texas will never abandon such a noble struggle. It will be made firm by the constant supporters of the constitution and the staunch enemies of your enemies. They will support the constitution and the authorities of their adopted country or his blood will water and enrich this soil. They will preserve inviable their rights as the constitution assures them or will leave Texas a terrible wasteland. But of such danger they [the Mexican authorities] have no knowledge, of the forces in Texas and outside of Texas. They know very well that they have ten thousand carbines for the defense of their rights that will not be returned to their peaceful homes until their rights have been made secure anew. There is not sufficient power in the Mexican Government to cast them out of the country, and they know that whatever force comes against them, it will find only the victorious revenge of a people who have always been brave and will always be free. For us we have nothing to fear. In Texas we are invincible, but we would like you all to become free, and we yearn for the memory of the freedom that up until now you had enjoyed; of the tyranny that you had before and had shaken; of the sweet, sacred, dear name of freedom; [page ends]

la vuestra. Solo teneis que resolver vuestra libertad y la
diosa descansará sobre vuestro estandarte. Nuestros
conciudadanos de Tejas jamas os abandonarán en
tan noble lucha. Los hallareis muy firmes é inva-
riables sostenedores de la Constitucion y los enemigos sa-
crificios de sus opositores. Sostendrán la constitucion
y las autoridades del pais de su adopcion ó su sangre
regará y enriquecerá este suelo. Preservarán invio-
lables sus derechos segun se los asegura la constitucion
ó tornarán á Tejas un horrible desierto. Pero semejante
peligro no temen conocen sus fuerzas en Tejas y fuera
de Tejas. Saven muy bien que diez mil carabinas
que tienen p.a la defensa de sus derechos no se han
de alsar en sus pacificas casas hasta que esos derechos
no se hallan asegurados de nuevo. No hay poder su-
ficiente en el Gobierno Mexicano p.a echarlos fuera del
pais y saven que cualesquiera fuerza que venga con-
tra ellos, solo vendrá á encontrar la victoriosa ven-
ganza de un pueblo que siempre ha sido valiente
y siempre será libre. Por nosotros nada
tenemos que temer. En Tejas somos inven-
cibles, pero desearíamos que vosotros fueseis li-
bres os rogamos por la memoria de la libertad
que hasta ahora habiais gozado por la tira-
nia que antes habeis sacudido; por el dulce
el sagrado el cariñoso nombre de Libertad,

[. . .] [we yearn that] you will return to wield your swords and work as the sons of liberty and as the worthy descendant of your patriotic ancestors! We beseech you not to make vain the hopes of our sister Republic of the North, which will always continue to believe that a people free and prosperous will not hand over their households, their altars, and their country to the enemy of their freedom.

Liberals of the Republic—the sons of the civilized world are with you. They are indignant in seeing the treacherous conduct of your enemies. They sympathize with your misfortunes, and all patriots in all parts of the world offer their prayers to heaven that you will still awaken from your apathy and you shall be free! Arise and replant the standard of freedom in your ground! Newly [illegible; *jurad*?] that will be sustained with your blood and treasure the federal republican system raising up republicans, and our country will be saved [*jurad*] from conquest or death, and the omnipotence of the truth will soon come to your favor as it has done before now. Our fight is against the enemy of constitutional freedom and ought not have to live when their form of republican federal government is destroyed. You ought to die before succumbing to the aristocracy. Fulfill your oaths [page ends]

que volvais á empuñar vuestras espadas y que
sereis como los hijos de los libres y como los dignos
descendientes de vuestros patrióticos antecesores. Os
suplicamos no hagais vanas las esperanzas de
vuestra hermana República del Norte á que
siempre continuareis creciendo un pueblo libre
y prospero no entregueis vuestros hogares, vuestros
altares y vuestro pais al enemigo de vuestra libertad.
= Liberales de la República !! los hijos del mundo
civilizado están sobre vosotros. Están indignados
de ver la conducta traicionera de vuestro enemigo.
Simpatizan en vuestras desgracias, y todo patriota
en todas partes del mundo ofrece sus oraciones al
cielo de que aun despertareis de vuestra apatía y
sereis libres! Animaos y plantad de nuevo en vues-
tro suelo la bandera de la libertad. De nuevo jurad
que sostendreis con vuestra sangre y tesoro el sis-
tema federativo Republicano levantaos republi-
canos y vuestro pais será salvo jurad conquistar
ó morir y la omnipotencia de la verdad pronto
acudirá á vuestro favor como lo ha hecho
antes de ahora. Vuestra lucha es contra el
enemigo de la libertad constitucional y no
debeis tener pª. el vivir cuando se destruya vues-
tra forma de Gobierno Republicano Federal.
Debeis primero morir que sucumbir á la
aristocracia. Cumplid pues vuestros juramtos.

[. . .] that you have made to the world and to the nation to sustain the constitution of the government that was adopted according to the test of all the nations that once justified to the Spanish that all men naturally are equal, and that all should be free to firmly embrace the pillars of the constitution, and [if you] only abandon it, it will be sacrificed in total ruin, taking up your last exclamation even in the hour of breathing these words of the constitution of the United States of Mexico.

Citizens of Texas, we have a sacred obligation to fulfill from our childhood what has been instilled when [*diosa*] tyranny. Your fathers were the first who planted in the soil of America the standard of freedom, and they purchased it with their blood and their fortune and you all were left in possession of such a [page ends]

que habeis hecho al mundo y á la Nacion de
sostener la constitucion del Gob.no segun fue
adoptada Dad esta prueva á todas las
naciones de que erais justificados cuando de-
clarasteis á la España que todos los hombres
por la naturaleza eran iguales, y que to-
dos devian ser libres abrazad fuertem.te los
pilares de la constitucion y solo la deveis
abandonar q.do seais sacrificados en su to-
tal ruina tomad por vuestra ultima
exclamacion aun en la hora de espirar es-
tas palabras la constitucion de los Estados
Unidos Mexicanos = Ciudadanos
en Tejas tenemos una obligacion
sagrada que cumplir desde vuestra
niñes se os ha inculcado cuan cara es
vuestra libertad y cuan odiosa la tira-
nia. Vuestros padres fueron los que
primero plantaron en el suelo de la
America el estandarte de la libertad.
con su sangre y con su tesoro os com-
praron y os dejaron en posecion de tan va-

[. . .] valuable heritage. You should sustain it firmly and tenaciously until death. The sympathies of all the world are with you all. Your brothers of the United States of the North desire very much the victory, and in the hour of danger they will come in the thousands to your support. Everywhere it will be said that your cause is just and your efforts plausible. Each mother and each brother will offer to heaven without prayers [?] that at the hour of danger none of their friends will become traitors to the country. Take for the motto of Texas the Federal Constitution and the Constitution of the State and God and Liberty.

San Felipe de Austin, June 22, 1835
R. M. Williamson, President
Moseley Baker, Secretary
This is a copy. San Felipe de Austin, June 22, 1835
Moseley Baker

This is a copy
J. M. Mendosa, Secretary[1]

00030

COMANDANCIA GENERAL E INSPECCION DE LOS ESTADOS INTERNOS DE ORIENTE.

34

tiosa herencia. Deveis sostenerla firme y tenazmente
hasta el morir. Las simpatias de todo el mundo es-
tan con vosotros. Vuestros hermanos de los Estados
Unidos del Norte os desean muy mucho la victoria
y en la ora del peligro ocurrirán en millares á
vuestro socorro. Por todas partes se os dirá que
vuestra causa es justa y vuestros esfuerzos plausi-
bles y cada madre y cada hermano ofrecerá al
cielo sus oraciones para que en la ora del peligro
ninguno de sus amigos sea traidor á su patria.
Firmad para el mote de Tejas la constitucion fe-
deral la constitucion del Estado y Dios y libertad
= San Felipe de Austin Junio 22 de 1835 = R.
M. Williamson presidente = Moseley Baker
Srio = Es copia S. Felipe de Austin Junio
22. de 1835. = Moseley Baker =

Es copia

J. Mr. Mendoza
Secret.o

APPENDIX 8

Columbia Meeting Proclamation

At a very large and respectable meeting of the citizens of the jurisdiction of Columbia, on the 28th day of June, 1835, held in pursuance of a previous call, for the purpose of considering the present situation of the country, and determining upon the course of conduct for the people of this jurisdiction to pursue, in the present and approaching crisis—Col. W. D. C. Hall was called to the chair, and Byrd B. Waller elected secretary.

The letter of the Political Chief of this department together with a number of documents throwing light upon the real situation of the country, having been read to the meeting, Messrs. John A. Wharton, W. D. C. Hall, H. Smith, J. F. Perry, J. H. Bell, S. Whiting, G. B. M'Kinstry, W. C. White, P. B. M'Neel, F. Bingham, J. AE. Phelps, Edwin Waller, E. Andrews, J. P. Caldwell, and E. G. Head were unanimously chosen to prepare a report and resolutions to be submitted for the consideration of this meeting. The committee retired but shortly returned with the following report and resolutions which were immediately adopted:—

To the citizens of the jurisdiction of Columbia:— Your committee having given the subject on which they were to report, as thorough an investigation as time and circumstances permit, beg leave to present the following report:

Your committee view [sic] with the deepest regret, and greatest alarm the present political situation of Texas, and recommend to this meeting and their fellow citizens generally, union, moderation, organization and a strict adherence to the laws and constitution of the land. Your committee protest [sic] against the conduct and acts of any set of individuals (less than a majority) calculated to involve the citizens of Texas in a conflict with the Federal Government of Mexico, and particularly protest against the proceedings of those persons at Anáhuac who gave the collector of customs, Don José Gonzales [*sic*],

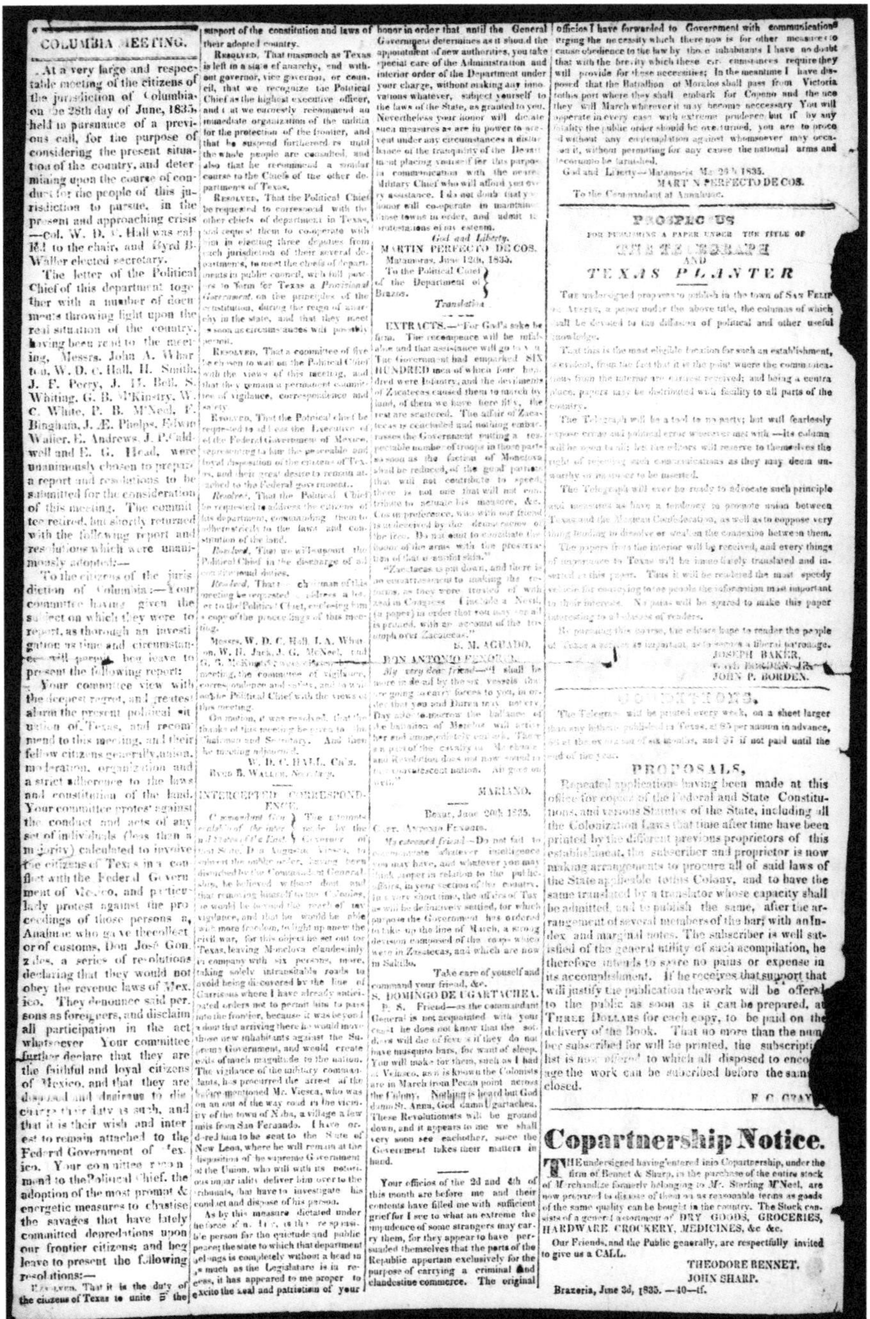

COLUMBIA MEETING.

At a very large and respectable meeting of the citizens of the jurisdiction of Columbia on the 28th day of June, 1835, held in pursuance of a previous call, for the purpose of considering the present situation of the country, and determining upon the course of conduct for the people of this jurisdiction to pursue, in the present and approaching crisis—Col. W. D. C. Hall was called to the chair, and Byrd B. Waller elected secretary.

The letter of the Political Chief of this department together with a number of documents throwing light upon the real situation of the country, having been read to the meeting, Messrs. John A. Wharton, W. D. C. Hall, H. Smith, J. F. Perry, J. H. Bell, S. Whiting, G. B. M'Kinstry, W. C. White, P. B. M'Neel, F. Bingham, J. Æ. Phelps, Edwin Waller, E. Andrews, J. P. Caldwell and E. G. Head, were unanimously chosen to prepare a report and resolutions to be submitted for the consideration of this meeting. The committee retired, but shortly returned with the following report and resolutions which were unanimously adopted:—

To the citizens of the jurisdiction of Columbia:—Your committee having given the subject on which they were to report, as thorough an investigation as time and circumstances will permit, beg leave to present the following report:

Your committee view with the deepest regret, and greatest alarm the present political situation of Texas, and recommend to this meeting, and their fellow citizens generally, union, moderation, organization and a strict adherence to the laws and constitution of the land. Your committee protest against the conduct and acts of any set of individuals (less than a majority) calculated to involve the citizens of Texas in a conflict with the Federal Government of Mexico, and particularly protest against the proceedings of those persons in Anahuac who gave the collector of customs, Don José Gonzales, a series of resolutions declaring that they would not obey the revenue laws of Mexico. They denounce said persons as foreigners, and disclaim all participation in the act whatsoever. Your committee further declare that they are the faithful and loyal citizens of Mexico, and that they are disposed and desirous to discharge their duty as such, and that it is their wish and interest to remain attached to the Federal Government of Mexico. Your committee recommend to the Political Chief, the adoption of the most prompt & energetic measures to chastise the savages that have lately committed depredations upon our frontier citizens; and beg leave to present the following resolutions:—

RESOLVED, That it is the duty of the citizens of Texas to unite in the support of the constitution and laws of their adopted country.

RESOLVED, That inasmuch as Texas is left in a state of anarchy, and without governor, vice governor, or council, that we recognize the Political Chief as the highest executive officer, and that we earnestly recommend an immediate organization of the militia for the protection of the frontier, and that he suspend further orders until the whole people are consulted, and also that he recommend a similar course to the Chiefs of the other departments of Texas.

RESOLVED, That the Political Chief be requested to correspond with the other chiefs of department in Texas, and request them to co-operate with him in electing three deputies from each jurisdiction of their several departments, to meet the chiefs of departments in public council, with full powers to form for Texas a *Provisional Government*, on the principles of the constitution, during the reign of anarchy in the state, and that they meet as soon as circumstances will possibly permit.

RESOLVED, That a committee of five be chosen to wait on the Political Chief with the views of this meeting, and that they remain a permanent committee of vigilance, correspondence and safety.

RESOLVED, That the Political chief be requested to address the Executive of the Federal Government of Mexico, representing to him the peaceable and loyal disposition of the citizens of Texas, and their great desire to remain attached to the Federal government.

Resolved, That the Political Chief be requested to address the citizens of his department, commanding them to adhere strictly to the laws and constitution of the land.

Resolved, That we will support the Political Chief in the discharge of all constitutional duties.

Resolved, That the chairman of this meeting be requested to address a letter to the Political Chief, enclosing him a copy of the proceedings of this meeting.

Messrs. W. D. C. Hall, I. A. Wharton, W. H. Jack, J. G. McNeel, and G. B. McKinstry were elected by the meeting, the committee of vigilance, correspondence and safety, and to wait on the Political Chief with the views of this meeting.

On motion, it was resolved, that the thanks of this meeting be given to the Chairman and Secretary. And then the meeting adjourned.

W. D. C. HALL, Ch'n.
BYRD B. WALLER, Secretary.

INTERCEPTED CORRESPONDENCE.

Commandant General of the Internal States of the East. } The attempts made by the Governor of that State, Don Augustin Viesca, to subvert the public order, having been disturbed by the Commandant Generalship, he believed without doubt and that removing himself to the Colonies, he would be beyond the reach of my vigilance, and that he would be able with more freedom, to light up anew the civil war, for this object he set out for Texas, leaving Monclova clandestinely in company with six persons, more, taking solely intransitable roads to avoid being discovered by the line of Garrisons where I have already anticipated orders not to permit him to pass into the frontier, because it was beyond a doubt that arriving there he would move those new inhabitants against the Supreme Government, and would create evils of much magnitude to the nation. The vigilance of the military commandants, has procurred the arrest of the before mentioned Mr. Viesca, who was on an out of the way road in the vicinity of the town of Naba, a village a few miles from San Fernando. I have ordered him to be sent to the State of New Leon, where he will remain at the disposition of the supreme Government of the Union, who will with its notorious impartiality deliver him over to the tribunals, that have to investigate his conduct and dispose of his person.

As by this measure dictated under the force of necessity, is the responsible person for the quietude and public peace; the state to which that department belongs is completely without a head in as much as the Legislature is in recess, it has appeared to me proper to excite the zeal and patriotism of your honor in order that until the General Government determines as it should the appointment of new authorities, you take special care of the Administration and interior order of the Department under your charge, without making any innovations whatever, subject yourself to the laws of the State, as granted to you. Nevertheless your honor will dictate such measures as are in power to prevent under any circumstances a disturbance of the tranquility of the Department placing yourself for this purpose in communication with the nearest Military Chief who will afford you every assistance. I do not doubt that your honor will co-operate in maintaining those towns in order, and admit the protestations of my esteem.

God and Liberty.
MARTIN PERFECTO DE COS.
Matamoras, June 12th, 1835.
To the Political Chief of the Department of Brazos.

Translation

EXTRACTS.—"For God's sake be firm. The recompence will be infallible and that assistance will go to you. The Government had embarked SIX HUNDRED men of which four hundred were Infantry, and the devilments of Zacatecas caused them to march by land, of them we have here fifty, the rest are scattered. The affair of Zacatecas is concluded and nothing embarrasses the Government putting a respectable number of troops in those parts as soon as the faction of Monclova shall be reduced, of the good patriots that will not contribute to speed, there is not one that will not contribute to actuate his measure, &c. Cos in preference, who with our friend is undeceived by the [illegible] of the [illegible]. Do not omit to conciliate the honor of the arms with the preservation of that [illegible] skin."

"Zacatecas is put down, and there is no embarrassment to making the reforms, as they were treated of with zeal in Congress. I include a Nevil, (a paper) in order that you may see all is praised, with an account of the triumph over Zacatecas."

S. M. AGUADO.

DON ANTONIO TENORIO.

My very dear friend—"I shall be more in detail by the six vessels that are going to carry forces to you, in order that you and Barra may not cry, Day after to-morrow the ballance of the battalion of Morelos will arrive here and immediately embark. There is a part of the cavalry at Matamoras and Revolution does not now sound to this convalescent nation. All goes on well."

MARIANO.

Bexar, June 20th 1835.
CAPT. ANTONIO TENORIO.

My esteemed friend—Do not fail to communicate whatever intelligence you may have, and whatever you may think proper in relation to the public affairs, in your section of the country. In a very short time, the affairs of Texas will be definitively settled, for which purpose the Government has ordered to take up the line of March, a strong devision composed of the corps which were in Zacatecas, and which are now in Saltillo.

Take care of youself and command your friend, &c.
S. DOMINGO DE UGARTACHEA.

P. S. Friend—as the commandant General is not acquainted with your coast he does not know that the soldiers will die of fevers if they do not have musquito bars, for want of sleep. You will make for them, such as I had at Velasco, as it is known the Colonists are in March from Pecan point across the Colony. Nothing is heard but God damn St. Anna, God damn Ugartachea. These Revolutionists will be ground down, and it appears to me we shall very soon see eachother, since the Government takes their matters in hand.

Your officios of the 2d and 4th of this month are before me and their contents have filled me with sufficient grief for I see to what an extreme the impudence of some strangers may carry them, for they appear to have persuaded themselves that the ports of the Republic appertain exclusively for the purpose of carrying a criminal and clandestine commerce. The original officios I have forwarded to Government with communications urging the necessity which there now is for other measures to cause obedience to the law by those inhabitants I have no doubt that with the brevity which these circumstances require they will provide for these necessities; In the meantime I have disposed that the Battallion of Morelos shall pass from Victoria to this port where they shall embark for Copano and thence they will March wherever it may become necessary. You will operate in every case with extreme prudence but if by any fatality the public order should be overturned, you are to proceed without any contemplation against whomsoever may occasion it, without permitting for any cause the national arms and decorum to be tarnished.

God and Liberty—Matamoris May 26th 1835.
MARTIN PERFECTO DE COS.
To the Commandant at Annahuac.

PROSPECTUS

FOR PUBLISHING A PAPER UNDER THE TITLE OF

THE TELEGRAPH AND TEXAS PLANTER

THE undersigned propose to publish in the town of SAN FELIPE DE AUSTIN, a paper under the above title, the columns of which shall be devoted to the diffusion of political and other useful knowledge.

That this is the most eligible location for such an establishment, is evident, from the fact that it is the point where the communications from the interior are earliest received; and being a central place, papers may be distributed with facility to all parts of the country.

The Telegraph will be a tool to no party; but will fearlessly expose error and political error wherever met with—its column will be open to all; but the editors will reserve to themselves the right of rejecting such communications as they may deem unworthy or improper to be inserted.

The Telegraph will ever be ready to advocate such principle and measures as have a tendency to promote union between Texas and the Mexican Confederation, as well as to oppose every thing tending to dissolve or weaken the connexion between them.

The papers from the interior will be received, and every things of importance to Texas will be immediately translated and inserted in this paper. Thus it will be rendered the most speedy vehicle for conveying to the people the information most important to their interests. No pains will be spared to make this paper interesting to all classes of readers.

By pursuing this course, the editors hope to render the people of Texas a service as important, as to secure a liberal patronage.

JOSEPH BAKER,
GAIL BORDEN, JR.
JOHN P. BORDEN.

CONDITIONS.

The Telegraph will be printed every week, on a sheet larger than any hitherto published in Texas, at $5 per annum in advance, $6 at the expiration of six months, and $7 if not paid until the end of the year.

PROPOSALS,

Repeated applications having been made at this office for copies of the Federal and State Constitutions, and various Statutes of the State, including all the Colonization Laws that time after time have been printed by the different previous proprietors of this establishment, the subscriber and proprietor is now making arrangements to procure all of said laws of the State applicable to this Colony, and to have the same translated by a translator whose capacity shall be admitted, and to publish the same, after the arrangement of several members of the bar; with an Index and marginal notes. The subscriber is well satisfied of the general utility of such a compilation, he therefore intends to spare no pains or expense in its accomplishment. If he receives that support that will justify the publication the work will be offered to the public as soon as it can be prepared, at THREE DOLLARS for each copy, to be paid on the delivery of the Book. That no more than the number subscribed for will be printed, the subscription list is now offered to which all disposed to encourage the work can be subscribed before the same is closed.

F. C. GRAY

Copartnership Notice.

THE undersigned having entered into Copartnership, under the firm of Bennet & Sharp, in the purchase of the entire stock of Merchandize formerly belonging to *Mr. Sterling M'Neel*, are now prepared to dispose of them on as reasonable terms as goods of the same quality can be bought in the country. The Stock consists of a general assortment of DRY GOODS, GROCERIES, HARDWARE, CROCKERY, MEDICINES, &c &c.

Our Friends, and the Public generally, are respectfully invited to give us a CALL.

THEODORE BENNET.
JOHN SHARP.

Brazoria, June 3d, 1835. —40—tf.

Columbia meeting proclamation, June 28, 1835, XI / 481.3 / expediente 1814, fojas 30–35, Archivo Histórico Militar.

a series of resolutions declaring that they would not obey the revenue laws of Mexico. They denounce said persons as foreigners and disclaim all participation in the act whatsoever. Your committee further declare [*sic*] that they are the faithful and loyal citizens of Mexico, and that they are disposed and desirous to discharge their duties as such, and that it is their wish and interest to remain attached to the Federal Government of Mexico. Your committee recommend [*sic*] to the Political Chief the adoption of the most prompt and energetic measures to chastise the savages that have lately committed depredations upon our frontier citizens; and beg [*sic*] leave to present the following resolutions:—

Resolved. That it is the duty of the citizens of Texas to unite in support of the constitution and laws of their adopted country.

Resolved, That inasmuch as Texas is left in a state of anarchy, and without governor, vice governor, or council, that we recognize the Political Chief as the highest executive officer, and that we earnestly recommend an immediate organization of the militia for the protection of the frontier, and that he suspend further orders until the whole people are consulted, and also that he recommend a similar course to the Chiefs of the other departments of Texas.

Resolved, That the Political Chief be requested to correspond with the other chiefs of department in Texas, and request them to co-operate with him in electing three deputies from each jurisdiction of the several departments, to meet with the chiefs of departments in public council, with full power to form for Texas a *Provisional Government* on the principles of the constitution, during the reign of anarchy in the state, and that they meet as soon as circumstances will possibly permit.

Resolved, That a committee of five be chosen to wait on the political chief with the views of this meeting, and that they remain a permanent committee of vigilance, correspondence and safety.

Resolved, That the Political Chief be requested to address the Executive of the Federal Government of Mexico, representing to him the peaceable and loyal disposition of the citizens of Texas, and their great desire to remain attached to the Federal Government.

Resolved, That the Political Chief be requested to address the citizens of his department, commanding them to adhere strictly to the laws and constitution of the land.

Resolved, That we will support the Political Chief in the discharge of all constitutional duties.

Resolved, That the Chairman of this meeting be requested to address a letter to the Political Chief, enclosing him a copy of the proceedings of this meeting.

Messrs. W. D. C. Hall, J. A. Wharton, W. H. Jack, J. G. McNeel, and G. B. McKinstry were charged by the meeting [to form] the committee of vigilance, correspondence and safety, and to wait on the Political Chief with the views of this meeting.

On motion, it was resolved, that the thanks for this meeting be given to the Chairman and Secretary. And then the meeting adjourned.

W. D. C. Hall, Ch'n.
Byrd B. Waller, Secretary.[1]

APPENDIX 9

Morelos Battalion Departure Report, July 2, 1835

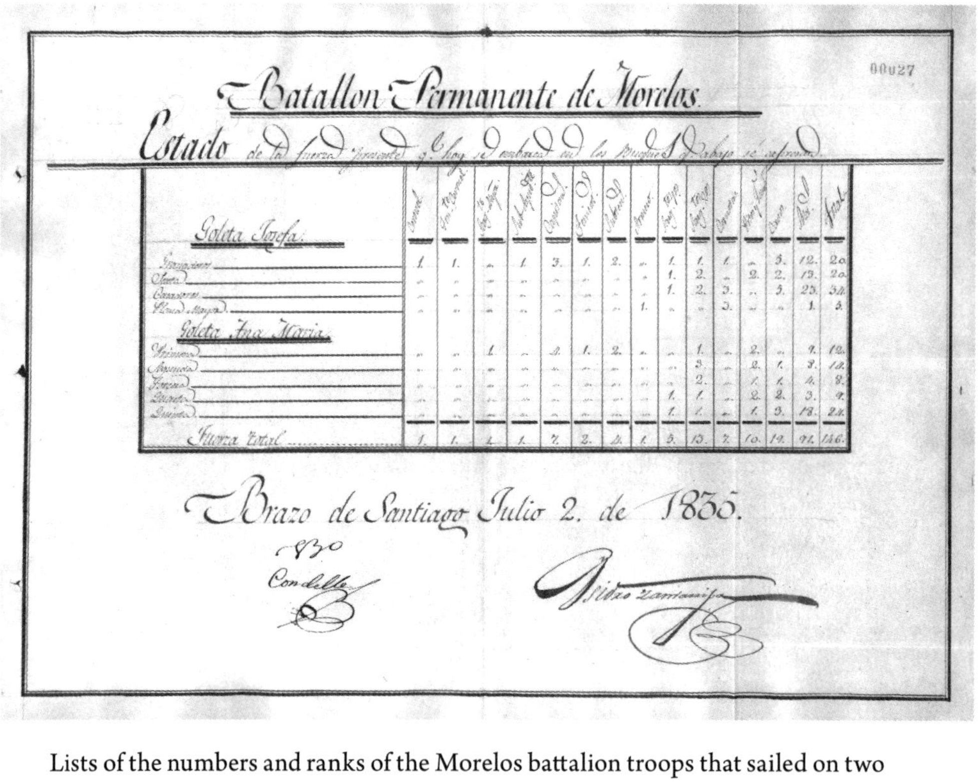

00027

Batallon Permanente de Morelos.

Estado de la fuerza presente q. hoy se embarca en los buques q. abajo se expresan.

	Coronel	Ten. Coronel	1er Ayud.	Subayud.	Capitanes	Tenientes	Subtenientes	Armero	Sarg. 1os	Sarg. 2os	Cornetas	[illegible]	Cabos	Sold.	Total
Goleta Josefa.															
Granaderos	1.	1.	–	1.	3.	1.	2.	–	1.	1.	1.	–	5.	12.	20.
Sexta	–	–	–	–	–	–	–	–	1.	2.	–	2.	2.	13.	20.
Cazadores	–	–	–	–	–	–	–	–	1.	2.	3.	–	5.	23.	34.
Plana Mayor	–	–	–	–	–	–	–	1.	–	–	3.	–	–	1.	5.
Goleta Ana Maria.															
Primera	–	–	1.	–	4.	1.	2.	–	–	1.	–	2.	–	9.	12.
Segunda	–	–	–	–	–	–	–	–	–	3.	–	2.	1.	8.	18.
Tercera	–	–	–	–	–	–	–	–	–	2.	–	1.	1.	4.	8.
Cuarta	–	–	–	–	–	–	–	–	1.	1.	–	2.	2.	3.	9.
Quinta	–	–	–	–	–	–	–	–	1.	1.	–	1.	3.	18.	24.
Fuerza total	1.	1.	1.	1.	7.	2.	4.	1.	5.	13.	7.	10.	19.	91.	146.

Brazo de Santiago Julio 2. de 1835.

Lists of the numbers and ranks of the Morelos battalion troops that sailed on two ships from Brazos de Santiago on July 2, 1835. Found in Brazos de Santiago, XI / 481.3 / expediente 1816, foja 37, Archivo Histórico Militar.

Permanent Battalion of Morelos

List of the force present that embarked today in the ships that are named below.

	Col.	Lt. Col.	Sgt. Maj.	Sub. Adj.	Capt.	Lt.	Sub. Lt.	Arm.	1 Sgt.	2 Sgt.	Corn.	Musc. and Drum.	Cpl.	Pvt.	Total
Schooner *Josefa*															
Grenadiers	1	1	x	1	3	1	2	---	1	1	1	---	5	12	20
6th Comp.	---	---	---	---	---	---	---	---	1	2	---	2	2	13	20
Lt. Inf. [Caz.]	---	---	---	---	---	---	---	---	1	2	3	---	5	23	34
Headquarters	---	---	---	---	---	---	---	1	---	---	3	---	---	1	5
Schooner *Ana Maria*															
1st Comp	---	---	1	---	4	1	2	---	---	1	---	2	---	9	12
2nd Comp	---	---	---	---	---	---	---	---	---	3	---	2	1	8	14
3rd Comp	---	---	---	---	---	---	---	---	---	2	---	1	1	4	8
4th Comp	---	---	---	---	---	---	---	---	1	1	---	2	2	3	9
5th Comp	---	---	---	---	---	---	---	---	1	1	---	1	3	18	24
Total Force	**1**	**1**	**1**	**1**	**7**	**2**	**4**	**1**	**5**	**13**	**7**	**10**	**19**	**91**	**146**

Brazo de Santiago, July 2, 1835
Condelle Ysidro Zamarripa

Morelos Battalion Strength Report, Béjar, October 1, 1835

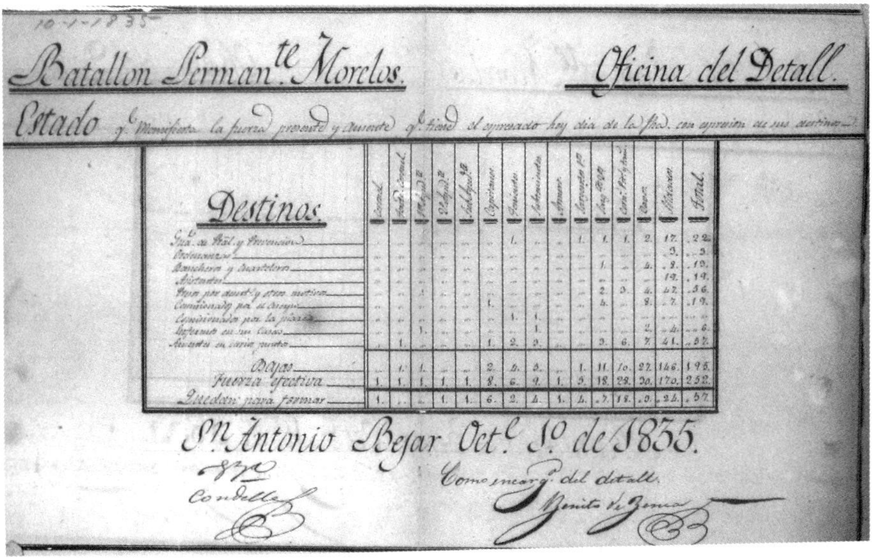

Morelos battalion strength report, Béjar, October 1, 1835, box 2S319, Bexar Archives, Dolph Briscoe Center for American History, University of Texas at Austin.

Permanent Battalion of Morelos Office of Details

Report that shows the force, present and absent, that the expressed [unit] has on today's date, with expressions of their assignments.

Destinations	Col.	Lt Col.	1st Adj.	2nd Adj.	Sub Adj.	Capt.	Lt.	Sub Lt.	Armorer	1st Sgt.	2nd Sgt.	Musc.	Cpl.	Pvt.	Total
Main guard and security guard	---	---	---	---	---	---	1	---	---	1	1	1	2	17	22
Orderlies	---	---	---	---	---	---	---	---	---	---	---	---	---	3	3
Cooks and barracks orderlies	---	---	---	---	---	---	---	---	---	---	1	---	4	8	13
Assistants	---	---	---	---	---	---	---	---	---	---	---	---	---	19	19
Prisoners for desertion and other reasons	---	---	---	---	---	---	---	---	---	---	2	3	4	47	56
Agents for the unit	---	---	---	---	---	1	---	---	---	---	4	---	8	7	19
Agents for the plaza	---	---	---	---	---	---	1	1	---	---	---	---	---	---	---
Sick in their houses	---		1	---	---	---	---	1	---	---	---	---	2	4	6
Absent at various places	---	1	---	---	---	1	2	3	---	---	3	6	7	41	57
Unavailable	---	1	1	---	---	2	4	5	---	1	11	10	27	146	195
Effective Force	1	1	1	1	1	8	6	9	1	5	18	28	30	170	252
Remaining to fill	1	---	---	1	1	6	2	4	1	4	7	18	3	24	57

S[a]n Antonio Béjar, Oct. 1, 1835
V [isto] B[uen]o[1]
As one in charge of details
Condelle [rubric]
Benito de Zenea [rubric]

APPENDIX 11

Morelos Battalion Criminal Replacements

GENERAL COMMAND OF THE STATE OF VERACRUZ

3RD DEPARTMENT

List of those individuals sentenced to the presidios of Texas and California with expression of those who are transported to the Port of Matamoros in the National Schooner of War *Bravo*, and those who remain in this plaza

Destined for the Presidio of Texas

Felipe Santiago	1	Diego Martin or Marvin	1
Narciso Perez	1	José del Carmen Gonzalez	1
Ysidro Benites	1	Cristoval Solis	1
Mariano Perez	1	Blas Barragan	1
Antonio Cuellar	1	Romualdo Luna	1
Euvenio Castillo	1	Rafael Torres	1
Librado Rodriguez	1	Apolonio Escobar	1
Pascual de los Reyes	1	Rafael Benebidez	1
Eduardo Palacios (deceased)	1	Juan Escalante	1
		Luis Sosa [Losa?]	1
Felipe Luna (á) el Chango	1	Bernardino Sanchez	1
Victor Martinez Amesquita	1	Justo Rosales	1
Luis Lindo	1	Teodoro Martin Leon	1
Martin Hernandez	1		
			26

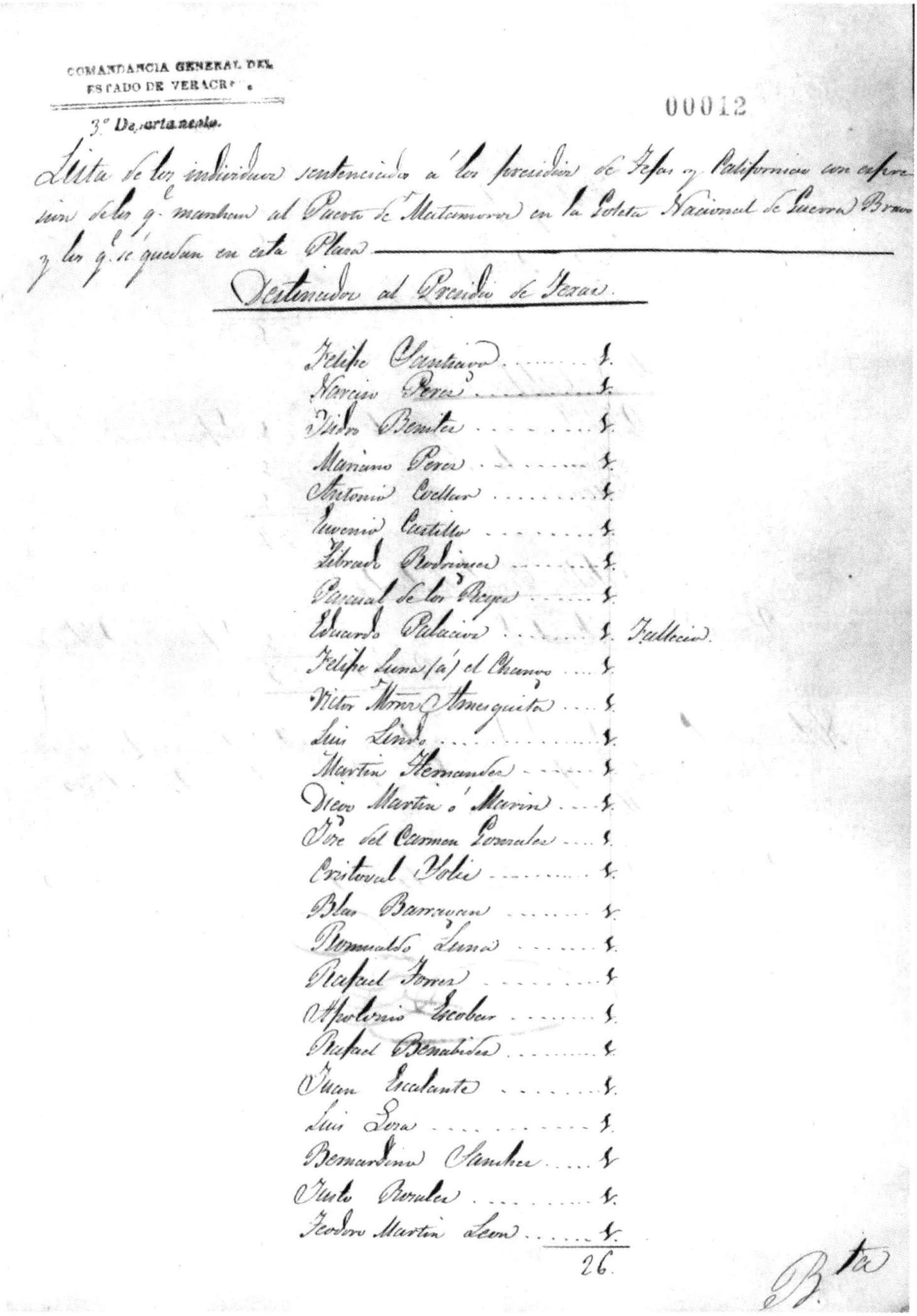
COMANDANCIA GENERAL DEL ESTADO DE VERACRUZ.

3.° Departamento.

00012

Lista de los individuos sentenciados á los presidios de Tejas y Californias con espresion de los q. marchan al Puerto de Matamoros en la Goleta Nacional de Guerra Bravo y los q.e se quedan en esta Plaza.

Destinados al Presidio de Tejas.

Felipe Santiago .... 1.
Narciso Perez .... 1.
Isidro Benitez .... 1.
Mariano Perez .... 1.
Antonio Cuellar .... 1.
Juvencio Castillo .... 1.
Liberado Rodriguez .... 1.
Pascual de los Reyes .... 1.
Eduardo Palacios .... 1. Falleció.
Felipe Luna (a) el Chamo .... 1.
Victor Moreno Amesquita .... 1.
Luis Lino .... 1.
Martin Hernandez .... 1.
Diego Martin ó Marin .... 1.
José del Carmen Gonzales .... 1.
Cristoval Velez .... 1.
Blas Barragan .... 1.
Romualdo Luna .... 1.
Rafael Torres .... 1.
Apolonio Escobar .... 1.
Rafael Benavides .... 1.
Juan Escalante .... 1.
Luis Lora .... 1.
Bernardino Sanchez .... 1.
Justo Morales .... 1.
Isidro Martin Leon .... 1.
26.

List of criminals sent to Texas and California as replacements for the Morelos battalion, October 14, 1835, XI / 481.3 / expediente 1111, fojas 19–20, Archivo Histórico Militar.

Andres Santa Anna	1
Agustín de la Rosa	1
Miguel Miranda	1
Castula Medina	1
Lazaro Ygnacio Valle	1
	31

To the Californias

José Tomas Páz y Puente	1 (Sick and in the Hospital)
Juan de la Pena	1
Dionicio Tinoco	1
	34

Permanent Morelos Battalion

Private deserter—	
Miguel Escovar	1 (sick in the hospital)
	Total 35

Note—those 32 individuals contained in this list, with this date [of] travel, [were] protected for 15 days.

Veracruz Oct. 14, 1835 Ramon Hernández

This is a copy. Veracruz. October, 15, 1835.

De la Buelta .... 26.

Andres Santa Anna .... 1.
Agustin de la Rosa .... 1.
Miguel Miranda .... 1.
Custodio Medina .... 1.
Lazaro Ygnacio Valle .... 1.

31.

Ptl. de Californias

Jose Tomas Perez y Puente .... 1. Enfermo en el Hospital
Juan de la Peña .... 1.
Dionicio Finoco .... 1.

34.

Batallon Perm.te de Morelos.

Soldado Desertor.. Miguel Escovar .... 1. Enfermo en el Hospital.

Total .... 35.

Nota.= Los treinta y dos individuos contenidos en esta lista, marchan con esta fecha socorridos por quince dias.= Veracruz Octubre 14. de 1835.= Ramon Hernandez.

Es Copia. Veracruz Octubre 15. de 1835.

San Luís Battalion Strength Report, November 17, 1835

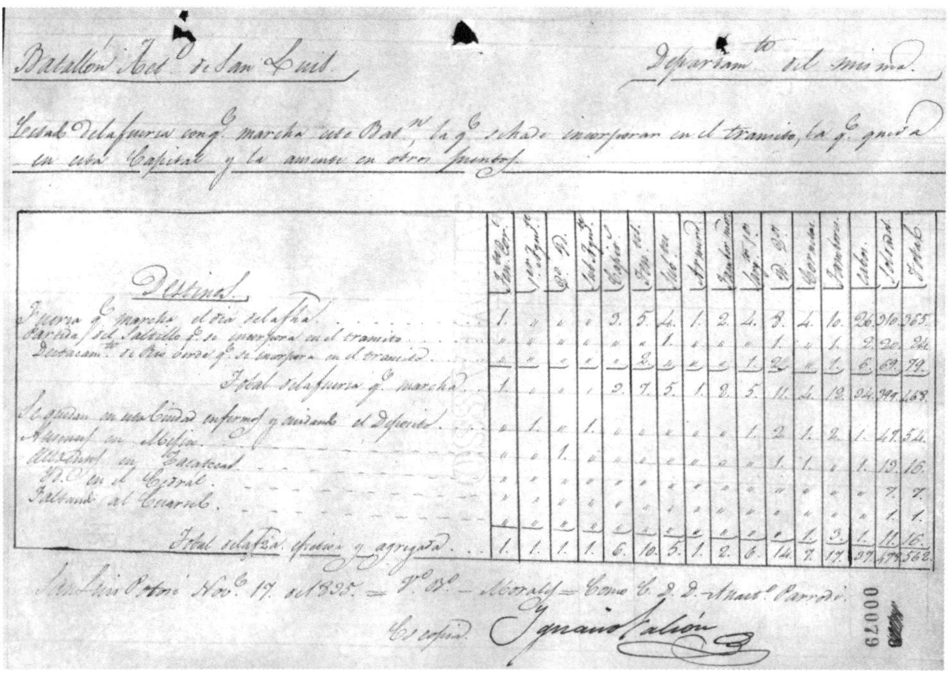

San Luís battalion strength report, November 17, 1835, XI / 481.3 / expediente 1823, foja 108, Archivo Histórico Militar.

ACTIVE BATTALION OF SAN LUÍS
DEPARTMENT OF THE SAME [SAN LUÍS]

State of the force with which this Battalion will march; that which will be incorporated in the transmission; that which remains in this capital, and the absent in other places

Destination	Lt. Col.	1st Adj.	2nd Adj.	Sub Adj.	Capt.	Lt.	Sub Lt.	gunsmith	Drum Maj.	1st Sgt.	2nd Sgt.	bugler	drummer	Corporal	Privates	Total
Force that marches this date	1	---	---	---	3	5	4	1	2	4	8	4	10	26	310	365
Party from Saltillo that will incorporate during the transit	---	---	---	---	---	---	1	---	---	---	1	---	1	2	20	24
Detachment from Rio Verde that will incorporate during the transit	---	---	---	---	---	2	---	---	---	1	2	---	1	6	69	79
Total of the force that will march	**1**	---	---	---	**3**	**7**	**5**	**1**	**2**	**5**	**11**	**4**	**12**	**34**	**399**	**468**
Those who remain in this city sick and caring for the deposit	---	1	---	1	---	---	---	---	---	1	2	1	2	1	47	54
Absent in Mexico [City]	---	---	1	---	---	---	---	---	---	---	1	1	---	1	13	16
Absent in Zacatecas	---	---	---	---	---	---	---	---	---	---	---	---	---	---	7	7
Same in Cedra'l	---	---	---	---	---	---	---	---	---	---	---	---	---	---	1	1
Missing [from] the barracks [AWOL?]	---	---	---	---	---	---	---	---	---	---	---	1	3	1	11	16
Total of the effective and aggregate force	**1**	**1**	**1**	**1**	**6**	**10**	**5**	**1**	**2**	**6**	**14**	**7**	**17**	**37**	**478**	**562**

San Luís Potosí *November 17, 1835* *V.o B.o Morales* *Como E. D. D Antonio Parrodi*
This is a copy *Ignacio Falcón*[1]

APPENDIX 13

Officers Ordered to Join the Mexican Army

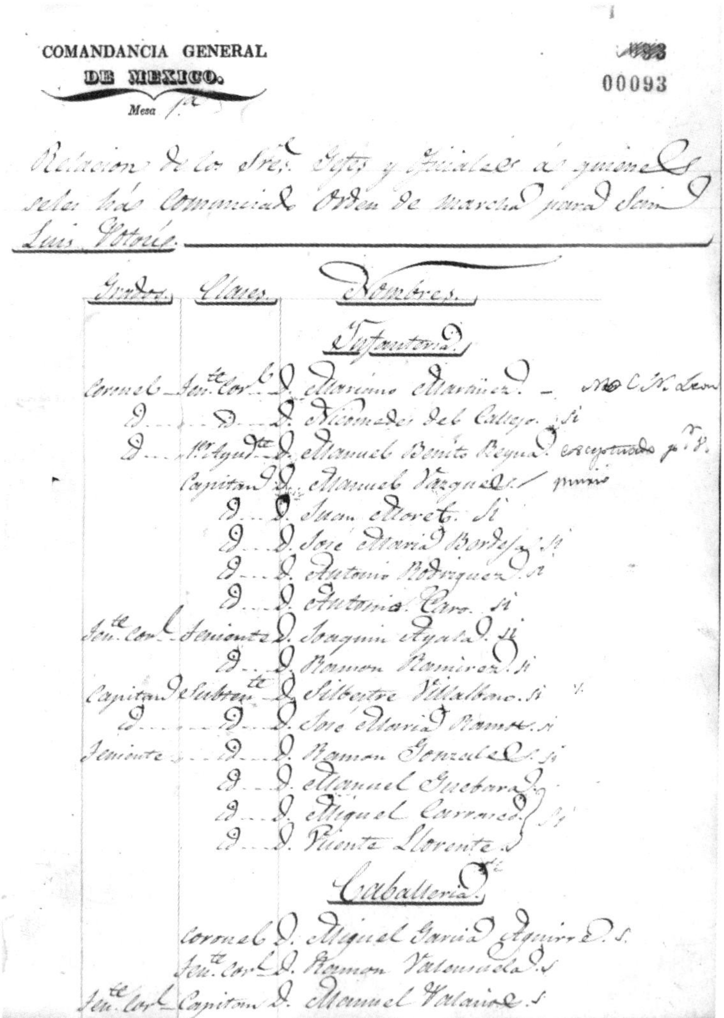

COMANDANCIA GENERAL
DE MEXICO.
Mesa 1a

00093

Relacion de los Sres. Gefes y Oficiales á quienes se les ha comunicado orden de marcha para San Luis Potosí.

Grados.	Clases.	Nombres.
		Infantería
Coronel	Ten.te Cor.l	D. Mariano Martinez
id.	id.	D. Nicomedes del Callejo
id.	1er Ayud.te	D. Manuel Benito Reyna
	Capitan	D. Manuel Vazquez
	id.	D. Juan Moret
	id.	D. José María Bordes
	id.	D. Antonio Rodriguez
	id.	D. Antonio Caro
Ten.te Cor.l	Teniente	D. Joaquin Ayala
	id.	D. Ramon Ramirez
Capitan	Subten.te	D. Silbestre Villalbano
id.	id.	D. José María Ramos
Teniente	id.	D. Ramon Gonzalez
	id.	D. Manuel Guebara
	id.	D. Miguel Carrasco
	id.	D. Vicente Llorente
		Caballería
	Coronel	D. Miguel Garcia Aguirre
	Ten.te Cor.l	D. Ramon Valenzuela
Ten.te Cor.l	Capitan	D. Manuel Valarino

Officers ordered to join the Mexican navy. expediente 1823, fojas 123–24, Archivo Historico Militar.

GENERAL COMMAND OF MEXICO

List of the Senior Commanders and officers who have been ordered to march for San Luís Potosí

Brevet Rank	Rank	Name	
		Infantry	
Colonel	Lt. Col	Mariano Martinez	no C. N. Leon
Id	Id	Nicomedes del Callejo	yes
Id	1st Adjutant	Manuel Benito Reyna	C 8 headed for 8 [?]
	Captain	Manuel Vazques	[illegible]
	Id	Juan Moreto	yes
	Id	José Maria Berdeja	yes
	Id	Antonio Rodriguez	yes
	Id	Antonio Caro	yes
Lt. Col	Lieutenant	Joaquin Ayala	yes
	Id	Ramon Ramirez	yes
Captain	Sub Lieutenant	Silbestre Villalbaso	yes
Id	Id	José Maria Ramos	yes
Lieutenant	Id	Ramon Gonzales	yes
	Id	Manuel Guebara	yes
	Id	Miguel Carrasco	yes
	Id	Vicente Llorente	yes
		Cavalry	
	Coronel	Miguel Garcia Aguirre	yes
	Lt. Colonel	Ramon Valensuela	yes
Lt. Col.	Captain	Manuel Palacios	yes

Grados	Clases	Nombres
[illegible]	Capitan D.	Manuel Patiño Gallardo. S
Ten.te Coron.l	id. D.	Catarino Barros. distrito.
	id. D.	Luis Medina. Comisario.
	id. D.	Gregorio Moreno. Si
Ten.te Cor.l	id. D.	José María Barberi. Con licencia.
	id. D.	Celso Cos. ——— Enfermo. no
	id. D.	Pedro Valenzuela. Si p.o Sinaloa
Ten.te Cor.l	id. D.	Pedro Patiño Gallardo. Si
	2.o Ayud.te D.	Angel Perez Castro. Si
Capitan	Teniente D.	Antonio Ponce de Leon. Si
	id. D.	Diego Pereda. S
	id. D.	Ventura Beran. S
	id. D.	Mariano Vazquez. S
	id. D.	Bernardo Parra. S
	Alferez D.	Manuel Bastian. } Si
	id. D.	Juan Iñiguez.
	id. D.	Juan Antonio Ruiz
	id. D.	Juan Ruiz Rojas.
	id. D.	Mariano Aubera.

Mexico Nov.e 23 de 1835.

Rem.do Lop. Um. [illegible]
[illegible]

Brevet Rank	Rank	Name	
	Captain	Manuel Patiño Gallardo	yes
Lt. Col.	Id	Catarino Barrosa	district [?]
	Id	Luis Medina [Modina?]	commissary
	Id	Gregorio Moreno	yes
Lt. Col.	Id	José Maria Barberi	with permission
	Id	Celso Cos	sick no
	Id	Pedro Walensuela	yes for [note is obscured]
	Id	Pedro Petiño Gallardo	yes
	2nd adjutant	Angel Perez Castro	yes
Captain	Lieutenant	Antonio Ponce de Leon	yes
	Id	Diego Peredo	yes
	Id	Mariano Velasquez	yes
	Id	Bernardo Parra	yes
	Subaltern [*alférez*]	Manuel Bastian	yes
	Id	Juan Yñiquez	yes
	Id	Juan Antonio Ruiz	yes
	Id	Juan Ruis Rojas	yes
	Id	Mariano Tabera	yes

Mexico [City], Nov. 23, 183   Fran.co Lupe [illegible]

APPENDIX 14

Luis Quintanar Broadside, November 13, 1835

Luis Quintanar,

Division General and Commanding General of the Department of Oaxaca, to his subordinates.

Soldiers: A miserable portion of adventurers and hypocrite settlers in Texas have dared to set foot hostilely in some of the towns of that territory. In these [towns] the magnanimous Mexican nation with liberal hands gave hospitality to those same monsters that today attempt to subjugate it and usurp one of the richest parts of its richest ground.

Is it the case that those ingrates have forgotten it was the Mexican soldiers who knew to destroy the Spanish armies and make them bite the dust? They [Mexican soldiers] are as numerous and disciplined as in 1821, when we achieved our independence and unquestionable rights. In these [the soldiers] have we appreciated life when dealing with these valuable objects? Those miserable people! What a short reign they are hoping for! To pulverize them we know to abandon everything, leaving the Supreme Government to surely turn them in front of its fearful bayonets. We will jump their weak barriers, in the manner that in Tampico, predicted by the Immortal Santa Anna, our valiant troops did against a more warlike enemy.

Soldiers of the Homeland: I feel the fire of indignation running in the blood of your veins, much more so if we do not occupy the first file in combat.

Companions in arms: the 9th of this month [November 1835] wielding these, we have solemnly sworn to sustain the constitutional bases sanctioned by the general congress. Let us also swear, before the creator

139

00139

LUIS QUINTANAR,

General de division y comandante general del Departamento de Oaxaca, á sus subordinados.

SOLDADOS: Una miserable porcion de aventureros é hipócritas colonos en Tejas han osado poner los pies hostilmente en algunos de los pueblos de aquel territorio, en que la magnánima nacion mexicana con mano liberal dió hospedage á los mismos monstruos que hoy pretenden sojuzgarla y usurparle una parte la mas rica de su fértil suelo.

¿Acaso habrán olvidado esos ingratos que los soldados mexicanos supieron destruir y hacer morder la tierra á los ejércitos españoles, tan numerosos como disciplinados, cuando se trató en 821 de nuestra independencia y derechos incuestionables? ¿En qué hemos apreciado la vida al versarse estos caros objetos? ¡Miserables!..... ¡Qué reinado tan corto se les espera!.... Para pulverizarlos sabrémos abandonarlo todo, dejando en seguro al Supremo Gobierno para volar delante de sus trémulas bayonetas: saltarémos sus débiles barreras, á la manera que en Tampico, presididos por el INMORTAL SANTA-ANNA, lo hicieron nuestras valientes tropas con enemigos mas belicosos.

SOLDADOS DE LA PATRIA: Yo os siento correr en la sangre de vuestras venas el fuego de la indignacion, mucho mayor si no hubiésemos de ocupar la primera fila en el combate.

COMPAÑEROS DE ARMAS: El 9 del actual empuñando éstas, hemos jurado solemnemente *sostener las bases constitucionales sancionadas por el congreso general:* juremos tambien ante el Creador del universo morir en torno del Supremo Gobierno, sosteniendo nuestros sacrosantos derechos.

Desde que tengola satisfcceionde mandaros, os he visto marchar por la senda del honor. Habeis sido inflecsibles para conservar el órden; moderados y generosos entre ambos partidos: léjos de vosotros han estado las venganzas personales, propias de almas viles y precarias. Esta conducta os ha grangeado la estimacion universal y la mia particularmente. Seguid como hasta aquí: olvidense épocas y resentimientos: formemos todos la fraternal columna en que se estrellen las maquinaciones de los anarquistas y de los enemigos esteriores: que no se oigan en el Departamento de Oaxaca otras voces que las siguientes: *¡Viva la independencia! ¡Viva la union! ¡Viva el Supremo Gobierno!* Esta será nuestra divisa y el estandarte con que se sacrificará gustoso vuestro antiguo amigo y camarada.

Oaxaca, Noviembre 13 de 1835.

Luis Quintanar.

OAXACA.—*Impreso por A. Valdes y Moya.*—1835.

Luis Quintanar broadside to subordinates, November 13, 1835, XI / 481.3 / expediente 1823, foja 189, Archivo Histórico Militar.

of the universe, to die in defense of the Supreme Government, sustaining our sacred rights.

Since I have the satisfaction of sending you, I have seen you march on the path of honor. You had been inflexible in order to conserve the order; moderate and generous between both parties: far from you has been personal vengeance, as owned by vile and precarious souls. This conduct has gained you universal estimation and mine particularly. Follow as up to here: forget times and resentments: Let us all for the fraternal column in which the machinations of the anarchists and outside enemies crash: that in the Department of Oaxaca there cannot be heard any other voices but the following: long live independence! Long live the union! Long live the Supreme Government! This will be our motto and the banner with which your old friend and comrade will be gladly sacrificed.

Oaxaca Nov. 13, 1835 Luis Quintanar

APPENDIX 15

Arms and Munitions Shipped from Veracruz to Texas

DIRECTOR GENERAL OF ARTILLERY

Plaza of Veracruz

List that states the arms, munitions, and other effects that under orders of the Commanding General of the State and the Senior Commanders of the Corps have embarked in the national sailboat *Mexico* commanded by 1st Lt. of the navy Blas Godines and with the purpose of transporting it to the Port of . . . . to place it at the disposition of the Commanding General of the Internal States of the East.

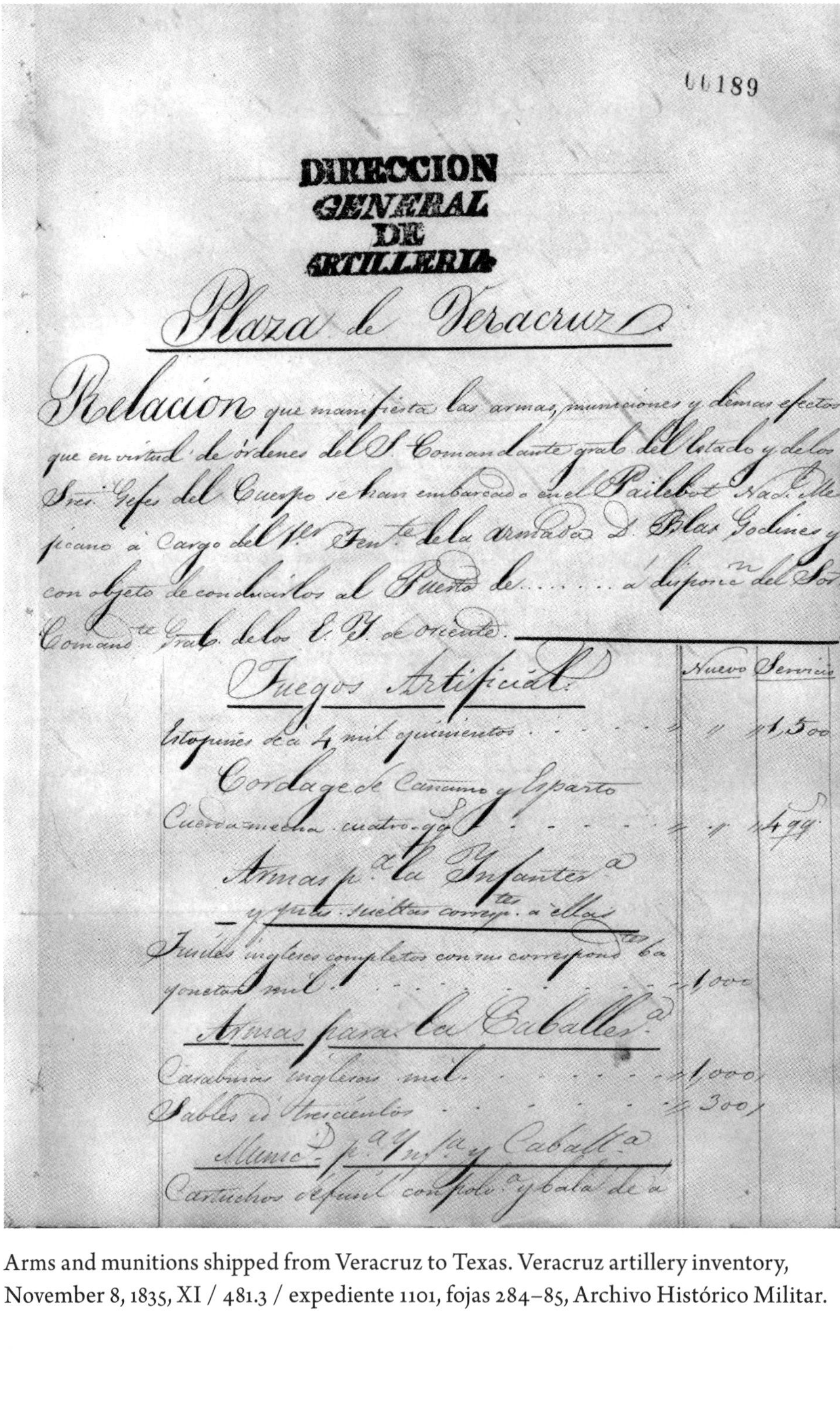

Arms and munitions shipped from Veracruz to Texas. Veracruz artillery inventory, November 8, 1835, XI / 481.3 / expediente 1101, fojas 284–85, Archivo Histórico Militar.

	New	Serviceable
Firing Devices		
Quick matches of 4 (1,500)		1,500
Cord of hemp and grass rope wick 4 *quintales*		499
Arms for the Infantry and loose things corresponding to them		
Complete English muskets with their corresponding bayonets (one thousand)	1,000	
Arms for the Cavalry		
English carbines (one thousand)	1,000	
English sabers (300)	300	
Munitions for Infantry and Cavalry		
Musket cartridges with gun powder and ball		

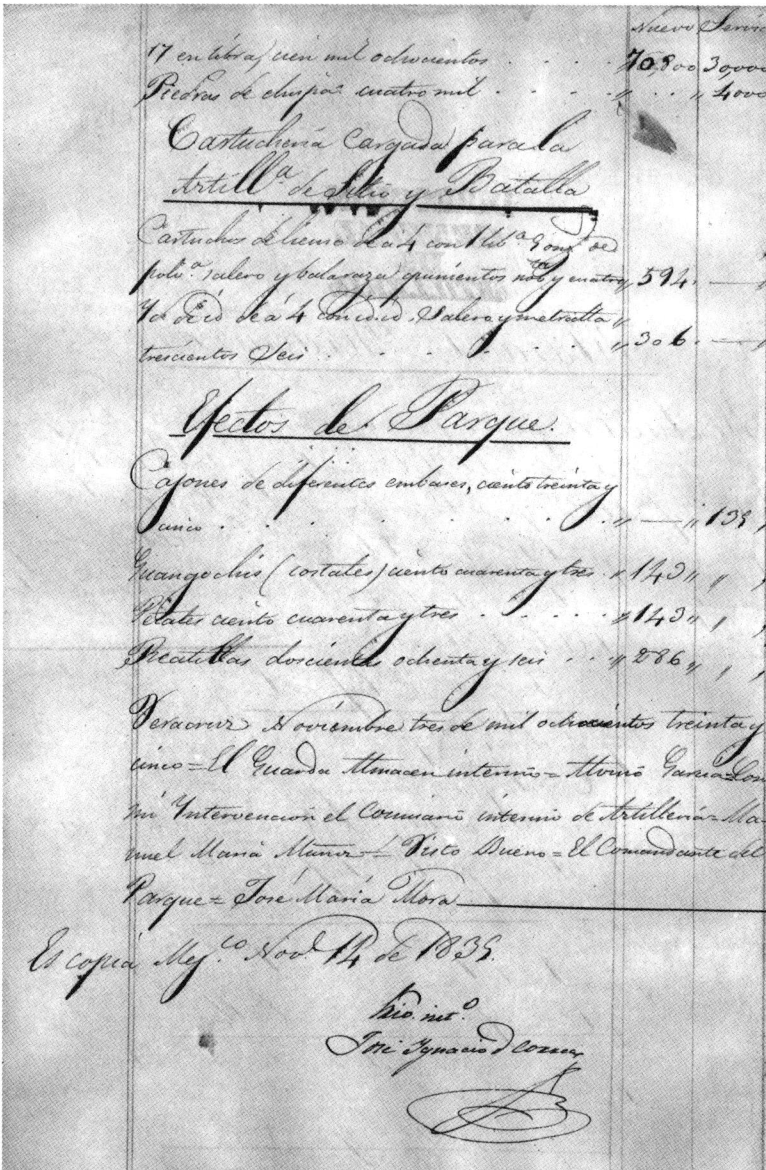

	Nuevo	Servi
17 en libras cien mil ochocientos . . .	70,800	30,000
Piedras de chispa cuatro mil	"	4000

Cartuchería Cargada para la Artill.a de Sitio y Batalla

Cartuchos de lienzo de a 4 con 1 lib.a 9 onz. de polv.a salero y balaraza quinientos noventa y cuatro	594	—
Id. de id. de a 4 con id. id. salero y metralla trescientos seis	306	—

Efectos de Parque

Cajones de diferentes embases, ciento treinta y cinco	" —	135
Guangochos (costales) ciento cuarenta y tres .	143	"
Petates ciento cuarenta y tres	143	"
Reatillas doscientas ochenta y seis . . .	286	"

Veracruz Noviembre tres de mil ochocientos treinta y cinco = El Guarda Almacen interino = Antonio Garcia = Con mi Intervencion el Comisario interino de Artilleria = Manuel Maria Muñoz = Visto Bueno = El Comandante del Parque = José María Mora

Es copia Mex.co Nov. 14 de 1835.

Srio. int.o
José Ygnacio de Lozano

	New	Serviceable
17 per pound (100,800)	70,800	30,000
Gun Flints (four thousand)		4,000
Loaded cartridges for the stationary and battle artillery		
Canvas cartridges for a four pounder with 1 pound 5 oz of gunpowder and a plain ball (594)	594	
Canvas cartridges for a four pounder with 1 pound 5 oz of gunpowder and canister (306)	306	
Effects from the [artillery] park		
Cases of different packaged things (135)		135
Sacking (sacks) (143)	143	
Backpacks (143)	143	
Twisted ropes (286)	286	

Veracruz, Nov. 3, 1835
The warehouse internal guard, Albino Garcia
With my intervention, the interim commissioner of Artillery, Manuel Maria Muñoz
Visto Bueno; Commander of the ammunition park, José María Mora,
This is a copy. Nov. 14, 1835

APPENDIX 16

Artillery to March from Zacatecas

SECRETARY OF WAR AND NAVY

Central Section

Permanent Artillery Park

By virtue of the orders from the Commanding General, Joaquín Ramírez y Sesma, the [artillery] pieces and stores that then are expressed [below] march at his orders

[Artillery] Battle Pieces		New	Used
	Cannon of 6 [pounder]	---	2
	Id of 4	---	2
Set of Nails [*clavason*]			
	Nails for spiking artillery	12	---
	Id. wheel rims	24	---
Gun carriages [*cureños*]			
	For a cannon of 6	---	2
	For id. of 4	---	2
Arms and implements for cannons			
	Bags of ramrods [*baquetas*] for cartridges	8	---
	Linstocks [with] iron trim [*herrados*]	---	4
	Cartridge boxes [*cartucheras*] for Quick match primers [*estopines*]	4	"
	Buckets [*cubetas*] for gun carriages of a 6 [pounder] and 4	---	4
	Portfire [drip] guard of tin [*Guarda lamafuegos de oja de lata*]	---	4
	Vent picks [*punzones*]	---	4

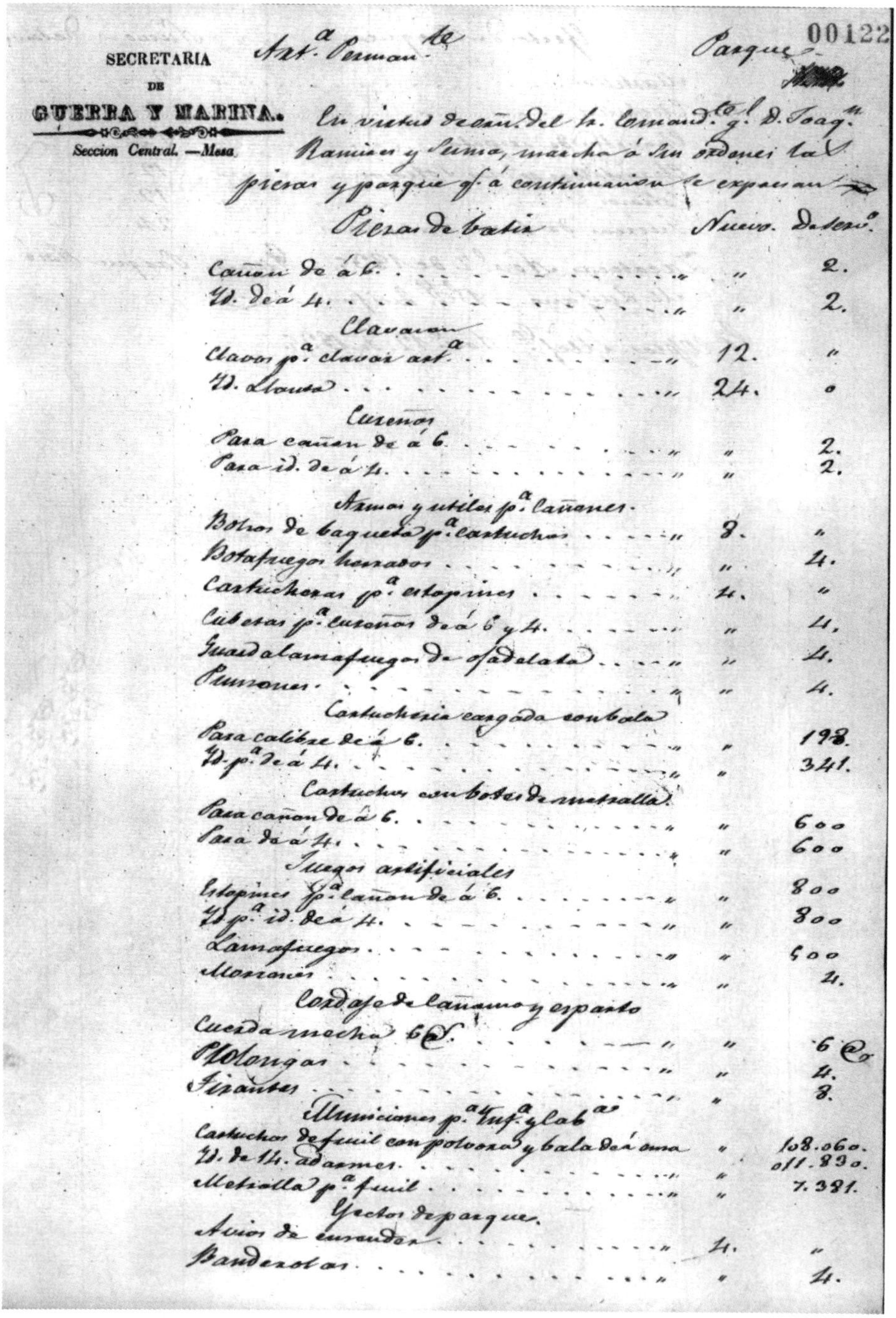

Artillery orders to march from Zacatecas. XI / 481.3 / expediente 1823, fojas 161–62, 164–65, Archivo Histórico Militar.

[Artillery] Battle Pieces		New	Used
Loaded cartridges with balls			
	For a 6 caliber	---	198
	Id. for a 4	---	341
Cartridges with cans of canister			
	For a cannon of 6	---	600
	Id. for a 4	---	600
Firing devices [*Fuegos artificiales*]			
	Quick matches for a cannon of 6	---	800
	Id. for id. of 4	---	800
	Portfires [*lamafuegos*]	---	500
	morrances	---	4
Cordage of burlap [*tow*] and grass [*esparto*]			
	Match [*cuerda mecha*] 6@	---	6@
	Artillery rope [*prolongas*]	---	4
	Traces [*tirantes*; to attach a horse to a coach or carriage]	---	8
Munitions for infantry and cavalry			
	Musket cartridges with powder and ball of one ounce	---	108,060
	Id. of 14 *adarmes* [about one ounce]	---	11,830
	Musket shot [*metralla para fusil*; buckshot or buck and ball]	---	7,381
Effects of [artillery] park			
	Provisions for lighting or setting fire [?] [*avios de encender*]	4	---
	Camp colors [*banderolas*]	---	4

Efectos de Parque. Nuevo — Deterio.

	Nuevo	Deterio.
Martillos	2	"
Cinchillos	4	"
Chavetas de repuesto	12	"
Chavetillas p.a los Sotrozos	12	"
Sotrozos	12	"
Tuercas de todos tamaños	24	"

Zacatecas Nov.e 7. de 1835. = Guarda Parque José M. Quijano. = B.F. Quijano

Es copia. Mex.co Nov.e 12. de 1835.

Effects of [artillery] park	**New**	**Used**
Hammers	2	---
Knives	4	---
Spare Forelock keys [*chavetas de respeto*; cotter pins?]	12	---
Small keys for *chavetillas para los sotrosos* [linchpins?]	12	---
Linchpins	12	---
Nuts [or female screws] of all sizes [*tuercas de todos tamanos*]	24	---

Zacatecas,Nov. 7. 1835, Guard of the artillery park
José Maria Quijano. V B Quijano [?]
This is a copy. Mexico [City]. Nov. 12, 1835

APPENDIX 17

Francisco Castañeda Battle Report, Gonzales, October 2, 1835

Today at five in the morning I was attacked at the habitation of la Perra by two hundred Americans, more or less. They had one medium piece [cannon] and a small piece of ordnance [*esmeril*]. So great was the superiority of the force opposing us, and as per your repeated orders, I began my retreat for this city, where I could give you an account of the circumstances of all that has occurred.

I suffered the loss of only one Private [page ends]

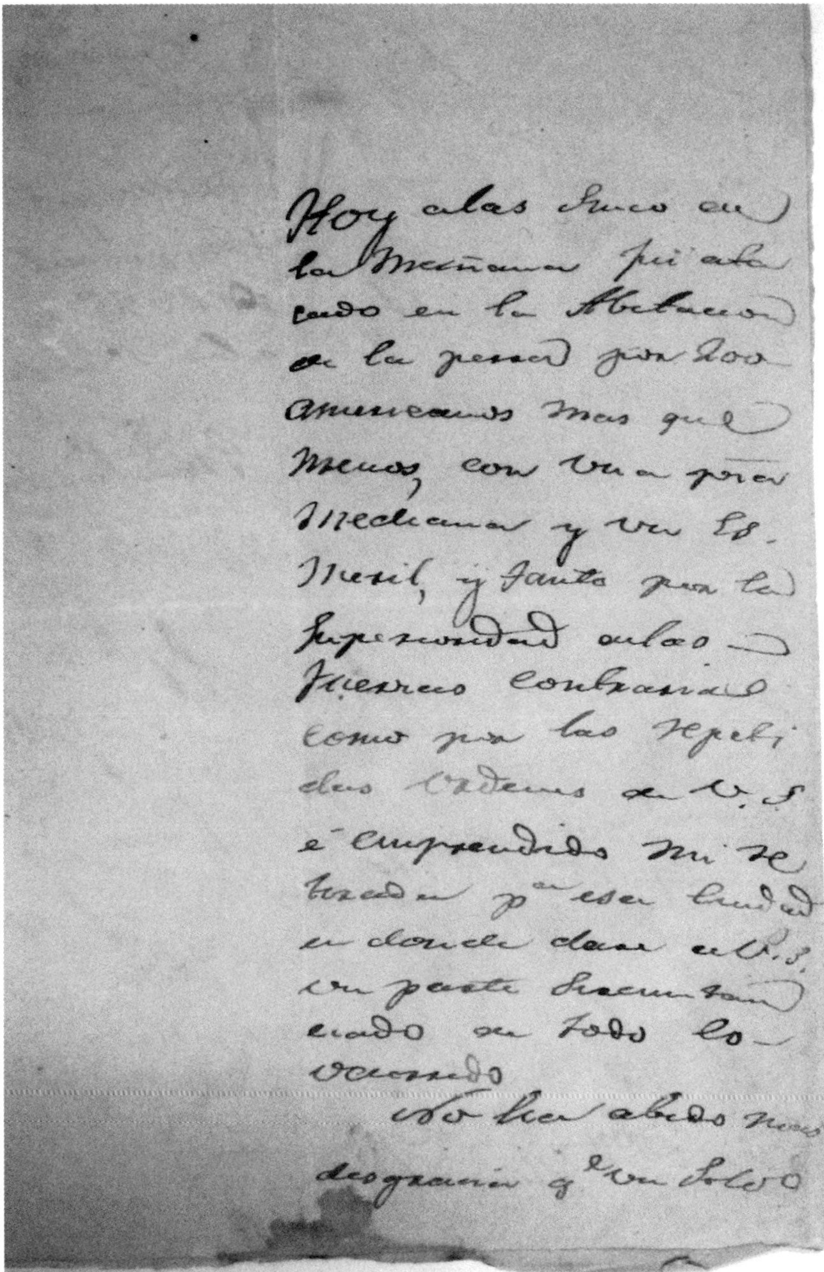

Hoy alas Sinco de
la Mañana fui ata
cado en la Abitacion
de la presa por 200
americanos mas que
menos, con una pieza
Mechanica y un Es.
Mesil, y tanto por la
Superioridad delas
Fuerzas contrarias
como por las repeti
das ordenes de V. S.
e emprendido mi re
tirada pa esa Ciudad
en donde dare a V. S.
un parte circunstan
ciado de todo lo
ocurrido
No ha abido nove
desgracia q. un solo

Francisco Castañeda battle report to José Domingo de Ugartechea, Gonzales, October 2, 1835, Muse Papers, Benson Latin American Collection, University of Texas at Austin.

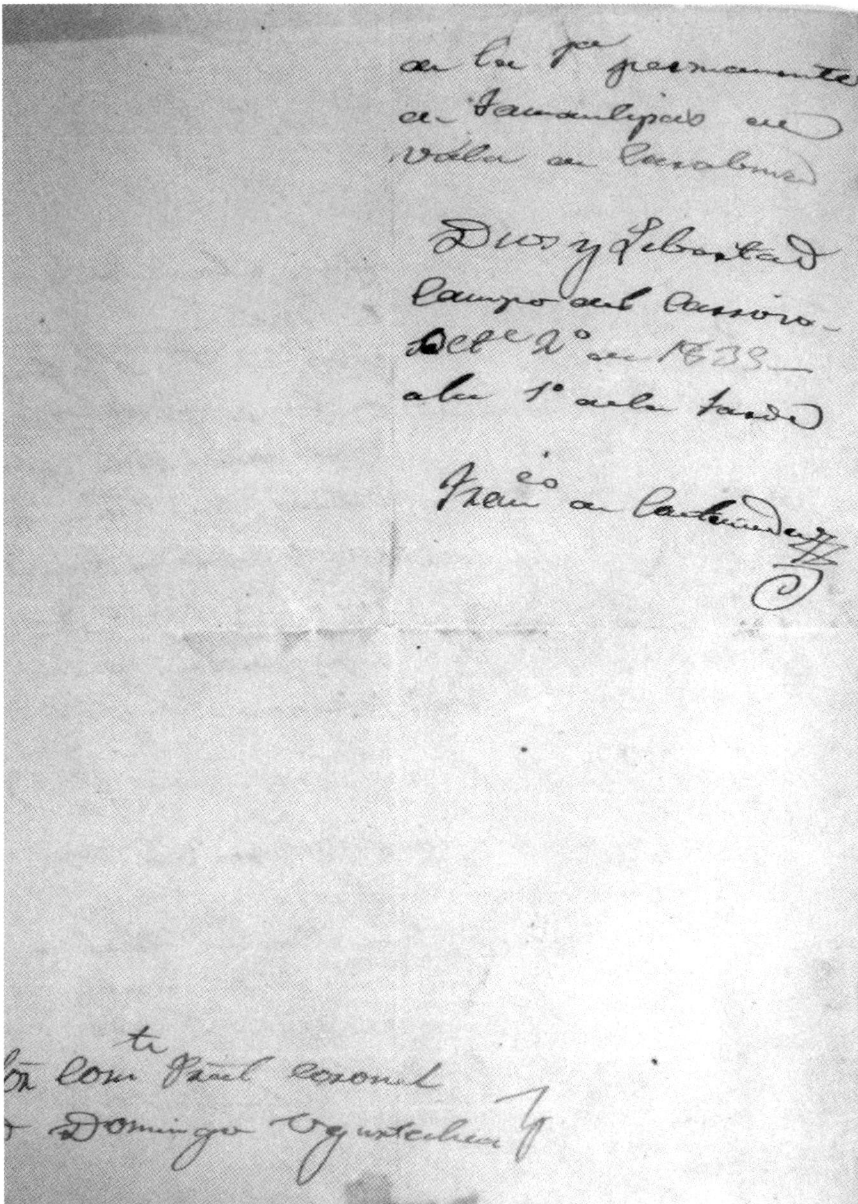
de la 1ª permanente
de Tamaulipas en
Villa de Cerralvo

Dios y Libertad
Campo del Arroyo
Octe 2º de 1835—
ala 1ª de la tarde

Franco de Castañeda

Sor. Comte Prl. Coronel
D. Domingo Ugartechea

[. . .] of the 1st Permanent [company] of Tamaulipas, from a carbine ball.

God and Liberty
Camp of the Carrizo
October 2, 1835
At 1 in the afternoon
Francisco de Castañeda

APPENDIX 18

Juan Zenteno's Oath to the Texans

Having been made prisoners in La Bahía by the Texas Division leading a pronunciamiento for the Constitution of 1824 and the Federal System, we are required to promise to not take up arms or take part against said pronunciamientos. [We do this] to obtain full liberty under our word of honor, and in proof that we will comply, we sign the present document. At Williams Camp along the Guadalupe River near Gonzales—Oct. 14, 1835

Juan Zenteno, Francisco Arzamendi, José Maria Rodríguez

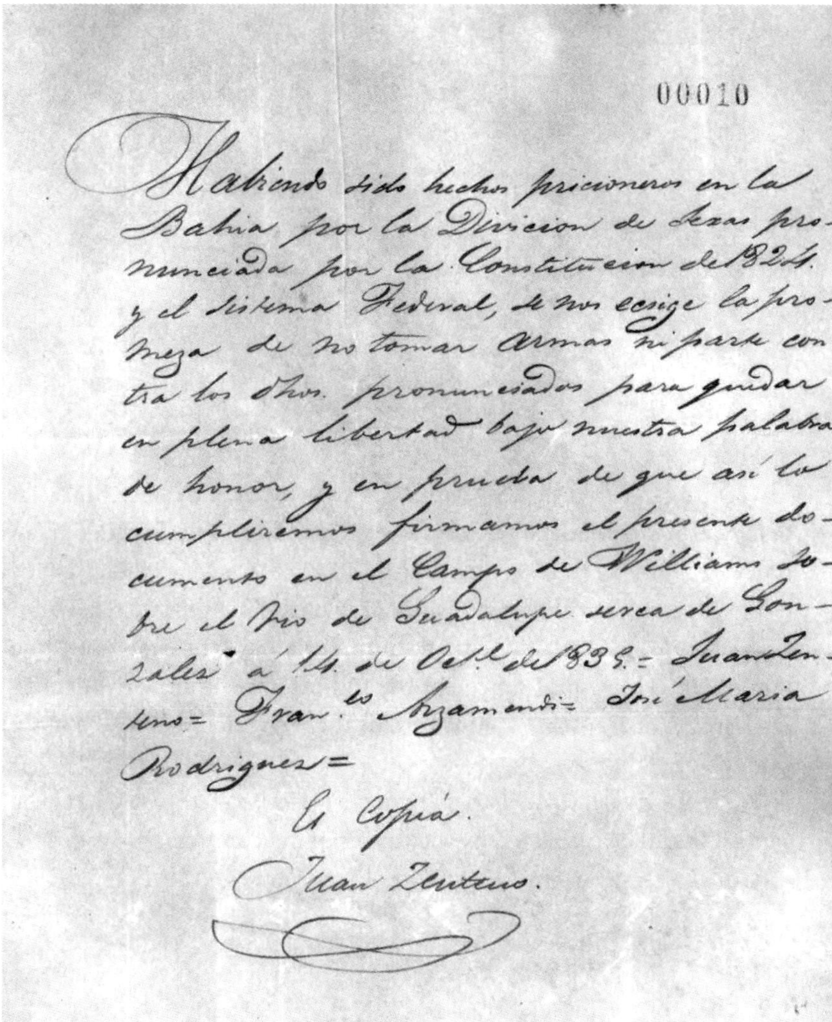

00010

Habiendo sido hechos pricioneros en la Bahia por la Division de Texas pronunciada por la Constitucion de 1824. y el sistema Federal, se nos ecsige la promeza de no tomar armas ni parte contra los dhos. pronunciados para quedar en plena libertad bajo nuestra palabra de honor, y en prueba de que así lo cumpliremos firmamos el presente documento en el Campo de Williams sobre el Rio de Guadalupe serca de Gonzales á 14. de Oct.e de 1835. = Juan Zenteno = Fran.co Arzamendi = José Maria Rodriguez =

Es Copia.

Juan Zenteno.

Juan Zenteno oath to the Texans, October 14, 1835, XI / 481.3 / expediente 1102, foja 14, Archivo Histórico Militar.

APPENDIX 19

Stephen F. Austin to Cos, October 17, 1835

Federal Army of Texas

Wishing to avoid the disastrous consequences of the civil war that disgracefully threatens Texas, I want to send to Your Excellency an officer with a flag to take a communication to Your Excellency that I hope will result in the reestablishment of peace and the trust in Texas.

As a consequence, I hope that Your Excellency will serve to tell me if you will receive said officer in the indicated manner with the corresponding guarantees for him and his escort, which will not be more than six or eight men.

He will carry a white flag, by which he will be recognized, and the same flag will be respected by the troops of my command.

God, Federation, and Liberty

Cibolo [Creek], Oct. 17, 1835

Estevan F. Austin

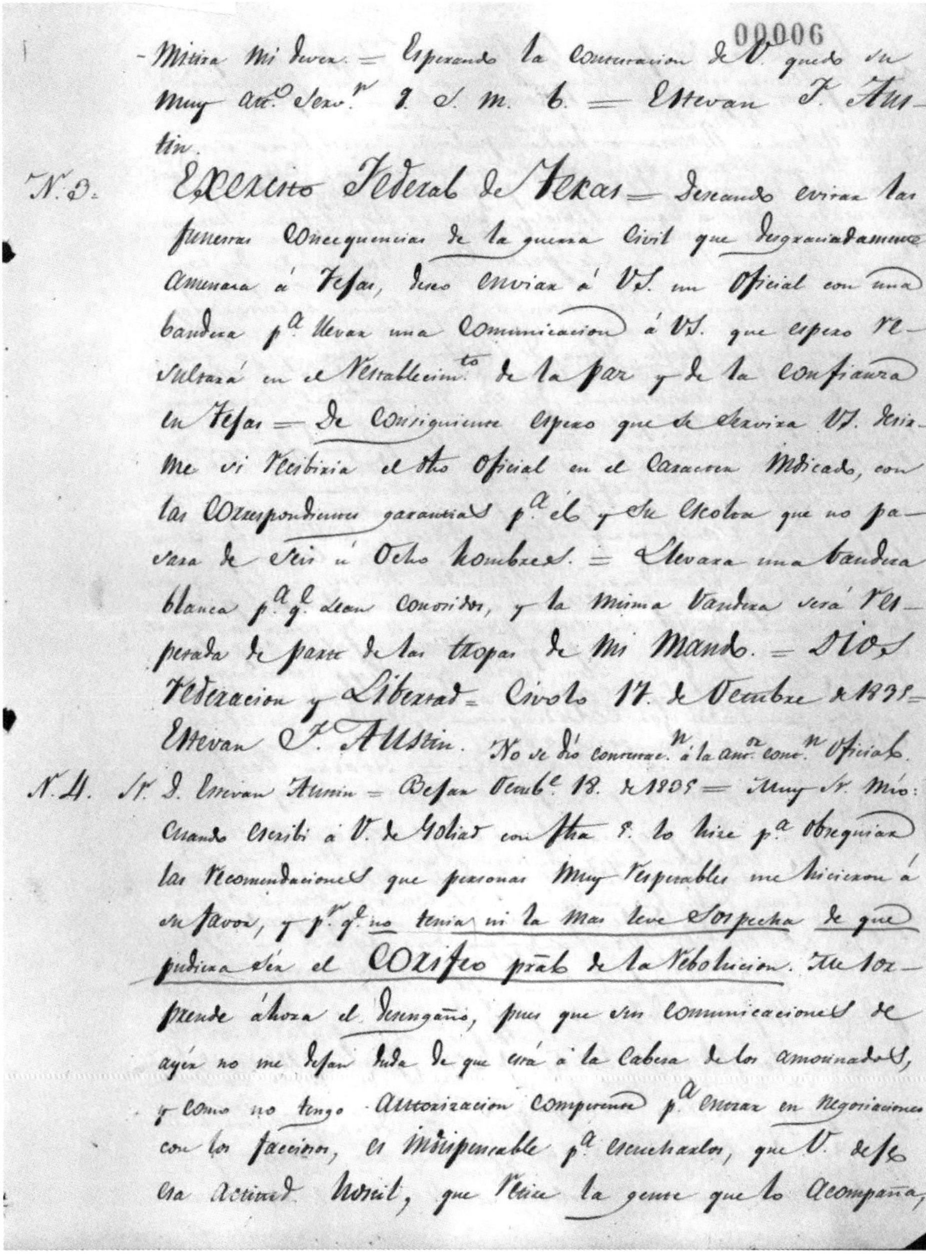

-mitira mi deber. = Esperando la contestacion de V. quedo su muy atto. servr. Q. S. M. B. = Estevan F. Austin.

N. 3. Exercito Federal de Texas = Deseando evitar las funestas consequencias de la guerra Civil que desgraciadamente amenaza á Texas, deseo enviar á VS. un Oficial con una bandera pa. llevar una comunicacion á VS. que espero resultará en el restablecimto. de la paz y de la confianza en Texas = De consiguiente espero que se servira VS. decirme si recibiria el dho. Oficial en el caracter indicado, con las correspondientes garantias pa. él y su escolta que no pasara de seis ú ocho hombres. = Llevara una bandera blanca pa. q. sean conocidos, y la misma bandera será respetada de parte de las tropas de mi mando. = Dios y Federacion y Libertad = Cibolo 17 de Octubre de 1835 = Estevan F. Austin. No se dió contestacn. á la antr. comn. oficial.

N. 4. Sr. D. Estevan Austin = Bexar Octbe. 18 de 1835 = Muy Sr. mio: Cuando escribí á V. de Goliad con fha. [illegible] lo hice pa. obsequiar las recomendaciones que personas muy respetables me hicieron á su favor, y pr. q. no tenia ni la mas leve sospecha de que pudiera ser el corifeo pral. de la revolucion. Me sorprende ahora el desengaño, pues que sus comunicaciones de ayer no me dejan duda de que está á la cabeza de los amotinados, y como no tengo autorizacion competente pa. entrar en negociaciones con los facciosos, es indispensable pa. escucharlos, que V. deje esa actitud hostil, que retire la gente que lo acompaña,

Stephen F. Austin to Cos, October 17, 1835 (two letters, only one translated), XI / 481.3 / expediente 1148, fojas 8–13, Archivo Histórico Militar.

Artillery Stores at Béjar, February 4, 1835

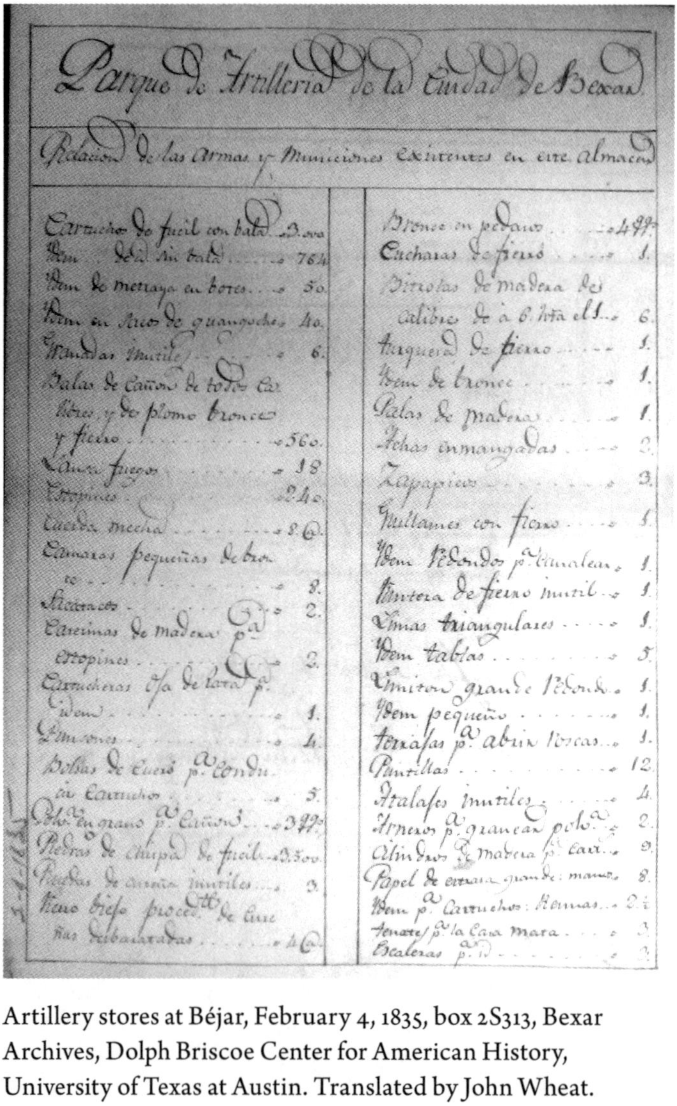
Parque de Artilleria de la Ciudad de Bexar

Relacion de las Armas y Municiones existentes en este almacen

Cartuchos de fusil con bala ... 3.000
Ydem de id. sin bala ... 764
Ydem de metralla en botes ... 50
Ydem en sacos de guangoche ... 40
Granadas inutiles ... 6
Balas de Cañon de todos calibres, y de plomo bronce y fierro ... 560
Lanza fuegos ... 18
Estopines ... 240
Cuerda mecha ... 8 @
Camaras pequeñas de bronce ... 8
Alcatraces ... 2
Caxetinas de madera pa. estopines ... 2
Cartucheras c/a de lata pa. ydem ... 1
[illegible] ... 4
Bolsas de cuero pa. conducir cartuchos ... 5
Polvo en grano pa. cañon ... 3 @
Piedras de chispa de fusil ... 3.500
Piezas de cureña inutiles ... 3
Fierro viejo procedente de cureñas desbaratadas ... 4 @

Bronce en pedazos ... 4 @
Cucharas de fierro ... 1
Birrolas de madera del calibre de a 6 hta el 1 ... 6
Horquetas de fierro ... 1
Ydem de bronce ... 1
Palas de madera ... 1
Achas enmangadas ... 2
Zapapicos ... 3
Martillos con fierro ... 1
Ydem redondos pa. remachar ... 1
[illegible] de fierro inutil ... 1
Limas triangulares ... 1
Ydem tablas ... 5
[illegible] grande redondo ... 1
Ydem pequeño ... 1
Tenazas pa. abrir roscas ... 1
[illegible] ... 12
Atalajes inutiles ... 4
Arneros pa. granear polvo ... 2
Cilindros de madera pa. cart. ... 9
Papel de estraza grande: manos ... 8
Ydem pa. cartuchos: resmas ... 2
Tenates pa. la casa mata ... 3
Escaleras pa. id. ... 3

Artillery stores at Béjar, February 4, 1835, box 2S313, Bexar Archives, Dolph Briscoe Center for American History, University of Texas at Austin. Translated by John Wheat.

Artillery Park of the City of Béxar			
Report on the arms and munitions in store at this magazine			
Musket cartridges with balls	3,000	Bronze in pieces	4 *quintales*
Musket cartridges without balls	764	Iron scoops	1
Canister shot in cans	50	Wooden *bitrolas* [?] for calibers 6 to 1	6
Id. in canvas bags	40		
Grenades, useless	6	Iron mold	1
Cannon balls of all calibers and of lead, bronze, and iron	560	Bronze mold	1
		Wooden shovels	1
		Hatchets with handles	2
Linstocks	18	Pickaxes	3
Primers	240	Rabbet planes with iron	1
Fuse cords	8 *arrobas*	Id. rounded for grooves	1
Small bronze breeches	8	Iron *runtera* [?], useless	1
Wad hooks	2	Triangular files	1
Wooden *cateimas* [?] for primers	2	Flat id.	5
		Large round *luniton* [?]	1
Tin cartridge boxes for id.	1	Small id.	1
		Threading machines to open screws	1
Punches [awls]	4	Small gun lock tumblers	12
Leather bags for carrying cartridges	5	Harnesses, useless	4
		Sieves for grinding gunpowder	2
Coarse gunpowder for cannons	3 *quintales*	Wooden cylinders for cartridges	9
Musket flints	3,500	Paper for wrapping large: [?]	8
Wheels for gun carriages, useless	3	Id. for cartridges: [?]	2 ½
Old iron from broken down gun carriages	4 *arrobas*	*Tenates* for the *casa mata*	3
		Ladders for id.	3

Sala de armas.

Esmeriles de buen uso	2.
Cañones de fucil inutiles	3.
Lanzas rectas	24.
Ydem medias lunas	3.
Bayonetas	20.

Piezas de Artilleria.

Cañones de á 6. muy maltratados	1.
Ydem de bronce de de á id	3.
Ydem de id. á 5.	1.
Ydem de á 4	2.
Ydem de á 3	5.
Ydem de á id. de bronce	1.
Ydem de á id. de á 2	2
Ydem de bronce de á 2 inutiles	4
Ydem de á 7. ½. Clavados	7.

Bexar Febrero 4. de 1835.

Fran.co Elera

Gun Room	
Small cannons [*esmiriles*] in good condition	2
Musket barrels, useless	3
Straight lances	24
Id. for fortifications	3
Bayonets	20
Artillery Pieces	
Six-pounder cannons, poorly maintained	1
The same of bronze [poorly maintained]	3
The same of a five-pounder [poorly maintained]	1
The same of a four-pounder [poorly maintained]	2
The same of a three-pounder [poorly maintained]	5
The same of bronze three-pounder [poorly maintained]	1
The same of a two-pounder [poorly maintained]	2
The same of bronze two-pounder, useless	4
The same of seven-pounder, spiked	7

Béjar, February 4, 1835
Fran.co Atesa [?]

APPENDIX 21

Munitions at Béjar, September 22, 1835

ARTILLERY PARK OF THE CITY OF BÉJAR

List that is shown to exist in the said park that is received by the Lt. of the Morelos Btn., Don Manuel Montero.

Musket cartridges with one-ounce balls	11,275
Same of same without balls	680
Musket powder in grain	7 *quintales* 5 [illegible]
Same of cannon in same	4 *quintales* 24 [illegible]
Gun flints	2,400
Leather matches	4 *arrobas*
Balls for Pedrazo cannon	75
Loose balls of one ounce	450
Knots	5
A box with instruments for constructing	
Flares	1
Canister for cannon	11 *quintales* 1 *arroba* 5 [illegible]
Unusable wheels for cannon	3
A small piece of a carriage	—

Béjar, September 22, 1835

Received ***Delivered***
Manuel Montero ***Francisco Mesa***

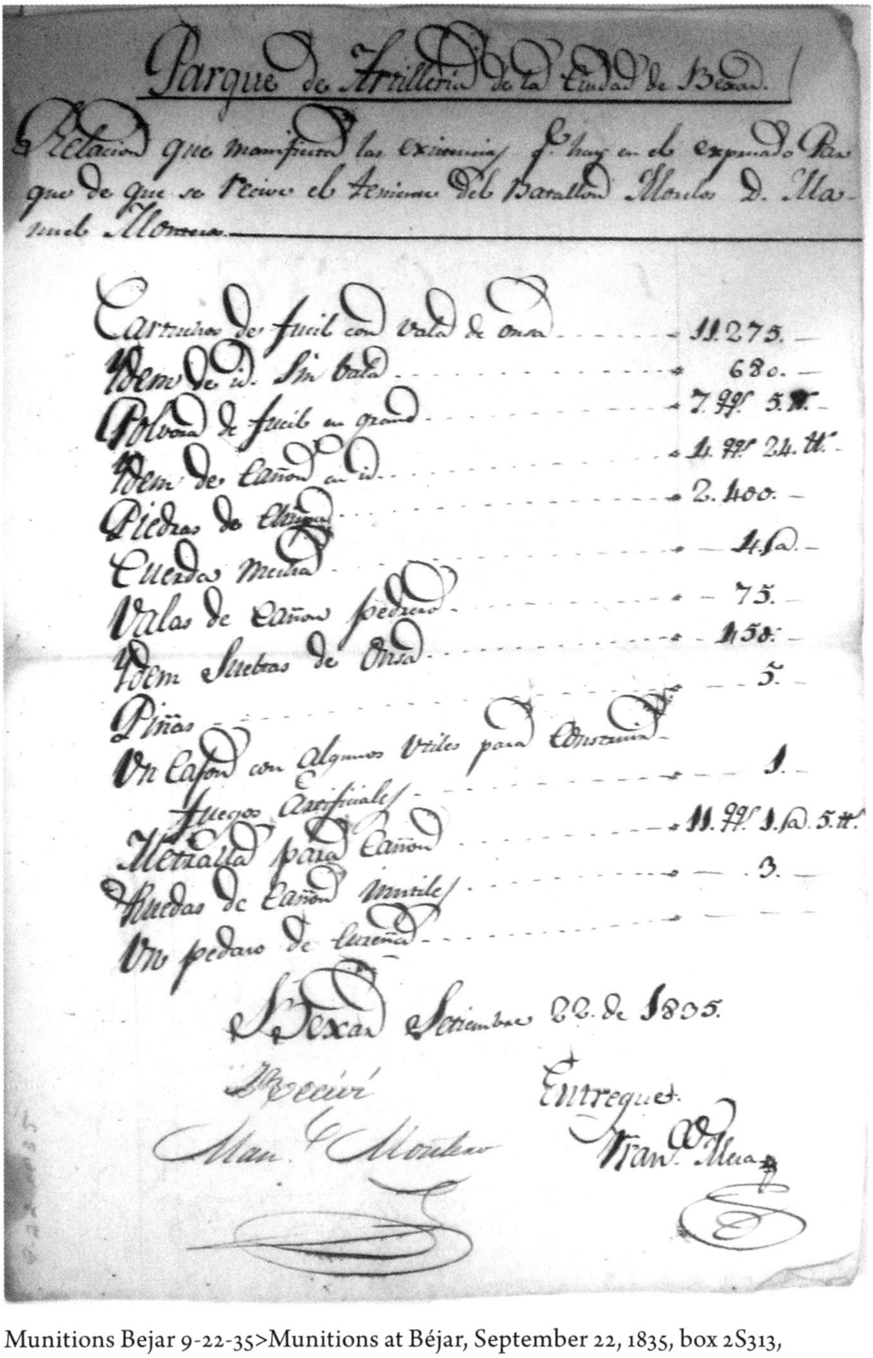

Parque de Artillería de la Ciudad de Bexar.

Relación que manifiesta las existencias q.e hay en el expresado Parque de que se recive el teniente del Batallón Morelos D. Manuel Montero.

Cartuchos de fusil con bala de onsa ---- 11.275.
Idem de id. sin bala ---- 680.
Polvora de fusil en grano ---- 7. @s 5. lb.
Idem de cañon en id. ---- 1. @s 24. lb.
Piedras de chispa ---- 2.400.
Cuerda mecha ---- 4 @.
Balas de cañon pedrero ---- 75.
Idem sueltas de onsa ---- 150.
Piñas ---- 5.
Un cajon con algunos utiles para construir fuegos artificiales ---- 1.
Metralla para cañon ---- 11. @s 1. @. 5. lb.
Ruedas de cañon inutiles ---- 3.
Un pedazo de cureña ----

S. Bexar Setiembre 22. de 1835.

Recibí
Man.l Montero

Entregué
Fran.co Mesa

Munitions Bejar 9-22-35>Munitions at Béjar, September 22, 1835, box 2S313, Bexar Archives, Dolph Briscoe Center for American History, University of Texas at Austin.

APPENDIX 22

Morelos Battalion Dead from the Battle of Concepción

PERMANENT MORELOS BATTALION STATE OF TEXAS

List of the senior officers and troops that were killed and made prisoner at the Mission Concepción on this date.

Company	Rank	Name	
Grenadier	Corporal	José Ma. Lara	1 deceased
1st	Private	Miguel Reyes	1 deceased
4th	Captain	Felipe Gonsáles Escalante	1 prisoner
6th	Private	Ygnacio Marques	1 prisoner
Cazadores	1st Sergeant	Felipe Figueroa	1 deceased
	Cazador [Private]	José Sanson	1 deceased
	Cazador [Private]	Fran.co Martínes	1 deceased
	Cazador [Private]	Pioquinto Duarte	1 deceased
	Cazador [Private]	Abran Gutierres	1 deceased
	Cazador [Private]	Juan Lopes	1 deceased
	Cazador [Private]	José Ma. Morales	1 deceased
	Cazador [Private]	José Ma. Gonsáles	1 deceased
Attached from the Jiménez Battalion			
	Corporal	Pedro Cuellar	1 deceased
Total			**12 [dead; 1 prisoner]**

San Antonio de Béjar   Oct. 28, 1835
Condelle   In charge of the detail   Benito de Zenea

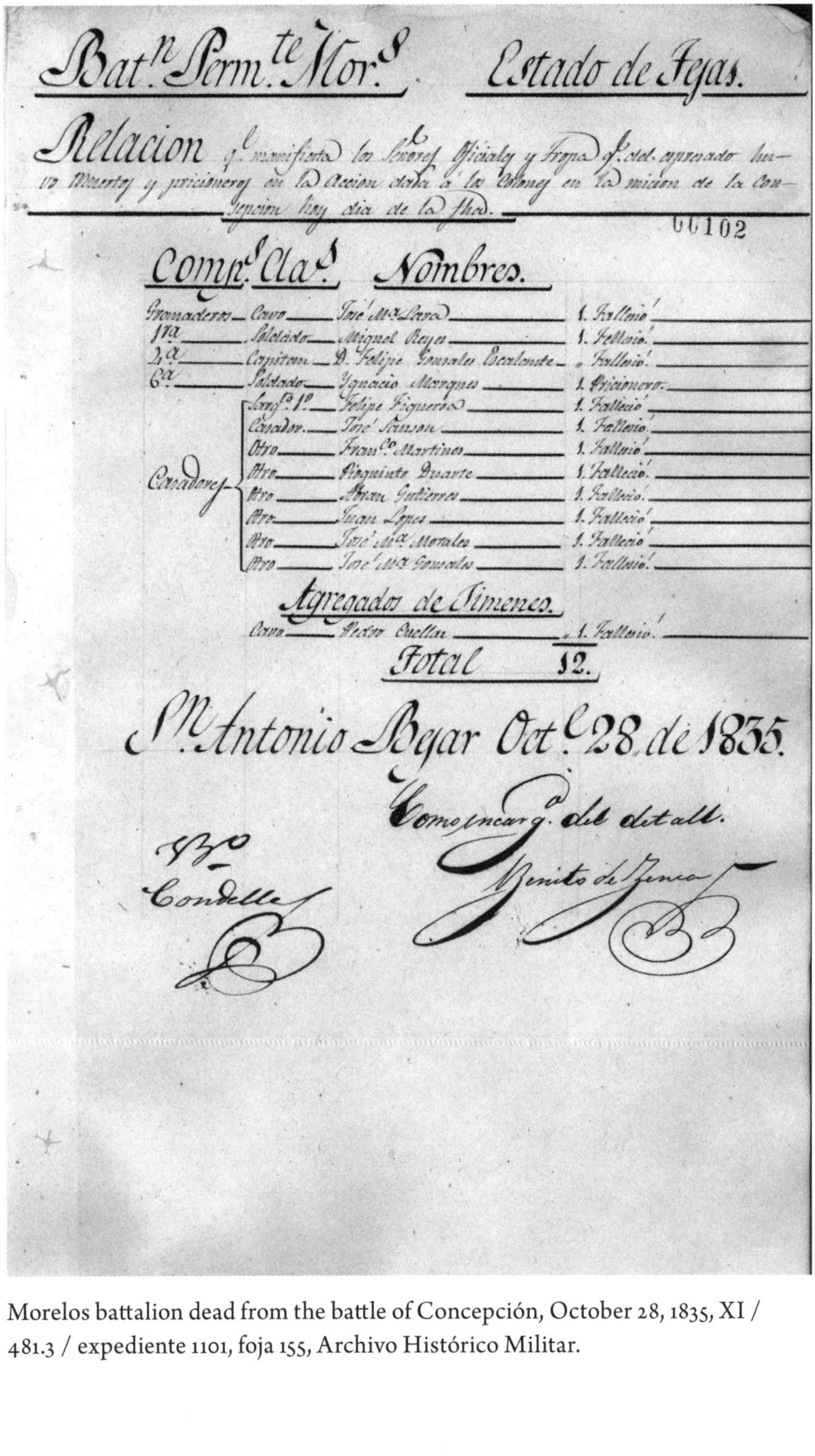

Bat.n Perm.te Mor.s — Estado de Tejas.

Relacion q.e manifiesta los Señores Oficiales y Tropa q.e del expresado hu-vo Muertos y pricioneros en la Accion dada á los Colonos en la mision de la Concepcion hoy dia de la fha.

00102

Comp.s	Clas.s	Nombres	
Granaderos	Cavo	José M.a Lara	1. Fallecio.
1.a	Soldado	Miguel Reyes	1. Fallecio.
2.a	Capitan	D. Felipe Gonsales Escalante	„ Fallecio.
6.a	Soldado	Ygnacio Marques	1. Pricionero.
Cazadores	Sarg.to 1.o	Felipe Figueroa	1. Fallecio.
	Cazador	José Sanson	1. Fallecio.
	Otro	Fran.co Martines	1. Fallecio.
	Otro	Pioquinto Duarte	1. Fallecio.
	Otro	Abran Gutierres	1. Fallecio.
	Otro	Juan Lopes	1. Fallecio.
	Otro	José M.a Morales	1. Fallecio.
	Otro	José M.a Gonsales	1. Fallecio.

Agregados de Jimenes.

	Cavo	Pedro Cuellar	1. Fallecio.
		Total	12.

S.n Antonio Bejar Oct.e 28 de 1835.

Como encarg.o del detall.
Benito de Zenea

V.o B.o
Condelle

Morelos battalion dead from the battle of Concepción, October 28, 1835, XI / 481.3 / expediente 1101, foja 155, Archivo Histórico Militar.

APPENDIX 23

Morelos Battalion Wounded from the Battle of Concepción

PERMANENT MORELOS BATTALION STATE OF TEXAS

List of the officers and troops who were wounded in the action against the colonists at the Mission Concepción on this date.

Company	Grades	Rank	Name	Wounds
Grenadier		2nd Sergeant	Consepción Chaves	1 by a bullet shot
		Cornetist	Juan Servantes	1 by a bullet shot
		Corporal	José Ma. Acosta	1 by a bullet shot
		Grenadier [Private]	Casiano Medina	1 by a bullet shot
			José Esquivel	1 by a bullet shot
			Fran.co Ramíres	1 by a bullet shot
			Ygn.o Dias	1 by a bullet shot
			Mariano Paredes	1 by a bullet shot
			Juan Navidad	1 by a bullet shot
3rd		Private	Bartolo Bueno	1 by a bullet shot
4th			Alejo Alvares	1 by a bullet shot
			Margarito Aldaco	1 by a bullet shot
5th		Sub Lieutenant	Fran.co Torres	1 by two bullet shots
		Private	Juan Castañeda	1 by a bullet shot
			José Reyes	1 by a bullet shot
			Antonio Aguilar	1 by a bullet shot
6th		Corporal	Mariano Romero	1 by a bullet shot
		Private	Mateo Chaves	1 by a bullet shot
			Julio Gonsáles	1 by a bullet shot

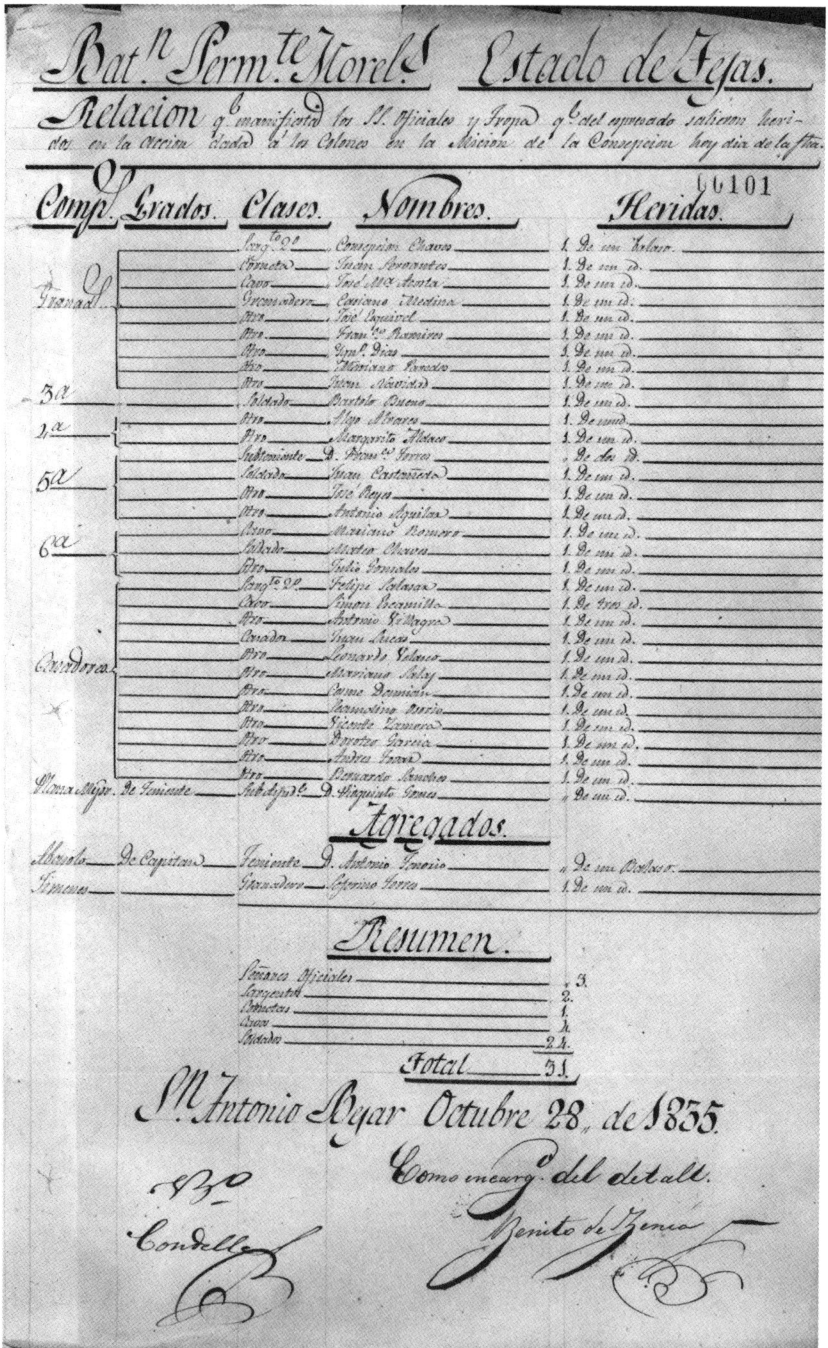
Bat.n Perm.te Morelos. Estado de Tejas.

Relacion q.e manifiesta los S.S. Oficiales y Tropa q.e del expresado salieron heridos en la Accion dada á los Colonos en la Mision de la Concepcion hoy dia de la fha.

Comp.s	Grados	Clases	Nombres	Heridas
Granad.s		Sarg.to 2.o	Concepcion Chaves	1. De un Balazo.
		Corneta	Juan Cervantes	1. De un id.
		Cabo	José M.a Acosta	1. De un id.
		Granadero	Casiano Medina	1. De un id.
		Otro	José Esquivel	1. De un id.
		Otro	Fran.co Ramirez	1. De un id.
		Otro	Ysm.l Dias	1. De un id.
		Otro	Mariano Paredes	1. De un id.
		Otro	Juan Navidad	1. De un id.
3.a		Soldado	Bartolo Bueno	1. De un id.
4.a		Otro	Albo Alvares	1. De un id.
		Otro	Margarito Velasco	1. De un id.
5.a		Subteniente	D. Fran.co Torres	„ De dos id.
		Soldado	Juan Castañeda	1. De un id.
		Otro	José Reyes	1. De un id.
		Otro	Antonio Aguilar	1. De un id.
6.a		Cabo	Mariano Romero	1. De un id.
		Soldado	Mateo Chaves	1. De un id.
		Otro	Julio Gonzales	1. De un id.
Cazadores		Sarg.to 2.o	Felipe Salazar	1. De un id.
		Cabo	Simon Escamilla	1. De dos id.
		Otro	Antonio Villagra	1. De un id.
		Cazador	Juan Lucas	1. De un id.
		Otro	Leonardo Velasco	1. De un id.
		Otro	Mariano Salas	1. De un id.
		Otro	Cosme Damian	1. De un id.
		Otro	Agustino Arrio	1. De un id.
		Otro	Vicente Zamora	1. De un id.
		Otro	Doroteo Garcia	1. De un id.
		Otro	Andres Ybarra	1. De un id.
		Otro	Bernardo Sanchez	1. De un id.
Plana Mayor	De Teniente	Subteniente	D. Hipolito Gomes	„ De un id.

Agregados.

Comp.s	Grados	Clases	Nombres	Heridas
Aldama	De Capitan	Teniente	D. Antonio Tenorio	„ De un Balazo.
Jimenez		Granadero	Ciprimo Torres	1. De un id.

Resumen.

Señores Oficiales	„ 3.
Sargentos	2.
Cornetas	1.
Cabos	4.
Soldados	24.
Total	31.

S.n Antonio Bejar Octubre 28„ de 1835.

V.o B.o Condelle

Como encarg.do del detall. Benito de Zenea

Morelos battalion wounded from the battle of Concepción, October 28, 1835, XI / 481.3 / expediente 1101, foja 154, Archivo Histórico Militar.

Company	Grades	Rank	Name	Wounds
Cazadores		2nd Sergeant	Felipe Salasar	1 by a bullet shot
		Corporal	Simon Escamilla	1 by three bullet shots
			Antonio Villagra	1 by a bullet shot
		Cazador [Private]	Juan Lucas	1 by a bullet shot
			Leonardo Velasco	1 by a bullet shot
			Mariano Salas	1 by a bullet shot
			Cosme Damion	1 by a bullet shot
			Secundino Osorio	1 by a bullet shot
			Vicente Zamora	1 by a bullet shot
			Doroteo Garcia	1 by a bullet shot
			Andres Tovar	1 by a bullet shot
			Bernardo Sánches	1 by a bullet shot
Headquarters	Sub Adjutant, Brevet Lt.		Pioquinto Gomes	1 by a bullet shot
		Attached		
Abasolo [Battalion]	Lt., Brevet Captain		Antonio Tenorio	1 by a bullet shot
Jiménez [Battalion]	Grenadier [Private]		Seferino Torres	1 by a bullet shot
Total				**31 [34 if officers included]**

San Antonio de Béjar, October 28, 1835

Condelle In charge of the detail Benito de Zenea

APPENDIX 24

Terms of Capitulation at Béjar, December 11, 1835

Capitulation entered into by general Martín Perfecto de Cos, of the Permanent troops, and general Edward Burleson, of the Colonial troops of Texas.

Being desirous of preventing the further effusion of blood and the ravages of civil war, [they] have agreed on the following stipulations:

1st. That general Cos and his officers retire into the interior of the republic, under parole of honor; that they will not in any way oppose the reestablishment of the federal Constitution of 1824.

2nd. That the one hundred infantry lately arrived with the convicts, the remnant of the battalion of Morelos, and the cavalry, retire with the general; taking their arms and ten rounds of cartridges for their muskets.

3nd. That the general take the convicts brought in by colonel Ugartechea, beyond the Rio Grande.

4th. That it is left to the discretion of the troops to follow their general, remain, or go to such point as they may deem proper: but in case they should all or any of them separate, they are to have their arms, etc.

5th. That all the public property, money, arms, and munitions of war be inventoried and delivered to general Burleson.

6th. That all private property be restored to its proper owners.

7th. That three officers of each army be appointed to make out the inventory, and see that the [page ends]

[. . .] terms of the capitulation be carried into effect.

8th. That three officers on the part of general Cos remain for the purpose of delivering over the said property, stores, etc.

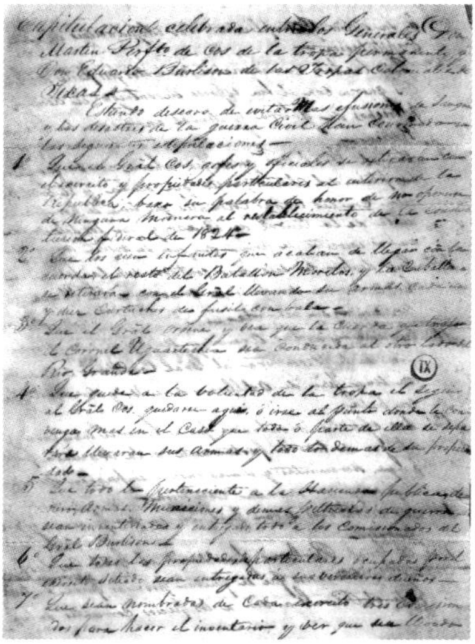

a.

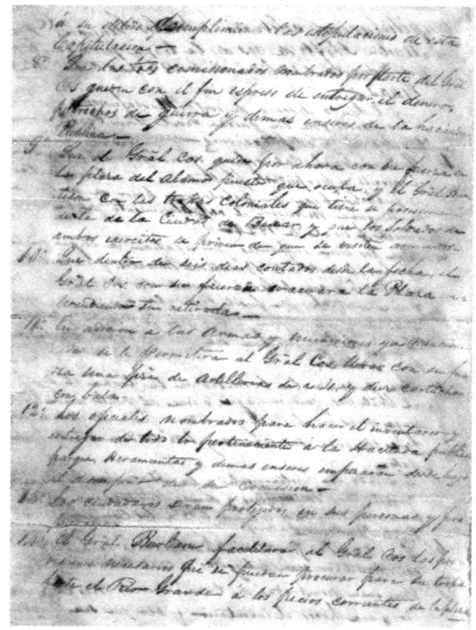

b.

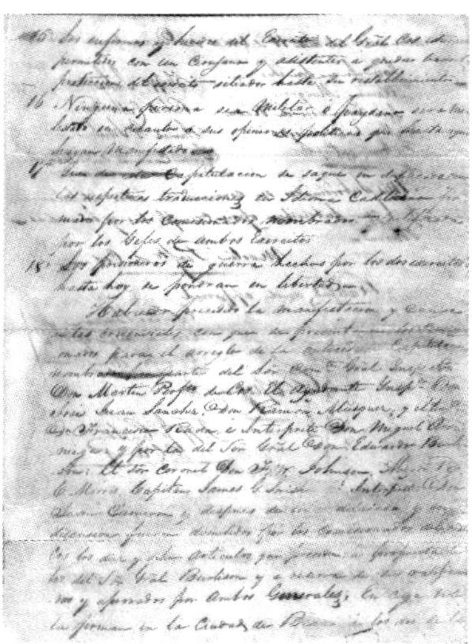

c.

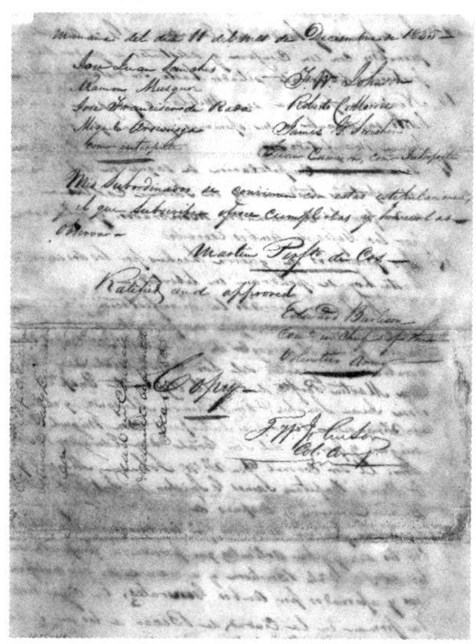

d.

Terms of capitulation at Béjar, December 11, 1835, Texas State Library and Archives Commission, accessed January 30, 2025, https://www.tsl.texas.gov/treasures/republic/bexar/cos1.html.

9th. That general Cos with his force, for the present, occupy the Alamo; and general Burleson, with his force, occupy the town of Béjar; and that the soldiers of neither party pass to the other armed.

10th. General Cos shall, within six days from the date hereof, remove his force from the garrison he now occupies.

11th. In addition to the arms before mentioned, general Cos shall be permitted to take a four-pounder and ten rounds of powder and ball with his force.

12th. The officers appointed to make the inventory and delivery of the stores, etc. shall enter upon the duties to which they have been appointed forthwith.

13th. The citizens shall be protected in their persons and property.

14th. General Burleson will furnish general Cos with such provisions as can be obtained, necessary for his troops to [travel to] the Río Grande, at the ordinary price of the country.

15th. The sick and wounded of general Cos's army, together with a surgeon and attendants, are permitted to remain.

16th. No person, either citizen or soldier, is to be molested on account of his political opinions hitherto expressed.

17th. That duplicates of this capitulation be made out in Castilian and English, and signed by the commissioners appointed, and ratified by the commanders of both armies.

18th. The prisoners of both armies, up to this day, shall be put at liberty.

The commissioners, José Juan Sánchez [Navarro], adjutant inspector; Don Ramón Múzquiz, lieutenant Francisco Rada, and interpreter Don Miguel Arciniega, appointed by the commandant and inspector, general Martín Perfecto de Cos; in connection with colonel F. W. Johnson, major R. C. Morris, and captain J. G. Swisher, and interpreter John Cameron, appointed on the part of general Edward Burleson: after a long and serious discussion, adopted the eighteen preceding articles, reserving their ratification by the generals of both armies.

In virtue of which, we have signed this instrument in the city of Béjar [page ends] on morning of the 11th day of December, 1835.

José Juan Sánchez	
Ramón Múzquiz	F. W. Johnson
José Francisco de Rada	Robert C. Morris
Miguel Arciniega	James G. Swisher
	Juan Cameron, Interpreter

I consent to, and will observe the above articles.
Martín Perf[ec]to de Cos
Ratified and approved
Edward Burleson
Commander in chief of the Volunteer Army.
[Copy of Capitulation between Gens Burleson & Cos]
[Dec. 18, 1835]
Copy
F. W. Johnson
Col. Army.

APPENDIX 25

Uniform Regulations

CONTRACT OF UNIFORMS

and other garments for the army, held by the board of money of this capital, on January 2, 1832, with orders and approval of the supreme government.

General Treasury of the Federation.—On the 15th of the current [month] the Secretary of Finance told us what follows.—Yesterday the Most Excellent Secretary of the office of War and Navy told me what follows.—Most Excellent Sir—assigning the supreme government the type of uniforms for the army and active militia, the corresponding arrangement is given so that the units are always provided, procuring the possible savings in national interests, and considering [at] the same time as continuing the contract that it [the government] held in the year 1824 with the well-known general staff, Colonel D. Manuel Barrera; every day the arrangement of this department becomes more difficult due to the confusion in which it is found, which may result in considerable damage to both the federal treasury and the contractor itself, without being able to achieve that all bodies are fully authorized; and on the other hand, in view of the fact that said contract must be already completed, the Most Excellent Mr. Vice President has served to prevent its termination, of course, by liquidating the respective account immediately by the federal treasury; and considering Your Excellency that due to the circumstances of the treasury, it is not possible at this time for the bodies to be paid the stipend indicated by ordinance for their wardrobes, making the consequent anticipations so that they could produce them; it has been helped to understand that, meanwhile, the income of the treasury is increased so that the units do not lack uniforms, but are provided with opportunity; [a] new contract is agreed upon by the respective authorities, and with the formalities established under the following conditions: First: that

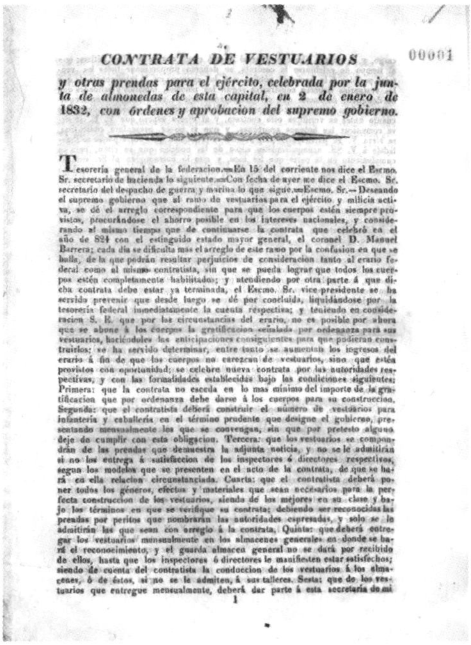
00001

CONTRATA DE VESTUARIOS

y otras prendas para el ejército, celebrada por la junta de almonedas de esta capital, en 2 de enero de 1832, con órdenes y aprobacion del supremo gobierno.

Tesorería general de la federacion.=En 15 del corriente nos dice el Escmo. Sr. secretario de hacienda lo siguiente.=Con fecha de ayer me dice el Escmo. Sr. secretario del despacho de guerra y marina lo que sigue.=Escmo. Sr.—Deseando el supremo gobierno que al ramo de vestuarios para el ejército y milicia activa, se dé el arreglo correspondiente para que los cuerpos estén siempre provistos, procurándose el ahorro posible en los intereses nacionales, y considerando al mismo tiempo que de continuarse la contrata que celebró en el año de 824 con el estinguido estado mayor general, el coronel D. Manuel Barrera; cada dia se dificulta mas el arreglo de este ramo por la confusion en que se halla, de la que podrán resultar perjuicios de consideracion tanto al erario federal como al mismo contratista, sin que se pueda lograr que todos los cuerpos estén completamente habilitados; y atendiendo por otra parte á que dicha contrata debe estar ya terminada, el Escmo. Sr. vice-presidente se ha servido prevenir que desde luego se dé por concluida, liquidándose por la tesorería federal inmediatamente la cuenta respectiva; y teniendo en consideracion S. E. que por las circunstancias del erario, no es posible por ahora que se abone á los cuerpos la gratificacion señalada por ordenanza para sus vestuarios, haciéndoles las anticipaciones consiguientes para que pudieran construirlos; se ha servido determinar, entre tanto se aumentan los ingresos del erario á fin de que los cuerpos no carezcan de vestuarios, sino que estén provistos con oportunidad; se celebre nueva contrata por las autoridades respectivas, y con las formalidades establecidas bajo las condiciones siguientes: Primera: que la contrata no esceda en lo mas mínimo del importe de la gratificacion que por ordenanza debe darse á los cuerpos para su construccion. Segunda: que el contratista deberá construir el número de vestuarios para infantería y caballería en el término prudente que designe el gobierno, presentando mensualmente los que se convengan, sin que por pretesto alguno deje de cumplir con esta obligacion. Tercera: que los vestuarios se compondrán de las prendas que demuestra la adjunta noticia, y no se le admitirán si no los entrega á satisfaccion de los inspectores ó directores respectivos, segun los modelos que se presenten en el acto de la contrata, de que se hará en ella relacion circunstanciada. Cuarta: que el contratista deberá poner todos los géneros, efectos y materiales que sean necesarios para la perfecta construccion de los vestuarios, siendo de los mejores en su clase y bajo los términos en que se verifique su contrata; debiendo ser reconocidas las prendas por peritos que nombrarán las autoridades espresadas, y solo se le admitirán las que sean con arreglo á la contrata. Quinta: que deberá entregar los vestuarios mensualmente en los almacenes generales en donde se hará el reconocimiento, y el guarda almacen general no se dará por recibido de ellos, hasta que los inspectores ó directores le manifiesten estar satisfechos; siendo de cuenta del contratista la conduccion de los vestuarios á los almacenes, ó de éstos, si no se le admiten, á sus talleres. Sesta: que de los vestuarios que entregue mensualmente, deberá dar parte á esta secretaría de mi

1

Uniform regulations, XI / 481.3 / expediente 1871, fojas 2–9, Archivo Histórico Militar.

the contract does not exceed in the least the amount of the allotment that by ordinance must be given to the units for their construction. Second: that the contractor must produce the number of uniforms for infantry and cavalry in the prudent term designated by the government, presenting monthly those that are agreed, without for any reason letting this obligation be [un]fulfilled. Third: that the uniforms will be made up of the garments shown in the attached notice and will not be accepted if it is not delivered to the satisfaction of the respective inspectors or directors, according to the models that are presented in the act of the contract, which will be done in the related circumstance. Fourth: that the contractor must use all the fabrics, effects, and materials that are necessary for the perfect construction of the uniforms, being one of the best in their class and under the terms in which they verify their contract; the garments must be recognized by experts who name the expressed authorities, and only those that are [compliant] with the contract will be accepted. Fifth: that they must deliver the uniforms monthly to the general warehouses where the survey will be made, and the general warehouse keeper will not be deemed to have received them until the inspectors or directors declare that they are satisfied; the contractors are responsible for the delivery of the uniforms to the warehouse workers, or of these, if not admitted, to their workshops. Sixth: that of the uniforms that I deliver monthly, this secretary in my [page ends]

[. . .] charge must report, and the warehouse guard general will keep an exact account of them. Seventh: that at the time of the contract, all possible advantages should be provided to the public treasury and the units; with the understanding that uniforms must be produced according to the designated models, sizes, and qualities; so that the army never ceases to be fully equipped with everything that corresponds to it.

The Most Excellent vice president wishes that this contract be verified as soon as possible, and for this purpose I hope that Your Excellency will be useful to communicate the pertinent orders, and that if no contractor should appear, Your Excellency will use it [the contract] to agree on the corresponding resolution.

[I] transfer it to Your Excellencies [*V. SS.*], accompanied by a copy of the news that is cited, for its fulfillment in the part that corresponds to them, and that they communicate it to the general commissioner of this city so that he may proceed to summon bidders under the conditions that are foreseen; in the hopes that the models in question will be passed to the secretary of the office of war and navy, for which purpose it will be officiated by this one [the secretary of the war and navy] in my charge.

Let us communicate it to Your Excellency, accompanying it with copies of the two news items cited (1) for the corresponding purposes.—God and Liberty. Mexico [City]. June 23, 1831.—Alone: for the death of my partner.—Simon Andonaegui. [To?] Señor Commissary General of Mexico

Secretary of War and Navy—fifth section—The Most Excellent vice president understands that proposals are going to be made in the next auction, contracted only to the garments that must come from the allotment of a complete uniform, excluding those that belong to other branches that must be provided by the respective estates; and consequently prevents His Excellency, who of course allows Your Excellency, those made by the highest bidder for the number of garments that constitute a complete uniform, excluding those belonging to the other branches [of the military], and reporting to the government with the proposals presented; but the precise condition that these must revolve in the concept that the maximum that the government must pay to the bidders,

(1) The notes of the garments referred to in this order are not inserted, since their number has been varied by subsequent orders, as shown below.

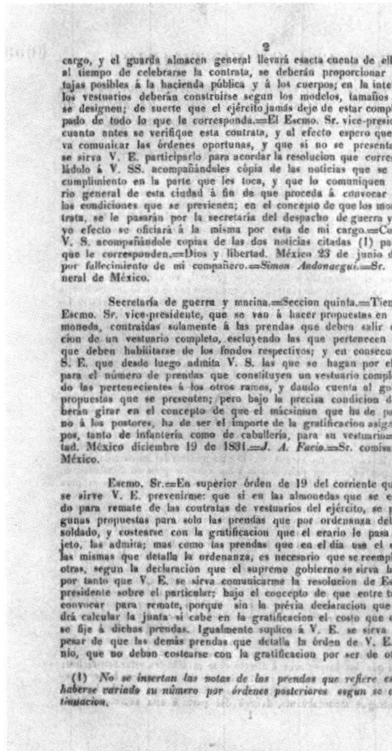

2

cargo, y el guarda almacen general llevará esacta cuenta de ellos. Sétima: que al tiempo de celebrarse la contrata, se deberán proporcionar todas las ventajas posibles á la hacienda pública y á los cuerpos; en la inteligencia de que los vestuarios deberán construirse segun los modelos, tamaños y calidades que se designen; de suerte que el ejército jamás deje de estar completamente equipado de todo lo que le corresponda.=El Escmo. Sr. vice-presidente desea que cuanto antes se verifique esta contrata, y al efecto espero que V. E. se sirva comunicar las órdenes oportunas, y que si no se presentare contratista, se sirva V. E. participarlo para acordar la resolucion que corresponda.=Trasládolo á V. SS. acompañándoles cópia de las noticias que se citan, para su cumplimiento en la parte que les toca, y que lo comuniquen al Sr. comisario general de esta ciudad á fin de que proceda á convocar postores bajo las condiciones que se previenen; en el concepto de que los modelos de que se trata, se le pasarán por la secretaría del despacho de guerra y marina, á cuyo efecto se oficiará á la misma por esta de mi cargo.=Comunicámoslo á V. S. acompañándole copias de las dos noticias citadas (1) para los efectos que le corresponden.=Dios y libertad. México 23 de junio de 1831.=Solo: por fallecimiento de mi compañero.=*Simon Andonaegui.*=Sr. comisario general de México.

Secretaría de guerra y marina.=Seccion quinta.=Tiene entendido el Escmo. Sr. vice-presidente, que se van á hacer propuestas en la próxima almoneda, contraidas solamente á las prendas que deben salir de la gratificacion de un vestuario completo, escluyendo las que pertenecen á otros ramos que deben habilitarse de los fondos respectivos; y en consecuencia previene S. E. que desde luego admita V. S. las que se hagan por el mejor postor para el número de prendas que constituyen un vestuario completo, esceptuando las pertenecientes á los otros ramos, y dando cuenta al gobierno con las propuestas que se presenten; pero bajo la precisa condicion de que éstas deberán girar en el concepto de que el mácsimun que ha de pagar el gobierno á los postores, ha de ser el importe de la gratificacion asignada á los cuerpos, tanto de infantería como de caballería, para su vestuario.=Dios y libertad. México diciembre 19 de 1831.=*J. A. Facio.*=Sr. comisario general de México.

Escmo. Sr.=En superior órden de 19 del corriente que recibí ayer se sirve V. E. prevenirme: que si en las almonedas que se están convocando para remate de las contratas de vestuarios del ejército, se presentaren algunas propuestas para solo las prendas que por ordenanza deben darse al soldado, y costearse con la gratificacion que el erario le pasa con este objeto, las admita; mas como las prendas que en el dia usa el ejército, no son las mismas que detalla la ordenanza, es necesario que se reemplacen unas con otras, segun la declaracion que el supremo gobierno se sirva hacer.=Espero por tanto que V. E. se sirva comunicarme la resolucion de Escmo. Sr. vice-presidente sobre el particular; bajo el concepto de que entre tanto suspendo convocar para remate, porque sin la prévia declaracion que pido, no podrá calcular la junta si cabe en la gratificacion el costo que en las posturas se fije á dichas prendas. Igualmente suplico á V. E. se sirva decirme si á pesar de que las demás prendas que detalla la órden de V. E. de 15 de junio, que no deban costearse con la gratificacion por ser de otros ramos, se

(1) *No se insertan las notas de las prendas que refiere esta órden, por haberse variado su número por órdenes posteriores segun se espresa á continuacion.*

must be the amount of the allotment assigned to the units, both infantry and cavalry, for their uniform. God and Liberty. Mexico [City]. December 19, 1831.

J. A. Facio [To?] Señor Commissary General of Mexico

Most Excellent Sir—In the superior order of the current [month] that I received yesterday, Your Excellency served to instruct me: that if in the papers that are being requested to auction off the contracts for army uniforms, some proposals will be presented for only the garments that by ordinance must be given to the soldier, and be paid for with the stipend that the treasury grants him [the soldier] for this object, [accept them]; but as the garments that the army wears [currently] are not the same as those detailed in the ordinance, it is necessary that they be replaced with the other, according to the declaration that the supreme government serves to make. I therefore hope that Your Excellency will serve to communicate to me the resolution of the Most Excellent vice president on the matter; under the concept that in the meantime I am suspending a call for auction because without the prior declaration that I request, the meeting will not be able to calculate if the allowance is fixed for the cost of such garments. I also ask Your Excellency to tell me if, despite the fact that the other orders detailed by Your Excellency's order of June 15, which should not be paid for with the stipend [designated] for being from other branches, [page ends]

[. . .] they must also be auctioned, as a bidder for all, assigning each one its price. God and Liberty. Mexico [City]. December 21, 1831. Ignacio Alas

[To] the Most Excellent Minister of War

Secretary of War and Navy—fifth section—The Most Excellent vice president is aware of Your Excellency's query [in] yesterday's dispatch, so that the garments of uniforms to be contracted are declared, since those worn by the army presently are not the same as those detailed in the general ordinance; His Excellency has served to declare that of the garments indicated by the government, and announced to the public in a notice of July 26 of this year, the infantry and cavalry are reflected in the attached list; verifying the contract of the complete uniform, with the garments that must compose it without exceeding in the least the amount that the treasury [has agreed to] spend with this object; expressing in the aforementioned contract, that I must come to this authority, the value or cost that is fixed for each of the garments when the auction is verified. In such a concept, His Excellency expects that, as soon as possible, he will inform Your Excellency of the auction of the uniform contract, under the terms provided by the government, and under all the conditions

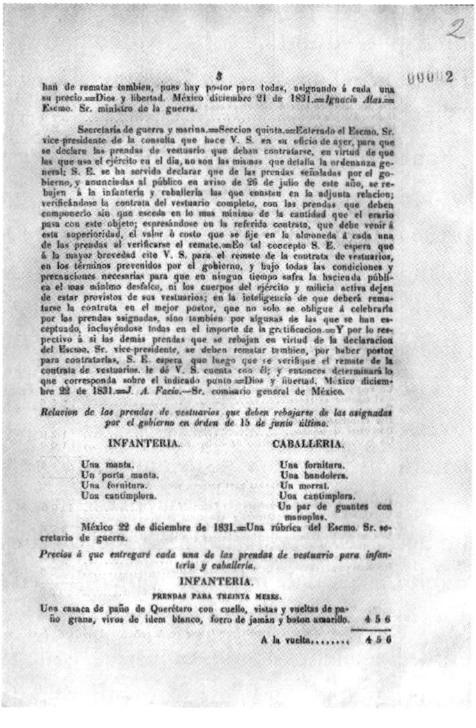
2

3 000 2

han de rematar tambien, pues hay postor para todas, asignando á cada una su precio.=Dios y libertad. México diciembre 21 de 1831.=*Ignacio Alas.*= Escmo. Sr. ministro de la guerra.

Secretaría de guerra y marina.=Seccion quinta.=Enterado el Escmo. Sr. vice-presidente de la consulta que hace V. S. en su oficio de ayer, para que se declare las prendas de vestuario que deban contratarse, en virtud de que las que usa el ejército en el dia, no son las mismas que detalla la ordenanza general; S. E. se ha servido declarar que de las prendas señaladas por el gobierno, y anunciadas al público en aviso de 26 de julio de este año, se rebajen á la infantería y caballería las que constan en la adjunta relacion; verificándose la contrata del vestuario completo, con las prendas que deben componerlo sin que esceda en lo mas mínimo de la cantidad que el erario pasa con este objeto; espresándose en la referida contrata, que debe venir á esta superioridad, el valor ó costo que se fije en la almoneda á cada una de las prendas al verificarse el remate.=En tal concepto S. E. espera que á la mayor brevedad cite V. S. para el remate de la contrata de vestuarios, en los términos prevenidos por el gobierno, y bajo todas las condiciones y precauciones necesarias para que en ningun tiempo sufra la hacienda pública el mas mínimo desfalco, ni los cuerpos del ejército y milicia activa dejen de estar provistos de sus vestuarios; en la inteligencia de que deberá rematarse la contrata en el mejor postor, que no solo se obligue á celebrarla por las prendas asignadas, sino tambien por algunas de las que se han exceptuado, incluyéndose todas en el importe de la gratificacion.=Y por lo respectivo á si las demás prendas que se rebajan en virtud de la declaracion del Escmo. Sr. vice-presidente, se deben rematar tambien, por haber postor para contratarlas, S. E. espera que luego que se verifique el remate de la contrata de vestuarios, le dé V. S. cuenta con él; y entonces determinará lo que corresponda sobre el indicado punto.=Dios y libertad. México diciembre 22 de 1831.=*J. A. Facio.*—Sr. comisario general de México.

Relacion de las prendas de vestuarios que deben rebajarse de las asignadas por el gobierno en órden de 15 de junio último.

INFANTERIA.	CABALLERIA.
Una manta.	Una fornitura.
Un porta manta.	Una bandolera.
Una fornitura.	Un morral.
Una cantimplora.	Una cantimplora.
	Un par de guantes con manoplas.

México 22 de diciembre de 1831.=Una rúbrica del Escmo. Sr. secretario de guerra.

Precios á que entregaré cada una de las prendas de vestuario para infantería y caballería.

INFANTERIA.

PRENDAS PARA TREINTA MESES.

Una casaca de paño de Querétaro con cuello, vistas y vueltas de paño grana, vivos de idem blanco, forro de jamán y boton amarillo.	4 5 6
A la vuelta........	4 5 6

and precautions necessary so that the public treasury never suffers the most minimum embezzlement, nor the units of the army and active militia are not provided with their uniforms; with the understanding that the contract must be auctioned off to the highest bidder, who is obliged not only to bid for the assigned garments, but also for some of those that have been excluded, all of which are included in the amount of the payment. And with regard to whether the other garments that are lowered by virtue of the declaration of the Most Excellent vice president, must also be auctioned, in order to have a bidder to contract them, His Excellency hopes that the auction of the uniform contract is verified. Your Excellency can count on it; and then it will determine the details of the contract. God and Liberty. Mexico [City]. December 22, 1831. J. A. Facio [To] the commissary general of Mexico.

List of uniform garments to be reduced from those assigned by the government in order of June 15 of the last [year].

INFANTRY	CAVALRY
A blanket	Leather straps [*fornitura*]
A blanket holder	A shoulder bag [*bandolera*]
Leather straps	Haversack [*moral*]
A canteen [*cantimplora*]	A canteen
	A pair of reinforced gloves [*par de guantes con manuplas*]

Mexico [City]. December 22, 1831. A rubric [in place of a signature] of the Most Excellent secretary of war.

Prices at which I will deliver each of the uniforms for infantry and cavalry.

INFANTRY	
GARMENTS FOR THIRTY MONTHS	
A *Querétaro* cloth [*paño*] jacket with a collar, facings [*vistas*], and cuff [*vueltas*] of scarlet [*grana*] cloth, decorated with white cloth, stuffed lining, and yellow buttons	456
On the back [i.e., the total]	456

this is the closest I can get the leaders due the table cells they stop me from placing them closer to the number.

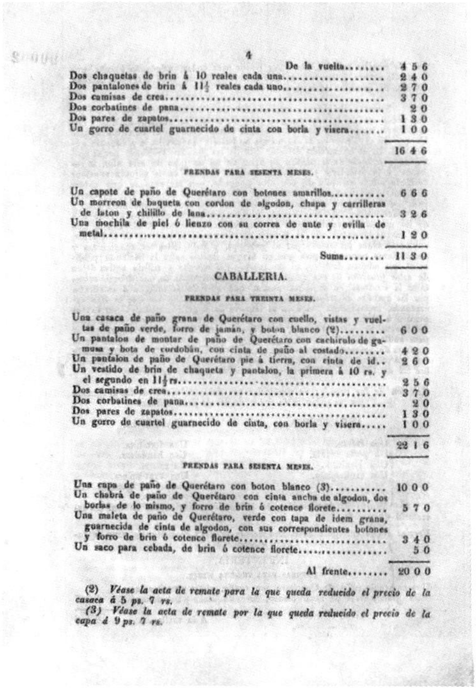

4

De la vuelta........	4 5 6
Dos chaquetas de brin á 10 reales cada una....................	2 4 0
Dos pantalones de brin á 11½ reales cada uno....................	2 7 0
Dos camisas de crea....................................	3 7 0
Dos corbatines de pana....................................	2 0
Dos pares de zapatos....................................	1 3 0
Un gorro de cuartel guarnecido de cinta con borla y visera.......	1 0 0
	16 4 6

PRENDAS PARA SESENTA MESES.

Un capote de paño de Querétaro con botones amarillos...........	6 6 6
Un morreon de baqueta con cordon de algodon, chapa y carrilleras de laton y chilillo de lana....................................	3 2 6
Una mochila de piel ó lienzo con su correa de ante y evilla de metal....................................	1 2 0
Suma........	11 3 0

CABALLERIA.

PRENDAS PARA TREINTA MESES.

Una casaca de paño grana de Querétaro con cuello, vistas y vueltas de paño verde, forro de jamán, y boton blanco (2).........	6 0 0
Un pantalon de montar de paño de Querétaro con cachirulo de gamusa y bota de cordobán, con cinta de paño al costado.........	4 2 0
Un pantalon de paño de Querétaro pie á tierra, con cinta de id..	2 6 0
Un vestido de brin de chaqueta y pantalon, la primera á 10 rs. y el segundo en 11½ rs....................................	2 5 6
Dos camisas de crea....................................	3 7 0
Dos corbatines de pana....................................	2 0
Dos pares de zapatos....................................	1 3 0
Un gorro de cuartel guarnecido de cinta, con borla y visera.....	1 0 0
	22 1 6

PRENDAS PARA SESENTA MESES.

Una capa de paño de Querétaro con boton blanco (3)............	10 0 0
Un chabrá de paño de Querétaro con cinta ancha de algodon, dos borlas de lo mismo, y forro de brin ó cotence florete..........	5 7 0
Una maleta de paño de Querétaro, verde con tapa de idem grana, guarnecida de cinta de algodon, con sus correspondientes botones y forro de brin ó cotence florete....................................	3 4 0
Un saco para cebada, de brin ó cotence florete..................	5 0
Al frente........	20 0 0

(2) *Véase la acta de remate para la que queda reducido el precio de la casaca á 5 ps. 7 rs.*

(3) *Véase la acta de remate por la que queda reducido el precio de la capa á 9 ps. 7 rs.*

From the back [previous page]	456
Two sailcloth [*brin*] jackets at 10 *reales* each..............................	240
Two sailcloth [*brin*] pants at 11½ *reales* each	270
Two medium-quality linen [*crea*] shirts	370
Two neckcloths [*corbatines de pana*; stocks]	20
Two pairs of shoes..	130
A ribbon-trimmed barracks cap with tassel and visor [*gorro del cuartel guarnecido de cinta con borla y visera*]	100
	1646

GARMENTS FOR SIXTY MONTHS

A cape [*capote*] of cloth from Querétaro with yellow button................	666
An attack helmet with cotton cords, metal sheets, and chinstraps of brass, and [*chilillo*] of wool	326
A knapsack of animal hide or linen cloth with its leather strap of buckskin and metal buckles	120
Total	**1130**

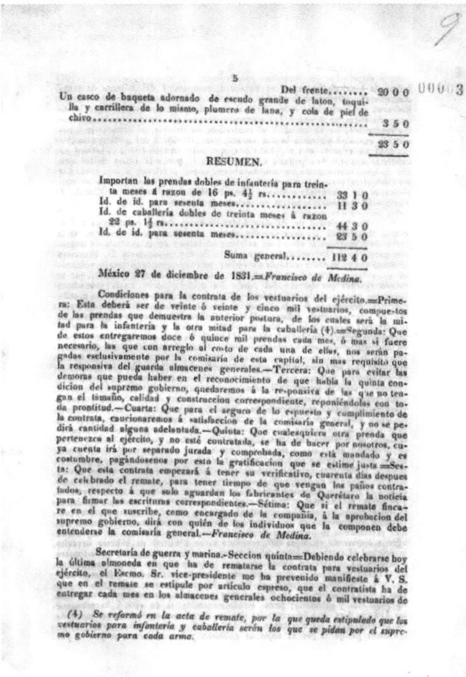

9

5

Del frente........	20 0 0
Un casco de baqueta adornado de escudo grande de laton, toquilla y carrillera de lo mismo, plumero de lana, y cola de piel de chivo........	3 5 0
	23 5 0

00003

RESUMEN.

Importan las prendas dobles de infantería para treinta meses á razon de 16 ps. 4½ rs............	33 1 0
Id. de id. para sesenta meses..................	11 3 0
Id. de caballería dobles de treinta meses á razon 22 ps. 1½ rs..................	44 3 0
Id. de id. para sesenta meses..................	23 5 0
Suma general........	112 4 0

México 27 de diciembre de 1831.=*Francisco de Medina.*

Condiciones para la contrata de los vestuarios del ejército.=Primera: Esta deberá ser de veinte ó veinte y cinco mil vestuarios, compuestos de las prendas que demuestra la anterior postura, de los cuales será la mitad para la infantería y la otra mitad para la caballería (4).=Segunda: Que de estos entregaremos doce ó quince mil prendas cada mes, ó mas si fuere necesario, las que con arreglo al costo de cada una de ellas, nos serán pagadas esclusivamente por la comisaría de esta capital, sin mas requisito que la responsiva del guarda almacenes generales.—Tercera: Que para evitar las demoras que pueda haber en el reconocimiento de que habla la quinta condicion del supremo gobierno, quedaremos á la responsiva de las que no tengan el tamaño, calidad y construccion correspondiente, reponiéndolas con toda prontitud.—Cuarta: Que para el seguro de lo espuesto y cumplimiento de la contrata, caucionaremos á satisfaccion de la comisaría general, y no se pedirá cantidad alguna adelantada.—Quinta: Que cualesquiera otra prenda que pertenezca al ejército, y no esté contratada, se ha de hacer por nosotros, cuya cuenta irá por separado jurada y comprobada, como está mandado y es costumbre, pagándosenos por esto la gratificacion que se estime justa.=Sesta: Que esta contrata empezará á tener su verificativo, cuarenta dias despues de celebrado el remate, para tener tiempo de que vengan los paños contratados, respecto á que solo aguardan los fabricantes de Querétaro la noticia para firmar las escrituras correspondientes.—Sétima: Que si el remate fincare en el que suscribe, como encargado de la compañía, á la aprobacion del supremo gobierno, dirá con quién de los individuos que la componen debe entenderse la comisaría general.—*Francisco de Medina.*

Secretaría de guerra y marina.-Seccion quinta=Debiendo celebrarse hoy la última almoneda en que ha de rematarse la contrata para vestuarios del ejército, el Escmo. Sr. vice-presidente me ha prevenido manifieste á V. S. que en el remate se estipule por artículo espreso, que el contratista ha de entregar cada mes en los almacenes generales ochocientos ó mil vestuarios de

(4) Se reformó en la acta de remate, por la que queda estipulado que los vestuarios para infantería y caballería serán los que se pidan por el supremo gobierno para cada arma.

[continued] from the front	2000
A *baqueta* [campaign?] helmet adorned with a large brass plate, ribbon and chinstrap of the same [brass], wool plumage, and a tail-end of young goat skin	350
	2350

GLOSSARY

adarme: Equivalent to one sixteenth of an ounce; the Mexican army had 17- and 19-*adarme* musket balls
alférez: Rank of a Mexican officer below a 2nd lieutenant
armero: Gunsmith
arriero: Muleteer
artilleros: Artillerymen; gunners
ayuntamiento: Body of magistrates of cities and towns, composed of an alcalde (mayor) and *regidores* (council members)
baqueta: Ramrod; the stick with which the charge is forced into firearms; drumstick
Batalla de Punta del Encinal del Perdido: The Mexican term for the battle of Coleto Creek (Fannin Battleground)
batallón activo: Active battalion, similar to a national guard unit that is called up in times of need
batallón permanente: A permanent battalion; regular army troops
Béjar (Béxar): San Antonio
botafuego: Linstock, a wooden staff with a match at the end of it, used by gunners in firing cannons
botes de Metrálla (*Metraya*): Tin cans filled with canister shot
caja: Stock of a musket
cajones de cartuchas: Boxes of cartridges
cantimplora: Canteen
carrillera: Chinstrap for a helmet
cazadores: Light infantrymen
cohetes á la Congrev: English Congreve rockets
corneta: Bugle; bugler

culebrina: Culverin (old style of cannon)
cureña: Gun carriage for a cannon
diana: A beat of the drum; reveille
esmeril: A small piece of ordnance (cannon)
Estados Unidos de Mejico: The United States of Mexico (including Texas prior to 1836)
Estados Unidos del Norte: The United States of the North (i.e., the United States of America)
estopín: Quick-match, which serves to fire a cannon
fusil: Smooth bore musket
granada: Hand grenade, a small hollow globe filled with fine powder; howitzer shell
granadero: Grenadier, a veteran foot soldier
habilitado: Paymaster of a regiment of the Mexican army
infantes: Infantrymen
instumentos de zapa: Entrenching tools
lanza fuegos: Another term for a linstock; see *botafuégo*
llave: Lock plate, the part of a gun by which the fire is struck; key
morrion: Helmet; shako
obus: Howitzer
parada: Bundle of paper cartridges tied together (usually about ten cartridges)
parque: Artillery depot; artillery park; ammunition
paso revista: Pass in review
piedras de chispa: Flints for a musket
plaza: Enlisted man; plaza
pólvora: Gunpowder, a composition of sulfur, saltpeter, and charcoal
pulgada: Inch (technically 0.916 English inches)
pronunciamiento: Military uprising
rancho: Army mess; ranch
rifle: Rifle
Río Bravo: Río Grande River
sacatrapos: Worm; an iron screw fastened to the end of a ramrod for drawing out a ball from barrel of a musket
salva: Salute; discharge of firearms
tambor: Drum; drummer
Tejano: Person of Spanish or Mexican descent living in Texas

tercerola: A short kind of carbine
tercio: Regiment of infantry
Texan (also Texian or Anglo): Immigrants who came to Texas from elsewhere (the United States, Europe, etc.)
trozo: Division of a column forming the vanguard or rear guard
zapador: Sapper; pioneer; one who builds bridges, fortifications, etc.

NOTES

ABBREVIATIONS

AGN: Archivo General de la Nación, Dolph Briscoe Center for American History, University of Texas, Austin, Texas

AHM: Archivo Histórico Militar, http:/www.archivohistorico2010sedena.gob.mx/busquedamenu

DBC: Dolph Briscoe Center for American History, University of Texas, Austin, Texas

PREFACE

1. Archivo Histórico Militar website, http://www.archivohistorico2010.sedena.gob.mx/busquedamenu.

2. Archivo General de Mexico, 1538–1849, DBC.

3. Vicente Filisola, *Memorias para la historia de la guerra de Tejas*, 2 vols. (Mexico: R. Rafael, 1848–49; repr., Mexico, D. F.: Editora Nacional, 1968), available in English as Vicente Filisola, *Memoirs for the History of the War in Texas*, trans. Wallace Woolsey, 2 vols. (Austin, TX: Eakin Press, 1987). Filisola wrote two separate versions of his memoirs but gave them the same title, *Memorias para la Historia de la Guerra de Tejas*. The first edition was published by R. Rafael in 1848–49. The second edition was published by Ignacio Cumplido in 1849 and is completely different from the Rafael edition. The Woolsey translation is primarily from the Rafael edition, but a few parts of the Cumplido edition are included in his work. Carlos Sánchez Navarro, ed., *La Guerra de Tejas: Memorias de un Soldado* (1st ed., Mexico: Editorial Polis, 1938; 2nd ed., Mexico: Editorial Jus, S.A., 1960).

4. Eugene C. Barker, "Difficulties of a Mexican Revenue Officer in Texas," *Quarterly of the Texas State Historical Association*, 4, no. 1 (1901): 192.

INTRODUCTION

1. Donald C. Cutter, trans. and ed., *The Defenses of Northern New Spain: Hugo O'Connor's Report to Teodoro de Croix, July 22, 1777* (Dallas: DeGolyer Library, 1994).

2. Filisola, *Memoirs for the History of the War*, vol. 1, 213.

3. To be precise, "the United States of the North" is the proper term, as Mexico was officially known as the United States of Mexico. For this work, "the United States of the North" will be shortened to the United States.

4. For a thorough look at Mier y Terán's inspection tour of Texas, see Manuel de Mier y Terán, *Texas by Terán: The Diary Kept by General Manuel de Mier y Terán on His 1828 Inspection of Texas*, ed. Jack Jackson, trans. John Wheat (Austin: University of Texas Press, 2000). Another official who accompanied Mier y Terán on his journey was José María Sánchez y Tapia, whose diary addresses the threat posed to Mexico by the Anglo occupants of Texas. Sánchez was "very suspicious of these people and found himself favorably impressed, often begrudgingly so, by only a few of them." José Maria Sánchez y Tapia, "A Trip to Texas in 1828," trans. Carlos E. Castañeda, *Southwestern Historical Quarterly* 29, no. 4 (April 1926): 249–88. A third journal of this expedition was written by the French naturalist Jean-Louis Berlandier, who accompanied Mier y Terán. It gives many details about the flora, fauna, geology, weather, etc. during the trip. Jean-Louis Berlandier, *Journey to Mexico during the Years 1826 to 1834*, vol. 2 (Austin: Texas State Historical Association, 1980).

5. Colonel Juan Nepomuceno Almonte was an aide to Santa Anna. His inspection tour to Texas in 1834 and his part in the Texas Revolution are documented in Jack Jackson, ed., *Almonte's Texas: Juan N. Almonte's 1834 Inspection, Secret Report, and Role in the 1836 Campaign*, trans. John Wheat (Austin: Texas State Historical Association, 2003).

6. For a thorough discussion of land speculation in Texas, see Eugene C. Barker, "Land Speculation as a Cause of the Texas Revolution," *Quarterly of the Texas State Historical Association* 10, no. 1 (July 1906): 76–95.

7. For more details on the misconception of slavery being permanently outlawed in 1829 in Mexico, see Andrew J. Torget, *Seeds of Empire: Cotton, Slavery, and the Transformation of the Texas Borderlands, 1800–1850* (Chapel Hill: University of North Carolina Press, 2015).

8. Tornel to Cos, October 31, 1835, XI / 481.3 / expediente 1101, fojas 86–89, AHM.

9. Mier y Terán, *Texas by Terán*, 178–79.

10. Filisola, an Italian by birth, joined the army in Spain as a young man and later moved to Mexico. He was second-in-command to Santa Anna in the Texas campaign and was the commander in chief after the Battle of San Jacinto. He was one of

the rare generals in the Mexican army who seemed to avoid politics and do his duty as a soldier.

11. Filisola, *Memoirs for the History of the War,* vol. 1, 189–96.

CHAPTER 1

1. Walter Edgar Hancock, "The Career of General Antonio López de Santa Anna (1794–1833)" (PhD diss., University of Texas at Austin, 1933), 1–4. Hancock's dissertation is confined to Santa Anna's career prior to 1833, but it gives a thorough account of his rise to power and of the politics and military campaigns from the royalist period through Santa Anna's presidency in 1833. Hancock gives a great deal of insight as to how Santa Anna became the man he was.

2. Manuel Rivera, *Historia Antigua y Moderna de Jalapa y de las Revoluciones del Estado de Veracruz,* vol. 1 (Mexico: Imprenta de Ignacio Cumplido, 1870), 308–11. Many writers of Texas history have claimed that Martín Perfecto de Cos was the brother-in-law of Santa Anna. It is possible that Cos was related to the owner of this counting firm and that there was some sort of relationship between Cos and Santa Anna. Santa Anna's brother-in-law did participate in the Texas campaign. His name was Ricardo Dromundo, the purveyor general of the army. This fact was documented by Colonel José de la Peña. See José Enrique de la Peña, *With Santa Anna in Texas: A Personal Narrative of the Revolution,* trans. and ed. Carmen Perry (College Station: Texas A&M Press, 1975; expanded ed., intro. James E. Crisp, College Station: Texas A&M University Press, 1997), 59. Gen. Vicente Filisola noted that Santa Anna had "family ties" with Dromundo. Filisola, *Memoirs for the History of the War,* vol. 2, 145.

3. Antonio López de Santa Anna, *Mi Historia Militar y Política, 1810–1874: memorias ínéditos* (Mexico: Vda de C. Bouret, 1905), available in the Genaro García Collection, vol. 9, Benson Manuscripts Collection, University of Texas at Austin; translated into English as Antonio López de Santa Anna, *The Eagle: The Autobiography of Santa Anna,* ed. Ann Fears Crawford (Austin, TX: State House Press, 1988). Santa Anna wrote his biography in 1876 in Nassau, Bahamas, during one of his many exiles. Unfortunately, the book contains little detail.

4. Rivera, *Historia Antigua y Moderna,* vol. 1, 309; Hancock, "Career of General Antonio López," 4.

5. Genaro García Collection, Benson Manuscripts Collection, University of Texas at Austin.

6. Hancock, "Career of General Antonio López," 18.

7. Arredondo's numbers were likely to have been exaggerated as he claimed that the rebel army numbered three thousand. Wilford Hardy Callcott, *Santa Anna:*

The Story of an Enigma Who Once Was Mexico (Norman: University of Oklahoma Press, 1936), 10–11.

8. Filisola, *Memoirs for the History of the War*, vol. 1, 32.

9. José María Luis Mora, *México y sus revoluciones*, vol. 4 (Mexico: Editorial Porrua, 1857), 268–70. It is very interesting that Mora noted that the citizens of the provinces who were terrorized by Arredondo held a "hatred of the deepest kind" because of the way they were treated. It is likely that it worked both ways. There were many Mexicans in Texas who refused to get involved in the revolution—very possibly attributable to fear of a repeat of Arredondo's treatment of the Béjar inhabitants. On the other hand, the Seguins, Navarros, etc. vigorously opposed Santa Anna and may well have done so due to the same memories. One might also argue that the Texans showed a "hatred of the deepest kind" when they had their chance for revenge at San Jacinto.

10. Callcott, *Santa Anna*, 11.

11. In November 1817, Santa Anna entered the town of Venta Arriba. He captured the insurgent rebel Francisco de Asís and immediately commanded that he be shot. There was never any explanation for this action. The "most atrocious" of the Royalist officers at the time was said to be Col. José Barradas. In a campaign in December 1817, he reported that he burned 162 ranches, two foundries, eighty-six corn granaries, and a variety of crops. In addition, he killed all the domestic animals that he encountered. Hancock, "Career of General Antonio López," 39–40.

12. Rivera, *Historia Antigua y Moderna*, 152–53; Hancock, "Career of General Antonio López," 71. This is an interesting reference to Santa Anna relying on fortune. In his first interview with Sam Houston, after his defeat at San Jacinto, Santa Anna was said to have commented that he was defeated by the fates.

13. Callcott, *Santa Anna*, 22.

14. Francisco Bulnes, *Las grandes mentiras de Nuestra historia: La Nación y el Ejército in las guerras extranjeras* (Paris: Librerìa de la Vda de Ch. Bouret, 1904), 772; Callcott, *Santa Anna*, 117–18.

15. Miguel Lerdo de Tejada, *Apuntes históricos de la historia de la ciudad histórica de Veracruz*, vol. 2 (Mexico, 1857), 76. Hancock notes that Don Carlos de Bustamante likely wrote this proclamation. Hancock, "Career of General Antonio López," 75. Bustamante was currently serving as Santa Anna's secretary. Callcott, *Santa Anna*, 24.

16. Rivera, *Historia Antigua y Moderna*, vol. 2, 176–77; Hancock, "Career of General Antonio López," 78.

17. Rivera, *Historia Antigua y Moderna*, vol. 2, 179; Hancock, "Career of General Antonio López," 80.

18. San Juan de Ulúa was a fortress in the harbor of Veracruz. The Spanish occupied this fortress at the time of Mexican independence and held it until the Spanish

general Coppinget surrendered to the Mexican general Miguel Barragán on November 18, 1825. Hancock, "Career of General Antonio López," 268.

19. Hancock, "Career of General Antonio López," 169.

20. On April 28, 1824, the Mexican congress passed a decree that if Iturbide ever tried to reenter Mexico he would be sentenced to death. Apparently unaware of this death decree, Iturbide landed at Soto la Marina on July 14, 1824. He was captured and executed on July 19 at Padilla. Santa Anna was later to have his remains brought to Mexico City and buried with honor. Hubert Howe Bancroft, *History of Mexico*, vol. 5, *1824–1861* (San Francisco: A. L. Bancroft, 1885), 804–10; Santa Anna, *The Eagle*, 258n15.

21. Hancock, "Career of General Antonio López," 191–92.

22. Callcott, *Santa Anna*, 57. Hancock adds an interesting story about Santa Anna's marriage. Apparently, Santa Anna was tricked into marrying the younger, less attractive of the two daughters of Señor García. When he discovered the ruse, Santa Anna was said to have commented: "This is not the one I wanted; I wanted the pretty one." Soon after he was said to have relented and said, "It does not matter; I'll adjust myself to it." Hancock says the story is recorded in Mirabeau Lamar's sketch of the life of Santa Anna, but he felt that it was likely fictitious. Hancock, "Career of General Antonio López," 304–6.

23. Tulancingo was the location of the skirmish where Guerrero defeated Bravo and essentially ended the Plan of Montaño.

24. Lorenzo de Zavala, *Ensayo histórico de las revoluciones de México desde 1808 hasta 1830*, vol. 2 (Mexico: Imprenta a cargo de M. N. de la Vega, 1845), 46; Hancock, "Career of General Antonio López," 334–35. Bancroft gave a similar opinion of Guerrero's biggest fault—his poor ancestry: "He was born in the town of Tixtla, then within the *intendencia* of Mexico, in 1782, of humble parents, Juan Pedro Guerrero and María Guadalupe Saldaña, belonging to the lowly race included in the term *castas*, utterly degraded both civilly and politically; for they were disqualified by law, custom, and prejudice for ever emerging from their low condition. To this fact should be ascribed Guerrero's defects, which have been so pitilessly and unjustly exaggerated by the very men that should have extolled his fortitude and exalted his services and personal merits." Bancroft, *History of Mexico*, vol. 5, 76–77.

25. For more on the politics of the Guerrero/Pedraza election in Veracruz, see Hancock, "Career of General Antonio López," 348–53.

26. De Zavala, *Ensayo histórico*, vol. 2, 65–71, 90–91; Hancock, "Career of General Antonio López," 359–61. Hancock also mentions an article written by Henry Ward, the minister from Great Britain, that strongly censured de Zavala's actions and concluded that he was guilty because he fled and refused to be tried. This is interesting since Ward and the British were actively supporting the Centralists (*escoceses*) while the Americans and Joel Poinsett favored the Federalists (*Yorkinos*).

Hancock, "Career of General Antonio López," 361–62, citing Henry Ward, "Politics in Mexico," *North American Review,* December 1830, 143.

27. Hancock, "Career of General Antonio López," 377–78.

28. Certainly, Houston did not have the superior numbers that Rincón had, but he was in a position where time was on his side. Santa Anna was getting further from his base, lower in supplies, and his soldiers more tired from the long marches. Houston, on the other hand, was still receiving aid and volunteers from the United States with each passing day. Hancock, "Career of General Antonio López," 390–91.

29. Hancock, "Career of General Antonio López," 391. For Rincón's complete account of his actions, see Manuel Rincón, "Manifiesto, El General Manuel Rincón justificado a los ojós de los Mexicans imparciales," in *Pronunciamiento de Perote por el general Antonio López de Sta. Anna, y sucesos de su campaña hasta la derogacion de la ley que lo proscribió escrito por un ciudadano que no tomó la más minima parte en aquellos acontecimientos* (Mexico: Imprenta de Aguila, 1829).

30. Hancock, "Career of General Antonio López," 405.

31. It is interesting to note that the rioting and looting that took place at this time in Mexico City would eventually lead to what was called the French Pastry War. The French invaded Mexico in 1839 because Mexico had refused to pay reparations for the damage French merchants had suffered during this revolt. This turned out to be very fortuitous for the Texans as it caused the second Texas campaign to be put on hold.

32. For Pedraza's account of this entire affair, see Manuel Gómez Pedraza, *Manifiesto, que Manuel Gómez Pedraza, ciudadano de la República de Méjico, dedica a sus compatriotas, o sea, Una reseña de su vida pública* (New Orleans: Imp. de B. Levy, 1831; repr., Guadalajara: Brambila, 1831).

33. Some sources give Barradas's first name as Isidoro.

34. Santa Anna to de Zavala, August 4, 1829, Portal to Texas History, University of North Texas, accessed June 24, 2008, http://texashistory.unt.edu/permalink/meta-pth-5994.

35. For more details on the Spanish invasion and the actions of Santa Anna and Mier y Terán, see Ohland Morton, "Life of General Don Manuel de Mier y Terán: As it Affected Texas-Mexican Relations," *Southwestern Historical Quarterly* 47, no. 3 (1944): 256–67; Bancroft, *History of Mexico,* vol. 5, 71–76; Hancock, "Career of General Antonio López," 459–80.

36. The Mexican losses were said to be 287 dead and wounded. Hancock, "Career of General Antonio López," 472.

37. Hancock, "Career of General Antonio López," 475–76.

38. Rivera, *Historia Antigua y Moderna,* vol. 2, 515.

39. Juan Suárez y Navarro, *Historia de México y del General Antonio López de Santa Anna* (Mexico: Imprenta de Ignacio Cumplido, 1850), 175–76; Hancock, "Career of General Antonio López," 498.

40. The prosecuting officer for the Guerrero trial was Lt. Col. Nicolás Condelle. Condelle was later to figure prominently in the Texas campaign. One of the accusations that Condelle made against Guerrero in the trial was that he had conspired with de Zavala and Joel Poinsett to borrow money from the United States and use Texas as collateral. Bancroft, *History of Mexico*, vol. 5, 98–99.

41. Santa Anna's letter was less than his best effort. It was written in response to a plea from Guerrero's wife. Guerrero had been executed before the letter was written. For a part of Santa Anna's letter to Bustamante, see Hancock, "Career of General Antonio López," 542.

42. Vital Fernández was to be an important player in the Texas campaign. Even though he did not go to Texas, he was the military commander of Nuevo Leon y Tamaulipas, stationed at Matamoros.

43. This march was reported to have covered sixty-three miles in thirty hours. Bancroft, *History of Mexico*, vol. 5, 120n58.

44. Suárez y Navarro, *Historia de México*, 371; Callcott, *Santa Anna*, 96.

45. Clarence W. Wharton, *El Presidente: A Sketch of the Life of General Santa Anna* (Austin, TX: Gammel's Book Store, [1926?]), 64; Callcott, *Santa Anna*, 108–9.

46. De Zavala, *Ensayo histórico*, vol. 1, 229–30; Hancock, "Career of General Antonio López," 249.

47. In archeological excavations on the San Jacinto battlefield under the direction of the Texas Parks and Wildlife Department and Dr. Roger Moore, I found an *ocho reales* silver coin. This dollar-sized coin was minted in Zacatecas in 1834 and was likely part of the above-mentioned loot. As will be further documented, this looting was basically a form of pay for the Mexican officers.

48. If Sánchez Navarro could have seen into the future, he might have added, "Or even worse, if he is captured." When Santa Anna was captured at San Jacinto, Filisola made it perfectly clear that he had no idea what the commander in chief's campaign plans were.

49. Sánchez Navarro, *La Guerra de Tejas*, 2nd ed., 76.

50. Sánchez Navarro, *La Guerra de Tejas*, 2nd ed., 77.

CHAPTER 2

1. William H. Wharton and J. B. Miller were to accompany him.

2. Bancroft, *History of the North Mexican States and Texas*, vol. 2, *1801–1889* (San Francisco: The History Company, 1889), 132–36.

3. Austin to Ayuntamiento, October 2, 1835, XI / 481.3 / expediente 1077, foja 59, AHM.

4. Eugene C. Barker, ed., *The Austin Papers*, 3 vols. (Washington: United States Government Printing Office, 1924–28), vol. 2, 1015–16.

5. Ayuntamiento to Austin, October 31, 1835, XI / 481.3 / expediente 1077, foja 59, AHM.

6. Several sources report that he was arrested in Monterrey, but Saltillo seems to be correct.

7. The Archivo Histórico Militar, as well as the Archivo General de la Nación, contain a plethora of letters back and forth between Viesca, Cos, Tornel, and many others who were involved in this conflict of cities.

8. Bancroft, *History of the North Mexican States and Texas*, vol. 2, 146–47. Article 11 of the law of April 30, 1830, required that a state have a population of eighty thousand to send a deputy to the national congress. Juan Almonte's report on the conditions in Texas showed that the population of Texas in 1834 was approximately twenty-one thousand.

9. Filisola wrote that in the new election no one could run for office who had served in office during the previous two years. Viesca had served as a legislator in the previous congress, thus making his election illegal. Filisola, *Memoirs for the History of the War*, vol. 2, 38–39.

10. Dr. James Grant was Scottish by birth. He settled in northern Mexico and was a staunch Federalist. For more information on Grant and the possibility that he was a secret British agent, see Stewart Reid, *The Secret War for Texas* (College Station: Texas A&M University Press, 2007).

11. Land sale law, March 11, 1835, XI / 481.3 / expediente 1094, foja 16, AHM.

12. Cos to Tornel, March 16, 1835, XI / 481.3 / expediente 1094, fojas 13–15, AHM.

13. Cos to political chiefs, September 3, 1835, in John H. Jenkins, ed., *The Papers of the Texas Revolution*, vol. 1 (Austin, TX: Presidial Press, 1973), 414.

14. The Mexican army was composed of three main classifications of troops. The permanent units were the regular professional soldiers. As a result of the ongoing pronunciamientos and revolts, they were very experienced, but they were undermanned, underpaid, and undersupplied because of the constant fighting. The second classification comprised the active units. These units were more like national guard units and would be called to service during times of need. They were generally less experienced and not as well trained as the permanent troops. The last class of soldiers was the presidial troops. For the most part these were cavalry companies who were stationed at the frontiers of the country. Some of them were excellent horsemen, but at this period in Mexico's history they were very undermanned. At times, these units were supplemented with conscripts and convicts.

15. Ugartechea was military commander at Velasco in 1832 when the Texans forced the Mexican soldiers there to surrender. He became the military commander of the state of Coahuila y Tejas in 1834 and was stationed at Béjar.

16. Ugartechea to Cos, April 27, 1835, XI / 481.3 / expediente 1097, fojas 16–17, AHM. On June 1, Ugartechea informed Cos that up to five hundred militiamen from Texas would be marching to Monclova. He requested that the presidial companies of Laredo and Lipantitlán come to Béjar to stop them.

17. Cos to Ugartechea, May 11, 1835, XI / 481. 3 / expediente 1097, fojas 18–20, AHM.

18. Cos to Tornel, May 28, 1835, in Jenkins, *Papers of the Texas Revolution*, vol. 1, 131.

19. Samuel May Williams worked closely with Stephen F. Austin and was often called his secretary. He had been in Monclova and was one of the partners in the four-hundred-league land deal. The Mexican authorities found it highly suspicious that Williams returned to San Felipe but bypassed the city of Béjar. The Samuel May Williams papers contain a great deal of information on many of these subjects and can be found at the Rosenberg Library in Galveston, Texas.

20. Cos to Lafuente, May 28, 1835, XI / 481.3 / expediente 1097, fojas 66–68, AHM.

21. Arreola to Cos, June 1, 1835, XI / 481.3 / expediente 1215, fojas 64–66, AHM.

22. Captured list, June 6, 1835, XI / 481.3 / expediente 1097, foja 128, AHM. Ben Milam was said to have been with him but escaped.

23. Ugartechea to Cos, June 15, 1835, XI / 481.3 / expediente 1098, foja 31, AHM. Ugartechea's spies also informed him that the colonists were willing to permit Mexican troops in their ports but not in the interior. On June 24 Cos replied to Ugartechea that the general command gave no merit as to what the colonists had resolved regarding where they would allow troops to be stationed. XI / 481.3 / expediente 1098, fojas 31–32, AHM.

24. For an excellent discussion of the Tejano situation in Nacogdoches at the time and the role of Vicente Cordova, the commander of the Tejano militia in that area, see Paul D. Lack, "The Córdova Revolt," in *Tejano Journey, 1770–1850*, ed. Gerald E. Poyo (Austin: University of Texas Press, 1996), 89–110.

25. Fray José Antonio Días de León came to Texas in 1816 and served at various times in Refugio, Béjar, and Nacogdoches. He was the last Franciscan monk in Texas and baptized Sam Houston in 1833. Aníbal A. González, "Diaz de Leon, Jose Antonio (ca. 1786–1834)," Handbook of Texas Online, last updated October 21, 2020, https://tshaonline.org/handbook/online/articles/fdi29.

26. Cos to Ugartechea, January 24, 1835, XI / 481.3 / expediente 1092, fojas 22–23, AHM. The phrase "respect the national honor" was used frequently in the letters of the Mexican officials. They seemed to be concerned that Mexican soldiers might do something that would start a major conflict, for which they were not yet prepared.

27. Ugartechea to Cos, December 15, 1834, XI / 481.3 / expediente 1092, foja 12, AHM. For more on the indigenous people of Texas, see Jean-Louis Berlandier, *The*

Indians of Texas in 1830, ed. John C. Ewers; trans. Patricia Reading Leclercq (Washington, DC: Smithsonian Institution Press, 1969).

28. Cos to Tornel, December 29, 1834, XI / 483.1 / expediente 1092, fojas 6–9, AHM.

29. Bean had taken part in the Nolan expedition and ended up in prison in Mexico. He fought with the insurgents in Mexico and was eventually appointed the Mexicans' Indian agent in Nacogdoches, where he helped keep the Cherokees neutral in the Fredonian Rebellion. Jack Jackson, *Indian Agent: Peter Ellis Bean in Mexican Texas* (College Station: Texas A&M University Press, 2005).

30. Cos to Tornel, May 26, 1835, vol. 331, box 2Q172, Texas 1834–35, pp. 186–87, AGN.

31. Rueg to Ugartechea, May 8, 1835, XI / 481.3 / expediente 1098, fojas 3–5, AHM.

32. Bean to Ugartechea, August 11, 1835, XI / 481.3 / expediente 1101, fojas 136–37, AHM.

33. Bean to Ugartechea, August 18, 1835, XI / 481.3 / expediente 1101, fojas 141–43, AHM. One gets the impression that Bean, at least at this point, was actually serious about his position as a colonel in the Mexican army and was trying his best to perform the duties of the military commander of the department.

34. Bean to Jackson, August 18, 1835, box 2Q173, vol. 332, p. 373, AGN.

35. By this time the land sales had been repealed, but Rueg was probably unaware of this at the time of writing the document.

36. Rueg to inhabitants, July 8, 1835, box 2Q224, book 568, fojas 34–36, AGN.

37. Cos to Rueg, August 17, 1835, box 2Q173, book 332, fojas 283, AGN.

38. Artillery park list, May 12, 1835, XI / 481.3 / expediente 1133, fojas 70–78, AHM.

39. John Linn to Thomas Henry, October 10, 1835, XI / 481.3 / expediente 1101, fojas 181–86, AHM (emphasis in original).

40. Robert McAlpin Williamson, address, June 22, 1835, in Jenkins, *Papers of the Texas Revolution*, vol. 1, 194–202.

41. Grace Grafton, "Leaves from a Ladies Journal: No. 7," *American Monthly Magazine*, July 1837, 233–42, https://books.google.com/books?id=vNsRAAAAYAAJ.

42. For an excellent documentation of the actions of Gómez Farías, de Zavala, and Mejía in New Orleans, see Edward L. Miller, *New Orleans and the Texas Revolution* (College Station: Texas A&M University Press, 2004), 19–36.

43. Many Texas history writers call him "Mexia," but in Mexican archival sources and in books written by Mexican authors his name is given as "Mejía."

44. Miller, *New Orleans and the Texas Revolution*, 30–31.

45. Filisola, *Memories for the History of the War*, vol. 2, 87.

46. Carbajal (spelled "Carabajal" in many of the archival documents and "Carvajal" in some others) was a Béjareño who lived for many years in the United States, where he was educated. He was involved in the first Anáhuac disturbance in 1832.

47. Ugartechea described him as a neighbor of Béjar. Note that this is not the Juan Sambrano (Zambrano) who was involved in the Casas revolt in 1811. XI / 481.3 / expediente 1099, fojas 7–10, AHM.

48. Frank W. Johnson was wanted for his part in the first disturbance at Anáhuac and possibly as a land speculator as well.

49. Robert McAlpin Williamson was an active leader of the war party in Texas. The members of this party were anxious to reinstate the constitution of 1824 or become independent from Mexico. As mentioned above, Williamson gave an impassioned speech at a meeting in San Felipe on June 22 that demonstrated his strong opposition to Santa Anna and the new Mexican government.

50. William Barret Travis arrived in Texas after the Mexican law of April 6, 1830, so technically he was an illegal immigrant. He became an active member of the war party in Texas and was arrested for his part in the first Anáhuac disturbance of 1832. Obviously, the main reason the Mexican officials wanted him arrested was for commanding the attack on Tenorio and his forces that June.

51. See n19 of this chapter.

52. Moseley Baker was another of the active leaders of the war party. He claimed to have been the first to speak for the independence of Texas from Mexico.

53. David Lee Child to Juan Almonte, September 15, 1835, in Jenkins, *Papers of the Texas Revolution*, vol. 1, 446. Almonte was exiled to New Orleans for a time and had also served in London, so he spoke perfect English.

54. Jackson, *Almonte's Texas*, 336–37.

55. Jackson, *Almonte's Texas*, 385–86.

56. Gene Brack, "Mexican Opinion and the Texas Revolution," *Southwest Historical Quarterly* 72, no. 2 (October 1968): 173.

57. Brack, "Mexican Opinion," 175.

58. Lorenzo de Zavala to Stephen F. Austin, September 17, 1835, in Jenkins, *Papers of the Texas Revolution*, vol. 1, 453–55. De Zavala also suggested that the Texans should establish themselves as a state of Mexican Federation, offer asylum to persecuted Mexicans, and offer to rejoin the Mexican confederation if, within two years, the other states of Mexico acted likewise and regained their rights.

CHAPTER 3

1. Located at the mouth of the Brazos River.

2. "Coke" and "Choate" are listed as two families who were early settlers of Galveston. Dr. J. O. Dyer, *The Early History of Galveston*, Centenary Edition, part 1 (Galveston, TX: Oscar Springer Print, 1916), 12.

3. Possibly John A. Williams, who was alcalde of Anáhuac in 1832 and was later labeled as a Mexican sympathizer. Margaret S. Henson, "Williams, John A.," Handbook of Texas online, last updated March 19, 2019, https://tshaonline.org/handbook/online/articles/fwi27.

4. There was a George Orr who lived in Liberty County. "George Orr," Republic of Texas Claims online, accessed December 2, 2018.

5. Probably John Moses Smith. He was considered a Tory by the locals of Liberty. Jean L. Epperson, "John Moses Smith," Handbook of Texas online, published July 1, 1995, https://tshaonline.org/handbook/online/articles/fsm66.

6. Cos to Campusáno, January 17, 1835, XI / 481.3 / expediente 1093, fojas 4–8, AHM.

7. Filisola, *Memoirs for the History of the War*, vol. 2, 35.

8. Tenorio to Ugartechea, May 18, 1835, XI / 481.3 / expediente 1820, fojas 36–37, AHM.

9. González was at Brazoria a short time before going to Anáhuac. Once again, because of a lack of forces to do otherwise he let the merchants there pay only duties on tonnage instead of the value of the goods. This upset the merchants at Anáhuac, who claimed they were being charged more, even though they were not paying.

10. A gunnade is a variant of a carronade. It was shorter than a regular cannon and thus had a shorter range. They were first introduced in about 1820. A "24-pounder" referred to a gunnade that would fire a ball weighing twenty-four pounds.

11. Tenorio to Cos, May 2, 1835, XI / 481.3 / expediente 1096, fojas 5–7, AHM. Notice that Tenorio reported that it was Alegria who appointed Gil Hernandez as the new commander of the guards of the customs; Gil Hernandez was also left with the register (a log of accounts).

12. Anáhuac troops and arms, April 23, 1835, box 2S315, Bexar Archives, DBC. The document shows thirty men, but there is a note that two of the soldiers were sick and in Matamoros.

13. Depositions of Martín de Alegria and José González, May 19, 27, 1835, XI / 481.3 / expediente 1820, fojas 5–13, AHM.

14. Tenorio to commissioner, May 4, 1835, XI / 481.3 / expediente 1096, fojas 3–4, AHM.

15. Tenorio to Cos, May 4, 1835, XI / 481.3 / expediente 1096, fojas 8–9, AHM.

16. Cos to Tornel, May 23, 1835, XI / 481.3 / expediente 1821, fojas 30–32, AHM.

17. The two Texans arrested were Andrew Briscoe and DeWitt Clinton Harris. The wounded man was William Smith.

18. Edward Gritten, an Englishman who served as a mediator between the Texans and Ugartechea, wrote in a note on July 11 from Gonzales, that the wounded

Texan did not die as had been rumored. Gritten to Ugartechea, July 11, 1835, in Jenkins, *Papers of the Texas Revolution*, vol. 1, 229–30.

19. Ugartechea to Cos, June 29, 1835, XI / 481.3 / expediente 1099, fojas 7–10, AHM.

20. Unknown to Ugartechea, June 25, 1835, box 331, p. 259, AGN.

21. Tenorio to Ugartechea, July 7, 1835, XI / 481.3 / expediente 1814, fojas 19–21, AHM.

22. James B. Miller to Cos, July 2, 1835, XI / 481.3 / expediente 1814, fojas 27–28, AHM.

23. "Intercepted Correspondence," *Texas Republican* (Brazoria, Texas), July 4, 1835, 4, available at Portal to Texas History online, accessed October 9, 2018, https://texashistory.unt.edu/ark:/67531/metapth80265/.

24. Citizens of [San Felipe de] Austin to citizens of Coahuila y Texas, June 22, 1835, XI / 481.3 / expediente 1814, fojas 42–50, AHM.

25. Robert M. Williamson, address, June 22, 1835, in Jenkins, *Papers of the Texas Revolution*, vol. 1, 194–202. It is not certain that the Mexican officials had this document, but the fact that it was printed in Brazoria on July 4 makes it likely.

26. Ramón Múzquiz was the legally elected vice governor, but the election results had been canceled by the Mexican government. A relative of Múzquiz, Rafael Ecay y Múzquiz, was appointed governor of Coahuila y Tejas after the arrest of Viesca. For more on Rafael Ecay y Múzquiz, see Jesús F. de la Teja, *Tejano Leadership in Mexican and Revolutionary Texas* (College Station: Texas A&M University Press, 2010), 138–39.

27. Cos to Ugartechea, July 20, 1835, XI / 481.3 / expediente 1814, fojas 39–41, AHM.

28. Columbia meeting, June 28, 1835, XI / 481.3 / expediente 1814, fojas 30–35, AHM; for an English translation, see "Columbia Meeting," *Texas Republican*, July 4, 1835, 4, available at Portal to Texas History online, accessed December 3, 2018, https://texashistory.unt.edu/ark:/67531/metapth80265.

29. Frank W. Johnson, *A History of Texas and Texans*, vol. 1 (Chicago: American Historical Society, 1914), 231–32. This letter was printed in the *Texas Republican*, August 22, 1835.

30. Ximenes and Flores were released from San Felipe and arrived in Béjar on July 24. Ugartechea to Cos, July 25, 1835, in Jenkins, *Papers of the Texas Revolution*, vol. 1, 276.

31. Martin to Ugartechea, August 5, 1835, XI / 481.3 / expediente 1100, fojas 163–65, AHM.

32. Cos to Francisco Pizarro Martínez, August 12, 1835, XI / 481.3 / expediente 1100, fojas 105–6, AHM.

33. Tenorio wrote that Travis had taken sixty-three muskets and twenty-five musket lock plates and cartridge boxes, with two packets of ten cartridges each. Tenorio to the chief of the department of the Brazos, July 26, 1835, in Jenkins, *Papers of the Texas Revolution*, vol. 1, 278.

34. Tenorio to Ugartechea, July 24, 1835, XI / 481.3 / expediente 1099, fojas 64–65, AHM.

CHAPTER 4

1. Ugartechea is referring to the presidio of San Antonio Bucareli de la Bavía (Babia). It was located in the state of Coahuila, near the Río Grande, and its troops were responsible for the area south of the Nueces.

2. Ugartechea to Cos, November 15, 1834, XI / 481.3 / expediente 1092, fojas 6–9, AHM.

3. He seems to be referring to the replacements for the Morelos battalion, which are described in more detail later in this chapter.

4. José Ygnacio Berdejo to commanding general of Jalisco, February 19, 1835, XI / 481.3 / expediente 1817, fojas 23–26, AHM.

5. Cos specifically noted that the cannons were bronze, with calibers of six and four. The English term for a 6-caliber cannon would have been a 6-pounder. A 6-pounder cannon would fire an iron ball that weighed six pounds, a 4-pounder cannon would fire a four-pound ball, etc. For the remainder of this work, the term "pounder" will be used instead of "caliber." Cos to Ugartechea, February 21, 1835, box 2S313, Bexar Archives, DBC. In the earlier document he had written that four cannons were coming, but in this dispatch he only mentioned three.

6. Cos to Ugartechea, March 19, 1835, box 2S314, Bexar Archives, DBC.

7. Gregorio Gómez Palomino was also the commander of the Tres Villas battalion, which was at Tampico prior to going to Texas. As commander at Tampico, he helped thwart the Mejía invasion.

8. Boca del Río refers to the mouth of the Brazos River, where Velasco was located.

9. Cos to Tornel, April 6, 1835 XI / 481.3 / expediente 1814, fojas 78–81, AHM.

10. Cos to Tornel, April 19, 1835, XI / 481.3 / expediente 1816, fojas 17–18, AHM.

11. Cos to Tornel, April 30, 1835, XI / 481.3 / expediente 1816, fojas 23–24, AHM.

12. Tornel to Cos, June 8, 1835, XI / 481.3 / expediente 1097, fojas 27–30, AHM.

13. Filisola wrote that they arrived on August 3 with 150 men and a 4-pounder cannon. No other support for presence of the artillery piece has been located. Filisola, *Memoirs for the History of the War*, vol. 2, 54.

14. Lipantitlán was a small fort on the Nueces River, a few miles upstream from San Patricio. It had been founded in response to the report of Manuel de Mier y Terán that documented the need for more Mexican troops in Texas.

15. Later in the campaign Peralta would serve as keeper of the orders for the 2nd brigade of the 2nd division. Col. Manuel Céspedes took command of the Guerrero battalion for most of the Texas campaign.

16. José Juan Sánchez Navarro Papers, vol. 2, p. 213, DBC.

17. Sánchez Navarro, *La Guerra de Tejas*, 2nd ed., 79–80.

18. In his memoirs Filisola mistakenly put December for many of the dates that should have been November.

19. *Obus* has occasionally been translated as "mortar," but it should be translated "howitzer." A howitzer was shorter than a cannon and took less gunpowder to fire. Unlike a mortar, its elevation could be adjusted.

20. It is possible that this was Erasmus "Deaf" Smith as he was living in Béjar at the time.

21. Morelos battalion strength report, October 1, 1835, box 2S319, Bexar Archives, DBC.

22. List of criminals sent to Texas and California, October 14, 1835, XI / 481.3 / expediente 1111, fojas 19–20, AHM.

23. Santa Anna was later informed that the 2nd active battalion of Mexico City was not fit to march, and it never did participate in the Texas Revolution. Another unit that Juan Almonte reported was involved in the Texas Revolution was the Morelia battalion. There was a document ordering four companies of the Morelia to march, but no evidence has been found that they did so.

24. Santa Anna to Tornel, October 26, 1835, XI / 481.3 / expediente 1101, fojas 196–206, AHM.

25. Castillo de San Juan de Ulúa was a fortress in the harbor of Veracruz. Santa Anna had already experienced the difficulty of trying to dislodge the Spanish from this fort, so he was probably anxious to avoid any repeat of this action.

26. As discussed previously, there is no evidence that Cos was the brother-in-law of Santa Anna, so the theory that he was trying to avenge Cos's defeat is invalid as well. The timing for this theory does not work, as the division of operations was marching north prior to the fall of Béjar.

27. Vital Fernández to Tornel, November 11, 1835, XI / 481.3 / expediente 1823, fojas 139–40, AHM.

28. The Tres Villas battalion was an active unit that came from three small villages near Mexico City, thus the name Tres Villas.

29. Tacubaya was an ancient city near Mexico City. During the time of the Texas Revolution, it was a popular area for the church and the rich. Santa Anna did much of his planning for the operation against Texas at Tacubaya.

30. Filisola, *Memoirs for the History of the War*, vol. 2, 54.

31. After the revolt in Zacatecas that Santa Anna put down in May 1835, Ramírez y Sesma was appointed governor and commanding general of that state.

32. Tornel to Felipe Cadallos, October 31, 1835, XI / 481.3 / expediente 1823, fojas 78–79, AHM. The Matamoros and Jiménez battalions were still in Zacatecas, maintaining order.

33. Sánchez Navarro, *La Guerra de Tejas*, 2nd ed., 86.

34. Sánchez Navarro, *La Guerra de Tejas*, 2nd ed., 84.

35. San Luís battalion strength report, November 17, 1835, XI / 481.3 / expediente 1823, foja 108, AHM. It should be noted that, for the most part, the strength reports of the units of the Mexican army listed the number of officers but did not include them in their total number of troops.

36. The Zapadores battalion was composed of sappers or diggers/builders. Technically they were not engineers as the Mexican army had its own engineer corps.

37. The reader should be aware that the active regiment of Guanajuato was a cavalry unit. This is not to be confused with the active *battalion* of Guanajuato, which was an infantry unit.

38. Tornel to Ramírez y Sesma, November 18, 1835, XI / 481.3 / expediente 1103, foja 18, AHM.

39. Brevet Gen. José Urrea was born at San Agustín de Tucson in the province of Sonora. He was an avid Federalist who was to be a significant participant in the Texas Revolution. Some Texas historians give his name as "de Urrea," but I have not found a document where he signs his name that way. For more information on Urrea, see Patricia Roche Herring, *General José Cosme Urrea: His Life and Times, 1797–1849*, Western Frontiersman Series 24 (Spokane, WA: Arthur H. Clark, 1995).

40. The last three names on the list, all enlisted men, were the secretaries for the staff.

41. Many of the officers were given a temporary promotion for the campaign. The brevet rank was a temporary promotion rank.

42. Not to be confused with his brother, José Nicolas de la Portilla, who will be introduced later in this work.

43. Headquarters staff, November 23, 1835, XI / 481.3 / expediente 1103, foja 4, AHM.

44. These are classic Napoleonic tactics. This is how the Mexican army was trained, but the Texans never would confront the Mexican army in the open, thus making their training useless.

45. Umberto Daniel Filizola, "Correspondence of Santa Anna during the Texas Campaign, 1835–1836" (master's thesis, University of Texas, 1939), 30–34.

46. Luis Quintanar to subordinates, November 13, 1835, XI / 481.3 / expediente 1823, foja 189, AHM.

47. Isidro Reyes to Tornel, November 6, 1835, box 331, p. 9, AGN.

CHAPTER 5

1. Moro was the director of artillery in Mexico City. The commanding general of artillery for the army of operations against Texas was Lt. Col. Pedro Ampudia. He was designated as commanding general even though he was not a general in rank.

2. Moro could be referring to Ampudia here, but it is likely that he was talking about the commander of the artillery foundry. In another document Moro calls him the "commanding general of artillery of this department."

3. One of the gunpowder factories was documented as being in Santa Fe, which at the time was a town just west of Mexico City.

4. Moro to Tornel, November 3, 1835, XI / 481.3 / expediente 1101, fojas 261–62, AHM.

5. The lack of copper for production of armaments has been verified by artifacts found in the Sea of Mud. Some of the canister shot is much smaller than most of the shot. These smaller shot were analyzed at the Texas A&M Conservation Research Laboratory. PXRF studies on the smaller canister shot showed that they had lead, iron, and even selenium added to the copper. Most of the canister shot found were almost pure copper.

6. On occasion this term has not been recognized by various translators. A *parada* of cartridges was a bundle of cartridges that would be carried in the cartridge box. When doing archeology at the Almonte surrender site near San Jacinto, the archeologists discovered that there were clusters of dropped balls that were highly likely to be dropped bundles.

7. Joe D. Hudgins, Terry Kieler, and Gregg Dimmick, *Tracking the Mexican Army through the Mar De Lodo (Sea of Mud): April 29–May 9, 1836; 41WH92, 41WH93, 41WH94, 41WH95, Wharton County, Texas,* Houston Archeological Society Report No. 16 (Houston: 2000), 13–14.

8. Terrence Wise and Richard Hook. *Artillery Equipments of the Napoleonic Wars,* Men-at-Arms Series (London: Osprey, 1979), 17.

9. Veracruz artillery inventory, November 8, 1835, XI / 481.3 / expediente 1101, fojas 284–85, AHM.

10. Ramírez y Sesma to Tornel, November 8, 1835, XI / 481.3 / expediente 1823, fojas 161–62, AHM; Ramírez y Sesma equipment list, November 7, 1835, XI / 481.3 / expediente 1823, fojas 164–65, AHM. Thanks to Mr. Rick Range for help in translating the inventory.

11. An inventory of the artillery, arms, and ammunition that were sent from Mexico City to Texas shows that the twelve artillery pieces included two 12-pounders, two 8-pounders, two 6-pounders, four 4-pounders, and two 6½-inch howitzers. All were recorded as being made of bronze. XI / 481.3 / expediente 1655, fojas 6–15, AHM.

12. Moro to Tornel, November 19, 1835, XI / 481.3 / expediente 1101, fojas 298–99, AHM.

13. Congreve rocket test, December 30, 1835, XI / 481.3 / expediente 1102, fojas 278–82, AHM.

14. Filisola, *Memoirs for the History of the War*, vol. 2, 149–51.

CHAPTER 6

1. The *Moctezuma* or *Montezuma* was a steam frigate built by Lizardi and Co. for the Mexican navy. It was renamed the *Bravo* in 1836. Jenkins, *Papers of the Texas Revolution*, vol. 1, 525n200.

2. Some sources list Calvi as the commander of the *Moctezuma*. However, in a letter of August 12, 1835, Cos wrote that the *Ingahm* vs. *Moctezuma* incident would have had a different result if its commander, 1st Lieutenant Marin, had been on board. He noted that the lieutenant was home in bed in Matamoros. Cos to Francisco Pizarro Martínez, August 12, 1835, XI / 481.3 / expediente 1100, fojas 105–6, AHM.

3. Tenorio to Ugartechea, June 25, 1835, in Jenkins, *Papers of the Texas Revolution*, vol. 1, 168.

4. See chapter 3 for details on the customs officials.

5. Unknown to the editor, June 1835, XI / 481.3 / expediente 1100, fojas 67–77, AHM. This document contains much more detail; only a summary is presented here.

6. The *Ingham* would later be sold to the Texas navy and renamed the *Independence*.

7. This was the entrance into the port of Matamoros.

8. In a separate document the captain of the port was named as Guillermo A. Wyse, 1st lieutenant of the Mexican fleet.

9. Variously called the *Correo de Mexico*, *Correo*, *Correo Mexicano*, and *Mexico Correo*.

10. Thompson to citizens, July 26, 1835, in Jenkins, *Papers of the Texas Revolution*, vol. 1, 278–79.

11. Besides the cargo that was unloaded, two passengers disembarked, Stephen F. Austin and Lorenzo de Zavala.

12. Declarations, September 23, 1835, XI / 481.3 / expediente 1114, fojas 37–63, AHM. This document also contains the depositions of William Morrison and Felipe Antonio Himenez (*sic*).

13. Prior to 1832, the Morelos battalion had been the 4th battalion, so he was serving as an escort for the Morelos battalion.

14. There are many more details in these depositions that are omitted here.

15. Francisco Pizarro Martínez to Henry Carleton, September 16, 1835, in Jenkins, *Papers of the Texas Revolution*, vol. 1, 449–50.

16. Henry Carleton to Francisco Pizarro Martínez, September 17, 1835, in Jenkins, *Papers of the Texas Revolution*, vol. 1, 452–53.

17. De P. Lopez to Tornel, October 21, 1835, XI / 481.3 / expediente 1114, fojas 23–24, AHM.

18. Thompson statement, October 1835, box 332, pp. 522–26, AGN.

19. Thompson was eventually released, as there was a hung jury. For other accounts of this encounter and the trial of Thompson in New Orleans, see Jonathan W. Jordan, *Lone Star Navy: Texas, the Fight for the Gulf of Mexico, and the Shaping of the American West* (Washington, DC: Potomac Books, 2006), 9–18; C. L. Douglas, *Thunder on the Gulf, or The Story of the Texas Navy* (Austin, TX: Graphic Ideas, 1936; rev. ed., 1972), 11–20.

20. As the letter is dated December 3, it is likely that Wyse meant to say the 24th of the previous month.

21. The American merchant ship was the *Hannah Elizabeth.*

22. Wyse to Tornel, December 3, 1835, box 333, p. 94, AGN; Wyse to Tornel, December 3, 1835, XI / 481.3 / expediente 1114, fojas 64–67, AHM.

23. Pizarro Martínez to secretary of state, December 13, 1835, box 528, p. 51, AGN.

CHAPTER 7

1. James Tumlinson receipt, March 10, 1835, Bexar Archives, DBC.

2. Navarro to Ponton, September 21, 1835, Bexar Archives, DBC. Navarro was now the political chief in Béjar. Translated by Dr. Frank de la Teja.

3. Andrew Ponton to Angel Navarro, September 26, 1835, box 2S319, Bexar County Archives, DBC.

4. DeWitt was in Monclova trying to get more land for his colony when he died of cholera on May 18, 1835.

5. Navarro to Ponton, September 30,1835, expediente 1101, foja 165, AHM.

6. Filisola wrote that it was eighty soldiers, and looking at the strength reports of the presidial companies in Béjar on October 1, it appears that there were about eighty-five soldiers marked as having gone to Gonzales; presidial companies strength reports, September 30–October 1, 1835, box 2S319, Bexar Archives, DBC.

7. Francisco de Castañeda to Ugartechea, September 29, 1835, box 2S319, 1548–52, Bexar County Archives, DBC.

8. Ugartechea to Castañeda, September 30, 1835, XI / 481.3 / expediente 1101, foja 170, AHM.

9. This is likely to be Launcelot Smither, a colonist who was sent by Ugartechea from Béjar to Gonzales to help negotiate the return of the cannon. In this dispatch,

dated September 30, Castañeda documents that Smith (Smither) was with the Texans but later notes that, like the Mexican couriers, he was a prisoner in Gonzales. In a document shown later in this chapter, dated November 1, Castañeda wrote about a Mr. Smitten who arrived that day with a pass from Ugartechea. It is difficult to know whether this is one or two individuals.

10. The mentioned communication has not been located in the archives.

11. Castañeda to Ugartechea, September 30, 1835, box 332, pp. 347–48, AGN.

12. The more the Mexicans wrote about the cannon the larger it seems to become.

13. Ugartechea was mistaken here: the *San Felipe* was not a steamboat. The steamboat was the *Laura*.

14. Ugartechea to Cos, September 30, 1835, expediente 1101, fojas 160–61, AHM.

15. Ugartechea actually wrote that this incident was in Nacogdoches, but it is obvious that he meant Gonzales.

16. Cos to Ugartechea, October 1, 1835, box 332, pp. 304–5, AGN.

17. Jenkins, *Papers of the Texas Revolution*, vol. 2, document 713, 7–8.

18. In the Mexican documents from this period the word for "loss" could refer to dead or wounded. From a later document we know that this soldier was only wounded.

19. Castañeda to Ugartechea, October 2, 1835, Muse Papers, Benson Latin American Collection, University of Texas at Austin; Castañeda to Ugartechea, October 2, 1835, box 332, p. 361, AGN.

20. Filisola, *Memoirs for the History of the War*, vol. 2, 64.

21. The bronze cannon was donated, through the efforts of Mr. Rick Range, to the conservancy by the family of John McRae, who had purchased the cannon from the Texas Historical Society at auction in 1986. The cannon not only has good (though not great) provenance but also has intentional damage similar to other known Alamo cannons.

22. Rosillo Creek is east of San Antonio on the road to Gonzales.

23. Some translators have read this as "la Peña." Texas history and battle of Gonzales researcher James Woodrick has postulated that this is the homesite of Ezekiel Williams. For more discussions on his theory of the use of "La Perra," see James Woodrick, *The Battle of Gonzales and Its Two Cannons* (self-pub., 2014), 31–32. Almonte called this location "la Perra" and added that it was the farm of Judge Williams. Jackson, *Almonte's Texas*, 393.

24. Likely to be the Carrizo (personal communication with James Woodrick).

25. Castañeda to Ugartechea, October 4, 1835, box 332, pp. 362–66, AGN.

26. Tejocotes Creek, also called El Durasno or Peach Creek. See Mier y Terán, *Texas by Terán*, 214n26, 214n28.

27. Cos to Tornel, October 4, 1835, box 332, pp. 313–14, AGN.

28. Ugartechea to Austin, October 4, 1835, box 332, pp. 351–55, AGN.

CHAPTER 8

1. Cos to Tornel, October 11, 1835, box 333, pp. 50–51, AGN.

2. Carronades were short, smooth bore, cast-iron cannons that were originally designed for merchant ships as anti-ship and anti-crew weapons. They used smaller powder loads and were powerful at short range.

3. Cos to Tornel, October 5, 1835, box 332, pp. 335–36, AGN.

4. Filisola, *Memoirs for the History of the War*, vol. 2, 62. Filisola noted that Sabaríego had only twenty-five presidial cavalrymen with him on this mission.

5. Cos to Tornel, October 5, 1835, box 332, pp. 337–38, AGN.

6. Juan Zenteno to Cos, October 11, 1835, box 331, pp. 20–21, AGN.

7. The military officers were first sent to Victoria and then on to Gonzales, where they met with Austin. They were eventually sent to San Felipe. Zenteno seems to have believed that he would be sent to San Felipe as well; however, based on later dispatches that will be discussed in this chapter, the customs officials were sent to Gonzales but never did go to San Felipe.

8. John Linn to brother, October 11, 1835, box 331, pp. 34–35, AGN.

9. John Linn to Thomas Henry, October 1835, box 331, pp. 33–32, AGN.

10. J. M. Guerra to Tornel, October 12, 1835, XI / 481.3 / expediente 1101, fojas 219–23, AHM.

11. Cos to Tornel, October 13, 1835, in Jenkins, *Papers of the Texas Revolution*, vol. 2, document 839, 110–11.

12. Cos to Tornel, October 13, 1835, Muse Papers, Benson Latin American Collection, University of Texas at Austin.

13. This was likely the same as the homesite of Ezekiel Williams, as the oath that Zenteno signed the next day was addressed as being at "Camp Williams." Also, the Texas army did not leave Williams's home until October 15. This was the same place that Castañeda called "la Perra" during the battle of Gonzales on October 2.

14. Juan Zenteno to Cos, October 17, 1835, XI / 481.3 / expediente 1102, fojas 15–16, AHM.

15. Juan Zenteno oath, October 14, 1835, XI / 481.3 / expediente 1102, foja 14, AHM.

16. Local ranchers and sometimes Irishmen from the San Patricio area would volunteer to help the Mexican army at times.

17. Several attempts have been made to find the two cannons abandoned by the Texans in the Nueces, but at the time of writing they have yet to be found.

18. Capt. Enrique Villareal was technically the military commander at Lipantitlán, but Rodríguez was the company commander. Villarreal was absent in Matamoros during the time this was taking place. José María Villareal is likely a separate individual. Muster roll for the 2nd active cavalry of Tamaulipas, October 1, 1835, Bexar Archives, DBC.

19. Guerra to Tornel, November 10, 1835, XI / 481.3 / expediente 1145, fojas 25–29, AHM.

20. Col. José María Gonzales was a staunch Federalist and was involved in the escape of Viesca and his party as they were being taken to prison after their arrest on the way to Texas. He sided with the Texans as a supporter of the constitution of 1824.

CHAPTER 9

1. Austin to Ugartechea, September 15, 1835, Muse Papers, Benson Latin American Collection, University of Texas at Austin.

2. Cos to Austin, October 5, 1835, XI / 481.3 / expediente 1148, fojas 8–13, AHM.

3. Cos to Tornel, October 9, 1835, box 332, pp. 344–45, AGN.

4. Austin to Cos, October 17, 1835 [two letters], XI / 481.3 / expediente 1148, fojas 8–13, AHM.

5. Cos to Austin, October 18, 1835. All four documents sent between Cos and Austin are included in one letter, apparently to Tornel.

6. There may have been a small group of Texans who arrived on October 12, but the main Texan army probably arrived there closer to October 16.

7. This tower was called the Powder House, or La Garita. It was built in 1807–10 when the Spanish were worried about an invasion by the United States after the Louisiana Purchase. The Texans controlled this tower during the siege of Béjar and the Mexicans controlled it during the 1836 battle. Jim Woodrick, personal communication.

8. De la Peña wrote that Mendoza was lieutenant colonel who was a defender of the Alamo in the 1835 campaign. De la Peña said that he later lost a limb from a cannonball while defending the Alamo and was saved, along with other wounded Mexicans, by Dr. James Grant. De la Peña, *With Santa Anna in Texas*, 83.

9. This would be consistent with the report that the Texans had buried the smaller cannon prior to arriving in Béjar.

10. Filisola gives a very comprehensive description of the Alamo and the fortifications that Cos constructed there. Filisola, *Memoirs for the History of the War*, vol. 2, 82–84.

11. Cos to Tornel, October 19, 1835, XI / 481.3 / expediente 1148, fojas 5–6, AHM.

12. Cos wrote that he was sending Rafael Ugartechea to Béjar to assist him. Cos to Ugartechea, January 8, 1835, in Jenkins, *Papers of the Texas Revolution*, vol. 1, 4.

13. Initially called Mission Nuestra Señora de la Purísima Concepción de Acuña, Mission Concepción was moved from East Texas to San Antonio in 1831. It is located on the San Antonio River south of the Alamo. In one of his accounts Sánchez Navarro called it Misión de Purísima. Sánchez Navarro, *La Guerra de Tejas*, 2nd ed., 60n1.

14. Rafael Ugartechea to Cos, October 28, 1835, box 332, p. 529, AGN.

15. Filisola, *Memoirs for the History of the War*, vol. 2, 68.

16. José María Mendoza to Cos, October 28, 1835, XI / 481.3 / expediente 1101, fojas 151–53, AHM.

17. Condelle was mentioned in a letter written by an anonymous author who referred to himself as "True Mexican." The author actually calls him "Colonel Cariaga" but identifies him as commander of the Morelos battalion who was to take over command from Ugartechea. The letter is dated August 15, 1835, and is addressed to persons known as Johnson, Baker, and Givens. In the letter, the author wrote that Ugartechea was a liberal who might begin a pronunciamiento against the Centralists. He noted that Santa Anna was afraid of Ugartechea. He called Cariaga (Condelle) a "blood-thirsty black son of a whore." Condelle took command of the Morelos battalion on July 3, 1835. Book 23, item 1431, Samuel M. Williams Papers, Rosenberg Library, Galveston, Texas.

18. Concepción dead, October 28, 1835, XI / 481.3 / expediente 1101, foja 155, AHM.

19. Concepción wounded, October 28, 1835, XI / 481.3 / expediente 1101, foja 154, AHM.

20. Cos to Tornel, October 29, 1835, XI / 481.3 / expediente 1101, fojas 147–50, AHM.

21. Tornel to Cos, December 2, 1835, XI / 481.3 / expediente 1148, fojas 51–52, AHM.

22. More than likely he meant to say San Luís Potosí or Leona Vicario, as there was no force that left Matamoros until mid-February.

23. Cos to Tornel, November 2, 1835, box 332, pp. 437–39, AGN.

24. Cos to Tornel, November 11, 1835, box 332, pp. 502–3, AGN.

25. Tornel to Cos, November 14, 1835, expediente 1148, fojas 14–16, AHM.

26. Ugartechea likely armed the Mexican citizens when he went to Laredo to meet the Morelos reinforcements.

27. This was likely the 12-pounder brought by the New Orleans Greys.

28. Cos to Tornel, November 27, 1835, box 332, pp. 516–17, AGN.

29. Sánchez Navarro, *La Guerra de Tejas*, 2nd ed., 47–74.

30. Filisola, *Memoirs for the History of the War*, vol. 2, 93.

31. This could be Erastus "Deaf" Smith or John William Smith (known as El Colorado). Both were residents of Béjar at the time and were immediately involved. It is more likely that this Smith is John Smith as Erastus Smith was severely wounded on the top of the Veramendi house on December 8. The Mexican writers did not describe Smith the translator as being wounded.

32. Major General Thompson was likely Francis "Frank" White Johnson, who served as the Texans' army inspector general and is documented to have been a

commissioner with Burleson. Robert C. Morris came to Béjar in 1835 as a member of the New Orleans Greys. The third commissioner for the Texans was Capt. James Gibson Swisher, which sounds nothing like Edelt.

33. Sánchez Navarro, *La Guerra de Tejas*, 117.

34. Cos is traditionally called the "oath breaker" in Texas history for breaking the pledge that he signed in Béjar. However, when one considers that he pledged not to fight against the constitution of 1824 and that the Texans, by the time he fought them again, were fighting for independence, he technically did not break his oath.

35. Mendoza was documented to have finally returned to Veracruz on December 30, 1836, on the English warship *Forte*. He was noted to have been wounded in defense of the Alamo. De Castro to Tornel, December 31, 1836, XI / 481.3 / expediente 1204, fojas 230–32, AHM.

36. Sánchez Navarro, *La Guerra de Tejas*, 2nd ed., 72–74. If the original list is consulted it should be noted that the headings for "Wounded" and "Dead" have been reversed.

37. Manuel Barragán to Santa Anna, December 13, 1835, XI / 481.3 / expediente 1102, fojas 221–24, AHM.

38. Juan José Galán to Santa Anna, December 13, 1835, XI / 481.3 / expediente 1102, fojas 228–30, AHM.

39. Since this name is quite rare it is possible that Luis de Ugartechea was the third member of the same Ugartechea family in Béjar at the time of the siege.

40. Sánchez Navarro, *La Guerra de Tejas, Memorias de un Soldado*, 122–25.

41. Santa Anna to Tornel, December 27, 1835, box 334, pp. 6–7, AGN.

42. Cos to Santa Anna, December 29, 1835, in Jenkins, *Papers of the Texas Revolution*, vol. 3, 358–59.

43. Sánchez Navarro, *La Guerra de Tejas, Memorias de un Soldado*, 125.

CHAPTER 10

1. Filisola, *Memoirs for the History of the War*, vol. 2, 118.

APPENDIX 1

1. Barker, *The Austin Papers*, vol. 2, 1016.

APPENDIX 7

1. This document is not the July 5 (given on June 22) address in Jenkins, *Papers of the Texas Revolution*, vol. 1, document 329, p. 194. It is the same date but seems totally different and is included only in the Mexican archives.

APPENDIX 8

1. "Columbia Meeting," *Texas Republican,* July 4, 1835, 4, Portal to Texas History, accessed January 28, 2025, https://texashistory.unt.edu/ark:/67531/metapth80265/.

APPENDIX 10

1. *Visto Bueno* is standard confirmation for official documents.

APPENDIX 12

1. The officers are not included in the totals.

SELECTED BIBLIOGRAPHY

ARCHIVAL DOCUMENTS

Archivo General de Mexico, 1538–1849, Dolph Briscoe Center for American History, University of Texas at Austin

Bexar Archives, Dolph Briscoe Center for American History, University of Texas at Austin

Dolph Briscoe Center for American History, University of Texas at Austin

Genaro García Collection, Benson Manuscripts Collection, University of Texas at Austin

José Juan Sánchez Navarro Papers, Dolph Briscoe Center for American History, University of Texas at Austin

Muse Papers, Benson Latin American Collection, University of Texas at Austin

Samuel M. Williams Papers, Rosenberg Library, Galveston, Texas

"Relacion de los señores, gefes y oficiales que perteneciente al ejército de operaciones sobre Tejas, pasaron revista en el mes de Marzo en la ciudad de San Antonio Béjar." [List of the senior commanders and officers who belonged in the army of operations over Texas that passed in review in the month of March in the city of San Antonio]. Archivo Historico de Secretaria de la Defensa Nacional (AHSDN), Operaciones, XI / 481.3 / 1713, Tomo 2, f. 383v. Mexico City, Mexico. Provided by Thomas Ricks Lindley and Jack Jackson.

NEWSPAPERS

Texas Republican (Brazoria, Texas)

THESIS

Hancock, Walter Edgar. "The Career of General Antonio López de Santa Anna (1794–1833)." PhD diss., University of Texas at Austin, 1933.

BOOKS AND PAMPHLETS

Bancroft, Hubert Howe. *History of Mexico*. Vol. 5, *1824–1861*. San Francisco: A. L. Bancroft, 1885.

———. *History of the North Mexican States and Texas*. Vol. 2, *1801–1889*. San Francisco: The History Company, 1886.

Barker, Eugene C., ed. The Austin Papers. 3 vols. Washington, DC: United States Government Printing Office, 1924–28.

Berlandier, Jean Louis. *The Indians of Texas in 1830*. Edited by John C. Ewers. Translated by Patricia Reading Leclercq. Washington, DC: Smithsonian Institution Press, 1969.

———. *Journey to Mexico during the Years 1826 to 1834*. 2 vols. Austin: Texas State Historical Association, 1980.

Bulnes, Francisco. *Las grandes mentiras de Nuestra historia: La Nación y el Ejército in las guerras extranjeras*. Paris: Librerìa de la Vda de Ch. Bouret, 1904.

Callcott, Wilfred Hardy. *Santa Anna: The Story of an Enigma Who Once Was Mexico*. Norman: University of Oklahoma Press, 1936.

Castañeda, Carlos E., trans. and ed. *The Mexican Side of the Texas Revolution, 1836, by the Chief Mexican Participants, General Antonio López de Santa Anna, Ramón Martínez Caro, General Vicente Filisola, General José Urrea, General José María Tornel*. Dallas: Graphic Ideas, 1970.

Cutter, Donald C., trans. and ed. *The Defenses of Northern New Spain: Hugo O'Connor's Report to Teodoro de Croix, July 22, 1777*. Dallas: DeGolyer Library, 1994.

De Zavala, Lorenzo. *Ensayo histórico de las revoluciones de México desde 1808 hasta 1830*. 2 vols. Mexico: Imprenta a cargo de M. N. de la Vega, 1845.

Diccionario Porrúa: Historia, Biografía y Geografía de Mexico. Mexico, D. F.: Editorial Porrúa, S.A., Ed. V, 1986.

Dyer, Dr. Jo. O. *The Early History of Galveston*. Centenary Edition. Galveston, TX: Oscar Springer Print, 1916.

Filisola, Vicente. *Análsis del diario mititar del General D. José Urrea durante la primera campaña de Tejas*. Matamoros: Mercurio a Cargo de Antonio Castañeda, 1838.

———. *Evacuation of Texas: Translation of the Representation Addressed to the Supreme Government by Vicente Filisola, in Defense of His Honor, and Explanation of His Operations as Commander-in-Chief of the Army against Texas*. Columbia, TX: G. & T. H. Borden, 1837. Reprint, Waco, TX: Texian Press, 1965.

———. *General Vicente Filisola's Analysis of José Urrea's Military Diary: A Forgotten 1838 Publication by an Eyewitness to the Texas Revolution*. Edited by Gregg J. Dimmick. Translated by John R. Wheat. Denton: Texas State Historical Association, 2007.

———. *Memoirs for the History of the War in Texas*. Translated by Wallace Woolsey. 2 vols. Austin, TX: Eakin Press, 1986–87.

———. *Memorias para la Historia de la Guerra de Tejas*. 2 vols. Mexico: R. Rafael, 1848–49. Reprint, *Historia de la Guerra de Tejas*. 2 vols. Mexico, D. F.: Editora Nacional, 1968.

———. *Memorias para la Historia de la Guerra de Tejas*. 2 vols. Mexico: Ignacio Cumplido, 1849. [This is a different book than the Rafael publication by the same name. The Cumplido publication has not been translated into English.]

Herring, Patricia Roche. *General José Cosme Urrea: His Life and Times, 1797–1849*. Western Frontiersman Series 24. Spokane, WA: Arthur H. Clark, 1995.

Hudgins, Joe D., and Gregg Dimmick. *A Campsite of the Retreating Mexican Army: April 1836; 41WH91, Wharton County, Texas*. Houston Archeological Society Report No. 13. Houston: 1998.

Hudgins, Joe D., Terry Kieler, and Gregg Dimmick. *Tracking the Mexican Army through the Mar de Lodo (Sea of Mud): April 29–May 9, 1836; 41WH92, 41WH93, 41WH94, 41WH95, Wharton County, Texas*. Houston Archeological Society Report No. 16. Houston: 2000.

Jackson, Jack, ed. *Almonte's Texas: Juan N. Almonte's 1834 Inspection, Secret Report, and Role in the 1836 Campaign*. Translated by John Wheat. Austin: Texas State Historical Association, 2003.

———. *Historical Background for Fort Lipantitlán State Historic Site 41NU54 Nueces County, Texas*. Study done for the cultural resources program of Texas Parks and Wildlife Department, Austin, Texas, 2002.

———. *Indian Agent: Peter Ellis Bean in Mexican Texas*. College Station: Texas A&M University Press, 2005.

Jenkins, John H. *The Papers of the Texas Revolution, 1835–1836*. 10 vols. Austin, TX: Presidial Press, 1973.

Johnson, Frank W. *A History of Texas and Texans*. 5 volumes. Edited by Eugene C. Barker. Chicago: American Historical Society, 1914.

Lerdo de Tejada, Miguel M. *Apuntes históricos de la historia de la ciudad histórica de Veracruz*. 2 vols. Mexico: Imprenta de Vicente Garcia Torres, 1857.

Mexico Congreso. *Manifest del Congreso general en el presente año*. Mexico: J. M. F. Lara, 1836.

Mier y Terán, Manuel de. *Texas by Terán: The Diary Kept by General Manuel de Mier y Terán on His 1828 Inspection of Texas*. Edited by Jack Jackson. Translated by John Wheat. Austin: University of Texas Press, 2000.

Miller, Edward L. *New Orleans and the Texas Revolution*. College Station: Texas A&M University Press, 2004.

Mora, José María Luis. *México y sus revoluciones*. 4 vols. Mexico: Editorial Porrua, 1857.

Pedraza, Manuel Gómez. *Manifiesto, que Manuel Gómez Pedraza, ciudadano de la República de Méjico, dedica a sus compatriotas, o sea, Una reseña de su vida pública.* New Orleans: B. Levy, 1831. Reprint, Guadalajara: Brambila, 1831.

Peña, José Enrique de la. *La Rebelión de Texas: Manuscrito Inedito de 1836 por un oficial de Santa Anna.* Edited by J Sánchez Garza. Mexico, 1955.

———. *With Santa Anna in Texas: A Personal Narrative of the Revolution.* Translated and edited by Carmen Perry. College Station: Texas A&M University Press, 1975. Expanded edition, with introduction by James E Crisp, College Station: Texas A&M University Press, 1997.

Poyo, Gerald E., ed. *Tejano Journey, 1770–1850.* Austin: University of Texas Press, 1996.

Reid, Stuart. *The Secret War for Texas.* College Station: Texas A&M University Press, 2007.

Rincón, Manuel. "Manifiesto, El General Manuel Rincón justificado a los ojós de los Mexicans imparciales." In *Pronunciamiento de Perote por el general Antonio López de Sta. Anna, y sucesos de su campaña hasta la derogacion de la ley que lo proscribió escrito por un ciudadano que no tomó la más minima parte en aquellos acontecimientos.* Mexico: Imprenta de Aguila, 1829.

Rivera, Manuel. *Historia Antigua y Moderna de Jalapa y de las Revoluciones del Estado de Veracruz.* 4 vols. Mexico: Imprenta de Ignacio Cumplido, 1870.

Sánchez Navarro, Carlos, ed. *La guerra de Tejas: Memorias de un Soldado.* Mexico: Editorial Polis, 1938; 2nd ed., Mexico: Editorial Jus, S.A., 1960.

Santa Anna, Antonio López de. *The Eagle: The Autobiography of Santa Anna.* Edited by Ann Fears Crawford. Austin, TX: State House Press, 1988.

———. *Manifiesto que de sus operaciones en la campaña de Tejas y en su cautiverio dirige á sus conciudadanos el General Antonio López de Santa Anna.* Veracruz: Imprenta Liberal, á Cargo de Antonio María Valdez, 1837.

———. *Mi historia militar y politica, 1810–1874: memorias* **inéditos**. Mexico: Vda de C. Bouret, 1905.

Suárez y Navarro, Juan. *Historia de México y del General Antonio López de Santa Anna.* Mexico: Imprenta de Ignacio Cumplido, 1850.

Teja, Jesús F. de la, ed. *Tejano Leadership in Mexican and Revolutionary Texas.* College Station: Texas A&M University Press, 2010.

Tijerina, Andrés. *Tejanos and Texas under the Mexican Flag, 1821–1836.* College Station: Texas A&M University Press, 1994.

Torget, Andrew J. *Seeds of Empire: Cotton, Slavery, and the Transformation of the Texas Borderlands, 1800–1850.* Chapel Hill: University of North Carolina Press, 2015.

Tornel y Mendivil, José María. *Breve reseña histórica de los acontecimientos mas notables de la Nación Mexicana.* Mexico: Imprenta de Cumplido, 1852.

Urrea, José. *Diario de las operaciones militares de la division que al mando del General José Urrea hizo la campaña de Tejas publicalo se Autor con algunas observaciones para vindicarse ante sus conciudadanos.* Victoria de Durango: Imprint of the government, 1838.

Wharton, Clarence R. *El Presidente: A Sketch of the Life of General Santa Anna.* Austin, TX: Gammel's Book Store, [1926?].

Wise, Terrence, and Richard Hook. *Artillery Equipments of the Napoleonic Wars.* Men-at-Arms Series. London: Osprey, 1979.

Woodrick, James. *The Battle of Gonzales and Its Two Cannons.* Self-published, 2014.

INTERNET SOURCES

Archivo Histórico Militar. http://www.archivohistorico2010.sedena.gob.mx/busquedamenu.

Handbook of Texas Online. Texas State Historical Association. http://www.tsha.utexas.edu/handbook/online/index.html.

Portal to Texas History. University of North Texas. https://texashistory.unt.edu.

Sons of DeWitt Colony Texas. http://www.tamu.edu/ccbn/dewitt/dewitt.htm.

PERIODICALS

Barker, Eugene C. "Difficulties of a Mexican Revenue Officer in Texas." *Quarterly of the Texas State Historical Association* 4, no. 1 (1901): 192.

———. "Land Speculation as a Cause of the Texas Revolution." *Quarterly of the Texas State Historical Association* 10, no. 1 (July 1906): 76–95.

Brack, Gene. "Mexican Opinion and the Texas Revolution." *Southwest Historical Quarterly* 72, no. 2 (October 1968): 170–82.

Grafton, Grace. "Leaves from a Ladies Journal: No. 7." *American Monthly Magazine,* July 1837, 233–42. https://books.google.com/books?id=vNsRAAAAYAAJ.

"La Guerra de Texas: Causa Formada al Gral. Filisola por Su Retirada en 1836." *Boletín del Archivo General de la Nación* 10, nos. 1–3 (1939).

Morton, Ohland. "Life of General Don Manuel de Mier y Terán: As It Affected Texas-Mexican Relations." *Southwestern Historical Quarterly* 47, no. 3 (1944): 256–67.

Sánchez y Tapia, José María. "A Trip to Texas in 1828." Translated by Carlos E. Castañeda. *Southwestern Historical Quarterly* 29, no. 4 (April 1926): 249–88.

Ward, Henry. "Politics in Mexico." *North American Review,* December 1830.

INDEX

Page numbers in italics refer to figures.